W9-BBI-284

JUN '89 $12.50

Embodiments of Mind

Embodiments of Mind

Warren S. McCulloch

The MIT Press
Cambridge, Massachusetts
London, England

New material © 1988 Massachusetts Institute of Technology

First M.I.T. Press Paperback Edition, March, 1970

Copyright © 1965 by
The Massachusetts Institute of Technology

All rights reserved. This book may not be reproduced,
in whole or in part, in any form
(except by reviewers for the public press),
without written permission from the publishers.

Library of Congress Cataloging-in-Publication Data

McCulloch, Warren S. (Warren Sturgis), b. 1898.
Embodiments of mind / Warren S. McCulloch.

   p. cm.
Includes index.
ISBN 0-262-63114-8 (pbk.)
1. Neuropsychology. 2. Human information processing. I. Title.
QP360.M352 1988   001.5'3—dc19   88-2987

Foreword

by Jerome Lettvin

There are two kinds of goals directing the current arts of artificial intelligence (AI), parallel distributed processing (PDP), and the hard-wired nets that process images or sounds. The first are products that are useful to industry and the military. This pays for the research. The second are ideas that play back into the study of brain. These ideas are most important because, while controversial, they represent the only successful notions so far in the study of brain as information processor.

The literature in neuroscience and psychology is now so large and growing so fast that no one can master what has been written or keep up with current work. That is because it is composed of endless empirics. There is no theory to give coherence to this mountain of data in terms of how the brain functions as a mechanism that sustains mental process. Since, in the end, that is the goal of neuroscience—to account for how such process can occur—the absence of working models points out how undeveloped is the discipline.

Some of the trouble comes from the physical intractability of nervous tissue. Signal-to-noise relations limit considerably the observations that can be made on a living system. What samples may be had are not enough, even in the simplest cases, to found a notion of the circuitry. But, even if ideally one could record from any element or part of an element in situ, it is not in the least obvious how the records could be interpreted. To a greater degree than in any other current science, we must know what to look for in order to recognize it. Precisely here is the deficit in neuroscience. We can observe the results of processing in the behavior of animals and in records taken from individual neurons, but we cannot account for either by mechanism.

This is where a prior art is needed, some understanding of process design. And that is where AI, PDP, and the whole investment in building neurosuccedanea enter in. Critics carp that the current golems do not resemble our friends Tom, Dick, or

Harry. But the brute point is that a working golem is not only preferable to total ignorance, it also shows how processes can be designed analogous to those we are frustrated in explaining in terms of nervous action. It suggests what to look for. After all, golems now are capable of doing contingent tasks, of changing adaptively, and of showing processes that resemble induction and learning in a vague way.

Enthusiasts in AI have long maintained that it is easier to build a human than to analyze one already in operation. That is essentially how Warren McCulloch thought, and it explains how he helped to lay the foundations of AI. But it is a more remarkable position than appears at first.

McCulloch knew very well that single neurons are not gates but rather that each is a complex analog processor of analog data. In the brain any neuron receives as input a variety of different concurrent messages from other neurons. As output it expresses the running state history of its input by a running time series of pulses that in a way is much like language. It is almost as if an observer on a complex scene sends what he sees expressed in a code that uses continuous variability of pulse interval. The pulses do not signify clocked logical operations but simply define the important variable, the time between pulses. This sort of device is hard to think about in ensembles of neurons that are massively interconnected. It is no surprise that there are few interesting models of real nerve nets.

Knowing this, McCulloch nevertheless felt that much could be learned simply from considering pulse generators of any description under broad interconnection. Accordingly he subverted the notion of a neuron in a way that I will describe shortly.

Neuroscience, as I remarked earlier, has long been in the doldrums with respect to understanding the mechanisms used for information processing in nervous tissue. The main progress in neuroscience is in the fine anatomy and chemistry of the brain—the material substrate for the machine. Thus AI and related fields have grown almost independent of biology. But recently, with the revival of the perceptron in layered form (PDP), there are signs of a new liaison. For now there is the image of self-organizing "neural nets" which modify themselves according to the sort of instruction that is little more than the remarking of error. This development has had a great impact on neuroscience, cognitive science, and related fields. From the biological view the products of PDP are not related to actual living systems any more than those that have issued from AI. But the idea that distributed processing has important properties has struck a loud chord, and McCulloch would have loved to have heard it.

Real nervous systems are characterized by widely distributed many-to-many connections between neurons. Such connectivity is the rule rather than the exception. One neuron in the brain receives its input from thousands of others and distributes its output to yet thousands of others. This massive connectivity accounts for the despair of those who sought to model real nervous nets and for the sudden enthusiasm with which PDP has been greeted. In a sense there are properties of such connected systems that are more or less independent of the intrinsic nature of the nonlinear elements used, whether gates or neurons.

By now it is clear that the immediate future of study in the modeling of the brain lies with the synthesis of gadgets more than with the analysis of data. Sooner or later the modelers will have to winnow the empirics of neuroscience and psychology. But as it stands today, they are the avant-garde and are rolling.

It is only natural that students in this burgeoning art should be curious about its origins and about what the originators thought. That is why this book has been reissued. And students can dream of how to rewrite "How We Perceive Universals" had Warren McCulloch known of PDP.

Warren McCulloch chose the writings in this collection. It is a sampler rather than an omnibus; many important works are not included. And that is as it should be since Warren preferred gesture and illusion to a full picture with everything spelled out. This made him a most enjoyable teacher, somewhat cryptic, but in a way that enhanced his ideas rather than obscured them. He wrote, talked, and comported himself as a cavalier. I do not think any of his friends would have been surprised had he shown with a rapier slung at his side and wearing a plumed hat askew.

But his ideas rather than his person are the substance of this book. Some of them call for a perspective rather than a commentary, and that may be the best service for a preface.

Two essays with Walter Pitts (one on the logical calculus possible with neuronal arrays, the other on perceiving universals) were, as best I know, the first attempt at a theory of how the mechanism of the brain can sustain mental process. These two papers are at the foundation of what later became known as artificial intelligence. Because Walter and I were living with Warren at the time the papers were spawned, I can provide some background.

The drive behind Warren and Walter's approach came from Leibnitz, who was Walter's favorite philosopher and whom Warren much admired. Leibnitz had shown that all logic could be reduced to an arithmetic and the arithmetic expressed in binary notation. Indeed he had done much of what was later issued independently by Boole. He conceived a logic engine that could compute any computable number by carrying out a chosen series of algebraic operations—what we now call algorithms. And he spent a fortune trying to realize it. At the same time Leibnitz was sharply aware that the very notion of such a machine raises some basic questions in epistemology. Some of his ideas are in part given in the Monadology, wherein he contrasts the principle of contradiction with the principle of sufficient reason, and the eternal truths of logic with the contingent truths of observation on the world. Such a dual approach to the nature of brain as meat machine (to use Minsky's epithet) begins in the seventeenth century with Descartes and Leibnitz, among others.

Once it was realized in the nineteenth century that nerve fibers conduct electrical pulses and that the pulse trains on these fibers carry meaningful messages, the problem was to account for how such information was processed by the brain as nerve net. Both excitation and inhibition had been shown as nervous actions before 1900, but it was not until David Lloyd's work in 1939–41 that the direct monosynaptic inhibitory and excitatory actions of nervous pulses were demonstrated. This finding, more than anything else, led Warren and Walter to conceive of single neurons as doing logical operations (à la Leibnitz and Boole) and acting as gates. Their concept was the first and most inspired attempt at a theory of nervous action that transcended Sherrington's earlier town-meeting model of central excitatory and inhibitory states, as if the strength of a proposed action could be measured by a simple continuous tally of yea and nay votes. Once this idea of neurons as logical gates was clear, Warren and Walter had to lay out the designing of them and then the ways of connecting them for specific operations; and this they did in engineering style with great verve. It doesn't matter that the rigor was not perfect—and the neurons very different from real ones—they were concerned more with the notion of working devices than with formal completeness of the system.

That ambition—to show how mental process is sustainable by nervous mechanism—comes to its height in the paper on how universals might be perceived. Here they took what was known of the architecture of the brain cortex to show how relations between the parts of a form could survive changes of scale of the form. It is a remarkable venture, as ingenious in its marriage of anatomy and function as it is purposely naive. Having devised the logical calculus of nervous activity, Walter and Warren were obliged to show how it could be used. And with gleeful hubris they chose as example not some simple reflex mediated by a system of not too great fine structure but rather what can be called a "higher function" processed by an unutterably complicated system. It doesn't matter whether the mechanism they describe actually occurs. That is beside the point. What matters is that such an engine can be designed using the methods they had laid down. They would rather have been clearly wrong than maunderingly vague, as was the accepted style. No point is served by elaborating further on this work. Other more extended appreciations and criticisms are well known.

Once this model of nervous function appeared, so apposite to the notions of digital computers already in the planning stage, great excitement spread among students of the emerging information sciences. But there was relatively little impact on nervous physiology. Warren and Walter were certainly alive to the kind of reservations that von Neumann later voiced in his essay "The Natural and Logical Theory of Automata" (thereby restating the duality in Leibnitz's thought). This important double view is usually caricatured in learned discussions of the mind-body problem. It is relevant here because Warren, who began as a gifted naturalist and remained so to the end, became entranced with alternative logics—three-valued logic, probabilistic logic, etc. At the same time Walter, who early in life dreamed of conquering the whole of natural science by logic, became ardently involved in empirics. In a sense they converted each other.

When Warren, Walter, Pat Wall, and I came to MIT, it was with the aim of marrying physiological data to advanced speculation on how a nervous system works. Norbert Wiener had already had an encounter with the problem. He had challenged Arturo Rosenblueth, saying that a few weeks of work would suffice to give an analytic expression to the input-output relations of a simple reflex. Whereupon Arturo mischievously invited him to design the experiments and to watch them being done in

Mexico City. Wiener's letter at the end of three weeks was a lively diatribe on noisy nonlinear systems that were clearly designed to frustrate right-thinking analysts.

After some initial work on spinal cord mechanisms, I shifted to the study of the frog's eye and then entrained Humberto Maturana from Harvard. When we collected the data put forth in one of the papers of this sampler, Warren, Walter, Humberto, and I gathered with Oliver Selfridge to hammer out the account. In line with our own perceptual experience we couched what we found in terms of universals of perception in the frog. The experiments had been done with that in mind. I remember well Walter's delighted despair at the results and Warren's almost bland acceptance of them as to have been expected. Warren never much shared Walter's and my enjoyment of Kant, and yet he admired Otto Magnus for the notion of the physiological a priori. So Walter, Oliver, Humberto, and I pushed strongly to couch the paper as the physiological demonstration of the synthetic a priori. Warren, with wry humor, gave in.

In this way Warren and Walter conspired to what seemed the idealistic obverse of their logical calculus. The universals are clear but hard to define, and the proper descriptions of them are fairly long even in precis because of the multiple contingencies. Now the challenge was to account for these distinct and clear but endlessly described universals or invariances in terms of a logical circuitry compatible with the retinal anatomy as then known.

As Warren pointed out, he accepted the synthetic a priori—he was not going to pretend to any tabula rasa notions like those of Locke or Bertrand Russell. But he still held that in the end there would be an algorithmic description of the processes that engendered what "perceptual" operations we found. There is no magic. And of course he is quite right. The retina is a machine, meaty and miraculous, but still a machine. Bit by bit the mechanism is coming to light, so to speak. The nervous engine is not had from neurons as logical gates but more as complex analog processors. Yet this does not contradict the spirit of the original essays on the logical calculus. It complements and augments those earliest notions.

Reminiscences may not be proper to a preface that ought to deal with the text in a dispassionate and thoughtful way. But Warren took such care with his words and sculpted his essays with so loving a hand that I could not rival his prose nor pretend disinterested judgment of it. On rereading his essays and poems, I find them as delightful as when I first read them fresh from his pen. Only one confession is due and it is my defect. He wrote many of his essays to be read aloud, but I always found them much harder to audit than to read—and that is because his allusions, which are transparent on paper, go by too quickly, as does his wordplay. He has an enviable style and is marvelously the cavalier that I remember.

Preface

This book presents our attempt to found a physiological theory of knowledge. It is gratefully dedicated to all my collaborators.

Except for three papers that were published in the *Journal of Mathematical Biophysics,* the articles were lectures, written over some twenty years for dissimilar audiences. Each can be read by itself.

It is in the interest of science to expose the formation of hypotheses to the criticism of fellow scientists in the hope of experimental contradiction. Facts have often compelled me to change my mind; but, to keep the record straight, no sins of commission or of omission have been corrected in these texts. You may hold me responsible, as principal author of all but one of these.

I have had about one hundred collaborators whom I must thank collectively without catalogue of their names or their contributions. My indebtedness to Walter Pitts is, of course, much greater than appears from our joint publications.

Jerome Lettvin, with Humberto Maturana, wrote "What the Frog's Eye Tells the Frog's Brain." I am delighted to have it included, for it is our first major step in experimental epistemology.

WARREN S. MCCULLOCH

Cambridge, Massachusetts
January 1965

Acknowledgments

The following have been reprinted with permission of the authors and publishers:

1. Warren S. McCulloch, "What Is a Number, that a Man May Know It, and a Man, that He May Know a Number?" (the Ninth Alfred Korzybski Memorial Lecture), *General Semantics Bulletin,* Nos. 26 and 27 (Lakeville, Conn.: Institute of General Semantics, 1961), pp. 7-18.

2. Warren S. McCulloch and Walter H. Pitts, "A Logical Calculus of the Ideas Immanent in Nervous Activity," *Bulletin of Mathematical Biophysics,* Vol. 5 (Chicago: University of Chicago Press, 1943), pp. 115-133.

3. Warren S. McCulloch, "A Heterarchy of Values Determined by the Topology of Nervous Nets," *Bulletin of Mathematical Biophysics,* Vol. 7 (Chicago: University of Chicago Press, 1945), pp. 89-93.

4. Walter Pitts and Warren S. McCulloch, "How We Know Universals: The Perception of Auditory and Visual Forms," *Bulletin of Mathematical Biophysics,* Vol. 9 (Chicago. University of Chicago Press, 1947), pp. 127-147.

5. Warren S. McCulloch, "Modes of Functional Organization of the Cerebral Cortex," *Federation Proceedi ɪgs,* Vol. 6 (Washington, D.C: Federation of American Societies for Experimental Biology, 1947), pp. 448-452.

6. Warren S. McCulloch, "Why the Mind Is in the Head," in L. A. Jeffress, ed., *Cerebral Mechanisms in Behavior,* the Hixon Symposium (New York: John Wiley, 1951), pp. 42-111. Copyright now held by the California Institute of Technology.

7. Warren S. McCulloch, "Through the Den of the Metaphysician," a lecture delivered to the Philosophical Club of the University of Virginia, March 23, 1948. English version of "Dans l'antre du métaphysicien," *Thales,* Vol. 7 (Paris: Presses Universitaires de France, 1951), pp. 37-49.

8. Warren S. McCulloch, *"Mysterium Iniquitatis* of Sinful Man Aspiring into the Place of God," *The Scientific Monthly,* Vol. 80, No. 1 (January 1955), pp. 35-39. Copyright 1955 by the American Association for the Advancement of Science.

9. P. D. Wall, W. S. McCulloch, J. Y. Lettvin, and W. H. Pitts, "Effects of Strychnine with Special Reference to Spinal Afferent

Fibres," *Epilepsia,* Series III, Vol. 4 (Amsterdam: Elsevier Publishing Company, 1955), pp. 29-40.

10. R. Howland, J. Y. Lettvin, W. S. McCulloch, W. Pitts, and P. D. Wall, "Reflex Inhibition by Dorsal Root Interaction," *Journal of Neurophysiology,* Vol. 18 (Washington D.C.: The American Physiological Society, 1955), pp. 1-17.

11. W. S. McCulloch, "Toward Some Circuitry of Ethical Robots or an Observational Science of the Genesis of Social Evaluation in the Mind-Like Behavior of Artifacts," *Acta Biotheoretica,* Vol. XI (1956), pp. 147-156.

12. W. S. McCulloch, "Agatha Tyche: Of Nervous Nets — the Lucky Reckoners," *Mechanisation of Thought Processes: Proceedings of a Symposium Held at the National Physical Laboratory,* November 24-27, 1958, No. 10, Vol. II (London: Her Majesty's Stationery Office, 1959), pp. 611-634.

13. Warren S. McCulloch, "Where Is Fancy Bred?" in Henry W. Brosin, ed., *Lectures on Experimental Psychiatry* (Pittsburgh, Pa.: University of Pittsburgh Press, 1961), pp. 311-324.

14. J. Y. Lettvin, H. R. Maturana, W. S. McCulloch, and W. H. Pitts, "What the Frog's Eye Tells the Frog's Brain," *Proceedings of the IRE,* Vol. 47, No. 11 (November 1959), pp. 1940-1959.

15. Warren S. McCulloch, "Finality and Form," Publication No. 11 in the American Lecture Series (Springfield, Ill.: Charles C Thomas, 1952).

16. Warren S. McCulloch, "The Past of a Delusion," copyright 1953 by the Chicago Literary Club.

17. Warren S. McCulloch, "Machines That Think and Want," originally entitled "Brain and Behavior," in Ward C. Halstead, ed., *Comparative Psychology Monograph* 20, No. 1, Series 103 (Berkeley, Cal.: University of California Press, 1950), pp. 39-50.

18. Warren S. McCulloch, "The Natural Fit," copyright 1959 by the Chicago Literary Club.

19. Warren S. McCulloch, "A Historical Introduction to the Postulational Foundations of Experimental Epistemology," in F. S. C. Northrop and Helen H. Livingston, eds., *Cross-Cultural Understanding: Epistemology in Anthropology* (New York: Harper & Row, Publishers, Incorporated, 1964), pp. 180-193. Copyright © 1964 by the Wenner-Gren Foundation for Anthropological Research, Incorporated.

20. Warren S. McCulloch, "Physiological Processes Underlying Psychoneuroses," *Proceedings of the Royal Society of Medicine,* Vol. 42 (1949), pp. 71-84.

21. Warren S. McCulloch, "What's in the Brain That Ink May Character?" presented at the International Congress for Logic, Methodology and Philosophy of Science, Jerusalem, Israel, August 28, 1964.

Contents

Contents

Introduction

Seymour Papert

When McCulloch's essays are hard to understand, the trouble lies less often in the internal logic of the individual arguments than in the perception of a unifying theme that runs, sometimes with exuberant clarity, sometimes in a tantalizingly elusive way, through the whole work. The consequent perplexity is partly intentional — McCulloch is at least as much concerned with questions as with answers — and partly the result of his way of expressing the general through the particular. But much of the difficulty exists because *we* come with habits based on more fashionable modes of thought, expecting philosophical questions to be discussed in the manner of the contemporary philosophers, and cybernetic questions with the same intention as they are given by other cyberneticists. On both counts we can be led seriously astray.

Embodiments of Mind must not be read as a more pleasing name for the set of puzzles sometimes called "the mind-body problem." The radical difference is marked by the possibility of discussion about whether these puzzles are "linguistic" rather than "genuine theoretical problems." Those that worry McCulloch are unquestionably genuinely theoretical, and linguistic only in the sense that they require as part of their solution the construction of a better theory of language than we possess today. Consider an example: A man has a mind to say something and says it. The embodiment problem is directed toward describing coherently, and relating on all levels of interpretation, the complex of events involved in such situations: the intention, the utterance, the reference of the utterance, the happenings in the man's brain.

It would be futile to discuss whether this enterprise belongs to philosophy, to neurology, or to psychology except that each of these disciplines has established traditions and modes of thought that preclude progress by deformation of the problem. The philosopher is skilled in the fine analysis of the logical structure of concepts but spurns all consideration of mechanisms and shies away from the formulation of general laws, while the tradition of the psychology of thinking leads to the choice of such simple experimental situations and theoretical models as to miss the philosophically interesting structural features of knowledge. There are, of course, good historical reasons for this polarization. Few thinkers in the mainstream of our philosophical tradition make any sharp distinction between what would today be classified as psychological and philosophical arguments. The dialogue between British "empiricist" philosophers and Continental rationalists about the existence of innate ideas constantly combines philosophical analysis with appeals to psychological evidence. Moreover, each side postulates mechanisms to account for the facts as it conceives them. A clear case in point is the associationist theory of knowledge. On the opposite side we find Kant making statements that would not be out of place in a discussion on techniques of programming: "our representation of things, as these are given to us, does not conform to these things as they are in themselves, but . . . these objects, as appearances, conform to our mode of representation." But while the embodiment of associationism poses no immediate conceptual problem, Kant's doctrine could neither be translated into material terms nor adequately developed on a clear, logical basis without concepts of representation and computation that would not come into being until our own period. The opposition between Hume and Kant is merely one example of a general process of growth in which epistemological sophistication outpaced the development of notions of logical and material mechanisms. A split had eventually to come between psychology, which was based on mechanism but unable to reach the complex properties of thought, and philosophy, which took the properties of thought seriously but could be satisfied with no conceivable mechanism.

We need no longer be trapped in this dilemma. Nevertheless, when the development of logic in the nineteen-thirties and of cybernetics in the next decade offered a way out, the opposition had, by the operation of one of the most general laws of the dynamics of systems of ideas, become categorized and built into many structural features of our thinking. The result was that a more thoroughgoing reconstruction than most men could tolerate was needed to reverse the process on an individual basis.

Thus McCulloch is not historically isolated in his plea for a *theoretical* epistemology, as opposed to the set of *analytical* and *critical* techniques to which the influential modern schools of philosophy restrict the theory of knowledge. And although this places him in a minority position among his contemporaries, he is not alone.

In listing some of his allies it is fitting to begin by mentioning the proposal for philosophical reform published in 1943 by a young British psychologist who was unable to live long enough to assume the role that should have been his in the development of cybernetic epistemology. The spirit of Kenneth Craik's thought is shown by the following quotation from his book *The Nature of Explanation*:

> Our question, to emphasize it once again, is not to ask what kind of thing a number is, but to think what kind of mechanism could represent so many physically possible or impossible, and yet self-consistent, processes as number does.

By a remarkable coincidence, which shows that these ideas were well rooted in that period, two important papers written in this spirit were published in the same year in the United States. One, by Julian Bigelow, Arturo Rosenblueth, and Norbert Wiener, set out the general principles for mechanisms that would embody the concept, no less difficult philosophically than number, of purpose. The other, by Warren McCulloch and Walter Pitts, described a logical calculus and the principles of construction for a class of computing machines that would permit the embodiment of any theory of mind or behavior provided only that it satisfied some very general principles of finitude and causality. These two papers introduce so clearly the new frame of thought that their publication could well be taken as the birth of explicit cybernetics. To that matter we shall return, after mentioning a fourth, rather different but equally important, focus of the new epistemological approach.

Jean Piaget, by origin a zoologist, set out to elucidate the mechanisms of knowledge by studying their development in small children. The advantages of this "genetic" approach are obvious. The structure of thinking in children is simple enough for ingenious experiments to lay bare its epistemological architectonics and show in operation processes similar in nature to those postulated by philosophers. One sees very clearly, for example, the way in which reality conforms to modes of representation characteristic of various stages of development. In a certain sense this confirms the correctness and utility of the Kantian principle cited earlier. On the other hand, the dynamic development of the modes of representation shows that Kant's theory must and can be refined and corrected in detail: the intuitions are not innate and unchangeable but can themselves be explained in terms of more fundamental processes. In his attempt to do so, Piaget is guided by his observation of children to formulate more precise theoretical tools for the conceptualization of the mechanisms of knowing than any classical epistemologist ever possessed.

The common feature of these proposals is their recognition that the laws governing the embodiment of mind should be sought among the laws governing information rather than energy or matter. This is clearest in the Bigelow-Rosenblueth-Wiener paper, but only because the situation they study is simpler than the others in its informational aspects. The principal conceptual step was the recognition that a host of physically different situations involving the teleonomic regulation of behavior in mechanical, electrical, biological, and even social systems should be understood as manifestations of one basic phenomenon: the return of information to form a closed control loop. It is perhaps slightly less evident that the key insight of the McCulloch and Pitts paper is essentially the same. A brief glance at the history of some aspects of the embodiment problem may make this clearer.

The theory of perception has been plagued by the idea that there must be in the brain some sort of geometrically faithful representation of the outside world. An early incident centered about this issue is the discussion of the problem of the inverted retinal image, which seems to have perplexed a number of clear thinkers including Leonardo da Vinci. The puzzle is essentially resolved in the hands of Descartes, who anticipates modern cybernetic ideas in his representation of the situation as a coding problem: there is no puzzle because no information is lost by the inversion. But if Descartes is able to think clearly about the transmission of information, in both senses, between the periphery and the brain, he is unable, for lack of a notion of computation, to say enough about intervening operations on it to provide a useful or intellectually satisfying model. This deficiency continues to make itself felt even in the first half of the twentieth century in the context of the perception of form. For although the infiltration of words like "isomorphism" and "topological" had eliminated the more elementary paradoxes, the only neurophysiological hypotheses about perception to be described in any detail during this period were those involving some sort of quasi-spatial model in the brain. The notion that the events in the brain could in every physical sense be arbitrarily unlike the perceived world had, of course, been considered; but no one had been able to develop it on a technical level into a sufficiently elaborated model to exert a competitive influence. McCulloch and Pitts were associated with two decisive acts that penetrated this barrier: their own 1943 paper which provides for the first time a set of mathematical instruments sufficiently powerful for the conceptual description of such hypotheses; and the investigation of the frog's visual system that culminated in the brilliant experiments carried out by their friends J. Y. Lettvin and H. R. Maturana and in the paper "What the Frog's Eye Tells the Frog's Brain."

The liberating effect of the mode of thinking characteristic of the McCulloch and Pitts theory can be felt on two levels. On the global level it permits the formulation of a vastly greater class of hypotheses about brain mechanisms. On the local level it eliminates all consideration of the detailed biology of the individual cells from the problem of understanding the integrative behavior of the nervous system. This is done by postulating a hypothetical species of neuron defined entirely by the computation of an output as a logical function of a restricted set of input neurons. The construction of neural circuits using schematic neurons specified by their conditions of firing was not in itself either original or profound; these had often been used diagrammatically to illustrate such simple things as reflex arcs. The step that needed boldness of conception and mathematical acumen was the realization that one could formalize the relations between neurons well enough to allow general statements about the global behavior of arbitrarily large and only partly specified nets to be deduced from assumptions about the form and connectivity of their components.

It is easy to fall into the error of reading "A Logical Calculus of Ideas Immanent in Nervous Activity" as a document of purely historical interest where contents have become obvious and commonplace. That this is true on a certain level of interpretation is proof of the results of the revolution in thought that has taken place since Rashevsky's valiant *Bulletin of Mathematical Biophysics* first presented the paper, twenty-one years ago, to a hostile or indifferent world. But if one looks behind the technical assertion at the style of thought and the intention of its authors, one soon discerns features that separate it sharply from typical current cybernetic writing. Of these the chief is its rationalist quest for necessity and comprehension as opposed to the merely pragmatic tests that so often satisfy those who build "models" of neural activities on psychological processes. The distinction is felt in the opening part of the paper. The authors will, as everyone knows, build their nets out of their now famous threshold neurons. But in doing so their first care is to make it clear that nothing of what they say is to be contingent on theoretically arbitrary choices of particular kinds of formal neuron; their first theorems assert the *invariance* of their basic definition with respect to a number of such choices; and if they restrict themselves to special cases, this is a matter of individual style and the lack of mathematical tools. When we reach the end of the paper, we are rewarded for the effort of struggling through its unfortunate logical notation by seeing the first birth of a true mathematical idea: Between the class of trivial combinational functions computable by simple Boolean logic and the too general class of functions computable by Turing machines, there are intermediate classes of computability determined by the most universal and natural mathematical feature of the net — its finiteness. This is pure mathematics. The theoretical assertion of the paper is that the behavior of any brain *must* be characterized by the computation of functions of one of these classes.

The point might be made more clearly by contrasting this statement with a widespread misinterpretation of this paper. It is often said that McCulloch and Pitts prove (critics say "only prove") some such proposition as: Whatever can be completely described can be realized by a net of neurons. This is misleading or false. For if the "description" is by complete explicit listing, then much simpler nets (without circles) would be sufficient; but if arbitrary constructive mathematical means may be used in the "description," one might need a Turing machine to realize the computation, and McCulloch and Pitts know perfectly well that their nets cannot compute all the functions computable by Turing machines. Any such attempt at simple statement misses the fundamental point that this paper introduces a *new concept,* for which we now have many formal definitions, but which can be related to simple intuitive concepts only in the sense that "force" as defined by physics is related to intuitive notions of force. The same issue arises, in material form, when it is said or denied that McCulloch and Pitts prove that the brain is a machine. A better formulation is to say that they provide a definition of "computing machine" that enables us to think of the brain as a "machine" in a much more precise sense than we could before. The advance is conceptual. From this step follows the possibility of formulating more precise particular hypotheses (as McCulloch and Pitts do themselves in "How We Know Universals" and many others have done since) about the specific structure of the net. From this also follows the familiar flood of attempts to dissolve away the problem of knowledge into simple processes of cybernetic fiddling with thresholds or random program generators. Perhaps this is the place to emphasize that McCulloch is not to blame for this. Indeed, he insists that to understand such complex things as numbers we must know how to embody them in nets of simple neurons. But he would add that we cannot pretend to understand these nets of simple neurons until we know — which we do not except for an existence proof — how they embody such complex things as numbers. We must, so to speak, maintain a dialectical balance between evading the problem of knowledge by declaring that it is "nothing but" an affair of simple neurons, without postulating "anything but" neurons in the brain. The point is, if I understand him well, that the "something but" we need is not of the brain but of our minds: namely, a mathematical theory of complex relations powerful enough to bridge the gap between the level of neurons and the level of knowledge in a far more detailed way than can any we now possess.

It would be very wrong to conclude that this mathematical deficiency in itself is any cause for skepticism about the value of the cybernetic method. On the contrary, the most convincing argument for its validity would be a demonstration that the problems and difficulties which have always faced men concerned with the nature of their own thinking — whether they are philosophers concerned with the presuppositions of knowledge, poets concerned with the mastery through simple words of man's complex relations, or architects concerned with the embodiment in matter of the abstract forms of the mind — come up in equivalent form in the new context. However, no demonstration of this sort could be completely formal and rigorous. Nor could it be produced by a rapid analysis of a small number of examples. It could come about only by insightful rethinking of old problems in the new terms, and to this, no less than to the initial tasks of forging fundamental concepts, Warren McCulloch has made an eminent contribution with a very personal flavor. In the nature of the case it is impossible to summarize or to generalize the conclusions to be drawn from such work — and it should be particularly noted that McCulloch himself scrupulously avoids forcing his ideas into prematurely categorical form. Like some of the Greeks he knows so well, and like Wittgenstein, whom he does not know, he is a master of the technique of speaking in such a way as to set the mind of the cooperative and active auditor into that motion which will lead him to insight. To members of his audience who are led to miss the point by their habit of expecting predigested conclusions, he is fond of saying: "Don't bite my finger, look where I am pointing."

Embodiments of Mind

What Is a Number,
that a Man May Know It,
and a Man,
that He May Know a Number?

Warren S. McCulloch

GENTLEMEN: I am very sensible of the honor you have conferred upon me by inviting me to read this lecture. I am only distressed, fearing you may have done so under a misapprehension; for, though my interest always was to reduce epistemology to an experimental science, the bulk of my publications has been concerned with the physics and chemistry of the brain and body of beasts. For my interest in the functional organization of the nervous system, that knowledge was as necessary as it was insufficient in all problems of communication in men and machines. I had begun to fear that the tradition of experimental epistemology I had inherited through Dusser de Barenne from Rudolph Magnus would die with me, but if you read "What the Frog's Eye Tells the Frog's Brain," written by Jerome Y. Lettvin, which appeared in the *Proceedings of the Institute of Radio Engineers,* November 1959, you will realize that the tradition will go on after I am gone. The inquiry into the physiological substrate of knowledge is here to stay until it is solved thoroughly, that is, until we have a satisfactory explanation of how we know what we know, stated in terms of the physics and chemistry, the anatomy and physiology, of the biological system. At the moment my age feeds on my youth — and both are unknown to you. It is not because I have reached what Oliver Wendell Holmes would call "our anecdotage" — but because all impersonal questions arise from personal reasons and are best understood from their histories — that I would begin with my youth.

I come of a family that, whether it be a corporeal or incorporeal *hereditimentum,* produces, with few notable exceptions, professional

1

men and women — lawyers, doctors, engineers, and theologians. My older brother was a chemical engineer. I was destined for the ministry. Among my teen-age acquaintances were Henry Sloan Coffin, Harry Emerson Fosdick, H. K. W. Kumm, Hecker — of the Church of All Nations — sundry Episcopalian theologians, and that great Quaker philosopher, Rufus Jones.

In the fall of 1917, I entered Haverford College with two strings to my bow — facility in Latin and a sure foundation in mathematics. I "honored" in the latter and was seduced by it. That winter Rufus Jones called me in. "Warren," said he, "what is thee going to be?" And I said, "I don't know." "And what is thee going to do?" And again I said, "I have no idea; but there is one question I would like to answer: What is a number, that a man may know it, and a man, that he may know a number?" He smiled and said, "Friend, thee will be busy as long as thee lives." I have been, and that is what we are here about.

That spring I joined the Naval Reserve and, for about a year of active duty, worked on problems of submarine listening, marlinspike seamanship, and semaphore, ending at Yale in the Officers' Training School, where my real function was to teach celestial navigation. I stayed there, majoring in philosophy, minoring in psychology, until I graduated and went to Columbia, took my M.A. in psychology, working on experimental aesthetics, and then to its medical school, for the sole purpose of understanding the physiology of the nervous system, at which I have labored ever since.

It was in 1919 that I began to labor chiefly on logic, and by 1923 I had attempted to manufacture a logic of transitive verbs. In 1928 I was in neurology at Bellevue Hospital and in 1930 at Rockland State Hospital for the Insane, but my purpose never changed. It was then that I encountered Eilhard von Domarus, the great philosophic student of psychiatry, from whom I learned to understand the logical difficulties of true cases of schizophrenia and the development of psychopathia — not merely clinically, as he had learned them of Berger, Birnbaum, Bumke, Hoche, Westphal, Kahn, and others — but as he understood them from his friendship with Bertrand Russell, Heidegger, Whitehead, and Northrop — under the last of whom he wrote his great unpublished thesis, "The Logical Structure of Mind: An Inquiry into the Philosophical Foundations of Psychology and Psychiatry." It is to him and to our mutual friend, Charles Holden Prescott, that I am chiefly indebted for my understanding of *paranoia vera* and of the possibility of making the scientific method applicable to systems of many degrees of freedom. From Rockland I went back to Yale's Laboratory of Neurophysiology to work with the erstwhile psychiatrist, Dusser de Barenne, on experimental epistemology; and only after his death, when I had finished the last job on strychnine neuronography to which he had laid his hand, did I go to Illinois as a Professor of Psychiatry, always pursuing the same theme, especially with Walter Pitts. I was there eleven years working on physiology in terms of anatomy, physics, and chemistry until, in 1952, I went to the Research Laboratory of Electronics of the Massachusetts Institute of Technology to work on the circuit theory of brains. Granted that I have never relinquished my interest in empiricism and am chiefly interested in the condition of water in living systems — witness the work of my collaborator, Berendsen, on nuclear magnetic resonance — it is with my ideas concerning number and logic, before 1917 and after 1952, that we are now concerned.

II

This lecture might be called, "In Quest of the Logos" or, more appropriately — perverting St. Bonaventura's famous title — "An Itinerary to Man." Its proper preface is that St. Augustine says that it was a pagan philosopher — a Neoplatonist — who wrote, "In the beginning was the Logos, without the Logos was not anything made that was made. . . . " So begins our Christian theology. It rests on four principles. The first is the eternal verities. Listen to the thunder of that saint, in about A.D. 500: "7 and 3 are 10; 7 and 3 have always been 10; 7 and 3 at no time and in no way have ever been anything but 10; 7 and 3 will always be 10. I said that these indestructible truths of arithmetic are common to all who reason." An eternal verity, any cornerstone of theology is a statement that is true regardless of the time and place of its utterance. Each he calls an idea in the Mind of God, which we can understand but can never comprehend. His examples are drawn chiefly from arithmetic, geometry, and logic, but he includes what we would now call the laws of Nature, according to which God created the world. Yet he did not think all men equally gifted, persistent, or perceptive to grasp their ultimate consequences, and he was fully aware of the pitfalls along the way. The history of Western science

3

would have been no shock to his theology. That it took a Galileo, a Newton, and an Einstein to lead us eventually to a tensor invariant, as it did, fits well with his theory of knowledge and truth. He would expect most men to understand ratio and proportion, but few to suspect the categorical implications of a supposition that simultaneity was not defined for systems moving with respect to one another. There is one passage that I can understand only by supposing that he knew well why the existence of horn angles had compelled Euclid's shift to Eudoxus' definition of ratio (I think it's in the fifth book), for things may be infinite with respect to one another and thence have no ratio. Be that as it may, we come next to authority.

Among the scholastic philosophers it is always in a suspect position. There are always questions of the corruption of the text; there are always questions of interpretations or of translations from older forms, or older meanings of the words, even of grammatical constructions. And who were the authorities? Plato, of course, and many a Neoplatonist and, later, Aristotle, known chiefly through the Arabs. Which others are accepted depends chiefly on the date, the school, and the question at issue. But the rules of right reason were fixed. One established first his logic — a realistic logic — despite nominalistic criticism such as Peter Abelard's, despite the Academicians invoking Aristotle's accusation of Plato that "he multiplied his worlds," a conclusion at variance with modern logical decisions and sometimes at variance with the Church. After logic, came being — ontology if you will, for being is a matter of definition, without which one never knows about what he speaks. To this, the apparent great exception is Thomas Aquinas, who takes existence as primary. This gives mere fact priority over the verities and tends to make his logic, although realistic, a consequence of epistemology — that is, to put fact ahead of reason and truth after it. Perhaps for this reason, although Roman law is clearly Stoic, he quotes Cicero more often than any other authority. His "God, in whom we live and move and have our being," is the existent. Therefore He alone knows us as we know ourselves. Consciousness, being an agreement of witnesses, becomes conscience, for while we may fool others, we cannot fool God; one ought to act as God knows him. The result is good ethics, but little contribution to science. His conception fits the Roman requirement of the agreement of witnesses required by law, as at the trial of Christ — and today in forensic medicine —

but not the scientist's requirement, who in the moment of discovery is the only one who knows the very thing he knows and has to wait until God agrees with him.

From that saint's day on, the battle rages between the Platonists and the Aristotelians. But the fourth principle in theology begins to take first place — witness Roger Bacon. One has the eternal verities (logic, mathematics, and to a less extent, the laws of Nature). One has the authorities, whom one tests against the verities by reason — and there, in the old sense, ended the "experiment." In the new sense, one had to look again at Nature for its laws, for they also are ideas in the Mind of the Creator. Of Roger Bacon's outstanding knowledge of mathematics and logic there can be no doubt, but his observations are such that one suspects he had invented some sort of telescope and microscope. Natural law began to grow. Duns Scotus was its last scholastic defender, and the last to insist on realistic logic, without which there is no science of the world. His subtle philosophy makes full use of Aristotle's logic and shows well its limitation. Deductions lead from rules and cases to facts — the conclusions. Inductions lead toward truth, with less assurance, from cases and facts, toward rules as generalizations, valid for bound cases, not for accidents. Abductions, the apagoge of Aristotle, lead from rules and facts to the hypothesis that the fact is a case under the rule. This is the breeding place of scientific ideas to be tested by experiment. To these we shall return later; for, nudged by Chaos, they are sufficient to account for intuition or insight, or invention. There is no other road toward truth. Through this period the emphasis had shifted from the eternal verities of mathematics and logic to the laws of Nature.

Hard on the heels of Duns Scotus trod William of Ockham, greatest of nominalists. He quotes "Entia non sint multiplicanda praeter necessitatem" against the multiplicity of entities necessary for Duns's subtleties. He demands that there be no collusion of arguments from the stern realities of logic with the stubbornnesses of fact. His intent is to reach deductive conclusions with certainty, but he suspected that the syllogism is a straitjacket. Of course he recognized that, and I quote him, "man thinks in two kinds of terms: one, the natural terms, shared with beasts; the other, the conventional terms (the logicals) enjoyed by man alone." By Ockham, logic, and eventually mathematics, are uprooted from empirical science. To ensure that nothing shall be in the conclusion that is not in the premise bars two roads that lead to the truth of the world and reduces the third road to the vacuous truth of circuitous tautology, "ὁ αὐτὸς λόγος." It is clear on reading him that he only sharpened a distinction between the real classes and classes of real things, but it took hold of a world that was becoming empirical in an uncritical sense. It began to look on logic as a sterile fugling with mere words and numbers, whereas truth was to be sought from experiment among palpable things. Science in this sense was born. Logic decayed. Law usurped the throne of Theology, and eventually Science began to usurp the throne of Law. Not even the intellect of Leibnitz could lee-bow the tide. Locke confused the ideas of Newton with mere common notions. Berkeley, misunderstanding the notions of objectivity for an excess of subjectivity, committed the unpardonable sin of making God a *deus ex machina,* who, by perennial awareness, kept the world together where and when we had no consciousness of things.

David Hume revolted. Left with only a succession of perceptions, not a perception of succession, causality itself for him could be only "a habit of the mind." Compare this with Duns Scotus' following proposition reposing in the soul: "Whatever occurs as in a great many things from some cause which is not free, is the natural effect of that cause." Clearly, Hume lacked the necessary realistic logic; and his notions awoke Kant from his dogmatic slumbers — but only to invent a philosophy of science that takes epistemology as primary, makes ontology secondary, and ends with a logic in which the thing itself is unknown, and perception itself embodies a synthetic *a priori.* Doubtless his synthetic *a priori* has been the guiding star of the best voyages on the sea of "stimulus-equivalence." But more than once it has misguided us in the field of physics — perhaps most obviously when we ran head-on into antimatter, which Leibnitz' ontology and realistic logic might have taught us to expect.

What is much worse than this is the long neglect of Hume's great gift to mathematics. At the age of twenty-three he had already shown that only in logic and arithmetic can we argue through any number of steps, for only here have we the proper test. "For when a number hath a unit answering to an unit of the other we pronounce them equal."

Bertrand Russell was the first to thank Hume properly, and so to give us the usable definition, not merely of equal numbers, but of number: "A number is the class of all of those classes that can be put into one-to-one correspondence to it." Thus 7 is the class of all of those classes that can be put into one-to-one correspondence with the days of the week, which are 7. Some mathematicians may question whether or not this is an adequate definition of all that the mind of man has devised and calls number; but it suffices for my purpose, for what in 1917 I wanted to know was how it could be defined so that a man might know it. Clearly, one cannot comprehend all of the classes that can be put into one-to-one correspondence with the days of the week, but man understands the definition, for he knows the rule of procedure by which to determine it on any occasion. Duns Scotus has proved this to be sufficient for a realistic logic. But please note this: The numbers from 1 through 6 are perceptibles; others, only countables. Experiments on many beasts have often shown this: 1 through 6 are probably natural terms that we share with the beasts. In this sense they are natural numbers. All larger integers are arrived at by counting or putting pebbles in pots or cutting notches in sticks, each of which is — to use Ockham's phrase — a conventional term, a way of doing things that has grown out of our ways of getting together, our communications, our logos, tricks for setting things into one-to-one correspondence.

We have now reached this point in the argument. First, we have a definition of number which is logically useful. Second, it depends upon the perception of small whole numbers. Third, it depends upon a symbolic process of putting things into one-to-one correspondence in a conventional manner. Such then is the answer to the first half of the question. The second is much more difficult. We know what a number is that a man may know it, but what is a man that he may know a number?

III

Please remember that we are not now concerned with the physics and chemistry, the anatomy and physiology, of man. They are my daily business. They do not contribute to the logic of our problem. Despite Ramon Lull's combinatorial analysis of logic and all of his followers, including Leibnitz with his universal characteristic and his persistent effort to build logical computing machines, from the death of William of Ockham logic decayed. There were, of course, teachers of logic. The forms of the syllogism and the logic of classes were taught, and we shall use some of their devices, but there was a general recognition of their inadequacy to the problems in hand. Russell says it was Jevons — and Feibleman, that it was DeMorgan — who said, "The logic of Aristotle is inadequate, for it does not show that if a horse is an animal then the head of the horse is the head of an animal." To which Russell replies, "Fortunate Aristotle, for if a horse were a clam or a hydra it would not be so." The difficulty is that they had no knowledge of the logic of relations, and almost none of the logic of propositions. These logics really began in the latter part of the last century with Charles Peirce as their great pioneer. As with most pioneers, many of the trails he blazed were not followed for a score of years. For example, he discovered the amphecks — that is, "not both . . . and . . ." and "neither . . . nor . . . ," which Sheffer rediscovered and are called by his name for them, "stroke functions." It was Peirce who broke the ice with his logic of relatives, from which springs the pitiful beginnings of our logic of relations of two and more than two arguments. So completely had the traditional Aristotelian logic been lost that Peirce remarks that when he wrote the *Century Dictionary* he was so confused concerning abduction, or apagoge, and induction that he wrote nonsense. Thus Aristotelian logic, like the skeleton of Tom Paine, was lost to us from the world it had engendered. Peirce had to go back to Duns Scotus to start again the realistic logic of science. Pragmatism took hold, despite its misinterpretation by William James. The world was ripe for it. Frege, Peano, Whitehead, Russell, Wittgenstein, followed by a host of lesser lights, but sparked by many a strange character like Schroeder, Sheffer, Gödel, and company, gave us a working logic of propositions. By the time I had sunk my teeth into these questions, the Polish school was well on its way to glory. In 1923 I gave up the attempt to write a logic of transitive verbs and began to see what I could do with the logic of propositions. My object, as a psychologist, was to invent a kind of least psychic event, or "psychon," that would have the following properties: First, it was to be so simple an event that it either happened or else it did not happen. Second, it was to happen only if its bound cause had happened — shades of Duns Scotus! — that is, it was to imply its temporal antecedent. Third, it was to propose this to subsequent psychons. Fourth, these were to be compounded to produce the equivalents of more complicated propositions concerning their antecedents.

In 1929 it dawned on me that these events might be regarded

as the all-or-none impulses of neurons, combined by convergence upon the next neuron to yield complexes of propositional events. During the nineteen-thirties, first under influences from F. H. Pike, C. H. Prescott, and Eilhard von Domarus, and later, Northrop, Dusser de Barenne, and a host of my friends in neurophysiology, I began to try to formulate a proper calculus for these events by subscripting symbols for propositions in some sort of calculus of propositions (connected by implications) with the time of occurrence of the impulse in each neuron. My difficulties then were five-fold: (1) There was at that time no workable notion of inhibition, which had entered neurophysiology from clerical orders to desist. (2) There was a confusion concerning reflexes, which — thanks to Sir Charles Sherrington — had lost their definition as inverse, or negative, feedback. (3) There was my own confusion of material implication with strict implication. (4) There was my attempt to keep a weather eye open for known so-called field effects when I should have stuck to synaptic transmission proper except for storms like epileptic fits. Finally, (5) there was my ignorance of modulo mathematics that prevented me from understanding regenerative loops and, hence, memory. But neurophysiology moved ahead, and when I went to Chicago, I met Walter Pitts, then in his teens, who promptly set me right in matters of theory. It is to him that I am principally indebted for all subsequent success. He remains my best adviser and sharpest critic. You shall never publish this until it passes through his hands. In 1943 he, and I, wrote a paper entitled "A Logical Calculus of the Ideas Immanent in Nervous Activity." Thanks to Rashevsky's defense of logical and mathematical ideas in biology, it was published in his journal [*Bulletin of Mathematical Biophysics*], where, so far as biology is concerned, it might have remained unknown; but John von Neumann picked it up and used it in teaching the theory of computing machines. I shall summarize briefly its logical importance. Turing had produced a deductive machine that could compute any computable number, although it had only a finite number of parts which could be in only a finite number of states and although it could move only a finite number of steps forward or backward, look at one spot on its tape at a time, and make, or erase, 1 or else 0. What Pitts and I had shown was that neurons that could be excited or inhibited, given a proper net, could extract any configuration of signals in its input. Because the form of the entire argument was strictly logical, and because Gödel had arithmetized logic, we had proved, in substance, the equivalence of all general Turing machines — man-made or begotten.

But we had done more than this, thanks to Pitts's modulo mathematics. In looking into circuits composed of closed paths of neurons wherein signals could reverberate, we had set up a theory of memory — to which every other form of memory is but a surrogate requiring reactivation of a trace. Now a memory is a temporal invariant. Given an event at one time, and its regeneration at later dates, one knows that there was an event that was of the given kind. The logician says, "There was some x such that x was a ψ. In the symbols of the *principia mathematica*, $(\exists x)\ (\psi x)$. Given this and negation, for which inhibition suffices, we can have $\sim(\exists x)\ (\sim\psi x)$, or, if you will, $(x)\ (\psi x)$. Hence, we have the lower-predicate calculus with equality, which has recently been proved to be a sufficient logical framework for all of mathematics. Our next joint paper showed that the ψ's were not restricted to temporal invariants but, by reflexes and other devices, could be extended to any universal, and its recognition, by nets of neurons. That was published in Rashevsky's journal in 1947. It is entitled "How We Know Universals." Our idea is basically simple and completely general, because any object, or universal, is an invariant under some groups of transformations and, consequently, the net need only compute a sufficient number of averages a_i, each an Nth of the sum for all transforms T belonging to the group G, of the value assigned by the corresponding functional f_i, to every transform T, as a figure of excitation ϕ in the space and time of some mosaic of neurons. That is,

$$a_i = \frac{1}{N} \sum_{\substack{\text{all} \\ T \epsilon G}} f_i[T\phi]$$

The next difficulty was to cope with the so-called value anomaly. Plato had supposed that there was a common measure of all values. And in the article entitled "A Heterarchy of Values Determined by the Topology of Nervous Nets" (1945), I have shown that a system of six neurons is sufficiently complex to suffer no such *"summum bonum."* All of these things you will find summarized in my J. A. Thompson lecture of May 2, 1946, "Finality and Form in Nervous Activity" (shelved by the publisher until 1952), including a prospectus of things to come — all written with Pitts's help. About this time he had begun to look into the problem of randomly connected nets. And, I assure you, what we proposed were constructions that were proof against minor perturbations of stimuli, thresholds, and connections. Others have published, chiefly by his inspiration, much of less moment on this score, but because we could not make the necessary measurements, he has let it lie fallow. Only once did he present it — at an early and unpublished Conference on Cybernetics, sponsored by the Josiah Macy, Jr., Foundation. That was enough to start John von Neumann on a new tack. He published it under the title "Toward a Probabilistic Logic." By this he did not mean a logic in which only the arguments were probable, but a logic in which the function itself was only probable. He had decided for obvious reasons to embody his logic in a net of formal neurons that sometimes misbehaved, and to construct of them a device that was as reliable as was required in modern digital computers. Unfortunately, he made three assumptions, any one of which was sufficient to have precluded a reasonable solution. He was unhappy about it because it required neurons far more reliable than he could expect in human brains. The piquant assumptions were: first, that failures were absolute — not depending upon the strength of signals nor on the thresholds of neurons; second, that his computing neurons had but two inputs apiece; third, that each computed the same single Sheffer stroke function. Let me take up these constraints one at a time, beginning with the first alone, namely, when failures are absolute. Working with me, Leo Verbeek, from the Netherlands, has shown that the probability of failure of a neural net can be made as low as the error probability of one neuron (the output neuron) and that this can be reduced by a multiplicity of output neurons in parallel. Second, I have proved that nets of neurons with two inputs to each neuron, when failures depend upon perturbations of threshold, stimulus strength, or connections, cannot compute any significant function without error — only tautology and contradiction without error. And last, but not least, by insisting on using but a single function, von Neumann had thrown away the great logical redundancy of the system, with which he might have bought reliability. With neurons of 2 inputs each, this amounts to 16^2; with 3 inputs each, to 256^3, etc.—being of the form $(2^{2^\delta})^\delta$, where δ is the number of inputs per neuron.

There were two other problems that distressed him. He knew that caffeine and alcohol changed the threshold of all neurons in the same direction so much that every neuron computed some wrong function of its input. Yet one had essentially the same output for the same input. The classic example is the respiratory mechanism, for respiration is preserved under surgical anesthesia where thresholds of all neurons are sky-high. Of course, no net of neurons can work when the output neuron's threshold is so high that it cannot be excited or so low that it fires continuously. The first is coma, and the second, convulsion; but between these limits our circuits do work. These circuits he called circuits logically stable under common shift of thresholds. They can be made of formal neurons, even with only two inputs, to work over a single step of threshold, using only excitation and inhibition on the output cell; but this is only a fraction of the range. Associated, unobtrusively, with the problem is this: That of the 16 possible logical functions of neurons with two inputs, two functions cannot by calculated by any one neuron. They are the exclusion "or," "*A* or else *B*," and "both or else neither" — the "if and only if" of logic. Both limitations point to a third possibility in the interactions of neurons, and both are easily explained if impulses from one source can gate those from another so as to prevent their reaching the output neuron. Two physiological data pointed to the same possibility. The first was described earliest by Matthews, and later by Renshaw. It is the inhibition of a reflex by afferent impulses over an adjacent dorsal root. The second is the direct inhibition described by David Lloyd, wherein there is no time for intervening neurons to get into the sequence of events. We have located this interaction of afferents, measured its strength, and know that strychnine has its convulsive effects by preventing it. This is good physiology, as well as logically desirable.

My collaborator Manuel Blum, of Venezuela, now has a nice proof that excitation and inhibition on the cell plus inhibitory interaction of afferents are necessary and sufficient for constructing neurons that will compute their logical functions in any required sequence as the threshold falls or rises. With them it is always possible to construct nets that are logically stable all the way from coma to convulsion under common shift of threshold.

The last of von Neumann's problems was proposed to the American Psychiatry Association in March 1955. It is this. The eye is only two logical functions deep. Granted that it has controlling signals from the brain to tell it what it has to compute, what sort of elements are neurons that it can compute so many different functions in a depth of 2 neurons (that is, in the bipolars and the ganglion cells)? Certainly, said he, neurons are much cleverer than flipflops or the Eccles-Jordan components of our digital computers. The answer to this is that real neurons fill the bill. With formal neurons of 2 inputs each and controlling signals to the first rank only, the output can be made to be any one of 15 of the possible 16 logical functions. Eugene Prange, of the Air Force Cambridge Research Center, has just shown that with neurons of 3 inputs each and controlling signals to all 4 neurons, the net can be made to compute 253 out of 256 possible functions.

IV

Gentlemen, I would not have you think that we are near a full solution of our problems. Jack Cowan, of Edinburgh, has recently joined us and shown that for von Neumann's constructions of reliable circuits we require Post's complete multiple-truth-value logic, for which Boole's calculus is inadequate. Prange has evolved a theory of incomplete mapping that allows us to use "don't-care" conditions as well as assertion and negation. This yields elegant estimations of tolerable segregated errors in circuits with neurons of large numbers of inputs. Captain Robert J. Scott, of the United States Air Force, has begun the computation of minimal nets to sequence the functions computed by neurons as thresholds shift. Many of our friends are building artificial neurons for use in industry and in research, thus exposing to experiment many unsuspected properties of their relations in the time domain. There is now underway a whole tribe of men working on artificial intelligence — machines that induce, or learn — machines that abduce, or make hypotheses. In England alone, there are Ross Ashby, MacKay, Gabor, Andrews, Uttley, Graham Russel, Beurle, and several others — of whom I could not fail to mention Gordon Pask and Stafford Beer. In France, the work centers around Schützenberger. The Americans are too numerous to mention.

I may say that there is a whole computing machinery group, followers of Turing, who build the great deductive machines. There is Angyon, the cyberneticist of Hungary, now of California, who had reduced Pavlovian conditioning to a four-bit problem, embodied in his artificial tortoise. Selfridge, of the Lincoln Laboratory, M.I.T. — with his Pandemonium and his Sloppy — is building abductive machinery. Each is but one example of many. We know how to instrument these solutions and to build them in hardware when we will.

But the problem of insight, or intuition, or invention — call it what you will — we do not understand, although many of us are having a go at it. I shall not here name names, for most of us will fail miserably and be happily forgotten. Tarski thinks that what we lack is a fertile calculus of relations of more than two relata. I am inclined to agree with him, and if I were now the age I was in 1917, that is the problem I should tackle. Too bad — I'm too old. I may live to see the youngsters do it. But even if we never achieve so great a step ahead of our old schoolmaster, we have come far enough to define a number so realistically that a man may know it, and a man so logically that he may know a number. This was all I promised. I have done more, by indicating how he may do it without error, even though his component neurons misbehave.

That process of insight by which a child learns at least one logical particle, *neither* or *not both,* when it is given only ostensively — and one must be so learned — is still a little beyond us. It may perhaps have to wait for a potent logic of triadic relations, but I now doubt it. This is what we feared lay at the core of the theoretical difficulty in mechanical translation, but last summer Victor Yngve, of the Research Laboratory of Electronics, M.I.T., showed that a small finite machine with a small temporary memory could read and parse English from left to right. In other languages the direction may be reversed, and there may be memory problems that depend on the parenthetical structure of the tongue. But unless the parenthetical structures are, as in mathematics, complicated repeatedly at both ends, the machine can handle even sentences that are finite — like "This is the house that Jack built." So I'm hopeful that with the help of Chaos similar simple machines may account for insight or intuition — which is more than I proposed to include in this text. I have done so perhaps not too well but at such speed as to spare some minutes to make perfectly clear to non-Aristotelian logicians that extremely non-Aristotelian logic invented by von Neumann and brought to fruition by me and my coadjutors.

My success arose from the necessity of teaching logic to neurologists, psychiatrists, and psychologists. In his letter to a German princess, Euler used circles on the page to convey inclusions and intersections of classes. This works for three classes. Venn, concerned

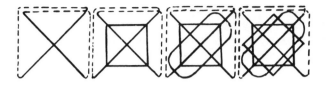

with four or five, invented his famous diagrams in which closed curves must each bisect all of the areas produced by previous closed curves. This goes well, even for five, by Venn's trick; six is tough; seven, well-nigh unintelligible, even when one finds out how to do it. Oliver Selfridge and Marvin Minsky (also of Lincoln Laboratory), at my behest, invented a method of construction that can be continued to infinity and remain transparent at a glance. So they formed a simple set of icons wherewith to inspect their contents to the limit of our finite intuitions. The calculus of relations degenerates into the calculus of classes if one is interested only in the one relation of inclusion in classes. This, in turn, degenerates into the calculus of propositions if one is interested only in the class of true, or else false, propositions, or statements in the realistic case. Now this calculus can always be reduced to the relations of propositions by pairs. Thanks to Wittgenstein we habitually handled these relations as truth tables to compare their logical values. These tables, if places are defined, can be reduced to jots for true and blanks for false. Thus every logical particle, represented by its truth table, can be made to appear as jots and

Contradiction $a \cdot \sim b$ $a \cdot b$ $\sim a \cdot b$ a $a \wedge b$ b $a \vee b$

$\sim a \cdot \sim b$ $\sim b$ $a \equiv b$ $\sim a$ $b \supset a$ $a \mid b$ $a \supset b$ Tautology

blanks in two intersecting circles. The common area jotted means

15

both; a jot in the left alone means the left argument alone is true; in the right, the right argument alone is true; and below, neither is true. Expediency simplifies two circles to a mere chi or X. Each of the logical relations of two arguments, and there are 16 of them, can then be represented by jots above, below, to right, and to left, beginning with no jots and then with one, two, and three, to end with four. These symbols, which I call Venn functions, can then be used to operate upon each other exactly as the truth tables do, for they picture these tables. A twelve-year-old boy who is bright

$$[\dot{X}] = [(\dot{X}\!\cdot) \;\dot{X}\; (\cdot\dot{X})]$$

$$[\dot{X}] = [(\dot{X}) \;\dot{X}\; (\dot{X})]$$

learns the laws in a few minutes, and he and his friends start playing jots and X's. A psychiatrist learns them in a few days, but only if he has to pay twenty-five dollars per hour for this psychotherapy. Next, since here we are generating probabilistic logic— not the logic of probabilities — we must infect these functions with the probability of a jot instead of a certain jot or a certain blank. We symbolize this by placing 1 for certain jots, 0 for certain blanks, and p for the probability of a jot in that place. These probabilistic Venn functions operate upon each other as those with jots and blanks, for true and false, utilizing products, instead of only $1 \times 1 = 1$ and $1 \times 0 = 0$ and $0 \times 0 = 0$ we get 1, p, p^2, p^3, 0, etc., and compute the truth tables of our complex propositions. This gives us a truly probabilistic logic, for it is the function, not merely the argument, that is infected by chance and is merely probable. This is the tool with which I attacked the problem von Neumann had set us.

A tool is a handy thing — and each has its special purpose. All-purpose tools are generally like an icebox with which to drive nails — hopelessly inefficient. But the discovery of a good tool often leads to the invention of others, provided we have insight into the operations to be performed. We have. Logicians may only be interested in tautology — an X with 4 jots — and contradiction — an X with none. But these are tautologically true or false. Realistic logic is interested in significant propositions — that is, in

16

those that are true, or false, according to whether what they assert is, or is not, the case. Nothing but tautology and contradiction can be computed certainly with any p's in every Venn function, so long as one makes them of two and only two arguments. This restriction disappears as soon as one considers Venn functions of more than two arguments in complex propositions. When we have functions of three arguments, Euler's three circles replace the two of conventional logic; but the rules of operations with jots and blanks — or with 1, p, 0 — carry over directly, and we have a thoroughly probabilistic logic of three arguments. Then Venn, and Minsky-Selfridge, diagrams enable us to extend these rules to 4, 5, 6, 7, etc., to infinitely many arguments. The rules of calculation remain unaltered, and the whole can be programmed simply into any digital computer. There is nothing in all of this to prevent us from extending the formulations to include multiple-truth-valued logics.

In the Research Laboratory of Electronics we report quarterly progress on our problems. In closing, I will quote from my carefully considered statement written a short while ago, so that you may learn how one words this for the modern logician working with digital computers, familiar with their logic and the art of programming their activity — for this is now no difficult trick. (I omit only the example and footnote.)

ON PROBABILISTIC LOGIC

[From *Quarterly Progress Report,* April 15, 1959,

Research Laboratory of Electronics, M.I.T.]*

Any logical statement of the finite calculus of propositions can be expressed as follows: Subscript the symbol for the δ primitive propositions A_j, with j taking the ascending powers of 2 from 2^0 to $2^{\delta-1}$ written in binary numbers. Thus: A_1, A_{10}, A_{100}, and so forth. Construct a V table with spaces S_i subscripted with the integers i, in binary form, from 0 to $2^\delta - 1$. Each i is the sum of one and

* The work of the Research Laboratory of Electronics, of which Dr. McCulloch is a staff member, is supported in part by the U.S. Army (Signal Corps), the U.S. Air Force (Office of Scientific Research, Air Research and Development Command), and the U.S. Navy (Office of Naval Research). The work of Dr. McCulloch's group also receives support from National Institutes of Health and Teagle Foundation, Incorporated.

only one selection of *j*'s and so identifies its space as the concurrence of those arguments ranging from S_0 for "None" to $S_2\delta_{-1}$ for "All." Thus A_1 and A_{100} are in S_{101}, and A_{10} is not, for which we write $A_1 \epsilon S_{101}$ and $A_{100} \epsilon S_{101}$ and $A_{10} \notin S_{101}$. In the logical text first replace A_j by V_h with a 1 in S_i if $A_j \epsilon S_i$ and with a 0 if $A_j \notin S_i$, which makes V_h the truth-table of A_j with $T = 1, F = 0$. Repeated applications of a single rule serve to reduce symbols for probabilistic functions of any δA_j to a single table of probabilities, and similarly any uncertain functions of these, etc., to a single V_r with the same subscripts S_r as the V_h for the A_j.

This rule reads: Replace the symbol for a function by V_k in which the k of S_k are again the integers in binary form but refer to the h of V_h, and the $p_k{}'$ of V_k betoken the likelihood of a 1 in S_k. Construct V_r and insert in S_r the likelihood $p_r{}''$ of a 1 in S_r computed thus:

$$p_r{}'' = \sum_0^{k*} p_k{}' \prod_{\substack{h \epsilon k \\ r=i}} p_{ih} \prod_{\substack{h \notin k \\ r=i}} (1 - p_{ih}) \quad k* \text{ is } k_{\max} \text{ of } V_k \quad (1)$$

Trivial — isn't it?

Gentlemen — you now know what I think a number is that a man may know it and a man that he may know a number, even when his neurons misbehave. I think you will realize that while I have presented you not with a mere logic of probabilities but with a probabilistic logic — a thing of which Aristotle never dreamed, yet the whole structure rests solidly on his shoulders — for he is the Atlas who supports the heaven of logic on his Herculean shoulders. In his own words, "Nature will not stand being badly administered."

Such is a number that man may know it and a man, made of fallible neurons, that may know it infallibly. That is more than I promised.

Good-by for the nonce.

A LOGICAL CALCULUS OF THE
IDEAS IMMANENT IN NERVOUS ACTIVITY*

Warren S. McCulloch and Walter H. Pitts

Because of the "all-or-none" character of nervous activity, neural events and the relations among them can be treated by means of propositional logic. It is found that the behavior of every net can be described in these terms, with the addition of more complicated logical means for nets containing circles; and that for any logical expression satisfying certain conditions, one can find a net behaving in the fashion it describes. It is shown that many particular choices among possible neurophysiological assumptions are equivalent, in the sense that for every net behaving under one assumption, there exists another net which behaves under the other and gives the same results, although perhaps not in the same time. Various applications of the calculus are discussed.

INTRODUCTION

THEORETICAL neurophysiology rests on certain cardinal assumptions. The nervous system is a net of neurons, each having a soma and an axon. Their adjunctions, or synapses, are always between the axon of one neuron and the soma of another. At any instant a neuron has some threshold, which excitation must exceed to initiate an impulse. This, except for the fact and the time of its occurrence, is determined by the neuron, not by the excitation. From the point of excitation the impulse is propagated to all parts of the neuron. The velocity along the axon varies directly with its diameter, from less than one meter per second in thin axons, which are usually short, to more than 150 meters per second in thick axons, which are usually long. The time for axonal conduction is consequently of little importance in determining the time of arrival of impulses at points unequally remote from the same source. Excitation across synapses occurs predominantly from axonal terminations to somata. It is still a moot point whether this depends upon irreciprocity of individual synapses or merely upon prevalent anatomical configurations. To suppose the latter requires no hypothesis *ad hoc* and explains known exceptions, but any assumption as to cause is compatible with the calculus to come. No case is known in which excitation through a single synapse has elicited a nervous impulse in any neuron, whereas any neuron may be excited by impulses arriving at a sufficient number of neighboring synapses within the period of latent addition, which lasts less than one quarter of a millisecond. Observed temporal summation of impulses at greater intervals is impossible for single neurons and empirically depends upon structural properties of the net. Between the arrival of impulses upon a neuron and its own propagated impulse there is a synaptic delay of more than half a millisecond. During the first part of the nervous impulse the neuron is absolutely refractory to any stimulation. Thereafter its excitability returns rapidly, in some cases reaching a value above normal from which it sinks again to a subnormal value, whence it returns slowly to normal. Frequent activity augments this subnormality. Such specificity as is possessed by nervous impulses depends solely upon their time and place and not on any other specificity of nervous energies. Of late only inhibition has been seriously adduced to contravene this thesis. Inhibition is the termination or prevention of the activity of one group of neurons by concurrent or antecedent activity of a second group. Until recently this could be explained on the supposition that previous activity of neurons of the second group might so raise the thresholds of internuncial neurons that they could no longer be excited by neurons of the first group, whereas the impulses of the first group must sum with the impulses of these internuncials to excite the now inhibited neurons. Today, some inhibitions have been shown to consume less than one millisecond. This excludes internuncials and requires synapses through which impulses inhibit that neuron which is being stimulated by impulses through other synapses. As yet experiment has not shown whether the refractoriness is relative or absolute. We will assume the latter and demonstrate that the difference is immaterial to our argument. Either variety of refractoriness can be accounted for in either of two ways. The "inhibitory synapse" may be of such a kind as to produce a substance which raises the threshold of the neuron, or it may be so placed that the local disturbance produced by its excitation opposes the alteration induced by the otherwise excitatory synapses. Inasmuch as position is already known to have such effects in the case of electrical stimulation, the first hypothesis is to be excluded unless and until it be substantiated, for the second involves no new hypothesis. We have, then, two explanations of inhibition based on the same general premises, differing only in the assumed nervous nets and, consequently, in the time required for inhibition. Hereafter we shall refer to such nervous nets as *equivalent in the extended sense*. Since we are concerned with properties of nets which are invariant under equivalence, we may make the physical assumptions which are most convenient for the calculus.

Many years ago one of us, by considerations impertinent to this argument, was led to conceive of the response of any neuron as factually equivalent to a proposition which proposed its adequate stimulus. He therefore attempted to record the behavior of complicated nets in the notation of the symbolic logic of propositions. The "all-or-none" law of nervous activity is sufficient to insure that the activity of any neuron may be represented as a proposition. Physiological relations existing among nervous activities correspond, of course, to relations among the propositions; and the utility of the representation depends upon the identity of these relations with those of the logic of propositions. To each reaction of any neuron there is a corresponding assertion of a simple proposition. This, in turn, implies either some other simple proposition or the disjunction or the conjunction, with or without negation, of similar propositions, according to the configuration of the synapses upon and the threshold of the neuron in question. Two difficulties appeared. The first concerns facilitation and extinction, in which antecedent activity temporarily alters responsiveness to subsequent stimulation of one and the same part of the net. The second concerns learning, in which activities concurrent at some previous time have altered the net permanently, so that a stimulus which would previously have been inadequate is now adequate. But for nets undergoing both alterations, we can substitute equivalent fictitious nets composed of neurons whose connections and thresholds are unaltered. But one point must be made clear: neither of us conceives the formal equivalence to be a factual explanation. *Per contra!*—we regard facilitation and extinction as dependent upon continuous changes in threshold related to electrical and chemical variables, such as after-potentials and ionic concentrations; and learning as an enduring change which can survive sleep, anaesthesia, convulsions and coma. The importance of the formal equivalence lies in this: that the alterations actually underlying facilitation, extinction and learning in no way affect the conclusions which follow from the formal treatment of the activity of nervous nets, and the relations of the corresponding propositions remain those of the logic of propositions.

The nervous system contains many circular paths, whose activity so regenerates the excitation of any participant neuron that reference to time past becomes indefinite, although it still implies that afferent activity has realized one of a certain class of configurations over time. Precise specification of these implications by means of recursive functions, and determination of those that can be embodied in the activity of nervous nets, completes the theory.

THE THEORY: NETS WITHOUT CIRCLES

We shall make the following physical assumptions for our calculus.

1. The activity of the neuron is an "all-or-none" process.

2. A certain fixed number of synapses must be excited within the period of latent addition in order to excite a neuron at any time, and this number is independent of previous activity and position on the neuron.

3. The only significant delay within the nervous system is synaptic delay.

4. The activity of any inhibitory synapse absolutely prevents excitation of the neuron at that time.

5. The structure of the net does not change with time.

To present the theory, the most appropriate symbolism is that of Language II of R. Carnap (1938), augmented with various notations drawn from B. Russell and A. N. Whitehead (1927), including the *Principia* conventions for dots. Typographical necessity, however, will compel us to use the upright '*E*' for the existential operator instead of the inverted, and an arrow ('$\rightarrow$') for implication instead of the horseshoe. We shall also use the Carnap syntactical notations, but print them in boldface rather than German type; and we shall introduce a functor *S*, whose value for a property *P* is the property which holds of a number when *P* holds of its predecessor; it is defined by '$S(P)\,(t)\,.\,\equiv\,.\,P(Kx)\,.\,t = x')$'; the brackets around its argument will often be omitted, in which case this is understood to be the nearest predicate-expression [*Pr*] on the right. Moreover, we shall write $S^2 Pr$ for $S(S(Pr))$, etc.

The neurons of a given net $\mathfrak{N}$ may be assigned designations 'c_1', 'c_2', ... , 'c_n'. This done, we shall denote the property of a number, that a neuron c_i fires at a time which is that number of synaptic delays from the origin of time, by '*N*' with the numeral *i* as subscript, so that $N_i(t)$ asserts that c_i fires at the time *t*. N_i is called the *action* of c_i. We shall sometimes regard the subscripted numeral of '*N*' as if it belonged to the object-language, and were in a place for a functoral argument, so that it might be replaced by a number-variable [*z*] and quantified; this enables us to abbreviate long but finite disjunctions and conjunctions by the use of an operator. We shall employ this locution quite generally for sequences of *Pr*; it may be secured formally by an obvious disjunctive definition. The predicates 'N_1', 'N_2', ... , comprise the syntactical class '*N*'.

Let us define the *peripheral afferents* of $\mathfrak{N}$ as the neurons of $\mathfrak{N}$ with no axons synapsing upon them. Let N_1, ... , N_p denote the actions of such neurons and N_{p+1}, N_{p+2}, ... , N_n those of the rest. Then a *solution of* $\mathfrak{N}$ will be a class of sentences of the form S_i: $N_{p+1}(z_1)\,.\,\equiv\,.\,Pr_i\,(N_1, N_2, ... , N_p, z_1)$, where Pr_i contains no free variable save z_1 and no descriptive symbols save the *N* in the argument [*Arg*], and possibly some constant sentences [*sa*]; and such that each S_i is true of $\mathfrak{N}$. Conversely, given a $Pr_1\,({}^1p^1{}_1, {}^1p^1{}_2, ... ,$ ${}^1p^1{}_p, z_1, s)$, containing no free variable save those in its *Arg*, we shall say that it is *realizable in the narrow sense* if there exists a net $\mathfrak{N}$

and a series of N_i in it such that $N_1 (z_1) . \equiv . Pr_1 (N_1, N_2, \ldots, z_1, sa_1)$ is true of it, where sa_1 has the form $N(0)$. We shall call it *realizable in the extended sense*, or simply *realizable*, if for some n $S^n (Pr_1)$ $(p_1, \ldots, p_p, z_1, s)$ is realizable in the above sense. c_{pi} is here the realizing neuron. We shall say of two laws of nervous excitation which are such that every S which is realizable in either sense upon one supposition is also realizable, perhaps by a different net, upon the other, that they are equivalent assumptions, in that sense.

The following theorems about realizability all refer to the extended sense. In some cases, sharper theorems about narrow realizability can be obtained; but in addition to greater complication in statement this were of little practical value, since our present neurophysiological knowledge determines the law of excitation only to extended equivalence, and the more precise theorems differ according to which possible assumption we make. Our less precise theorems, however, are invariant under equivalence, and are still sufficient for all purposes in which the exact time for impulses to pass through the whole net is not crucial.

Our central problems may now be stated exactly: first, to find an effective method of obtaining a set of computable S constituting a solution of any given net; and second, to characterize the class of realizable S in an effective fashion. Materially stated, the problems are to calculate the behavior of any net, and to find a net which will behave in a specified way, when such a net exists.

A net will be called *cyclic* if it contains a circle: i.e., if there exists a chain c_i, c_{i+1}, $\ldots$ of neurons on it, each member of the chain synapsing upon the next, with the same beginning and end. If a set of its neurons c_1, c_2, $\ldots$, c_p is such that its removal from $\mathfrak{N}$ leaves it without circles, and no smaller class of neurons has this property, the set is called a *cyclic* set, and its cardinality is the *order of* $\mathfrak{N}$. In an important sense, as we shall see, the order of a net is an index of the complexity of its behavior. In particular, nets of zero order have especially simple properties; we shall discuss them first.

Let us define a *temporal propositional expression* (a *TPE*), designating a *temporal propositional function* (*TPF*), by the following recursion:

1. A $^1p^1$ $[z_1]$ is a TPE, where p_1 is a predicate-variable.

2. If S_1 and S_2 are TPE containing the same free individual variable, so are SS_1, $S_1 v S_2$, $S_1.S_2$ and $S_i. \sim S_2$.

3. Nothing else is a TPE.

Theorem I

Every net of order 0 can be solved in terms of temporal propositional expressions.

Let c_i be any neuron of $\mathfrak{N}$ with a threshold $\theta_i > 0$, and let c_{i1}, $c_{i2}, \ldots , c_{ip}$ have respectively n_{i1}, $n_{i2}, \ldots , n_{ip}$ excitatory synapses upon it. Let c_{j1}, $c_{j2}, \ldots , c_{jq}$ have inhibitory synapses upon it. Let κ_i be the set of the subclasses of $\{n_{i1}, n_{i2}, \ldots , n_{ip}\}$ such that the sum of their members exceeds θ_i. We shall then be able to write, in accordance with the assumptions mentioned above,

$$N_i(z_1) \, . \, \equiv \, . \, S \left\{ \prod_{m=1}^{q} \sim N_{jm}(z_1) \, . \sum_{\alpha \in K_i} \prod_{s \in \alpha} N_{is}(z_1) \right\} \tag{1}$$

where the '$\sum$' and '$\prod$' are syntactical symbols for disjunctions and conjunctions which are finite in each case. Since an expression of this form can be written for each c_i which is not a peripheral afferent, we can, by substituting the corresponding expression in (1) for each N_{jm} or N_{is} whose neuron is not a peripheral afferent, and repeating the process on the result, ultimately come to an expression for N_i in terms solely of peripherally afferent N, since $\mathfrak{N}$ is without circles. Moreover, this expression will be a TPE, since obviously (1) is; and it follows immediately from the definition that the result of substituting a TPE for a constituent $p(z)$ in a TPE is also one.

Theorem II

Every TPE is realizable by a net of order zero.

The functor S obviously commutes with disjunction, conjunction, and negation. It is obvious that the result of substituting any S_i, realizable in the narrow sense (i.n.s.), for the $p(z)$ in a realizable expression S_1 is itself realizable i.n.s.; one constructs the realizing net by replacing the peripheral afferents in the net for S_1 by the realizing neurons in the nets for the S_i. The one neuron net realizes $p_1(z_1)$ i.n.s., and Figure 1-a shows a net that realizes $Sp_1(z_1)$ and hence SS_2, i.n.s., if S_2 can be realized i.n.s. Now if S_2 and S_3 are realizable then $S^m S_2$ and $S^n S_3$ are realizable i.n.s., for suitable m and n. Hence so are $S^{m+n} S_2$ and $S^{m+n} S_3$. Now the nets of Figures 1b, c and d respectively realize $S(p_1(z_1) \text{ v } p_2(z_1))$, $S(p_1(z_1) \cdot p_2(z_1))$, and $S(p_1(z_1) \cdot \sim p_2(z_1))$ i.n.s. Hence $S^{m+n+1} (S_1 \text{ v } S_2)$, $S^{m+n+1} (S_1 \cdot S_2)$, and $S^{m+n+1} (S_1 \cdot \sim S_2)$ are realizable i.n.s. Therefore $S_1 \text{ v } S_2 S_1 \cdot S_2 S_1 \cdot \sim S_2$ are realizable if S_1 and S_2 are. By complete·induction, all TPE are realizable. In this way all nets may be regarded as built out of the fundamental elements of Figures 1a, b, c, d, precisely as the temporal propositional expressions are generated out of the operations of precession, disjunction, conjunction, and conjoined negation. In particular, corresponding to any description of state, or distribution of the values *true* and *false* for the actions of all the neurons of a net save that which makes them all false, a single neuron is constructible whose firing is a necessary and sufficient condition for the validity of that description. Moreover, there is always an indefinite number of topologically different nets realizing any TPE.

Theorem III

Let there be given a complex sentence S_1 built up in any manner out of elementary sentences of the form $\mathbf{p}(z_1 - zz)$ where zz is any numeral, by any of the propositional connections: negation, disjunction, conjunction, implication, and equivalence. Then S_1 is a TPE and only if it is false when its constituent $\mathbf{p}(z_1 - zz)$ are all assumed false—i.e., replaced by false sentences—or that the last line in its truth-table contains an 'F',—or there is no term in its Hilbert disjunctive normal form composed exclusively of negated terms.

These latter three conditions are of course equivalent (Hilbert and Ackermann, 1938). We see by induction that the first of them is necessary, since $p(z_1 - zz)$ becomes false when it is replaced by a false sentence, and $S_1 \text{ v } S_2$, $S_1 \cdot S_2$ and $S_1 \cdot \sim S_2$ are all false if both their constituents are. We see that the last condition is sufficient by remarking that a disjunction is a TPE when its constituents are, and that any term

$$S_1 \cdot S_2 \ldots \ldots S_m \cdot \sim S_{m+1} \cdot \sim \ldots \ldots \sim S_n$$

can be written as

$$(S_1 . S_2 . . . . S_m) . \sim (S_{m+1} v\ S_{m+2} v . . . . v\ S_n),$$

which is clearly a TPE.

The method of the last theorems does in fact provide a very convenient and workable procedure for constructing nervous nets to order, for those cases where there is no reference to events indefinitely far in the past in the specification of the conditions. By way of example, we may consider the case of heat produced by a transient cooling.

If a cold object is held to the skin for a moment and removed, a sensation of heat will be felt; if it is applied for a longer time, the sensation will be only of cold, with no preliminary warmth, however transient. It is known that one cutaneous receptor is affected by heat, and another by cold. If we let N_1 and N_2 be the actions of the respective receptors and N_3 and N_4 of neurons whose activity implies a sensation of heat and cold, our requirements may be written as

$$N_3(t) : \equiv\ : N_1(t-1) . v . N_2(t-3) . \sim N_2(t-2)$$
$$N_4(t) . \equiv . N_2(t-2) . N_2(t-1)$$

where we suppose for simplicity that the required persistence in the sensation of cold is, say, two synaptic delays, compared with one for that of heat. These conditions clearly fall under Theorem III. A net may consequently be constructed to realize them, by the method of Theorem II. We begin by writing them in a fashion which exhibits them as built out of their constituents by the operations realized in Figures 1a, b, c, d: i.e., in the form

$$N_3(t) . \equiv . S\{N_1(t) \text{ v } S[(SN_2(t)) . \sim N_2(t)]\}$$
$$N_4(t) . \equiv . S\{[SN_2(t)] . N_2(t)\}.$$

First we construct a net for the function enclosed in the greatest number of brackets and proceed outward; in this case we run a net of the form shown in Figure 1a from c_2 to some neuron c_a, say, so that

$$N_a(t) . \equiv . SN_2(t).$$

Next introduce two nets of the forms 1c and 1d, both running from c_a and c_2, and ending respectively at c_4 and say c_b. Then

$$N_4(t) . \equiv . S[N_a(t) . N_2(t)] . \equiv . S[(SN_2(t)) . N_2(t)].$$
$$N_b(t) . \equiv . S[N_a(t) . \sim N_2(t)] . \equiv . S[(SN_2(t)) . \sim N_2(t)].$$

27

Finally, run a net of the form 1b from c_1 and c_b to c_3, and derive

$$N_3(t) . \equiv . S[N_1(t) \mathbf{v} N_b(t)]$$
$$. \equiv . S\{N_1(t) \mathbf{v} S[(SN_2(t)) . \sim N_2(t)]\}.$$

These expressions for $N_3(t)$ and $N_4(t)$ are the ones desired; and the realizing net *in toto* is shown in Figure 1e.

This illusion makes very clear the dependence of the correspondence between perception and the "external world" upon the specific structural properties of the intervening nervous net. The same illusion, of course, could also have been produced under various other assumptions about the behavior of the cutaneous receptors, with correspondingly different nets.

We shall now consider some theorems of equivalence: i.e., theorems which demonstrate the essential identity, save for time, of various alternative laws of nervous excitation. Let us first discuss the case of *relative inhibition*. By this we mean the supposition that the firing of an inhibitory synapse does not absolutely prevent the firing of the neuron, but merely raises its threshold, so that a greater number of excitatory synapses must fire concurrently to fire it than would otherwise be needed. We may suppose, losing no generality, that the increase in threshold is unity for the firing of each such synapse; we then have the theorem:

Theorem IV

Relative and absolute inhibition are equivalent in the extended sense.

We may write out a law of nervous excitation after the fashion of (1), but employing the assumption of relative inhibition instead; inspection then shows that this expression is a *TPE*. An example of the replacement of relative inhibition by absolute is given by Figure 1f. The reverse replacement is even easier; we give the inhibitory axons afferent to c_i any sufficiently large number of inhibitory synapses apiece.

Second, we consider the case of extinction. We may write this in the form of a variation in the threshold θ_i after the neuron c_i has fired; to the nearest integer—and only to this approximation is the variation in threshold significant in natural forms of excitation—this may be written as a sequence $\theta_i + b_j$ for j synaptic delays after firing, where $b_j = 0$ for j large enough, say $j = M$ or greater. We may then state

Theorem V

Extinction is equivalent to absolute inhibition.

For, assuming relative inhibition to hold for the moment, we need merely run M circuits $\mathfrak{I}_1, \mathfrak{I}_2, \ldots \mathfrak{I}_M$ containing respectively $1, 2, \ldots, M$ neurons, such that the firing of each link in any is sufficient to fire the next, from the neuron c_i back to it, where the end of the circuit $\mathfrak{I}_j$ has just b_j inhibitory synapses upon c_i. It is evident that this will produce the desired results. The reverse substitution may be accomplished by the diagram of Figure 1g. From the transitivity of replacement, we infer the theorem. To this group of theorems also belongs the well-known

Theorem VI

Facilitation and temporal summation may be replaced by spatial summation.

This is obvious: one need merely introduce a suitable sequence of delaying chains, of increasing numbers of synapses, between the exciting cell and the neuron whereon temporal summation is desired to hold. The assumption of spatial summation will then give the required results. See e.g. Figure 1h. This procedure had application in showing that the observed temporal summation in gross nets does not imply such a mechanism in the interaction of individual neurons.

The phenomena of learning, which are of a character persisting over most physiological changes in nervous activity, seem to require the possibility of permanent alterations in the structure of nets. The simplest such alteration is the formation of new synapses or equivalent local depressions of threshold. We suppose that some axonal terminations cannot at first excite the succeeding neuron; but if at any time the neuron fires, and the axonal terminations are simultaneously excited, they become synapses of the ordinary kind, henceforth capable of exciting the neuron. The loss of an inhibitory synapse gives an entirely equivalent result. We shall then have

Theorem VII

Alterable synapses can be replaced by circles.

This is accomplished by the method of Figure 1i. It is also to be remarked that a neuron which becomes and remains spontaneously active can likewise be replaced by a circle, which is set into activity by a peripheral afferent when the activity commences, and inhibited by one when it ceases.

THE THEORY: NETS WITH CIRCLES

The treatment of nets which do not satisfy our previous assumption of freedom from circles is very much more difficult than that case. This is largely a consequence of the possibility that activity may be set up in a circuit and continue reverberating around it for an indefinite period of time, so that the realizable Pr may involve reference to past events of an indefinite degree of remoteness. Consider such a net $\mathfrak{N}$, say of order p, and let $c_1, c_2, \ldots, c_p$ be a cyclic set of neurons of $\mathfrak{N}$. It is first of all clear from the definition that every N_s of $\mathfrak{N}$ can be expressed as a TPE, of $N_1, N_2, \ldots, N_p$ and the absolute afferents; the solution of $\mathfrak{N}$ involves then only the determination of expressions for the cyclic set. This done, we shall derive a set of expressions $[A]$:

$$N_i(z_1) \, . \, \equiv \, . \, Pr_i[S^{n_{i1}} N_1(z_1), S^{n_{i2}} N_2(z_1), \ldots, S^{n_{ip}} N_p(z_1)], \qquad (2)$$

where Pr_i also involves peripheral afferents. Now if n is the least common multiple of the n_{ij}, we shall, by substituting their equivalents according to (2) in (3) for the N_j, and repeating this process often enough on the result, obtain S of the form

$$N_i(z_1) \, . \, \equiv \, . \, Pr_1[S^n N_1(z_1), S^n N_2(z_1), \ldots, S^n N_p(z_1)]. \qquad (3)$$

These expressions may be written in the Hilbert disjunctive normal form as

$$N_i(z_1) \, . \, \equiv \, . \, \sum_{\substack{\alpha \varepsilon k \\ \beta_\alpha \varepsilon k}} S_\alpha \prod_{j \varepsilon k} S^n N_j(z_1) \prod_{j \varepsilon \beta_\alpha} \sim S^n N_j(z_1), \text{ for suitable } \kappa, \qquad (4)$$

where S_α is a TPE of the absolute afferents of $\mathfrak{N}$. There exist some 2^p different sentences formed out of the pN_i by conjoining to the conjunction of some set of them the conjunction of the negations of the rest. Denumerating these by $X_1(z_1)$, $X_2(z_1)$, ..., $X_{2p}(z_1)$, we may, by use of the expressions (4), arrive at an equipollent set of equations of the form

$$X_i(z_1) \cdot \equiv \cdot \sum_{j=1}^{2p} Pr_{ij}(z_1) \cdot S^n X_j(z_1). \tag{5}$$

Now we import the subscripted numerals i, j into the object-language: i.e., define Pr_1 and Pr_2 such that $Pr_1(zz_1, z_1) \cdot \equiv \cdot X_i(z_1)$ and $Pr_2(zz_1, zz_2, z_1) \cdot \equiv \cdot Pr_{ij}(z_1)$ are provable whenever zz_1 and zz_2 denote i and j respectively.
Then we may rewrite (5) as

$$(z_1)zz_p : Pr_1(z_1, z_3)$$
$$\cdot \equiv \cdot (Ez_2)zz_p \cdot Pr_2(z_1, z_2, z_3 - zz_n) \cdot Pr_1(z_2, z_3 - zz_n) \tag{6}$$

where zz_m denotes n and zz_p denotes 2^p. By repeated substitution we arrive at an expression

$$(z_1)zz_p : Pr_1(z_1, zz_n zz_2) \cdot \equiv \cdot (Ez_2)zz_p (Ez_3)zz_p \ldots (Ez_n)zz_p.$$
$$Pr_2(z_1, z_2, zz_n (zz_2 - 1)) \cdot Pr_2(z_2, z_3, zz_n (zz_2 - 1)) \ldots \tag{7}$$

$Pr_2(z_{n-1}, z_n, 0) \cdot Pr_1(z_n, 0)$, for any numeral zz_2 which denotes s.

This is easily shown by induction to be equipollent to

$$(z_1)zz_p : . Pr_1(z_1, zz_n zz_2) : \equiv : (Ef) (z_2) zz_2 - 1 f(z_2 zz_n)$$
$$\leqq zz_p \cdot f(zz_n zz_2) = z_1 \cdot Pr_2(f(zz_n (z_2 + 1))), \tag{8}$$
$$f(zz_n z_2)) \cdot Pr_1(f(0), 0)$$

and since this is the case for all zz_2, it is also true that

$$(z_4) (z_1)zz_p : Pr_1(z_1, z_4) \cdot \equiv \cdot (Ef) (z_2) (z_4 - 1) \cdot f(z_2)$$
$$\leqq zz_p \cdot f(z_4) = z_1 f(z_4) = z_1 \cdot Pr_2[f(z_2 + 1), f(z_2), z_2] \cdot \tag{9}$$
$$Pr_1[f(\text{res } (z_4, zz_n)), \text{res } (z_4, zz_n)],$$

where zz_n denotes n, res (r, s) is the residue of r mod s and zz_p denotes 2^p. This may be written in a less exact way as

$$N_i(t) \cdot \equiv \cdot (E\phi) (x)t - 1 \cdot \phi(x) \leqq 2^p \cdot \phi(t) = i \cdot$$
$$P[\phi(x + 1), \phi(x) \cdot N_{\phi}(_0) (0)],$$

where x and t are also assumed divisible by n, and Pr_2 denotes P. From the preceding remarks we shall have

31

Theorem VIII

The expression (9) *for neurons of the cyclic set of a net $\mathfrak{N}$ together with certain* TPE *expressing the actions of other neurons in terms of them, constitute a solution of $\mathfrak{N}$.*

Consider now the question of the realizability of a set of S_i. A first necessary condition, demonstrable by an easy induction, is that

$$(z_2)z_1 \cdot p_1(z_2) \equiv p_2(z_2) \cdot \to \cdot S_i \equiv S_i \begin{Bmatrix} p_1 \\ p_2 \end{Bmatrix} \tag{10}$$

should be true, with similar statements for the other free p in S_i: i.e., no nervous net can take account of future peripheral afferents. Any S_i satisfying this requirement can be replaced by an equipollent S of the form

$$(Ef)\ (z_2)z_1\ (z_3)zz_p : f\epsilon\ Pr_{mi}$$
$$: f(z_1, z_2, z_3\ = 1\ .\ \equiv\ .\ p_{z3}(z_2) \tag{11}$$

where zz_p denotes p, by defining

$$Pr_{mi} = \hat{f}[(z_1)\ (z_2)z_1(z_3)zz_p : .\ f(z_1, z_2, z_3) = 0\ .\ \mathbf{v}\ .\ f(z_1, z_2, z_3)$$
$$= 1 : f(z_1, z_2, z_3) = 1\ .\ \equiv\ .\ p_{z3}(z_2) : \to\ :\ S_i].$$

Consider now these series of classes α_i, for which

$$N_i(t) : \equiv\ :\ (E\phi)\ (x)t(m)q : \phi\epsilon\alpha_i : N_m(x)\ .\ \equiv\ .\ \phi(t, x, m) = 1.$$
$$[i = q + 1, \cdots, M] \tag{12}$$

holds for some net. These will be called *prehensible* classes. Let us define the *Boolean ring* generated by a class of classes κ as the aggregate of the classes which can be formed from members of κ by repeated application of the logical operations; i.e., we put

$$\mathcal{R}(\kappa) = p\hat{\ }\hat{\lambda}[(\alpha, \beta) : \alpha\epsilon\kappa$$
$$\to \alpha\epsilon\lambda : \alpha, \beta\epsilon\lambda\ .\ \to\ .\ -\alpha, \alpha\ .\ \beta, \alpha\ \mathbf{v}\ \beta\epsilon\lambda].$$

We shall also define

$$\overline{\mathcal{R}}(\kappa)\ .\ =\ .\ \mathcal{R}(\kappa) - \iota{}^{\prime}p^{\prime} - {}^{\prime\prime}\kappa,$$
$$\mathcal{R}_e(\kappa)\ = p^{\prime}\ \hat{\lambda}[(\alpha, \beta) : \alpha\epsilon\kappa \to \alpha\epsilon\lambda\ .\ \to\ .\ -\alpha, \alpha\ .\ \beta, \alpha\ \mathbf{v}\ \beta, S\ {}^{\prime\prime}\alpha\epsilon\hat{\lambda}$$
$$\overline{\mathcal{R}}_e(\kappa)\ =\ \mathcal{R}_e(\kappa) - \iota{}^{\prime}p^{\prime} - {}^{\prime\prime}\kappa,$$

and

$$\sigma(\psi, t) = \hat{\phi}[(m)\ .\ \phi(t + 1, t, m) = \psi(m)].$$

The class $\mathcal{R}_e(\kappa)$ is formed from κ in analogy with $\mathcal{R}(\kappa)$, but by repeated application not only of the logical operations but also of that which replaces a class of properties $P \, \epsilon \, \alpha$ by $S(P) \, \epsilon \, S \, ``\alpha$. We shall then have the

LEMMA

$Pr_1(p_1, p_2, \ldots, p_m, z_1)$ is a TPE if and only if

$$(z_1) \, (p_1, \ldots, p_m) \, (Ep_{m+1}) : p_{m+1} \, \epsilon \, \overline{\mathcal{R}}_e(\{p_1, p_2, \ldots, p_m\})$$
$$p_{m+1}(z_1) \equiv Pr_1(p_1, p_2, \ldots, p_m, z_1) \tag{13}$$

is true; and it is a TPE not involving 'S' if and only if this holds when '$\mathcal{R}_e$' is replaced by '$\mathcal{R}$', and we then obtain

Theorem IX

A series of classes α_1, α_2, ... α_s is a series of prehensible classes if and only if

$$(Em) \, (En) \, (p)n(i) \, (\psi) : . \, (x)m\,\psi(x) = 0 \, \mathrm{v} \; \psi(x \; = 1 : \rightarrow : (E\beta)$$
$$(Ey)m \, . \; \psi(y) = 0 \, . \; \beta\epsilon\mathcal{R}[\hat{\gamma}((Ei) \, . \, \gamma = \alpha_i)) \, . \, \mathrm{v} \, . \, (x)m \, .$$
$$\psi(x) \; = 0 \, . \; \beta\epsilon\overline{\mathcal{R}}[\hat{\gamma}((E_i) \, . \, \gamma = \alpha_i)] : (t) \, (\phi) : \phi\epsilon\alpha_i \, . \tag{14}$$
$$\sigma(\phi, nt + p) \, . \rightarrow \, . \, (Ef) \, . \; f\epsilon\beta \, . \; (w)m(x)t - 1 \, .$$
$$\phi(n(t + 1) + p, nx + p, w) = f(nt + p, nx + p, w).$$

The proof here follows directly from the lemma. The condition is necessary, since every net for which an expression of the form (4) can be written obviously verifies it, the ψ's being the characteristic functions of the S_a and the β for each ψ being the class whose designation has the form $\prod_{i\epsilon\alpha} Pr_i \prod_{j\epsilon\beta} Pr_j$, where Pr_k denotes α_k for all k. Conversely, we may write an expression of the form (4) for a net $\mathfrak{N}$ fulfilling prehensible classes satisfying (14) by putting for the $Pr_a \, Pr$ denoting the ψ's and a Pr, written in the analogue for classes of the disjunctive normal form, and denoting the α corresponding to that ψ, conjoined to it. Since every S of the form (4) is clearly realizable, we have the theorem.

It is of some interest to consider the extent to which we can by knowledge of the present determine the whole past of various special nets: i.e., when we may construct a net the firing of the cyclic set of whose neurons requires the peripheral afferents to have had a set of past values specified by given functions ϕ_i. In this case the classes α_i of the last theorem reduced to unit classes; and the condition may be transformed into

$$(E\ m,\ n)\ (p)n(i,\ \psi)\ (Ej) : .\ (x)m : \psi(x) = 0\ .\ \mathbf{v}\ .\ \psi(x) = 1 :$$
$$\phi_{i\epsilon\sigma}(\psi,\ nt + p) : \rightarrow : (w)m(x)t - 1\ .\ \phi_i(n(t+1)$$
$$+ p,\ nx + p,\ w) = \phi_j(nt + p,\ nx + p,\ w) : .$$
$$(u,\ v)\ (w)m\ .\ \phi_i(n(u + 1) + p,\ nu + p,\ w)$$
$$= \phi_i(n(v + 1) + p,\ nv + p,\ w).$$

On account of limitations of space, we have presented the above argument very sketchily; we propose to expand it and certain of its implications in a further publication.

The condition of the last theorem is fairly simple in principle, though not in detail; its application to practical cases would, however, require the exploration of some 2^{2n} classes of functions, namely the members of $\mathcal{R}(\{\alpha_1,\ \ldots,\ \alpha_s\})$. Since each of these is a possible β of Theorem IX, this result cannot be sharpened. But we may obtain a sufficient condition for the realizability of an **S** which is very easily applicable and probably covers most practical purposes. This is given by

Theorem X

Let us define a set of **K** of **S** by the following recursion:

1. Any *TPE* and any *TPE* whose arguments have been replaced by members of **K** belong to **K**;

2. If $Pr_1(z_1)$ is a member of **K**, then $(z_2)z_1\ .\ Pr_1(z_2)$, $(Ez_2)z_1\ .\ Pr_1(z_2)$, and $C_{mn}(z_1)\ .\ s$ belong to it, where C_{mn} denotes the property of being congruent to m modulo n, $m < n$.

3. *The set* **K** *has no further members.*

Then every member of **K** is realizable.

For, if $Pr_1(z_1)$ is realizable, nervous nets for which

$$N_i(z_1)\ .\ \equiv\ .\ Pr_1(z_1)\ .\ SN_i(z_1)$$
$$N_i(z_1)\ .\ \equiv\ .\ Pr_1(z_1)\ \mathbf{v}\ SN_i(z_1)$$

are the expressions of equation (4), realize $(z_2)z_1\ .\ Pr_1(z_2)$ and

$(E\,z_2)z_1$. $Pr_1(z_2)$ respectively; and a simple circuit, $c_1, c_2, \ldots, c_n$, of n links, each sufficient to excite the next, gives an expression

$$N_m(z_1) \,.\, \equiv \,.\, N_1(0) \,.\, C_{mn}$$

for the last form. By induction we derive the theorem.

One more thing is to be remarked in conclusion. It is easily shown: first, that every net, if furnished with a tape, scanners connected to afferents, and suitable efferents to perform the necessary motor-operations, can compute only such numbers as can a Turing machine; second, that each of the latter numbers can be computed by such a net; and that nets with circles can be computed by such a net; and that nets with circles can compute, without scanners and a tape, some of the numbers the machine can, but no others, and not all of them. This is of interest as affording a psychological justification of the Turing definition of computability and its equivalents, Church's λ — definability and Kleene's primitive recursiveness: If any number can be computed by an organism, it is computable by these definitions, and conversely.

CONSEQUENCES

Causality, which requires description of states and a law of necessary connection relating them, has appeared in several forms in several sciences, but never, except in statistics, has it been as irreciprocal as in this theory. Specification for any one time of afferent stimulation and of the activity of all constituent neurons, each an "all-or-none" affair, determines the state. Specification of the nervous net provides the law of necessary connection whereby one can compute from the description of any state that of the succeeding state, but the inclusion of disjunctive relations prevents complete determination of the one before. Moreover, the regenerative activity of constituent circles renders reference indefinite as to time past. Thus our knowledge of the world, including ourselves, is incomplete as to space and indefinite as to time. This ignorance, implicit in all our brains, is the counterpart of the abstraction which renders our knowledge useful. The role of brains in determining the epistemic relations of our theories to our

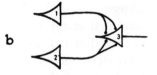

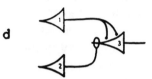
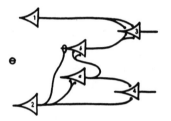
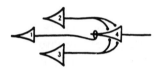
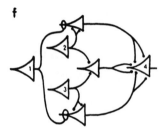
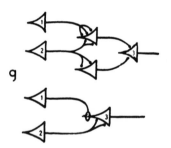
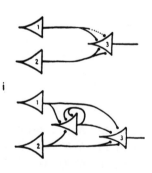
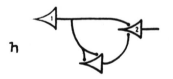

FIGURE 1

observations and of these to the facts is all too clear, for it is apparent that every idea and every sensation is realized by activity within that net, and by no such activity are the actual afferents fully determined.

There is no theory we may hold and no observation we can make that will retain so much as its old defective reference to the facts if the net be altered. Tinnitus, paraesthesias, hallucinations, delusions, confusions and disorientations intervene. Thus empiry confirms that if our nets are undefined, our facts are undefined, and to the "real" we can attribute not so much as one quality or "form." With determination of the net, the unknowable object of knowledge, the "thing in itself," ceases to be unknowable.

To psychology, however defined, specification of the net would contribute all that could be achieved in that field—even if the analysis were pushed to ultimate psychic units or "psychons," for a psychon can be no less than the activity of a single neuron. Since that activity is inherently propositional, all psychic events have an intentional, or "semiotic," character. The "all-or-none" law of these activities, and the conformity of their relations to those of the logic of propositions, insure that the relations of

---

←   **EXPRESSION FOR THE FIGURES**

In the figure the neuron c_i is always marked with the numeral i upon the body of the cell, and the corresponding action is denoted by 'N' with i as subscript, as in the text.

Figure 1a $N_2(t) . \equiv . N_1(t - 1)$

Figure 1b $N_3(t) . \equiv . N_1(t - 1) \mathbf{v} N_2(t - 1)$

Figure 1c $N_3(t) . \equiv . N_1(t - 1) . N_2(t - 1)$

Figure 1d $N_3(t) . \equiv . N_1(t - 1) . \sim N_2(t - 1)$

Figure 1e $N_3(t) : \equiv : N_1(t - 1) . \mathbf{v} . N_2(t - 3) . \sim N_2(t - 2)$
    $N_4(t) . \equiv . N_2(t - 2) . N_2(t - 1)$

Figure 1f $N_4(t) : \equiv : \sim N_1(t - 1) . N_2(t - 1) \mathbf{v} N_3(t - 1) . \mathbf{v} . N_1(t - 1) \cdot$
    $N_2(t - 1) . N_3(t - 1)$
    $N_4(t) : \equiv : \sim N_1(t - 2) . N_2(t - 2) \mathbf{v} N_3(t - 2) . \mathbf{v} . N_1(t - 2) .$
    $N_2(t - 2) . N_3(t - 2)$

Figure 1g $N_3(t) . \equiv . N_2(t - 2) . \sim N_1(t - 3)$

Figure 1h $N_2(t) . \equiv . N_1(t - 1) . N_1(t - 2)$

Figure 1i $N_3(t) : \equiv : N_2(t - 1) . \mathbf{v} . N_1(t - 1) . (Ex)t - 1 . N_1(x) . N_2(x)$

psychons are those of the two-valued logic of propositions. Thus in psychology, introspective, behavioristic or physiological, the fundamental relations are those of two-valued logic.

Hence arise constructional solutions of holistic problems involving the differentiated continuum of sense awareness and the normative, perfective and resolvent properties of perception and execution. From the irreciprocity of causality it follows that even if the net be known, though we may predict future from present activities, we can deduce neither afferent from central, nor central from efferent, nor past from present activities—conclusions which are reinforced by the contradictory testimony of eye-witnesses, by the difficulty of diagnosing differentially the organically diseased, the hysteric and the malingerer, and by comparing one's own memories or recollections with his contemporaneous records. Moreover, systems which so respond to the difference between afferents to a regenerative net and certain activity within that net, as to reduce the difference, exhibit purposive behavior; and organisms are known to possess many such systems, subserving homeostasis, appetition and attention. Thus both the formal and the final aspects of that activity which we are wont to call *mental* are rigorously deducible from present neurophysiology. The psychiatrist may take comfort from the obvious conclusion concerning causality—that, for prognosis, history is never necessary. He can take little from the equally valid conclusion that his observables are explicable only in terms of nervous activities which, until recently, have been beyond his ken. The crux of this ignorance is that inference from any sample of overt behavior to nervous nets is not unique, whereas, of imaginable nets, only one in fact exists, and may, at any moment, exhibit some unpredictable activity. Certainly for the psychiatrist it is more to the point that in such systems "Mind" no longer "goes more ghostly than a ghost." Instead, diseased mentality can be understood without loss of scope or rigor, in the scientific terms of neurophysiology. For neurology, the theory sharpens the distinction between nets necessary or merely sufficient for given activities, and so clarifies the relations of disturbed structure to disturbed function. In its own domain the difference between equivalent nets and nets equivalent in the narrow sense indicates the appropriate use and importance of temporal studies of nervous activity: and to mathematical biophysics the theory contributes a tool for rigorous symbolic treatment of known nets and an easy method of constructing hypothetical nets of required properties.

REFERENCES

1. Carnap, R.: *The Logical Syntax of Language.* New York, Harcourt, Brace and Company, 1938.
2. Hilbert, D., und Ackermann, W.: *Grundüge der Theoretischen Logik.* Berlin, J. Springer, 1927.
3. Whitehead, A. N., and Russell, B.: *Principia Mathematica.* Cambridge, Cambridge University Press, 1925.

A HETERARCHY OF VALUES DETERMINED BY THE
TOPOLOGY OF NERVOUS NETS

WARREN S. McCULLOCH

Because of the dromic character of purposive activities, the closed circuits sustaining them and their interaction can be treated topologically. It is found that to the value anomaly, when A is preferred to B, B to C, but C to A, there corresponds a diadrome, or circularity in the net which is not the path of any drome and which cannot be mapped without a diallel on a surface sufficient to map the dromes. Thus the apparent inconsistency of preference is shown to indicate consistency of an order too high to permit construction of a scale of values, but submitting to finite topological analysis based on the finite number of nervous cells and their possible connections.

The term "reflex" originally meant a disturbance which, initiated by an extra-nervous organ, returned by a nervous path to that same organ. The law of Bell-Magendie, that impulses enter the nervous system by dorsal and emerge by ventral roots, specified the direction of conduction of these circular disturbances. Circular propagation in this direction was called dromic, in the opposite, antidromic. With the possible exception of phenomena comparable to that described by Porter, no response of any effector has ever indicated an antidromic reflex although conduction in the reverse direction has been demonstrated in both the dorsal and ventral roots.

The term "reflex" has latterly been used of any activity in which one pylon was extra-neural regardless of whether or not it was somatic. Lack of anatomic continuity about the external pylon let aftercomers ignore the essential circularity. All reflexes are dromes, activities of feed-back mechanisms, and consequently their function includes all purposive activity.

In addition to reflexes, there exist within the central nervous system reverberating circuits which for brevity are called endromes. Endromes are not in general so related to reflexes as to be uniquely syndromic or antidromic. Their temporal importance in determining the formal properties of nervous activity has been previously discussed (McCulloch and Pitts, 1943). Concerning endromes as well as reflexes, it is well to recall that a given feed-back circuit may be regenerative for one temporal combination of excitations and degenerative for another.

Obviously any number of parallel circuits may be utilized by a single drome and these circuits may divide and unite without the disturbance ceasing to be dromic. Anatomically, the nervous components of their paths consist of neurons so related that the disturbance passes from neuron to neuron over a synapse from the axonal terminations of one neuron to the cell body of the next. With questionable propriety, the terms dromic and antidromic have been applied to passage across a synapse in this and the reverse direction respectively. The impropriety arises from the interrelation of two or more dromes. Conduction in each is dromic, in both, syndromic, but from one to the other, whether it facilitates or inhibits, it is properly neither syn- nor anti-, but heterodromic. Without heterodromic activity reflexes would occur independently of one another. It is therefore to these that one must look for sub-, super-, or co-ordination of reflexes; and, therefore, for behavior, including all relevant aspects of purposive activity.

For the following discussion, it is unnecessary to distinguish homeostatic from appetitive activity. One may even ignore the asymmetry of adversion and aversion, but it is essential to remember that the circuit, whether regenerative or degenerative, must be closed for its activity to be purposive. Thus, in its simplest form, any drome maps in a plane as in Figure 1.

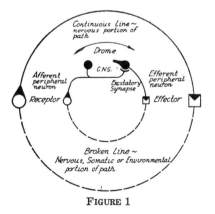

FIGURE 1

For a theory of valuation to be scientific, it must rest on observation and lead to prediction. Empirically, one must observe choice. Choice implies that two or more potential acts are incompatible. The observation requires some overt act with inhibition of incompatibles.

There must then be two complete circuits and an inhibitory, hetero-dromic influence from the one (for an overt act) to the other (for an incompatible act). The circuit maps as indicated in Figure 2.

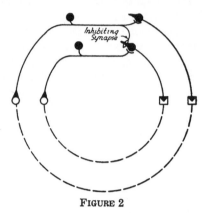

Inhibiting Synapse

FIGURE 2

This scheme can be elaborated for any number of circuits arranged in order of dominance of dromes of each over all within it as in Figure 3.

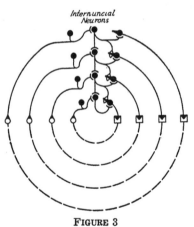

Internuncial Neurons

FIGURE 3

This figure in which heterodromic paths between parallel circuits require no diallels, or "crossovers", demonstrates that any hierarchy of values indicated by choice requires only a nervous net that maps on a plane. The term "hierarchy" in this context has two implications; each drome determines some aim, goal or end, and no two dromes determine exactly the same end. Because organisms live for these ends, they are appreciated by them neither as means to other ends nor as conduct forced upon them, but rather as having that kind of power or importance which culminated in the notion of the sacred or holy—this is the religious implication of "hierarchy" as applied to values. The second implication, arising from the sacerdotal structure of the church, is that the many ends are ordered by the right of each to inhibit all inferiors. The number of ends, although large, is finite. The order is such that there is some end preferred to all others, and another such that all are preferred to it, and that of any three if a first is preferred to a second and a second to a third, then the first is preferred to the third. Logically, therefore, to assert a hierarchy of values is to assert that values are magnitudes of some one kind. Summarily, if values were magnitudes of any one kind, the irreducible nervous net would map (without diallels) on a plane.

Ever since theories of value deserted the inadequate, rational or proportional, Platonic approach, they have been notably inferior to intuition in inferring the outcome of an untried choice. Examination of the theories uncovers that values have been subsumed to be magnitudes of some one kind. Experimental aesthetics, economics, and conditioned reflexology have produced instances in which, under constant condition, preference was circular. One such instance would have been sufficient basis for categorical denial of the subsumption that values were magnitudes of any one kind. Thus, for values there can be no common scale.

Consider the case of three choices, *A* or *B*, *B* or *C*, and *A* or *C* in which *A* is preferred to *B*, *B* to *C*, and *C* to *A*. The irreducible nervous net is shown in Figure 4.

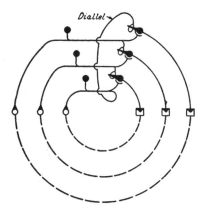

FIGURE 4

It requires one diallel in the plane. Its three heterodromic branches link the dromes so as to form a circle in the net which is distinguished from an endrome in that it is not the circuit of any drome but transverse to all dromes, i.e., diadromic. The simplest surface on which this net maps topologically (without a diallel) is a tore. Circularities in preference instead of indicating inconsistencies, actually demonstrate consistency of a higher order than had been dreamed of in our philosophy. An organism possessed of this nervous system—six neurons— is sufficiently endowed to be unpredictable from any theory founded on a scale of values. It has a heterarchy of values, and is thus internectively too rich to submit to a *summum bonum*.

Topological analysis of the intricacies of values implied by interlocking circularities of preference or of the equivalence of diallels in circuits to the surface on which the nets map without diallels are alike beyond the scope of the present article. Yet, it seems pertinent to note that, however complicated, the ultimate solution is finite even in man. The number of neurons in the brain is some 10^{10} and the number of irreducible diallels is presumably smaller. Let us suppose the worst of possible conditions. In the case of a circular preference, for 3 items, 1 diallel mediates 1 diadrome; for 4 items, 3 diallels mediate 4 diadromes; for 5 items, 6 diallels mediate 7 diadromes; for 6 items, 10 diallels mediate 15 diadromes; for 7 items, 15 diallels mediate 31 diadromes; and so on. Thus, from simple topological considerations, it is clear that if d be the number of diallels and D, the number of diadromes, and if the diallels be arranged in such a manner as to produce the maximum possible number of diadromes, then $D = 2^{-1/2 + \sqrt{1/4 + 2d}} - 1$. For an astronomically large number of diallels $D \to 2^{\sqrt{2d}}$, but d is less than 10^{10}. Therefore, D, is less than 10^{12000}.

This investigation has been aided by a grant from the Josiah Macy, Jr. Foundation.

LITERATURE

McCulloch, W. S. and W. Pitts. 1943. "A Logical Calculus of the Ideas Immanent in Nervous Activity." *Bull. Math. Biophysics*, 5, 115-133.

LETTER TO THE EDITOR

THE HETERARCHY OF VALUES DETERMINED BY THE
TOPOLOGY OF NERVOUS NETS

Since you received the article on the above topic (*Bull. Math. Biophysics,* Vol. 7, No. 2), questions have arisen concerning the dependence of the anomaly on the topology of nets. It would be helpful if you could publish the following note:

Given three dromes, each of which goes over one synaptic connection which is singly insufficient to fire its subsequent neuron but which may be reinforced from one other drome, an organism which fails to respond appetitively to any one of three sensory queues singly may respond to two by what appears to be a preference for one; and three such specious choices may exhibit the circularity of the value anomaly.

Consider three dromes—*A, B,* and *C*—so connected that no one sustains activity without summation from the afferent component of one other drome and let the net be such that *B* (and only *B*) necessarily contributes to *A*; similarly, *C* (and only *C*) to *B*, and *A* (and only *A*) to *C*. Presented with a stimulus *a, b,* or *c* separately, there will be no response; but given any pair, *a* and *b,* or *b* and *c,* or *c* and *a,* the organism will appropriate *a, b,* or *c,* respectively; and given *a, b,* and *c,* the organism will appropriate all three. Obviously the net resembles Figure 4 of the article in question except that the threshold of the afferent neurons is now such as to require impulses from the terminations of two axons, and that the heterodromic actions are summative instead of inhibitory. The same topological considerations apply. The preference, whether or not it be a true choice, is determined by a diadrome, which is no less a diadrome because its heterodromic connections are summative instead of inhibitory.

WARREN S. McCULLOCH, M.D.

HOW WE KNOW UNIVERSALS
THE PERCEPTION OF AUDITORY AND VISUAL FORMS

WALTER PITTS

AND

WARREN S. MCCULLOCH

Two neural mechanisms are described which exhibit recognition of forms. Both are independent of small perturbations at synapses of excitation, threshold, and synchrony, and are referred to particular appropriate regions of the nervous system, thus suggesting experimental verification. The first mechanism averages an apparition over a group, and in the treatment of this mechanism it is suggested that scansion plays a significant part. The second mechanism reduces an apparition to a standard selected from among its many legitimate presentations. The former mechanism is exemplified by the recognition of chords regardless of pitch and shapes regardless of size. The latter is exemplified here only in the reflexive mechanism translating apparitions to the fovea. Both are extensions to contemporaneous functions of the knowing of universals heretofore treated by the authors only with respect to sequence in time.

To demonstrate existential consequences of known characters of neurons, any theoretically conceivable net embodying the possibility will serve. It is equally legitimate to have every net accompanied by anatomical directions as to where to record the action of its supposed components, for experiment will serve to eliminate those which do not fit the facts. But it is wise to construct even these nets so that their principal function is little perturbed by small perturbations in excitation, threshold, or detail of connection within the same neighborhood. Genes can only predetermine statistical order, and original chaos must reign over nets that learn, for learning builds new order according to a law of use.

Numerous nets, embodied in special nervous structures, serve to classify information according to useful common characters. In vision they detect the equivalence of apparitions related by similarity and congruence, like those of a single physical thing seen from various places. In audition, they recognize timbre and chord, regardless of pitch. The equivalent apparitions in all cases share a common figure and define a group of transformations that take the equiva-

46

lents into one another but preserve the figure invariant. So, for example, the group of translations removes a square appearing at one place to other places; but the figure of a square it leaves invariant. These figures are the *geometric objects* of Cartan and Weyl, the *Gestalten* of Wertheimer and Köhler. We seek general methods for designing nervous nets which recognize figures in such a way as to produce the same output for every input belonging to the figure. We endeavor particularly to find those which fit the histology and physiology of the actual structure.

The epicritical modalities map the continuous variables of sense into the neurons of a fine cortical mosaic that strikingly imitates a continuous manifold. The visual half-field is projected continuously to the *area striata*, and tones are projected by pitch along Heschl's gyrus. We can describe such a manifold, say $\mathscr{M}$, by a set of coordinates $(x_1, x_2, \cdots, x_n)$ constituting the point-vector x, and denote the distributions of excitation received in $\mathscr{M}$ by the functions $\phi(x, t)$ having the value unity if there is a neuron at the point x which has fired within one synaptic delay prior to the time t, and otherwise, the value zero. For simplicity, we shall measure time in mean synaptic delays, supposed equal, constant, and about a millisecond long. Indications of time will often not be given.

Let G be the group of transformations which carry the functions $\phi(x, t)$ describing apparitions into their equivalents of the same figure. The group G may always be taken finite, as is seen from the atomicity of the manifold; let it have N members. We shall distinguish four problems of ascending complexity:

1) The transformation T of G can be generated by transformations t of the underlying manifold $\mathscr{M}$, so that $T\phi(x) = \phi[t(x)]$; e.g., if G is the group of translations, then $T\phi(x) = \phi(x + a_T)$, where a_T is a constant vector depending only upon T. If G is the group of dilatations, $T\phi(x) = \phi(a_T x)$, where a_T is a positive real number depending only upon T. All such transformations are linear:

$$T[\alpha\phi(x) + \beta\psi(x)] = \alpha\phi[t(x)] + \beta\psi[t(x)]$$
$$= \alpha T\phi(x) + \beta T\psi(x).$$

2) The transformations T of G cannot be so generated, but are still linear and independent of the time t. An example is to take the gradient of $\phi(x)$, or to replace $\phi(x)$ by its average over a certain circle surrounding x.

3) The transformations T of G are linear, but depend also upon the time. For example, they take a moving average over the preceding five synaptic delays or take some difference as an approximation to the time-derivative of $\phi(x, t)$.

4)   Not all T of G are linear.

Our special nets are essays in problem 1. The simplest way to construct invariants of a given distribution $\phi(x,t)$ of excitation is to average over the group G. Let f be an arbitrary functional which assigns a unique numerical value, in any way, to every distribution $\phi(x,t)$ of excitation in $\mathcal{M}$ over time. We form every transform $T\phi$ of $\phi(x,t)$, evaluate $t[T\phi]$, and average the result over G to derive

$$a = \frac{1}{N} \sum_{\substack{\text{all} \\ T\varepsilon G}} f[T\phi] . \tag{1}$$

If we had started with $S\phi$, S of G, instead of ϕ, we should have

$$\frac{1}{N} \sum_{T\varepsilon G} f[TS\phi] = \frac{1}{N} \sum_{\substack{\text{All } T \\ \text{such that} \\ TS^{-1}\varepsilon G}} f[T\phi] = a , \tag{2}$$

for TS^{-1} is in the group when, and only when, T is in the group; that is, the terms of the sum (1) are merely permuted.

To characterize completely the figure of $\phi(x,t)$ under G by invariants of this kind, we need a whole manifold $\varXi$ of such numbers a for different functionals f, with as many dimensions in general as the original $\mathcal{M}$; if we describe $\varXi$ by coordinates $(\xi_1, \xi_2, \cdots, \xi_m) = \xi$, we may fulfill this requirement formally with a single f which depends upon ξ as a parameter as well as upon the distribution ϕ which is its argument, and write

$$\phi_{f,G}(\xi) = \frac{1}{N} \sum_{T\varepsilon G} f[T\phi\xi] . \tag{3}$$

If the nervous system needs less than complete information in order to recognize shapes, the manifold $\varXi$ may be much smaller than $\mathcal{M}$, have fewer dimensions, and indeed reduce to isolated points. The time t may be one dimension of $\varXi$, as may some of the x_j representing position in $\mathcal{M}$.

Suppose that G belongs to problems 1 or 2 and that the dimensions of $\varXi$ are all spatial; then the simplest nervous net to realize this formal process is obtained in the following way: Let the original manifold $\mathcal{M}$ be duplicated on $N-1$ sheets, a manifold $\mathcal{M}_T$ for each T of G, and connected to $\mathcal{M}$ or its sensory afferents in such a way that whatever produces the distribution $\phi(x)$ on $\mathcal{M}$ produces the transformed distribution $T\phi(x)$ on $\mathcal{M}_T$. Thereupon, separately for each value of ξ for each $\mathcal{M}_T$, the value of $f[T\phi\xi]$ is computed by a suitable net, and the results from all the $\mathcal{M}_T$'s are added by convergence on

48

the neuron at the point ξ of the mosaic Ξ. But to proceed entirely in this way usually requires too many associative neurons to be plausible. The manifolds $\mathcal{M}_T$ together possess the sum of the dimensions of $\mathcal{M}$ and the degrees of freedom of the group G. More important is the number of neurons and fibers necessary to compute the values of $f[T\phi, \xi]$, which depends, in principle, upon the entire distribution $T\phi$, and therefore requires a separate computer for every ξ for every T of G. This difficulty is most acute if f be computed in a structure separated from the $\mathcal{M}_T$, since in that case all operations must be performed by relatively few long fibers. We can improve matters considerably by the following device: Let the manifolds $\mathcal{M}_T$ be connected as before, but raise their thresholds so that their specific afferents alone are no longer able to excite them; cause adjuvant fibers to ramify throughout each $\mathcal{M}_T$ so that when active they remedy the deficiency in summation and permit $\mathcal{M}_T$ to display $T\phi(x)$ as before. Let all the neurons with the same coordinate x on the N different $\mathcal{M}_T$'s send axons to the neuron at x on another recipient sheet exactly like them, say Q — this Q may perfectly well be one of the $\mathcal{M}_T$'s — and suppose any one of them can excite this neuron. If the adjuvant neurons are excited in a regular cycle so that every one of the sheets $\mathcal{M}_T$ in turn, and only one at a time, receives the increment of summation it requires for activity, then all of the transforms $T\phi$ of $\phi(x)$ will be displayed successively on Q. A single f computer for each ξ, taking its input from Q instead of from the $\mathcal{M}_T$'s, will now suffice to produce all the values of $f[T\phi, \xi]$ in turn as the "time-scanning" presents all the $T\phi$'s on Q in the course of a cycle. These values of $f(T\phi, \xi)$ may be accumulated through a cycle at the final Ξ-neuron in any way.

This device illustrates a useful general principle which we may call the *exchangeability of time and space*. This states that any dimension or degree of freedom of a manifold or group can be exchanged freely with as much delay in the operation as corresponds to the number of distinct places along that dimension.

Let us consider the auditory mechanism which recognizes chord and timbre independent of pitch. This mechanism, or part of it, we shall suppose situated in Heschl's gyrus, a strip of cortex two to three centimeters long on the superior surface of the temporal lobe. This strip receives afferents from lower auditory mechanisms so that the position on the cortex corresponds to the pitch of tones, low tones exciting the outer and forward end, high tones the inner and posterior. Octaves span equal cortical distances, as on the keyboard of a piano. The afferents conveying this information from the medial geniculate slant upward through the cortex, branching into telodendria in the principal recipient layer IV, which consists of vertical columns of fifty or more neurons concerning the course of whose ramifying axons there is no certain knowledge except that their activity eventually excites columns of cells situated beneath the recipient layers. Their axons converge to a layer of small pyramids whose axons terminate principally in the secondary auditory cortex or adjacent parts of the temporal lobe. To the layers above and below the receptive layers also come "associative" fibers from elsewhere in the cortex, particularly from nearby. There is no good Golgi picture of the primary auditory cortex in monkeys, but unless it is unlike all the rest of the cortex, it also receives nonspecific afferents from the thalamus, which ascend to branch indiscriminately at every level. A picture of the primary auditory cortex stained by Nissl's method is given in Figure 1, and a schematic version in Figure 2.

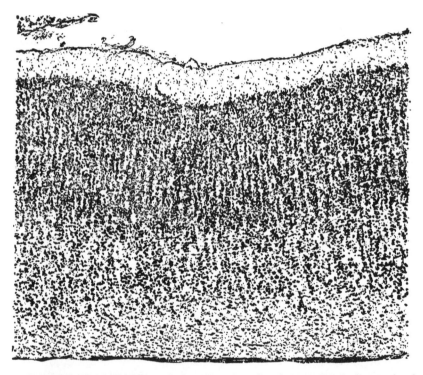

FIGURE 1. Vertical section of the primary auditory cortex in the long axis of Heschl's gyrus, stained by Nissl's method which stains only cell bodies. Note that the columnar cortex, typical of primary receptive areas, shows two tiers of columns, the upper belonging to the receptive layer IV and the lower, lighter stained, to layer V.

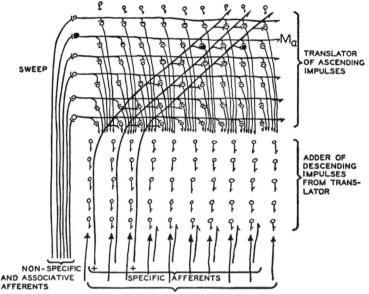

FIGURE 2. Impulses of some chord enter slantwise along the specific afferents, marked by plusses, and ascend until they reach the level $\mathcal{M}_a$ in the columns of the receptive layer activated at the moment by the nonspecific afferents. These provide summation adequate to permit the impulses to enter that level but no other. From there the impulses descend along columns to the depth. The level in the column, facilitated by the nonspecific afferents, moves repetitively up and down, so that the excitement delivered to the depths moves uniformly back and forth as if the sounds moved up and down together in pitch, preserving intervals. In the deep columns various combinations are made of the excitation and are averaged during a cycle of scansion to produce results depending only on the chord.

The secondary auditory cortex has separate specific afferents and the same structure as the primary except for possessing some large pyramids known to send axons to distant places in the cortex such as the motor face and speech areas.

In this case, the fundamental manifold $\mathcal{M}$ is a one-dimensional strip, and x is a single coordinate measuring position along it. The group G is the group of uniform translations which transform a distribution $\phi(x, t)$ of excitation along the strip into $T_a\phi = \phi(x + a, t)$. The group G is thus determined by adding the various constants to the coordinate x, and therefore belongs to problem 1. The set of manifolds $\mathcal{M}_T$ is a set of strips $\mathcal{M}_a$ that could be obtained by sliding the whole of $\mathcal{M}_a$ back and forth various distances along its length. The same effect is obtained by slanting the afferent fibers upward, as in Figure 2, and in the auditory cortex itself where the levels in the

51

columnar receptive layer constitute the $\mathcal{M}_T$. These send axons to the deeper layer, a mass capable of reverberation and summation over time, that may well constitute the set of $f(T\phi, \xi)$ computers for the various ξ, or part of them.

To complete the parallel with our general model, we require adjuvant fibers to activate the various levels $\mathcal{M}_a$ successively. It is to the nonspecific afferents that modern physiology attributes the well-known rhythmic sweep of a sheet of negativity up and down through the cortex—the alpha-rhythm. If our model fits the facts, this alpha-rhythm performs a temporal "scanning" of the cortex which thereby gains, at the cost of time, the equivalent of another spatial dimension in its neural manifold.

According to Ramón y Cajal (1911), Lorente de Nó (1922), and J. L. O'Leary (1941), the specific visual afferents originate in the lateral geniculate body and travel upward through the calcarine cortex, to ramify horizontally for long distances in the stripe of Gennari. This is called the *granular layer* by Brodmann from Nissl stains, and is also called the *external stria of Baillarger*, from its myeloarchitecture. (Zunino, 1909). It is the fourth, or receptive, layer of Lorente de Nó. It may be divided into a superior part IVa, consisting of the larger star-cells and star-pyramids, and an inferior part IVb, consisting of somewhat smaller star-cells, arranged in columns, although the distinction of parts is not always evident (O'Leary, 1941, p. 141). The stripe of Gennari is the sole terminus of specific afferent fibers in the cat and higher mammals, although not in the rabbit. Its neurons send numerous axons horizontally and obliquely upward and downward within the layer; others ascend to the plexiform layer at the surface or descend to the subjacent fifth layer of efferent cells; and axons from the large star-pyramids even enter the subjacent white matter.

The electrical records of J. L. O'Leary and G. H. Bishop (1941) indicate that the normal response of the striate cortex to an afferent volley is triphasic, commencing in layer IV, shown by a surface-positive potential. Next it rises to the surface, making it negative; then as the surface becomes positive, it descends first to the third layer to project to other cortical areas, and then reaches the fifth layer, whence it goes to the pulvinar, the superior colliculus (Barris, Ingram, and Ranson, 1935), and tegmental oculo-motor nuclei, especially to the para-abducens nucleus, which subserves conjugate deviation of the eyes. (Personal communication from Elizabeth Crosby.) This triphasic response, having the period of the alpha-rhythm, is too long to be easily envisaged as a single cycle of purely internal reverberation in the striate cortex. This opinion is confirmed by the superimposed faster response to more intense afferent volleys. It is more reasonable to regard efferents to undifferentiated thalamic nuclei and nonspecific afferents from them (Dempsey and Morrison, 1943) as responsible for the sustention of this triphasic rhythm. As in the auditory mechanism, we assign them the function of "scanning" by exciting sheets seriatim in the upper layers of the cortex.

A version of the visual cortex which agrees with these facts and which constitutes a mechanism of the present type for securing invariance to dilatation and constriction of visual forms is diagrammed in Figure 3. For comparison with this scheme some drawings by Cajal (1900) from Golgi preparations are shown in Figure 4 with the original captions.

Figure 3 is a diagram of part of the neurons in a vertical section of cortex taken radially outward from that cortical point to which the center of the fovea projects. The lowest tier of small cells in IVb is the primary receptive manifold $\mathcal{M}$; the upper tiers of inter-

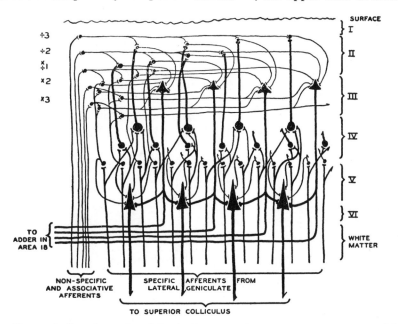

FIGURE 3. Impulses relayed by the lateral geniculate from the eyes ascend in specific afferents to layer IV where they branch laterally, exciting small cells singly and larger cells only by summation. Large cells thus represent larger visual areas. From layer IV impulses impinge on higher layers where summation is required from nonspecific thalamic afferents or associative fibers. From there they converge on large cells of the third layer which relay impulses to the parastriate area 18 for addition. On their way down they contribute to summation on the large pyramids of layer V which relays them to the superior colliculus.

nuncials in I, II, and III, to which the upper tiers of layer IVa separately project, constitute the manifolds $\mathcal{M}_a$ for uniform constriction of all the coordinates of an apparition by factors $0 < a < 1$. This reduplication of the layers of IVa in additional upper internuncial tiers is of course unnecessary since the nonspecific afferents might equally well scan the layers of star-pyramids themselves. The magnifications of the apparition are represented on the internuncial tiers drawn beneath the efferents in the third layer. It is quite likely that these are in reality the small star-cells of IVb, or even the long horizontal extensions of the specific afferents within the outer stria of Baillarger. Histological sections of the visual cortex are now being cut radial to the projection of the center of the fovea and perpendicular to it. It is evident that many details of this and the other hypothetical nets of this paper might be chosen in several ways with equal reason; we

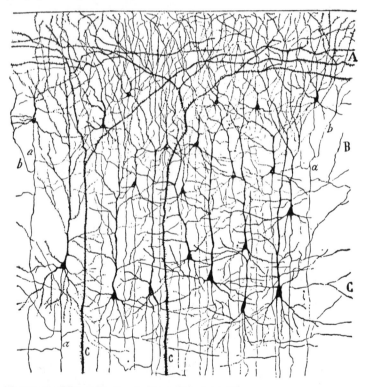

FIGURE 4a. The following is the original caption.
Kleine und mittelgrosse Pyramidenzellen der Sehrinde eines 20 tägigen Neugeborenen (Fissura calcarina). *A*, plexiforme Schicht; *B*, Schicht der kleinen Pyramiden; *C*, Schicht der mittelgrossen Pyramiden; *a*, absteigender Axencylinder; *b*, rückläufige Collateralen; *c*, Stiele von Riesenpyramiden.

have only taken the most likely in the light of present knowledge. The sheet of excitement from nonspecific afferents sweeping up and down the upper three layers, therefore, produces all magnifications and constrictions seriatim on the efferent cells of layer III, traveling from there to the parastriate cortex where the functionals f are made of them and the results added.

It is worth observing again, when special example can fix it, that the group-invariant spatio-temporal distribution of excitations which represents a figure need not resemble it in any simple way. Thus, purely for illustration, we might suppose that the efferent pyramids in the layer III of our diagram project topographically upon another cortical mosaic, which only responds to corners, and accumulates over a cycle of scansion. A square in the visual field, as it moved in and out in successive constrictions and dilatations in Area 17, would trace out four spokes radiating from a common center upon the recipient mosaic. This four-spoked form, not at all like a square, would then be the size-invariant figure of square. In fact, Area 18 does not act like this, for during stimulation of a single spot

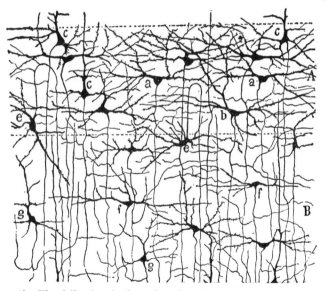

FIGURE 4b. The following is the original caption.
Schichten der Sternzellen der Sehrinde des 20 tägigen Neugeborenen (Fissura calcarina). A, Schicht der grossen Sternzellen; a, halbmondförmige Zellen; b, horizontale Spindelzelle; c, Zellen mit einem zarten radiären Fortsatz; e, Zelle mit gebogenem Axencylinder; B, Schicht der kleinen Sternzellen; f, horizontale Spindelzellen; g, dreieckige Zellen mit starken gebogenen Collateralen; h, Pyramiden mit gebogenem Axencylinder, an der Grenze der fünften Schicht; C, Schicht der kleinen Pyramiden mit gebogenem Axencylinder.

in the parastriate cortex, human patients report perceiving complete and well-defined objects, but without definite size or position, much as in ordinary visual mental imagery. This is why we have situated the mechanism of Figure 3 in Area 17, instead of later in the visual association system. This also makes it likely that one of the dimensions of the apperceptive manifold $\varXi$, upon whose points the group-averages of various properties of the apparition are summed, is time.

This point is especially to be taken against the Gestalt psychologists, who will not conceive a figure being known save by depicting it topographically on neuronal mosaics, and against the neurologists of the school of Hughlings Jackson, who must have it fed to some specialized neuron whose business is, say, the reading of squares. That language in which information is communicated to the homunculus who sits always beyond any incomplete analysis of sensory mechanisms and before any analysis of motor ones neither needs to be nor is apt to be built on the plan of those languages men use toward one another.

Besides the mechanisms which compute invariants as averages, there is another variety of nervous net that can perceive universals. These nets we call *reflex-mechanisms*. Consider the reflex-arc from the eyes through the tectum to the oculomotor nuclei and so to the muscles which direct the gaze. We propose that the superior colliculus computes by double integration the lateral and vertical coordinates of the "center of gravity of the distribution of brightness" referred to the point of fixation as origin, and supplies impulses at a rate proportional to these coordinates to the lateral and vertical eye-muscles in such a way that these then turn the visual axis toward the center of gravity. As the center of gravity approaches the origin, its ordinate and abscissa diminish, slowing the eyes and finally stopping them when the visual axes point at the "center of brightness." This provides invariants of translation. If a square should appear anywhere in the field, the eyes turn until it is centered, and what they see is the same, whatever the initial position of the square. This is a reflex-mechanism, for it operates on the principle of the servo-mechanism, or "negative feedback."

We find considerable support for this conjecture in the profuse anatomical and physiological literature on the corpora quatrigemina anteriora. Histologically, in mammals they are arranged in nine laminae, composed alternately of grey and white matter. Aside from the central grey of the aqueduct, we may enumerate these as follows, from the most superficial inward, naming them with C. V. Ariëns-Kappers, G. C. Huber, and E. C. Crosby (1936):

1)   A superficial layer of fine white myelinated fibers running

antero-posteriorly. These arise in the posterior end of the middle temporal gyrus, about Area 37 of Brodmann, in the part of the temporal lobe which associates visual and auditory material. (E. Crosby, unpublished.) This is the *stratum zonale*, so called by Cajal (1911).

2) A *stratum griseum superficiale*, composed of radially directed cells of sundry types, each with dendrites ramifying near one or both of the adjacent layers, and an axon plunging down into the fourth layer.

3) The *stratum opticum*. This dense layer of myelinated fibers courses antero-posteriorly and constitutes the major afferent supply to the colliculus. The upper portion comes directly from the optic chiasm, as fibers from the nasal side of the contralateral retina and the temporal side of the ipsilateral, and pierces the rostral surface. These direct fibers diminish in number and importance in the higher mammals, giving place to fibers from the occipital cortex beneath them in the layer. These come up from the depths with the radiation from Area 17 somewhat caudal to that from Area 18 or 19 or both (Barris, Ingram, and Ransom, 1935). There are some other cortical fibers of unknown origin in this stratum also, but none from the frontal eye-fields of Area 8 (*ibid.*), which projects directly to oculomotor nuclei (Ward and Reed, 1946). The fibers of the stratum opticum end in bushy terminal arborizations in the grey matter above and below it.

4) A *stratum griseum mediale*, which, together with the three laminae beneath—the *stratum album mediale*, and the two *strata alba et grisea profunda*—makes up Cajal's (1911) "Zone ganglionaire ou des fibres horizontales." Here lie the principal bigeminate efferents. The dendrites of these cells pervade the superficial grey, the stratum opticum, and their own layer. Fibers reach their somata from all the upper strata and the commissure of the superior colliculus. Their axons course horizontally, laterally, and then somewhat caudally, descend to the stratum album profundum, and leave the tectum laterally or else pierce the medial surface as commissural fibers to the other colliculus. The former comprises the "uncrossed" bundle of tecto-pontine fibers (not tecto-spinal: *ibid.*) besides the main "voie optique reflexe" of Cajal. The latter leaves the tectum to spiral ventrad and caudad around the aqueduct and the third and fourth nerve nuclei, decussates, and passes caudad under the medial longitudinal fasciculus to the para-abducens and VI-th nerve nuclei, and to the cervical cord (Cajal, 1911). As it passes, it gives collaterals to all the oculomotor nuclei, mostly crossed at the rostral end and mostly uncrossed posteriorly (E. Crosby, unpublished). As we proceed caudally, the oculomotor nuclei innervate the ocular muscles in this order: superior rectus, medial rectus, inferior oblique, inferior rectus,

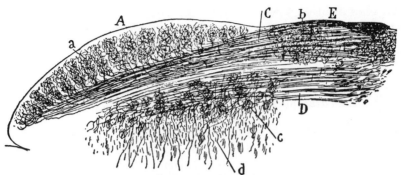

FIGURE 5*a*. The following is the original caption.
Coupe sagittale montrant l'ensemble des fibres optiques du tubercule quadri-jumeau antérieur; souris âgée de 24 heures. Méthode de Golgi. *A*, écorce grise du tubercule antérieur; *C*, courant superficiel des fibres optiques; *D*, courant pro-fond; *E*, région postérieure du corps genouillé externe; *b*, foyer où se terminent des collatérales des fibres optiques; *c*, nids péricellulaires formés par les fibres optiques; *d*, fibres transversales de la couche ganglionnaire.

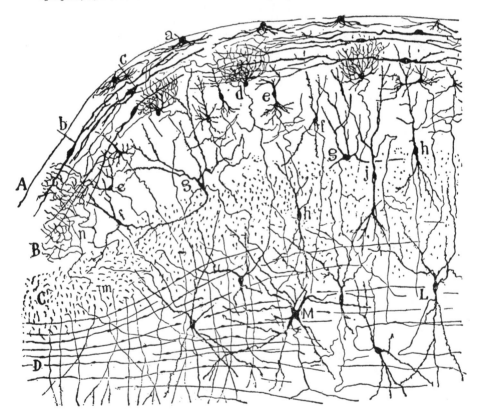

and thence the superior oblique and the lateral rectus, substantiating the scheme of B. Brouwer (1917). These nuclei are interconnected by the medial longitudinal fasciculus, whereby axonal collaterals presumably inhibit antagonists and facilitate synergists. They are aided in this by modest interstitial nuclei such as the para-abducens, subserving conjugate deviation, and perhaps one between the medial recti, for convergence. Such nuclei also serve to transmit the cortical, striatal, acoustic, and vestibular impulses to the oculomotor nerves (*ibid.*, and Lorente de Nó, 1933). Some drawings by Ramón y Cajal from Golgi preparations of the superior colliculus are reproduced, with his captions, in Figure 5.

Julia Apter (1945, 1946), by illuminating small spots on the retina of the cat and finding the tectal point of maximum evoked potential, has demonstrated that each half of the visual field, seen through the nasal half of one eye and the temporal half of the other, maps point-by-point upon the contralateral colliculus. The contours of projection, in angular degrees lateral and vertical from the visual axis, are drawn on the right colliculus as dotted lines in Figure 6. Presumably the calcarine cortex would map similarly, although this has not been tried. In addition, by strychninizing a single point on the collicular surface and flashing a diffuse light on the retina, she obtained change in gaze so as to fix a certain constant point in the visual field. The points for various strychninized places are sketched in solid lines on the right colliculus of Figure 6. It is clear that they nearly coincide with the retinal points which project to the strychninized spot. She showed that if the diffuse light on the retina were

---

FIGURE 5*b* . The following is the original caption.
Coupe transversale du tubercule quadrijumeau antérieur; lapin âgé de 8 jours. Méthode de Golgi. *A*, surface du tubercule tout près de la ligne médiane; *B*, couche grise superficielle ou couche cendrée de Tartuferi comprenant les zones des cellules horizontales et des cellules fusiformes verticales; *C*, couche des fibres optiques; *D*, couche des fibres transversales ou zone blanc cendré profonde de Tartuferi; *L*, *M*, cellules de la couche ganglionnaire ou des fibres transversales; *a*, cellules marginales; *b*, cellules fusiformes transversales ou horizontales; *c*, autre cellule de même espèce, montrant bien son cylindre-axe; *d*, petites cellules à bouquet dendritique compliqué; *e*, cellules fusiformes verticales; *f*, *g*, differents types cellulaires de la couche grise superficielle; *h*, *j*, cellules fusiformes de la zone des fibres optiques; *m*, collatérale descendante allant à la substance grise centrale; *n*, arborisation terminale des fibres optiques.

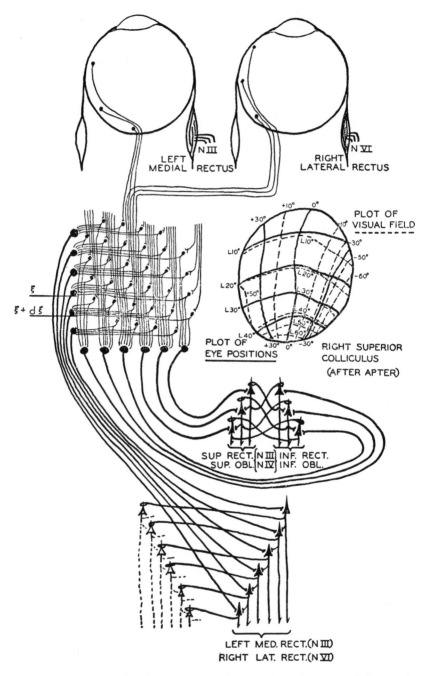

FIGURE 6. A simplified diagram showing occular afferents to left superior colliculus, where they are integrated anteroposteriorly and laterally and relayed to the motor nuclei of the eyes. A figure of the right superior colliculus mapped for visual and motor response by Apter is inserted. An inhibiting synapse is indicated as a loop about the apical dendrite. The threshold of all cells is taken to be one.

replaced by a localized one, the response would occur if, and only if, the points projecting to the strychninized spot were illuminated—apart from certain other smaller effects from the fovea.

All these results agree well with our initial hypothesis. If x and y are respectively lateral and vertical coordinates in the visual field, and $\phi(x, y)$ is the brightness inhabiting the point (x, y)—that is, the response of the spot in the optic nerve which images (x, y)—the coordinates $\bar{x}$ and $\bar{y}$ of the center of brightness are

$$\bar{x} = \int_V dy \int x\phi(x, y)\, dx,$$

$$\bar{y} = \int_V dy \int y\phi(x, y)\, dx,$$

(4)

where integration is over the whole visual field V. If ξ_R, η_R are respectively sagittal and lateral coordinates measuring position on the right colliculus C_R, and ξ_L and η_L their mirror images on the left colliculus C_L, there will be a mapping

$$x = x_R = p(\xi_L, \eta_L),$$

$$y = y_R = q(\xi_L, \eta_L), \quad \text{if } x > 0,$$

(5)

and

$$x = x_L = p(\xi_R, \eta_R),$$

$$y = y_L = q(\xi_R, \eta_R), \quad \text{if } x \leqq 0.$$

To transform equations (4) into the coordinates of the colliculus will then yield

$$\bar{x} = \bar{x}_R - \bar{x}_L,$$

$$\bar{y} = \bar{y}_R + \bar{y}_L,$$

$$\bar{x}_R = \int_{C_L} \int \Phi_L(\xi, \eta) p(\xi, \eta) J(\xi, \eta)\, d\xi d\eta,$$

$$\bar{y}_R = \int_{C_L} \int \Phi_L(\xi, \eta) q(\xi, \eta) J(\xi, \eta)\, d\xi d\eta,$$

$$\bar{x}_L = \int_{C_R} \int \Phi_R(\xi, \eta) p(\xi, \eta) J d\xi d\eta,$$

$$\bar{y}_L = \int_{C_R} \int \Phi_R(\xi, \eta) q(\xi, \eta) J d\xi d\eta;$$

where

$$J(\xi,\eta)=\begin{vmatrix}\dfrac{\partial p}{\partial \xi} & \dfrac{\partial p}{\partial \eta}\\[2mm]\dfrac{\partial q}{\partial \xi} & \dfrac{\partial q}{\partial \eta}\end{vmatrix}$$

and

$$\Phi_L(\xi,\eta)=\phi[-p(\xi,\eta),q(\xi,\eta)],$$
$$\Phi_R(\xi,\eta)=\phi[p(\xi,\eta),q(\xi,\eta)]$$

are the distributions of brightness on the surface of the colliculus.

Now it clearly makes no difference to the final result whether the true center of gravity $(\bar{x},\bar{y})$ determines the net frequency of impulses sent into the eye-muscles, or whether it is some other pair of numbers u and v that increase monotonically with x and y respectively and vanish with them. For in any case, the eyes must be moved in such a direction as to diminish (u,v), and *pari passu* $(\bar{x},\bar{y})$; and finally they must remove (u,v), and therefore $(\bar{x},\bar{y})$, to the origin at the visual axes. Thus, if the two quantities computed from $\phi(x,y)$ to determine lateral and vertical motion respectively have the form

$$u=u_R-u_L,\quad v=v_R+v_L,$$

$$u_R=\int_{c_L}\int U(\xi,\eta)\Phi_L(\xi,\eta)\,d\xi d\eta,\qquad(6)$$

$$v_R=\int_{c_L}\int V(\xi,\eta)\Phi_L(\xi,\eta)\,d\xi d\eta,$$

with a similar integral with Φ_R for u_L and v_L, and any U and V fulfilling the condition that for every η, $U(\xi,\eta)$ is properly monotonic in η, and for every ξ, $V(\xi,\eta)$ is properly monotonic in η, then u and v will have the required properties that they shall vanish and vary monotonically with $\bar{x}$ and $\bar{y}$ respectively. J. Apter (1945, 1946) shows that one can write, approximately,

$$x=p(\xi),$$
$$y=q(\eta),\qquad(7)$$

with $p(\xi)$ and $q(\eta)$ both properly monotonically increasing, neglecting the other variable. This would yield

$$U(\xi,\eta)=p(\xi)p'(\xi)q'(\eta),$$
$$V(\xi,\eta)=q(\eta)q'(\eta)p'(\xi),$$

How We Know Universals

so that

$$u_R = \int_{C_L} p(\xi)\,dp(\xi) \int \Phi_L(\xi,\eta)\,q'(\eta)\,d\eta,$$

$$v_R = \int_{C_L} q(\eta)\,dq(\eta) \int \Phi_L(\xi,\eta)\,p'(\xi)\,d\xi,$$

together with the corresponding expressions for u_L and v_L involving Φ_R, furnish an approximation to $(\bar{x},\bar{y})$. Most general of this type is

$$u = u_R - u_L = \int_C R_1(\xi)\,d\xi \int [\Phi_L(\xi,\eta) - \Phi_R(\xi,\eta)]\,S_1(\eta)\,d\eta, \qquad (8)$$

$$v = v_R + v_L = \int_C R_2(\eta)\,d\eta \int [\Phi_L(\xi,\eta) + \Phi_R(\xi,\eta)]\,S_2(\eta)\,d\eta, \qquad (9)$$

where S_1 and S_2 are non-negative and R_1 and R_2 are properly monotonic and vanish at the origin. The integration is taken over the range of the collicular coordinates. If $S_1 = S_2 = 1$, $R_1(\xi) = \xi = R_2(\xi)$, this is the center of gravity of the afferent excitement upon the colliculi. The simplest schematic way of computing expressions (8) and (9) is actually to carry out the double "integration" on the colliculus, as in Figure 6, so that to compute expression (8) we first add all the afferent impulses within a thin transverse strip, $(\xi, \xi + d\xi)$, to compute

$$d\xi \int \Phi_L(\xi,\eta)\,d\eta.$$

This quantity, for most caudal or greatest ξ, is fed highest into a chain of successively exciting oculomotor neurons; for most anterior, smallest ξ, it comes in lowest. This process provides a net frequency of impulses to the right lateral and medial recti which is certainly weighted by some monotonic factor $R_1(\xi)$. Reciprocal inhibition by axonal collaterals from the nuclei of the antagonist eye-muscles, which are excited similarly by the other colliculus, serves to perform the algebraic subtraction to obtain $u = u_R - u_L$. The computation of the vertical position v of the quasi-center of gravity is done similarly. It is also possible, in whole or in part, that the difference $\Phi_L(\xi,\eta) - \Phi_R(\xi,\eta)$ in equation (8), or the sum $\Phi_L(\xi,\eta) + \Phi_R(\xi,\eta)$ in (9), is computed by commissural fibers running between contralateral tectal points with the same coordinates, instead of in the oculomotor nuclei.

We have omitted to divide the final results u and v by the total luminous flux $A = \int_V \int \Phi(x,y)\,dx\,dy$ before calling (u,v) the "quasi-

63

center of gravity." For the reflex this makes no difference, since (u, v) finally lies at the origin, which does not change on multiplication by A. Similarly, Apter's single-point strychninizations are not relevant to the question. But if several distinct points are strychninized on the colliculus at once, then equation (8) requires gaze to deviate by a lateral distance which is the *sum* of the deviations evoked from the points separately. This may happen; but it seems more likely that the total excitation from the colliculus is in fact kept constant by compensatory variations in the background of facilitation or inhibition, produced perhaps by reverberation with the periaqueductal grey, if not internally in the tectum. H. Klüver's observation (1942) should be recalled here, that even decorticate monkeys whose corpora quadrigemina are not otherwise deafferented detect and discriminate total luminous flux.

But if the colliculus takes a "weighted center of gravity" of an impingent distribution of light, in our most general sense, for suitably chosen partially monotonic positive functions $U(\xi, \eta)$, $V(\xi, \eta)$, so dividing it by the total luminous flux, then, and only then, by a theorem of Reisz, whenever a finite (or infinite) number of points of the colliculus are simultaneously strychninized, the consequent gaze will lie within the smallest convex polygon (or simplex) containing all the points whose projections are strychninized.

This example may be straightforwardly generalized to provide a uniform principle of design for reflex-mechanisms which secure invariance under an arbitrary group G. In some way, out of 'the whole series of transforms $T\phi$ of an apparition, one of them ϕ_0 is elected to be standard—e.g., one of a standard overall size—and when presented with ϕ, the mechanism computes one or more suitable parameters $a(\phi)$, $b(\phi)$, $\cdots$, which define its position within the series of $T\phi$'s in a univocal way so that their simultaneous equality $a(\phi) = a(S\phi)$, $b(\phi) = b(S\phi)$, etc., is sufficient to entail $S = I$, the identity. The errors

$$E_1(\phi) = a(\phi) - a(\phi_0),$$
$$E_2(\phi) = b(\phi) - b(\phi_0),$$

if they do not already all vanish, then impel the mechanism to perform a suitable operation $T\phi$ so determined as to diminish the parameters $E(T\phi)$ as compared to $E(\phi)$. This process may be repeated many times, reducing the $E(\phi)$ at every stage, until the $E(\phi)$'s all vanish and $\phi = \phi_0$, its standard. The mechanism is circular: it follows the scheme

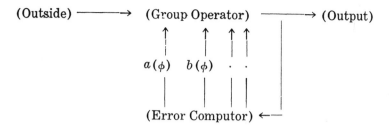

(Outside) ⟶ (Group Operator) ⟶ (Output)

$a(\phi)$ $b(\phi)$ · ·

(Error Computor) ←—

In the case of the colliculus, the group is the two-dimensional translation-group, and the two quantities $a(\phi)$ and $b(\phi)$ are the coordinates of the "weighted center of gravity" of equation (6). For any general group of the type we are considering, quantities $a(\phi)$ of this type may always be found, as is shown in the theory of the irreducible representations of the group G.

We have focussed our attention on particular hypothetical mechanisms in order to reach explicit notions about them which guide both histological studies and experiment. If mistaken, they still present the possible kinds of hypothetical mechanisms and the general character of circuits which recognize universals, and give practical methods for their design. These procedures are a systematic development of the conception of reverberating neuronal chains, which themselves, in preserving the sequence of events while forgetting their time of happening, are abstracted universals of a kind. Our circuits extend the abstraction to a wide realm of properties. By systematic use of the principle of the exchangeability of time and space, we have enlarged the realm enormously. The adaptability of our methods to unusual forms of input is matched by the equally unusual form of their invariant output, which will rarely resemble fhe thing it means any closer than a man's name does his face.

The authors wish to express their great indebtedness to Professor Elizabeth Crosby for her generous assistance and more especially for permission to quote her as yet unpublished observations.

This work was aided by grants from the Josiah Macy, Jr. Foundation and the Rockefeller Foundation.

LITERATURE

Apter, J. 1945. "The Projection of the Retina on the Superior Colliculus of Cats." *J. Neurophysiol.*, 8, 123–134.

Apter, J. 1946. "Eye Movements Following Strychninization of the Superior Colliculus of Cats." *J. Neurophysiol.*, 9, 73–85.

Ariëns-Kappers, C. V., G. C. Huber, and E. C. Crosby. 1936. *The Comparative Anatomy of the Nervous System of Vertebrates.* New York: The Macmillan Co.

Barris, R. W., W. R. Ingram, and S. W. Ranson. 1935. "Optic Connections of the Diencephalon and Midbrain in Cat." *J. Comp. Neur.*, 62, 117–144.

Brouwer, B. 1917. "Klinisch-Anatomische Onderzoekingen Over de Oculomotoriuskern." Voordracht, Gehouden in de Vergadering der Amsterdamsche Neurologenvereeniging op 7 December 1916, in het Binnen-Gasthuis, Collegekamer voor Neurologie. *Neder. Tijdschrift voor Geneeskunde*, Eerste Helft, 14, 1–11.

Dempsey, E. W., and R. S. Morison. 1943. "The Electrical Action of a Thalamo-Cortical Relay System." *Amer. Jour. of Physiology*, 138, 2, 283–296.

Huber, G. C., E. C. Crosby, R. T. Woodburne, L. A. Gillilan, J. O. Brown, and B. Tamthai. 1943. "The Mammalian Midbrain and Isthmus Regions. I. The Nuclear Pattern." *J. Comp. Neur.*, 78, 129–534.

Klüver, H. 1942. "Functional Significance of the Geniculo-Striate System." *Visual Mechanisms*, Pennsylvania: J. Cattell Press, 253–299.

Lorente de Nó, R. 1922. "La Corteza Cerebral del Raton." *Trab. Lab. Invest. Biol. Univ. Madr.*, 20, 41–78.

Lorente de Nó, R. 1933. "The Vestibulo-Ocular Reflex Arc." *Arch. Neurol. and Psychiat.*, 30, 245–291.

Morison, R. S., and E. W. Dempsey. 1942. "The Production of Rhythmically Recurrent Cortical Potentials After Localized Thalamic Stimulation." *Amer. Jour. of Physiol.*, 135, 293–300.

Morison, R. S., and E. W. Dempsey. 1943. "Mechanism of Thalamo-Cortical Augmentation and Repetition." *Amer. Jour. of Physiol.*, 138, 297–308.

O'Leary, J. L., and G. H. Bishop. 1941. "The Optically Excitable Cortex of the Rabbit." *J. Comp. Neur.*, 68, 423–478.

Ramón y Cajal, S. 1911. *Histologie du Système Nerveux*. Paris: Maloine.

Ramón y Cajal, S. 1900. *Die Sehrinde*. Leipzig: Barth.

Ward, A. A. and H. L. Reed. 1946. "Mechanism of Pupillary Dilatation Elicited Cortical Stimulation." *J. Neurophysiol.*, 9, 329–336.

Woodburne, K. T., E. C. Crosby and R. E. McCotter. 1946. "The Mammalian Midbrain and Isthmus Region. II. The Fibre Connections." *J. Comp. Neur.*, 85, 67–92.

Zunino, G. 1909. "Die Myeloarchitektonische Differenzierung der Grosshirnrinde beim Kaninchen." *J. Psych. u. Neur.*, 14, 38–70.

MODES OF FUNCTIONAL ORGANIZATION OF THE CEREBRAL CORTEX*

WARREN S. McCULLOCH

The experiments that gave rise to the following notions were all performed on the primates, *Macaca mulatta* and *Pan satyrus*, although the counts of neurons are usually on man. In all of them the cerebral cortex has come to outweigh and, in neurons, to out-number the rest of the central nervous system. As in all such evolutions of the cephalic end of the dorsal plate, mere size permits greater distinction of functionally dissimilar portions and of their various paths of communication. But with its majority has come not only an undertaking of selected functions of more caudal portions of ,the dorsal plate and a control of their activity by impulses projected upon them (1), but also interference with the execution of their functions by impulses upon one or more of the systems relaying their signals toward the final common path (2). Some of those systems, say the cortico-ponto-cerebello-dentato-rubro-spinal (3), have lost so much of their projection upon the cord that the output of their remnants returns in no small measure to the cortex (4), so relating its events indirectly. In primates, the plurality of all lower neurons are thus re-entrantly involved. Among remaining caudad systems, I know none which does not receive, directly or indirectly, signals from the cortex, nor any sector of the cortex that does not signal to some of them. But, as they still receive their proper peripheral afferents their output is the result of at least two streams—one from the cortex and one or more from elsewhere in the dorsal plate (5, 6).

To that *great* extent to which its afferents inform it of the peripheral consequences of the action of its own efferents (7, 8, 9), any system is part of the path of a reflex. And most if not all purely reflexive action is negative feedback (10) tending to reduce all deviation from an intended peripheral state measured by the afferents (11). Left to itself each such circuit is homeostatic (9). But, to *that* extent to which its central nervous components can be influenced from elsewhere, notably the cerebrum, it can be made to seek other states or, to use an engineer's term, be reduced to a *servo-mechanism* (11). Nothing but the name is new.

* This work was aided by grants from the Joseph and Mary Markle Foundation, Josiah Macy, Jr. Foundation and the Rockefeller Foundation. The author wishes to thank Mr. Walter Pitts for his careful revisions of the manuscript and Dr. Jerome Lettvin for the preparation of the references.

In 1826 Sir Charles Bell read his famous paper on the nervous circle (7) before the Royal Society; and in 1868 Clerk Maxwell read his on the governors of steam-engines (12), with much of the mathematics required for these negative feedback, or reflexive, systems (13). Had Hughlings Jackson founded his hypothesis (14, 15) upon their ideas instead of resting it on Herbert Spencer's Epicurean psychology (16) he would certainly not have pictured the second level (17), especially the motor cortex, as the bass of a piano-accordion whose every button sounds a chord (17, 18). Nor does he save his theory in admitting cooperation or competition from other structures, notably the cerebellum (19), for "it make no great part" of his account of the motor cortex and the pyramidal tact (14).

Let experiment have frozen proper activities of servo-mechanisms by fixing bones, muscles, joints, etc., then excitation of one or few Betz' cells will evoke what Jackson called movements (16), that is to say contraction of few muscles (20) and, perhaps, relaxation of antagonists—a complexity not allowed by the classical description of the motor cortex as a harpsichord with a cell to pluck each string (21, 22, 23, 24). No better is Walshe's notion (25) that these cortical efferents, like the push-buttons of some monstrous "juke-box", serve each to evoke entire some innate or learned "pattern of movement", (26, 27) which dwells in one such efferent at least and is not else effectable (27).

These inept conceits—accordion, harpsichord and juke-box—alike failed to predict the disparate consequences of stimulation at diverse frequencies (28). Percival Bailey has shown us that from all parts of Face Area 4, where twelve or more impulses per second regularly evoke contraction of facial muscles innervated by the seventh nerve, ten or less per second ilicit only movements of the tongue, innervated by the twelfth alone (29). As he excited the efferents directly, and impulses descending conserve frequency (30), only filters in lower structures accomplish their diversion.

In familiar phrase, we might concede that frequency as well as place must enter our "idea" of the mode of representation of motion, and conceive the cortex an English horn. This opinion, as sweet, equivocal and perfidious as its three precedents, is as legitimate. For the lexicographer (31) will allow all four, and twenty others like them, quite impartially, each with a good sense of "to represent." All are metaphorical, compatible, assert little, predict nothing. It were less deceptive to have cortex

67

"represent" that internuncial ocean where its axons end—better, to do nothing of the kind (32). Now nothing from the cortex partakes in the functional organization of the cortex unless the recipient internuncials affect the cortex again, and only so much as the corticifugal activity informs the return. We shall treat such feedback under Indirect Functional Organization, merely remarking that the cortex does thus affect its sensory input (33, 34).

The number of corticipetal fibres has been variously estimated, but I can find no one but Earl Walker brave enough to make it a hundred million, even in man. From the relative density of thalamic to extrinsic cortico-cortical fibres we may admit of the latter as many more, i.e. 10^8. The number of cortical neurons to be connected we may likewise round off at 10^{10} again in man (35). Thus indirect and extrinsic fibres together are no more than a fiftieth of the associators of cortical events, for we can estimate the actual number of intrinsic cortico-cortical axons by recalling that less than one in a hundred leaves the cortex. This gives us again a hundred intrinsic to one extrinsic and one indirect cortico-cortical connection. To the ramification of axons we look for the multiplication of synapses required for summation.

We turn, therefore, to the grey mass of the cortex. Histological pictures by Cajal (36) and Lorente de Nó (37) show we can separate its vertical from its horizontal constitution. Conceive, then, the cortex as a mass of cells, say a hundred in depth 38, 39), divisible into ill-defined layers containing principally neurons of given kinds, so connected from layer to layer that there are skip-distances of one layer in their vertical synapsis except in the outermost and innermost where cells of the odd and even series associate (37). In the intermediate layers are chiefly neurons whose axons are vertical with only subsidiary horizontal ramifications. Such vertical systems of neurons can reverberate (39, 40, 41) longer than if all layers were equally thoroughly interconnected by single axons. They can easily tolerate rhythms whose period is determined by a full circulation through the hundred cells, for this, with reasonable allowance for slow conduction and synaptic delays, demands but ten impulses per second in each neuron. And we know some neurons that fire for long periods at twenty times that frequency (42, 43).

Yet, it has become increasingly evident that this rhythm usually recorded from idle cortex may not be attributable to it alone (44, 45), but rather to its ability to follow without loss that frequency imparted to it by unspecific afferents from undifferentiated thalamic structures (46, 47, 48, 49, 50, 51, 52). As yet there is nothing to suggest that it is anything more than a happy coincidence of the natural periods of intrinsic and indirect functional organizations, which may become unhappy when

three per second impulses appear (53, 54), leading to *petit mal*, with its spike and dome (55) that block all proper function of cortex and thalamus (56). These gross fluctuations of voltage through the cortex, having properties largely dependent simply on distance, resemble all disorders which introduce "fields" (57, 58, 59), be they physical or chemical or both, into mosaics of cells each capable of a discrete decision—impulse or nóne—and thereby consume the effective degrees of freedom without contributing to the precise ordering of their decisions, that is, to information (60). In 1936 Bishop showed that even the mild fluctuations, or alpha rhythm, of idle brain have a somewhat similar effect (52).

To him we are yet more indebted for the first proof of any function of the largest single bundle of extrinsic cortico-cortical connections, the corpus callosum, for he showed that, on cutting the visual cortices loose from the geniculate bodies, it swept them into phase (52). Van Wagenen and Akelaitis (61, 62, 63, 64, 65, 66) have proved its unimportance by exhibiting the relative normality, including the continuity of visual perception (65), after its section in epileptics, in whom the section frequently prevented spread of grand mal convulsions across the midline. Its ability to sweep the other hemisphere into such seizures, Erickson proved (67), and I can confirm, with all paths through lower structures interrupted. Had Van Wagenen included the anterior commissure in his transsections probably all his operations would have succeeded (68). Although I have spent much time strychninizing one square millimeter of cortex in primates under Dial and recording the impulses over the extrinsic system (69), I for one am convinced that, although it alone can keep the cortex promptly informed of its own remote activity, no more specific task can yet be surely ascribed to any part of it. To generalize convulsions is scarcely its duty. Our inability to discover its role is exasperating, for with 10^{10} neurons organized vertically by hundreds, there are some 10^8 such vertical groups and hence nearly enough extrinsic axons for one to go to each group.

But before we return to these groups whose numbers and arrangement ultimately determine the cytoarchitecture of the cortex, let me say that Bailey and von Bonin have completed their study of this aspect of *Macaca Mulatta* (70) and are well along on *Pan Satyrus* (71), that histological facts have compelled them to adopt von Economo's cartography (35) and that all our neuronographic findings on these extrinsic connections when so plotted show regularities we sought in vain in Brodmann's scheme (72). Sooner or later we shall adjust nomenclature to the ineducable vertical structure of the *cortex cerebri*.

We have seen that this structure could support rhythms requiring say 100 synaptic delays—but we know that the time for reflections through the thick of the cortex is often less than 10 synaptic delays (52, 73, 74) with due allowance for conduction. An incoming volley of specific afferents initiates a surface-position wave of say 2 milliseconds (52). This is followed by 4 or more milli-seconds of surface-negativity (52) while it inhabits and spreads in superficial layers. Then it descends, taking perhaps 2 more milliseconds (52). A primary sensory area bombarded by such afferents properly timed at lower levels might then be driven at 120 cycles per second, if output and input did not interfere. Presumably they do, for its highest recorded frequency is that at which flicker fuses, about 53 per second (75, 76, 77, 78). Now there can be but one corticifugal fibre for the whole 100 cells of which some or all have come into play to determine, in a matter of say 5 synaptic delays, whether that efferent shall fire or no.

The maximum information (60) that may enter such a decision of the corticifugal fibre in this short time is the time in synaptic delays multiplied by the number of neurons, i.e. 5 × 100, or as much information as can be conveyed in twenty five-lettered words. Since these neurons are arranged in reverberating chains (39, 40), a second impulse, following a first within any period during which their reverberations are still informed by the first, has a fate determined in part by that active memory (78). Moreover, these columns are not merely linked with remote columns by one extrinsic fibre, but with adjacent columns by numerous fibres (39, 40, 79) and with others in the neighborhood by fewer, the number decreasing with increasing distance. Thus, the information brought to bear in determining the twenty words-worth of information is many times more. It increases with the duration of a figure in the impinging world; and all our perceptions of tone, chords, positions, shapes, etc. become blurred (43, 80) when one figure of excitement succeeds another at say 10 per second.

This demands a process which shall, from information radiating through the cortex out of the many channels that report the world, abstract one or more universals, or ideas (81). These may be found by scanning the recipient volume of cortex to discover figures of excitement regardless of position or size. To scan that space we shall detect and relay to fixed points the coincidence of the information with a horizontal plane of excitement that sweeps up and down the volume. Let it step but a cell's height per synaptic delay, and the time for clear perception, be jt form seen or chord heard, becomes the required tenth of a second. Large electrodes on a cortex uninformed detect the sweep of scansion (82, 83), but on a cortex informed, the sweep is lost in the twinkle of details comprised in the perception (82, 83).

This fancy cleaves to fact, prescribes experiment, predicts outcome, invites refutation. It does not strain credulity, for mere statistical order suffices for nets to embody this process, inasmuch as small perturbation of threshold, of excitement, even of synapsis has little or no effect on the average that is the figure, or idea. These nets are random in detailed synapsis, for genes do not predestine termini to all neuronal ramification.

If connections in the felt-work of the cortex be random they are suitable to explain that surface-negative wave which expands in a circle about a mildly stimulated point in the cortex. Rosenblueth measured its rate of propagation from a strychninized spot under chloralose (84). The circle expands too slowly to be spread by anything but repeated synaptic relay. It diminishes as it spreads. But weak strychninization of an area near its origin renders that area hyper-excitable and then radial symmetry is lost, for the wave, with greater size and steeper front, races across the strychninized area (85). I could make little of this until Walter Pitts set up the mathematics for conduction in the random net (86). Now it appears as a verification of his theory that its velocity of propagation is determined by the rate at which spatial summation reaches a critical value in a random net and, therefore, by the threshold of the cells.

We have theories now that will force us to many experiments that may reveal to what extent the nets of the cortex are ordered, but none that will account for the ordering of these nets by learning, for this, like crystallization, is a change of state, and for such stochastic processes the mathematics is not yet (87, 88).

In closing, let me rehearse the general order that can be seen. Sectors of cortex, defined by their connections with thalamic nuclei (89), severally exhibit a receptive area or a pair juxtaposed but oriented reversely (90, 91, 92) each surrounded by a zone to which it gives many extrinsic axons. From each of these composite fields arises a projection whose activity affects that part of the body in which its organs of sense are situate. Thus the *area striata* (93) and its surrounding zones (94) move the eyes toward the place in the visual field corresponding to the position of excitation. The first and second somaesthetic areas and the zone anterior to the former and deep to the latter (95) in the Sylvian fissure, extending on to the Island of Reil, direct the carriers of their appropriate receptors, and the superior surface of the second temporal convolution pricks up the ipsilateral ear (96).

This close cortical coupling of each sensory input to output affecting that sensory input by moving the organ of sense is a mode of functional organization whose circuit leaves and returns to the body. It is more indirect than the interception of sensory impulses to cortex which area 4s achieves *via nuclei caudati* by blocking thalamic relay (97, 98,

99). Yet circuits through the external world are but extensions of what Bell proposed merely through muscles in The Nervous Circle. On these re-entrant activities Cannon founded his conception of homeostasis (9), and Rosenblueth and Wiener, their theory of purposive behavior (100).

In primates these appetitive circuits pervade the cortex wherein their dominance is ordered and whence their dominion is effected. Yet the general plan of the cortex makes its own functional organization imperfect without control of input by output, over links beyond the present scope of physiology. They are to be sought wherever appetitive circuits traverse the public world. Unlike unicorns some of these links are always to be found in Parliament Square (101).

BIBLIOGRAPHY

(1) LE GROS CLARK, W. E., Physiol. Reviews **22**: 205, 1942. (2) WARD, A. A., JR., AND REED, H. L., J. Neurophysiol. **9**: 4, 329, 1946. (3) BUCY, P., J. Neuropath. & Exp. Neurol. **1**: 2, 224, 1942. (4) CRESCITELLI, F. AND GILMAN, A., Am. J. Physiol. **147**: 127, 1946. (5) LORENTE DE NO, R., J. Neurophysiol. **2**: 5, 402–464, 1939. (6) LORENTE DE NO, R., J. Neurophysiol. **1**: 3, 195, 1938. (7) BELL, C., On the nervous circle, etc. Read before the Royal Society, February 16, 1826. (8) MAGENDIE, T., Mémoire sur quelques découvertes récentes rélatives aux factions du système nerveux. Lu à la séance publique de l'Acadamie des Sciences. Paris, 1823. (9) CANNON, W., Physiol. Reviews **9**: 399, 1929. (10) BLACK, H. S., Elec. Eng. **53**: 114, January, 1934. (11) McCOLL, H., Servo Mechanisms, 1945—Van Nostrand. (12) MAXWELL, C., Proc. Royal Soc. **100**: 1868 (On Governors). (13) HEAVISIDE, O., Electromagnetic Theory, **1,2** and **3**: Electrician Pub. Co., 1893, et seq. (14) HUGHLINGS JACKSON, J., Med. Press and Circ. **10**: 1, 329, 1881. (15) HUGHLINGS JACKSON, J., Lancet, **1**: 79, 1898. (16) SPENCER, H., Principals of Psychology, 1855—Publisher not listed. (17) HUGHLINGS JACKSON, J., Med. Press and Circ. **2**: 411, 1882. (18) HUGHLINGS JACKSON, J., Croonian Lecture, Part 1, March, 1884 (Lancet, **1**: 535, 1884. (19) HUGHLINGS JACKSON, J., Brain **22**: 621, 1899. (20) CHANG, H., RUCH, T. AND WARD, A. A. JR., J. Neurophysiol. **10**: 1, 39, 1947. (21) FRITSCH, G. AND Hitzig, E., Arch. Anat. Physiol. wiss Med. **37**: 300–332, 1870. (22) HITZIG, E., Untersuchungen uber das Gehirn, Berlin, Hirschwald, 1874. (23) BEEVOR, E. C. AND HORSLEY, V., Phil. Tr. **181**: 129, 1890–91. (24) SHERRINGTON, C. AND LEYTON, A.S.F., Quart. J. Exp. Physiol. **11**: 135, 1917. (25) WALSHE, F.M.R., Oliver Sharpey Lecture No. 2, Royal Coll. of Physicians, of London, May 2, 1929. (26) WALSHE, F.M.R., Brain **50**: 377, 1927. (27) WALSHE, F.M.R., Brain **56**: 104, 1943. (28) WYSS, O.A.M. AND CROZIER, W. J., Helv. Physiol. Pharmacol. Acta **1**: 89, 1943. (28a) DELGADO, J.M.R., FULTON, J. AND LIVINGSTON, R. B., Fed. Proc. **6**: 1, 1947. (29) BAILEY, P., Personal communication. (30) ADRIAN, E. D. AND MORUZZI, S., J. Physiol. **97**: 153–199, 1939. (31) CRAIGIE, E. W., Oxford English Dictionary ("Represent" ca. 1910). (32) BARNARD, R., J. Comp. Neurol. **73**: 235, (1940). (33) HEAD, H. AND HOLMES, G., Brain **34**: 102, 1912. (34) DUSSER DE BARENNE, J. G. AND McCULLOCH, W. S., J. Neurophysiol. **1**: 2, 177, 1938. (35) VON ECONOMO, C. AND KOSKINAS, G. N., Die Cytoarchitektonik, J. Springer, Vienna, 1925. (36) RAMON Y CAJAL, S., Histologie du système nerveux, Paris, Maloine, 1909–1911. (37) LORENTE DE NO, R., Chap. XV in Physiology of the Nervous System, Fulton —Oxford University Press, 1943. (38) VON BONIN, G., Personal communication. (40) LORENTE DE NO, R., J. f Psych. u Neur. **45**: H 6, 381, 1934. (41) LORENTE DE NO, R., J. f Psych. u Neur. **46**: H 2 u 3, 113, 1934. (42) LORENTE DE NO, R., J. Neurophysiol. **1**: 3, 207, 1938. (43) STEVENS, S. S. AND DAVIS, H., Hearing—Wiley, 1938. (44) DUSSER DE BARENNE, J. G. AND McCULLOCH, W. S., Am. J. Physiol. **127**: 620, 1939. (45) DUSSER DE BARENNE, J. G. AND McCULLOCH, W. S., J. Neurophysiol. **4**: 4, 304, 1941. (46) LEWY, F. H. AND CANNON, W., J. Neurophysiol. **3**: 388, 1940. (47) MORISON, R. AND DEMPSEY, W., Am. J. Physiol. **135**: 2, 281, (48) DEMPSEY, W. AND MORISON, R., Am. J. Physiol. **135**: 2, 293, 1942. (49) DEMPSEY, W. AND MORISON, R., Am. J. Physiol. **138**: 42, 283, 1943. (50) MORISON, R. AND DEMPSEY, W., Am. J. Physiol. **138**: 42, 297, 1943. (51) MORISON, R. AND BASSETT, D. L., J. Neurophysiol. **8**: 304, 1945. (52) BISHOP, G., Symposia on Quan. Biol. Cold Spring Harbor **4**: 305, 1946. (53) WARD, A. A. JR., J. Neurophysiol. **10**: 2, 104, 1947. (54) JASPER, H., PENFIELD, W. AND DROOGLEEVER-FORTUYN, J., 26th Annual Meeting Assn. for Research in Nerv. and Ment. Dis., December 13, 1946. (55) GIBBS, F., LENNOX, W. AND GIBBS, E., Arch. Neurol. and Psychiat. **46**: 613, 1941. (56) PENFIELD, W. AND JASPER, H., 26th Annual Meeting, Assn. for Research in Nerv. and Ment. Dis., December 13, 1946. (57) GERARD, R. AND LIBET, B., Livro de Homenagem, Rio de Janeira, Brasil, 1939. (58) LIBET, B. AND GERARD, R., J. Neurophysiol. **4**: 438, 1941. (59) KOHLER, W. AND WALLACH, Proc. Amer. Phil. Soc. **88**: 269, 1944. (60) WIENER, N., Time, Communication and the Nervous System, Mss. in preparation for Northrop. (61) AKELAITIS, T., Am. J. Psychiat. **98**: 409, 1941-42. (62) AKELAITIS, T., Arch. Neurol. and Psychiat. **48**: 914, 1942. (63) AKELAITIS, A. J., RISTEEN, W. A., HERREN, R. Y. AND VAN WAGENEN, W. P., Arch. Neurol. and Psychiat. **47**: 971, 1942. (64) AKELAITIS, A. J., RISTEEN, W. A., HERREN, R. Y. AND VAN WAGENEN, W. P., Arch. Neurol. and Psychiat. **49**: 820, 1943. (65) AKELAITIS, A. J., J. Neu-

ropath. Exper. Neurol. **2**: 226, 1943. (66) AKELAITIS, A. J., J. Neurosurg. **1**: 94, 1944. (67) ERICKSON, T., Arch. Neurol. and Psychiat. **43**: 429, 1940. (68) McCULLOCH, W. S. AND GAROL, H., J. Neurophysiol. **4**: 7, 555, 1941. (69) McCULLOCH, W. S., Corticocortical Connections—Chap. VIII in "The Precentral Motor Cortex"—Ed. P. Bucy, University of Illinois Press, 1944. (70) BAILEY, P. AND VON BONIN, G., Neocortex of Macaca Mulatta, University of Illinois Press, 1947. (71) BAILEY, P., VON BONIN, G. AND McCULLOCH, W. S. Studies on Neocortex of the Chimpanzee. Mss. in preparation. University of Illinois Press. (72) BRADMANN, K., Vergleichende Loakalisationslehre der Grosshirnrinde, etc. Leipzig, Barth, 1909. (73) MARSHALL, WOOLSEY, c. AND BARD, P., J. Neurophysiol. **4**: 1, 1941. (74) BARTLEY, S. H., O'LEARY, J. L. AND BISHOP, G., Am. J. Physiol. **120**: 604, 1937. (75) CROZIER, W. J., WOLF, C., ZERRAHN, G. AND WOLF., J. Gen. Physiol. **21**: 203, 1937. (76) HECHT, S. AND SCHLAER, S., J. Gen. Physiol. **19**: 965, 1936. (77) BARTLEY, S. H., Vision—van Nostrand, 1941. (78) McCULLOCH, W. S., Finality and Form—Fifteenth James Arthur Lecture, N. Y. Acad. of Science, May 2, 1946. (79) RAMON Y CAJAL, S., Die Sehrinde—Leipzig, Barth, 1900. (80) WALLS, G. L., The Vertebrate Eye—Cranbrook Inst. of Science, August 1942 (pp. 356–365). (81) McCULLOCH, W. S. AND PITTS, W., Bull. Math. Biophys. September 1947. (82) BERGER, H., Das Elektrenkephalogramm des Menschen—Nova Acta Leopoldina **6**: 38, 173, 1938, Halle (Saale). (83) GIBBS, F. AND GIBBS, E., Atlas of Electroencephalography. (84) ROSENBLUETH, A. AND CANNON, W., Am. J. Physiol. **135**: 3, 690, 1942. (85) McCULLOCH, W. S., mss. in preparation. (86) PITTS, W., Ph.D. Thesis in preparation—M.I.T. Dept. of Mathematics. (87) WIENER, N., The Homogeneous Chaos, Am. J. Math. 1938. (88) WIENER, N. AND WINTNER, A., The Discrete Chaos, Am. J. Math. 1940. (89) McCULLOCH, W. S., Physiol. Reviews **24**: 3, 390, 1944. (90) WOOLSEY, C. AND WALZL, E. M., Bull. Johns Hopkins Hosp. **71**: 315, 1942. (91) TALBOT, C. N., WOOLSEY, C. AND THOMPSON, W. G., Fed. Proc. Am. Soc. Exper. Biol. **5**: 103, 1946. (92) WOOLSEY, C. AND FAIRMAN, Surgery **19**: 684, 1946. (93) WALKER, A. E. AND WEAVER, T., J. Neurophysiol. **3**: 353, 1940. (94) FOERSTER, O., Lancet **2**: 309, 1931. (95) CHUSID, J. AND SUGAR, O., demonstration. (96) SUGAR, O. AND CHUSID, J., demonstration. (97) DUSSER DE BARENNE, J. G. AND McCULLOCH, W. S., J. Neurophysiol. **1**: 364, 1938. (98) GELLHORN, E., J. Neurophysiol. **10**: 2, 125, 1947. (99) BARKER, S. H. AND GELLHORN, E., J. Neurophysiol. **10**: 2, 133, 1947. (100) ROSENBLUETH, A., WIENER, N. AND BIGELOW, J., Philosophy of Science **10**: 1, 18, 1943. (101) WALSHE, F. H. R., Brit. Med. J. **1**: 514, 1931.

Why the Mind Is in the Head

WARREN S. McCULLOCH

As the industrial revolution concludes in bigger and better bombs, an intellectual revolution opens with bigger and better robots. The former revolution replaced muscles by engines and was limited by the law of the conservation of energy, or of mass-energy. The new revolution threatens us, the thinkers, with technological unemployment, for it will replace brains with machines limited by the law that entropy never decreases. These machines, whose evolution competition will compel us to foster, raise the appropriate practical question: "Why is the mind in the head?"

Coming as I do between psyche anatomized and psyche synthesized, I must so define my terms that I can bridge the traditional gulf between mind and body and the technical gap between things begotten and things made.

By the term "mind," I mean ideas and purposes. By the term "body," I mean stuff and process. Stuff and process are familiar to every physicist as mass and energy in space and time, but ideas and purposes he keeps only in the realm of discourse and will not postulate them of the phenomena he observes. In this I agree with him. But what he observes is some sort of order or invariance in the flux of events. Every object he detects in the world is some sort of regularity. The existence of these objects is the first law of science. To detect regularities in the relations of objects and so construct theoretical physics requires the disciplines of logic and mathematics. In these fundamentally tautological endeavors we invent surprising regularities, complicated transformations which conserve whatever truth may lie in the propositions they transform. This is invariance, many steps removed from simple sensation but not essentially different. It is these regularities, or invariants, which I call ideas, whether they are theorems of great abstraction or qualities simply sensed. The reason for excluding them from physics is that they must not be supposed to be either stuff or process in the causal sequences of any part of the world. They are neither material nor efficient. So, to my mind Newton, Planck, and Jeans sin by introducing God as a sort of mind at large in the world to account for physical effects, like the action of gravity at a distance.

But let us now compel our physicist to account for himself as a part of the physical world. In all fairness, he must stick to his own rules and show in terms of mass, energy, space, and time how it comes about that he creates theoretical physics. He must then become a neurophysiologist (that is what happened to me), but in so doing he will be compelled to answer whether theoretical physics is something which he can discuss in terms of neurophysiology (and *that* is what happened to me). To answer "no" is to remain a physicist undefiled. To answer "yes" is to become a metaphysician—or so I am told.

But is that just? The physicist believes entropy to be somehow in or of physical systems. It may or must increase with time. But it is neither material nor efficient, in fact it is a number, namely, the logarithm of the probability of the state. It is, therefore, a measure of the disorder of an ensemble—or collection of systems. Now Norbert Wiener has proposed that information is orderliness and suggests that we measure it by negative entropy, the logarithm of the reciprocal of the probability of the state. Let us, for this argument, accept his suggestion. Ideas are then to be construed as information. Sensation becomes entropic coupling between us and the physical world, and our interchange of ideas, entropic coupling among ourselves. Our knowledge of the world, our conversation—yes, even our inventive thought —are then limited by the law that information may not increase on going through brains, or computing machines.

The attempt to quantify the information leads to a search for an appropriate unit, which, in turn, forces us to distinguish between two types of devices. In so-called logical, or digital, contrivances, a number to be represented is replaced by a number of things—as we may tally grain in a barn by dropping a pebble in a jug for each sheaf. The abacus is such a device. The nervous system is par excellence a logical machine. In so-called analogical contrivances a quantity of something, say a voltage or a distance, is replaced by a number of whatnots or, conversely, the quantity replaces the number. Sense organs and effectors are analogical. For example, the eye and the ear report the continuous variable of intensity by discrete impulses the logarithm of whose frequency approximates the intensity. But this process is carried to extremes in our appreciation of the world in pairs of opposites. As Alcmaeon, the first of experimental neurophysiologists, so well observed, "the majority of things human are two"—white-black, sweet-bitter, good-bad, great-small. Our sense organs, detecting regularities the same in all respects save one, create dichotomies and decide between opposites. These the "brain somehow fits together." From this sprang associationalism, culminating in Mill's evolutionary hypothesis that things are similar for us which have occurred together in the experience of our progenitors, and Kapper's law that nervous structures associated in action become associated in position. Neither proposes any mechanism other than random variation and the survival of those in whom the happy concatenation occurred. We inherit a nervous system so structured that we do perceive similarities (or have ideas) and these, not isolated, but conjoined within the system in many useful ways. That synthetic a priori is the theme of all our physiological psychology, learning excepted.

How, in all these processes, can we "quantify" the amount of information? In analogical devices it is best done by examining the numerical component. They all suffer from a peculiar limitation of accuracy which can usually not be pushed beyond one part in a thousand and almost never beyond one part in a million, even in such a simple matter as weighing. Moreover, analogical devices can not be combined in any way to push the decimal point. By measuring carefully the diameter and circumference of a circle, we might analogically estimate the ratio π to six significant figures. With a digital device, say an abacus, we can compute it to any number of places.

What characterizes a digital, or logical, device is that its possible states are separated sharply. In the simplest case there are only two. Wiener proposes that, for these bivalent systems, we define the unit of information as the decision *which* state it shall occupy. Notice, now, that this system has one degree of freedom—say, go or no-go—until it receives one unit of information, whereupon it has none. Next consider an ensemble of two such systems. It can be in any one of four states, and two units of information are required to match its degrees of freedom. If it were composed of three systems it might be in any one of eight states, and would require three units of information to fix it. Thus the number of possible states is 2 raised to the power which is the number of systems and each unit of information subtracts one from that exponent. Here Wiener's unit of information is exactly the logarithm to the base 2 of the reciprocal of the probability of the state, which, of course, is the negative entropy of an ensemble of bivalent systems. Neurons are bivalent systems.

Let me define "corruption" as the ratio of information in the input to that in the output. Each eye has something like a hundred million photoreceptors, each of which in a given millisecond can emit one or no impulse. In other words, it is an ensemble which can be in any

74

one of $2^{100,000,000}$ possible states, or the amount of information it has is a hundred million units per millisecond.

Now Pitts and I have computed the information in the output of a piano player surpassing any ever known. We have given him a keyboard of a hundred keys, let him strike independently with each finger with any one of ten strengths ten times per second, and let each hand span ten keys. That sounds like a lot of information, but on computing it we find it is only about two units per millisecond.

Recent telephonic devices have sampled waves every thousandth of a second and passed on one pip if the wave was then of a given deviation from the mean, otherwise no pip. These are relayed to a smearing device and heard. It is better than 90 per cent as intelligible as the original voice. Three such pips per millisecond determined by eight possible values of the wave reproduce an orchestra. So much information at most may we hope to convey.

Whether we figure the ratio of input to output from our impossible player or from human speech, the corruption is of the order of a hundred million to one. Part of this corruption is referable to the coupling of our nervous system to our muscles and is avoided in some of the Crustacea. They use axons of several sizes, and by varying the frequency of discharge obtain more degrees of contraction than there are possible synchronous states of the nerves to their muscles. The viscosity of muscle smears the result in time, so that the rate at which impulses can come over the nerve is wasted by the inability of muscle to follow. In us a nerve of a thousand axons can be in 2^{1000} possible states, whereas the muscle, because it can only add tensions, has only a thousand possible states. 1000 is about 2^{10}; so the corruption in passing from nerve to brawn is 100 to 1.

What becomes of all the rest of the information? To answer that, conceive neurons as telegraphic relays. Each one may be tripped by some combination of signals provided these are very nearly synchronous. It detects the coincidence and only then emits a signal to subsequent relays. Now the threshold of the photoreceptors of the eye is always varying. At any one millisecond it may be tripped by a single photon, and, at another, fail to fire in response to many. By connecting many of these to a coincidence detector set to require a reasonable number of impulses simultaneously, we have a signal which corresponds to a statistically significant fraction of its receptors and so we wash out the random variation of threshold. Thus using the relayed information that fails to agree with other information, we achieve a high probability that what goes on through the nervous system does correspond to something in the world. Perhaps it will be clearer to say it this way. The logical probability that a neuron will have an impulse in one millisecond is $1/2$, that two neurons of an ensemble in the same millisecond $1/2 \times 1/2$. The chance that both will fire by chance simultaneously is the product of their probabilities separately; that is, it is smaller; $1/4$. Therefore, in the nervous system, by repeatedly demanding coincidence we vastly increase the probability that what is in the output corresponds to something in the input. We pay for certainty with information. The eye relays to the brain about the hundredth part of the information it receives. The chance that what it does relay is due to chance is fantastically small, 2^{-100}, a billionth of a billionth of a billionth of a tenth of one per cent.

Here, then, is the first technically important difference between us and robots. In them we cannot afford to carry out any computations, no matter how simple, in a hundred parallel paths and demand coincidence. Consequently, no computing machine is as likely to go right under conditions as various as those we undergo.

Accordingly to increase certainty every hypothesis should be of minimum logical, or a priori, probability so that, if it be confirmed in experiment, then it shall be because the world is so constructed. Unfortunately for those who quest absolute certainty, a hypothesis of zero logical probability is a contradiction and hence can never be confirmed. Its neurological equivalent would be a neuron that required infinite coincidence to trip it. This, in a finite world, is the same as though it had no afferents. It never fires.

In all of this I take it for granted that you are familiar with the all-or-none law of the nervous impulse, with the brevity of latent addition, with the duration of synaptic delay, with the evidence for spatial summation and for inhibition at a synapse, and with the local origin of energy from metabolism, all of which together insure that the principal circuit actions of the nervous system are those of the digital, or logical, kind. My reason for letting time flow in lapses of a millisecond is based on the work of Lorente de Nó, who has given us some of the best measures of the other properties of conduction. It is probable that no neuron can sustain more impulses than a thousand per second, even under the healthiest conditions, and one millisecond will include synaptic delay, or absolute refractory period, or the front of the pulse itself. These permit us to treat the nervous impulse as an atomic event.

But a nervous impulse is also a signal. It is true if what it proposes is true, otherwise it is false. It is false if it arises from any cause other than the adequate, or proper, excitation of the cell. The threshold of the dark-adapted eye for light is about a photon in several seconds. Pressure applied to the eye will evoke impulses, but the energy required is many million times more. Press on the eye and you see light when there is no light. The signals are false. Thus nervous impulses are atomic signals, or atomic propositions on the move. To them the calculus of propositions applies provided each is subscripted for the time of its occurrence and implication given a domain only in the past. In terms of such a calculus applied to nervous nets, Pitts and I have been able to prove that even nets devoid of circles can realize any proposition which is a logical consequence of its input. As this is the most that *any* net *can* do it is obviously an adequate theory. We know, of course, that facilitation and extinction occur, and we showed that whatever these can effect can be done digitally, or discretely, by go, no-go devices. In our first essay, we were unable to obtain much more than the calculus of atomic propositions; but, by introducing circles in which a train of impulses patterned after some fact could circulate, we did get existential operators for time past.

This is the argument: In a net in which there are no re-entrant paths a signal anywhere in the net implies a signal in a neuron nearer to receptors, and so backward in time until we arrive at the receptors. The signal here and now in this net implies the signal sent there just then. But once set going, a disturbance in a closed chain implies that there was a signal in its input at some time but does not indicate at what time. In short, the reverberating activity patterned after something that happened retains the form of the happening but loses track of when it happened. Thus it shows that there was some time at which such and such occurred. The "such and such" is the idea wrenched out of time.

It is an eternal idea in a transitory memory wherein the form exists only so long as the reverberation endures. When that ceases, the form is no longer anywhere. Only this kind of memory remains to aged brains in which no new abiding traces can be made and old ones fade. While we are young, use leaves some sort of change, as freshets cut their channels in the hills so that aftercoming waters follow and enlarge their beds. Yet all other forms of memory, including written records, do nothing which cannot also be achieved by mere reverberation, and hence add nothing to the theory.

There are other closed paths important in the origin of ideas, circuits which have "negative feedback." In terms of them reflexes were first defined as actions starting in some part of the body, setting up impulses to the central nervous system, whence they were reflected to those structures in which they arose, and there stopped or reversed the process that gave rise to them. All inverse feedbacks have this in common, that each establishes some particular state of the system, for they bring it back toward that state by an amount which increases with their deviation from that state. They are, as we say, error-operated. The state toward which they return the system is the goal, or aim, or end *in and of* the operation. This is what is meant by function. On these circuits Cannon founded his theory of homeostasis, and Rosenblueth and Wiener their theory of teleological mechanisms.

Any such circuit becomes a servomechanism as soon as the particular state it is to seek can be determined for it. Thus the stretch reflex tends to keep our muscles at constant length, but *that* length is determined for these circuits by more complicated arcs which traverse almost all parts of the central nervous system and require the reflex to seek those states which permit us to stand and move.

One reflex turns the eyes toward anything that enters the visual field. Its path runs from the eye by fibers that bypass the geniculate to enter the superior colliculi upon which they map the visual field. Here local circuits compute the vector from the center of gaze to the center of gravity of the apparition and send this information to the oculomotor nuclei which, in turn, relay orders to the appropriate muscles and turn the eyes so as to decrease that vector. As it reaches zero the eyes come to rest with the apparition centered. This reflex, I am told, will operate even in a man who has lost one-half his visual cortex, if he is dark adapted and a light, unseen by him, is placed in his blind field. If two are placed there the eyes turn toward a position intermediate. Under these conditions but with cortex *intact,* the eyes turn similarly but then snap from spot to spot, for the reflex is then subservient to impulses from the cerebrum. By turning the eyes so as to center the form, the reflex rids the apparition of the gratuitous particularity of the place at which it appeared. Every reflex, by running through a series of intermediate states to that established by it, rids some item to be observed of some fortuitous specificity. In the case of the collicular reflex, it has selected the centered form from among all possible exemplifications. Once in this, the canonical position, the system is ready for the computation of the form. There is little doubt that in us this computation occurs in the cerebral cortex, notably the visual areas. What happens then as the eyes turn rapidly is a series of on and off signals from most portions of the eye. These serve to clean the slate for the centered form unencumbered by blurring due to motion. The latter we suffer only when the eyes turn slowly; for instance, when we are very tired.

There are negative feedbacks within the brain. One of these resembles the automatic volume control in the radio. It tends to keep constant the sensory input to the cerebral cortex. In so doing it gives us another existential operator, for it detects that there was some intensity such that it was of this-or-that figure. In the case of vision, this circuit follows two other devices serving the same end; namely, the slow adaptation of the retina and the rapid change of pupillary diameter. All together these enable us to detect the form though the intensity of its illumination range through 39 decibels, that is, from faint starlight to full daylight—only we may not look at the sun without closing our eyes.

There are also appetitive circuits with a part of their path, from receptors to effectors, inside us, and the rest through the world outside. They are said to be inverse feedbacks over the target. Given any two inverse feedbacks which working together would destroy us, like swallowing and inhaling, there is built into us some connection between their paths whereby, when both are set going, one stops the other. In the case of learned modes of appetitive behavior, similar inhibitory links must be acquired or we perish. If we have three incompatible circuits in which *A* dominates *B* and *B* dominates *C*, the chances are equal whether *A* will dominate *C* or *C*, *A*. We speak of the end-in-operation of the dominant as of *greater* value. We have even tried to construct scales of value for diverse ends, but, since dominance is sometimes circular, values are not magnitudes of a single kind, and the terms "greater" and "less" are simply inapplicable. What we have called the value anomaly and regarded as evidence of a lack of order or system bespeaks, in fact, order of a kind we had not imagined, and a system tighter knit. Here endeth the psychological blind alley and Plato's theory of the Good. We cannot make one scale of value that predicts choice. Only knowledge of mechanism permits such prophecy.

I drew a circuit to move a figure, given anywhere in a mosaic of relays, to all positions in one direction. From each relay impulses ascended diagonally in the required direction through sheets of relays resembling the original mosaic and so spaced that their constituent relays formed columns perpendicular to the planes. And I set the threshold of all relays so that none would fire except when a slanting impulse coincided with one in the plane of that relay. I brought the output of every relay vertically all the way down to the original mosaic. Now when there is a simultaneous volley of the required figure at the given place in the original mosaic and at the same time a simultaneous volley to all the relays of any one of the sheets above, the figure is reproduced on that sheet by a volley in the relays where the slanting volley hits the sheet. Thence it projects straight down on the original mosaic. This reproduces the figure at a distance which steps off in the direction of the slant by a number of relays proportional to the height of the excited sheet. Now let the figure endure by a series of volleys at its origin, and excite the sheets successively upward, and the figure will be translated step by step from the origin to all possible positions in the direction of the slant. Whatever shape is present in the input to this circuit is preserved in these successive representations and, as the output descends vertically, the shape is translated without distortion. Von Bonin, who had worked with me on the auditory cortex, when he saw the diagram mistook it for a drawing of that cortex. Certainly we had but to replace the relays by pictures of neurons and the similarity was startling. The parallel functions are even more alike. We can center a form seen by turning our eyes, but there is no way we can tune our ears so as to translate a chord up and down the scale. Our brain receives it at a fixed key or pitch. In the primate these pitches map longitudinally on the input to Heschl's gyrus, so spaced that octaves span nearly equal distances. If this, the primary auditory cortex, worked like my circuit it would move the output up and down the axis of pitch while it preserved the interval, and so the chord. Here is an existential operator for chord regardless of pitch. The output asserts that there were pitches such that there was this or that chord.

Is there anything in physiology corresponding to the sequential excitation of the sheets? And, if so, how fast can it complete a cycle? There is the familiar alpha rhythm of the cortex, a shift of voltage that rises and falls through the cortex ten times per second. Although the correspondence *may* be entirely fortuitous, this is about the rate at which chords can be distinguished—ten per second. Now we need excellent histological studies by the Golgi method to know whether the detailed connections of cells in this area are what the hypothesis requires. These must be made in specified planes to match our physiological data. Because incoming signals and outgoing signals, like the pulse of scansion, ascend and descend through the cortex, when the cortex is at work the sweep of scansion should disappear, as it does, in the twinkle of details.

There are at least two ways that the output of this primary cortex may convey a chord regardless of pitch. There may be an inverse feedback which stops the figure of excitation when it reaches a canonical position along the axis of pitch, but there is no evidence that this exists. The other way is suggested by anatomy. Beneath the receptive layers of the cortex are columns of cells where properly timed impulses may be accumulated through a time equal to the sum of their synaptic delays to coincide upon efferent cells whose axons go to the adjacent, or secondary, auditory cortex.

If they terminate there at random, and if the cells there merely require coincidence to fire, we will have for every chord regardless of pitch a corresponding spot of maximal coincidence. The activity of this spot proposes the required universal, or idea. If we were to excite this spot electrically in waking man at operation, he should report hearing the chord. He does, but unfortunately no one has asked him whether he hears it at some particular pitch. The experiment is difficult because the primary auditory cortex is buried deep, and the secondary adjacent to it almost as deep, in the fissure of Sylvius. Moreover, I have not been able to map well the projection of the primary upon the secondary; and, finally, the interpretation is complicated by a direct projection upon the second with the sequence of pitches reversed. Fortunately these difficulties are not present in the visual area of man or monkey.

I drew a circuit to extract shape regardless of size, and this was mistaken by both von Bonin and Percival Bailey for a schematic representation of the outer strip of Baillarger which makes the visual cortex the "area striata." We start again with a mosaic. Select a point to represent the center of gaze and map the visual field as a set of concentric circles whose radii are proportional to the logarithm of the angles at the eye. From the mosaic let impulses proceed along branching channels spraying outward as they ascend through sheets of relays in which the density of relays decreases but their threshold increases as we go from below upward. From all of these relays let signals rise to corresponding upper layers of relays where coincidence with sweeping pulses is required, and let the signals of these layers converge on relays of low threshold, thence descend to leave the area striata. Now, with the pulse of scansion we shall have successively in this output all possible dilatations and constrictions of any figure in the input. The possibilities are limited by the grain and gross dimensions of the cortex, but these limit input and output equally. Since we have, in the output, all sizes made from a given one it makes no difference which size was given in the input.

Had we not conformed to present knowledge by mapping radial angles by their logarithms we would be compelled to require that the branching ascent of the input take a radial direction, but as it is it may branch nearly equally in all directions. Hence we cannot hope to detect much difference in histological study, even by silver stains of fibers, between sections cut radially and others, tangentially, in the visual cortex, or even in ones parallel to the surface. Thanks to Ramon y Cajal and Lorente de Nó, we know that the anatomical connections are at least sufficient for the theory. Here, as in audition, if the alpha rhythm evinces the scansion, we should be able to see ten forms per second. We can. Faster, they blur, merge, or glide into one another. Moreover, a rise of metabolic rate with fever or hyperthyroidism causes a rise in alpha frequency and a rise in the number of distinguishable frames per second.

When strychnine is applied locally to a spot on the cortex it causes the cells there to fire almost in unison. The fibers leaving that area then carry nearly synchronous volleys of impulses. These can be traced to the ends of the axons if there are enough of them near together. When these axons turn up again into the cortex anywhere, we can detect them there as a sharp change in voltage, the so-called "strychnine spike." When Dusser de Barenne and I strychninized a pinhead spot on the area striata, strychnine spikes appeared at many points in the secondary visual area as if the output from each spot in the area striata were scattered at random in the secondary visual area. Hence, from any particular set of spots in the primary area there will arise by chance some spot of maximum excitation in the secondary area. Activity at this spot implies activity in some figure of spots output by the primary; hence some shape regardless of size. Electrical stimulation of a spot on the primary visual cortex in waking man is reported by him as a blurred circle of light, whereas similar excitation of a spot in the secondary area is reported as a form. Moreover, this form, while it has a position in space, in the sense that he can point at it, has none in the visual field. Nor does it seem to have size there, any more than the recalled image of the moon seems to subtend one particular angle at the eye.

The mechanism we propose for abstracting chord and form is really computing a kind of average, and that average will not be seriously affected by small perturbations of excitation, of threshold, or even of particular connections as long as they are to cells in the right neighborhood. This conforms to clinical findings. A man may have several holes in his visual cortex, as big as or bigger than, the hole in his retina called the optic disk, and, except in a small number of cases, the forms seen will be unaffected. Although in such a case we can map these blind spots, he will not see them and the things seen will appear to be continuous through the blind spots. Scrutiny of the hypothesis even suggests that this process may account for much relational determination, for the four corners of a square in the input would be completed as a square, whereas parts of the sides might well flop, seeming now a maltese cross and now a square, etc. These flops would be the outcome of rivalry between two maxima for dominance over subsequent areas. Thus, for vision, our hypothesis fits well all known facts.

Older schools of physiological psychology and of neurology, guided by atomistic associational doctrines, tended to think in terms of neurons, each of which had one duty, for example, to know squares. This seems to be at least partially true of spots in the secondary visual cortex. Gestalt psychologists have treated the mosaic of relays of the cortex as if it were a field on which sensations mapped synchronously. This seems more likely true of receptors like the retina, for even its cortical replica is bisected by a line down the middle of the field and the halves mapped far asunder. Now it is easy to show that both of these "caricature" the nervous process. We need only note that a nervous net can take any figure in space, requiring an ensemble of a given number of neurons simultaneously, and convert it into a figure of impulses over a single neuron requiring as many relay times as there were neurons in the ensemble, and vice versa. From this alone it is clear that we cannot tell what kind of thing we must look for in a brain when it has an idea, except that it must be invariant under all those conditions in which that brain is having that idea. So far we have considered particular hypotheses of cortical function. They are almost certainly wrong at some point. Because they have already had to fit many disparate data, they are of little a priori probability. They prophesy the outcome of an infinite number of experiments, some of which are almost certain to refute them.

But with respect to the underlying theory, which is merely glorified tautology, there is no such possibility. It is, in fact, little more than a simple application of the theory of groups of transformations. For any figure in the input of a computing machine it is always possible to calculate an output invariant under a group of transformations. We calculate a set of averages, for all members of the group, of numerical values assigned by an arbitrary functional to each transform of the information conceived as the distribution of excitation at all points and times in an appropriate manifold. To define the figure completely under these transformations, we would need a whole manifold of such averages for various functionals, and this manifold would have to have as many dimensions as our original one; but, for practical purposes, we usually need only a few averages. Since in the finite net of relays the number of transformations in finite time is finite, we may use simple sums instead of averages.

This general theory describes all processes of securing invariants, or having ideas, which we have discovered or invented to date; and one mechanism differs from another in the nature of its arbitrary functional. For example, in the cerebral circuits proposed the functional may always assign the value one to any vector in the manifold if the particular point had a signal in the previous relay time, and, if not, assign it zero, whereas, in the reflex circuit for centering an apparition the functional clearly depends upon the figure of excitation in the manifold, and changes as the form centers; in effect, it assigns the value zero to all save the last transform on the cortex.

We may, of course, make the output of any calculator of invariants (or of several of them) the input to another and so have an idea of ideas, which is what Spinoza calls consciousness, and thus get far away from sensation. But our most remote abstractions are all ultimately reducible to primitive atomic propositions and the calculus of the lowest level. The domain of their implication lies only in time past. If their domain extended into the future, our sensations would imply our thoughts and our thoughts imply deeds. They do not, for even if the threshold of every cell in the nervous system were fixed, between the time we conceive an act and the time the impulses reach the motor horn cell, other signals from the world may get there first, and so often thwart us. We note the failure in the fact and are forced to distinguish between what we will and what we shall do. Hence the notion of the will.

But we do guess at things to come. When we run to catch a baseball we run not toward it but toward the place where it will be when we get there to grab it. This requires prediction. We behave as if there were some law compelling the world to act hereafter as it did of yore. Only one of our predictive circuits has been carefully studied by physiologists. It is responsible for optokinetic nystagmus. It has a tendency to persist, which may be seen when a train stops, for it then attributes motion in the opposite direction to the ties and rails. The earmark of every predictive circuit is that if it has operated long uniformly it will persist in activity, or overshoot; otherwise it could not project regularities from the known past upon the unknown future. This is what, as a scientist, I dread most, for as our memories become stored, we become creatures of our yesterdays—mere has-beens in a changing world. This leaves no room for learning.

Neurons are cheap and plentiful. If it cost a million dollars to beget a man, one neuron would not cost a mill. They operate with comparatively little energy. The heat generated raises the blood in passage about half a degree, and the flow is half a liter per minute, only a quarter of a kilogram calorie per minute for 10^{10}, that is, 10 billion neurons. Von Neumann would be happy to have their like for the same cost in his robots. His vacuum tubes can work a thousand times as fast as neurons, so he could match a human brain with 10 million tubes; but it would take Niagara Falls to supply the current and the Niagara River to carry away the heat. So he is limited to about the thousandth part of man's computer. He has to be very careful to specify in detail which relays are to be connected to a given relay to trip it. That is not the case in human brains. Wiener has calculated that the maximum amount of information our chromosomes can convey would fill one volume of the *Encyclopaedia Britannica,* which could specify all the connections of ten thousand neurons if that was all it had to do. As we have 10^{10} neurons, we can inherit only the general scheme of the structure of our brains. The rest must be left to chance. Chance includes experience which engenders learning. Ramon y Cajal suggested that learning was the growing of new connections.

I do not doubt that the cerebral cortex may be the most important place in primates. But it is certainly the most difficult place to look for change with use. Think of it as a laminated felt of fibers which serve to associate neighboring rough columns of cells nearly a hundred high and linked together vertically by their axons. These columns are then connected to distant columns by axons which dip into the white matter and emerge elsewhere into the cortex. These last connections I have studied for many years but have at best a general picture of how areas are related, certainly nothing that could give the detail necessary to distinguish between its connections before and after learning.

To understand its proper function we need to know what it computes. Its output is some function of its input. As yet we do not know, even for the simplest structure, what that function is. We have only a few input-output curves for the monosynaptic reflex arc obtained by David Lloyd, and now a few more by Arturo Rosenblueth. Walter Pitts is analyzing them mathematically at the present moment and has as yet no very simple answer. There is no chance that we can do even this for the entire cortex. That is why we need such a hypothesis as we have proposed for particular areas, for these may be disproved by records of electrical activity recorded concurrently at a few specified places.

Contrast our ignorance of its proper function with the detailed present knowledge of the projection of the sensory system upon it. For on at least two-thirds of its surface we can map the surface of the body, outside, and, to some extent, inside, so as to assign to every square millimeter of cortex the origin of its specific afferents and through them the exact position of the organs of sense. Beginning last summer, and continuing right now, the surface of the cerebellum, upon which the body maps similarly, is being stimulated and its projection to the so-called motor and sensory cortex, primary and secondary, explored and plotted millimeter by millimeter. Also now the projections of so-called non-specific afferents are receiving similar attention. Thus within a year or so we will know the geometry of its input and will be ready to seek in loci well defined the temporal pattern of its input.

I wish we could say half as much for our knowledge of its output. Since the days of Bubnoff and Heidenhain it has been electrically stimulated and the resultant change in muscle and gland carefully observed and elaborately recorded. But these responses depend upon the state of all subservient circuits which have yet to be analyzed. Hardly a month passes but what we are confronted by surprises. Frequency as well as shape of electrical pulses have been shown to determine the very path of the descending pulses from one and the same cortical focus. For example, volleys of impulses from the so-called face motor cortex, if more than ten or twelve per second, play principally through the nucleus of the seventh nerve upon the muscles of the face; whereas, if less than ten per second they are relayed almost exclusively through the nucleus of the twelfth to the tongue. Finally, the response to one and the same form of stimulation of a single focus in the motor cortex for one limb is determined both in amplitude and in direction by the motion and by the position of the limb at the time of stimulation. Clearly, to understand the significance of the output of the cerebral cortex we must know, for every sub-servient structure, the input-output curves. Even that will not be enough, for when several of them form a re-entrant circuit we must know their relations. Until we do so we will be in danger of attributing to the cerebral cortex functions proper to lower structures.

Last, but not least, the cortex is itself part of many re-entrant systems, and what our hypothesis attributes to cortex alone in securing invariants, or having ideas, may well depend upon loops joining it and the thalamus. From all these uncertainties I would turn to something simple as the monosynaptic arc of the stretch reflex and, by procedures far from normal, try to teach it something. It will be difficult, for in it the connections are as certainly determined as in a man-made computing machine; and we will have to break old connections before we can form new ones.

This brings us back to what I believe is the answer to the question: Why is the mind in the head? Because there, and only there, are hosts of possible connections to be formed as time and circumstance demand. Each new connection serves to set the stage for others yet to come and better fitted to adapt us to the world, for through the cortex pass the greatest inverse feedbacks whose function is the purposive

86

life of the human intellect. The joy of creating ideals, new and eternal, in and of a world, old and temporal, robots have it not. For this my Mother bore me.

REFERENCES

1. Barker, S. H., and Gellhorn, E. Influence of suppressor areas on afferent impulses. *J. Neurophysiol.*, 1947, **10**, 125–132.
2. Bell, Charles. On the nervous circle which connects the voluntary muscles with the brain. *Proc. Roy. Soc.*, 1826, **2**, 266–267.
3. Cajal, Ramon y, S. *Histologie du système nerveux.* 2 vols. Paris: Maloine, 1909, 1911.
4. Lorente de Nó, R. Sections in J. F. Fulton's *Physiology of the nervous system.* London: Oxford University Press, 1943.
5. Maxwell, C. On governors. *Proc. Roy. Soc.*, 1868, **16**, 270–283.
6. McColl, H. *Servo-mechanisms.* New York: D. Van Nostrand Co., 1945.
7. McCulloch, W. S. A heterarchy of values determined by the topology of nerve nets. *Bull. of Math. Biophys.*, 1945, **7**, 89–93.
8. McCulloch, W. S. *Finality and form.* Fifteenth James Arthus Lecture, New York Academy of Science, May 2, 1946.
9. McCulloch, W. S. *Machines that think and want.* Lecture at the American Psychological Association, September 9, 1947.
10. McCulloch, W. S. *Through the den of the metaphysician.* Lecture at the University of Virginia, March 23, 1948.
11. McCulloch, W. S. Teleological mechanisms. *Ann. New York Acad. Sci.*, 1948, **50**, 4.
12. McCulloch, W. S., and Lettvin, J. Y. Somatic functions of the central nervous system. *Ann. Rev. Physiol.*, 1948, **10**, 117–132.
13. McCulloch, W. S., and Pitts, W. How we know universals. *Bull. Math. Biophys.*, 1947, **9**, 127–147.
14. McCulloch, W. S., and Pitts, W. The statistical organization of nervous activity. *J. Amer. Statistical Assoc.*, 1948, **4**, 91–99.
15. Rosenblueth, A., Wiener, N., and Bigelow, J. Behavior, purpose, and teleology. *Philos. of Science*, 1943, **10**, 18–24.
16. Wiener, N. *Cybernetics.* New York: John Wiley and Sons, 1948.
17. Wittgenstein, L. *Tractus Logico-Philosophicus.* London: Paul, 1922.

DISCUSSION

DR. LORENTE DE NÓ: The main question in our minds is whether the theory as a whole is going to stand or not. I think that probably many of the details will not stand, but that the main concept will certainly remain. I'm quite sure that all of my colleagues will agree that Dr. McCulloch has brought what we know of both the anatomy and the physiology of the brain closer to an integrated whole than it has ever been before, and I want to congratulate Dr. McCulloch very much and very sincerely.

DR. VON NEUMANN: I would not like to attempt a detailed discussion of the very beautiful and very interesting presentation made by Dr. McCulloch, perhaps something like that can be done in the general discussion. I will, however, ask two questions, both dealing with only one aspect of the matter. You have emphasized that you are giving *sufficient* mechanisms and that it is in conflict with your entire philosophy at this time to claim that these are necessarily the ones that are used. You give proofs of possibility. There is, nevertheless, one point where the question of the actual mechanism is especially burning, and that is the question of memory. You have pointed out that there are positive feedbacks—reverberating circuits—built out of switching organs which are quite adequate as memory. If there were nothing else in the world except neurons, you could build memory out of neurons. My own feeling is that if one were really to construct in this way a nervous system with its known attributes it would probably take more neurons than there are, but this is an aside. My real question is this: First of all, I have observed that all neurologists seem very certain that the reverberating circuit trick is not used in making the actual memory. Amorphous intuition points in the same direction. In surmising this is not so, I have always had a bad conscience. I am not sure why they are so positive. What is the best evidence one can give for this?

The second question is this. Most neurologists with whom I have had an opportunity to talk seem to be equally convinced that memory is due to some lasting changes somewhere on the body of the nerve cell, somehow connected with alterations of thresholds. Is it not better to say that there probably is a memory organ somewhere, but that we are absolutely ignorant as to where it is—probably as ignorant as the Greeks, who located the whole intelligence in the diaphragm?

DR. MC CULLOCH: I'm afraid my answer is necessarily a bit lengthy. In the first place, I would like to contrast as sharply as possible the maximum length of what I consider reverberative memory, with the enduring memories which we bring on from childhood. I have seen a man over 80 years of age walk into a meeting of a Board of Directors and for 8 hours work out from scratch all of the details necessary for the sale of a complete railroad. He pushed the other men so as to get every piece of evidence on the table. His judgment was remarkably solid. The amount of detail involved in the transaction was enormous, and it actually took over 6 hours to get all of the requisite details on the map. He summarized that detail at the end of the meeting, in a period of a half an hour, very brilliantly, and when he came out he sat down, answered two letters that were on his desk, turned to his secretary, and said, "I have a feeling that I should have gone to a Board of Directors Meeting." He was not then, or at any later time, able to recall one iota of that meeting, and he was in that state for nearly a year before he died. This is the picture of what we call "presbyophrenia." In that state, whatever our memory organ is, we are unable to make any new record in it. Actually, the recent paths begin to fade, leaving only earlier memories to pop up. So, at that period, one is more likely to remember in detail and individually, the things that happened in childhood rather than the things of later years. Such a memory goes, quits, stops, the minute the brain is used for something else, or the minute that it comes to rest. Here is a span of at least 8 hours of high cerebral activity in carrying the details from the first moment of the meeting to the end of the meeting.

Per contra, not all memory can be of this reverberative kind. It is obvious that, although this kind of memory is carried reverberatively in the brain, it cannot endure during very deep sleep and it cannot endure during narcosis. It goes out, when the brain has a seizure and it goes out in sleep. In the one case, it goes out because the whole apparatus is pervaded by what I will call shock waves which go through it and through it and through it in the fit. In the other case, it goes out because it has no signals traveling—the brain is "shut down." I believe that only lower mechanisms are really busy in deep sleep. Now then, why do we want to attribute the memory to the brain at all? Why may it not be in the spleen or somewhere else? The answer is because injuries of the brain, but not injuries of other things, do result in losses of memory, and that is the fundamental reason for pinning it on the brain.

The next question is: Why does one attribute this, the enduring memory, to a growth process—change with use—somewhere in the excitability in neurons rather than elsewhere? Well, first, because it is a relatively lively process, and when things are growing, one tries to pin it on growth processes. Second, because it has the peculiarity that what we learn later is only a modification of what is already laid down. It is an accumulative affair of this sort. Why attribute it to the junctions of cells? Because there is where we imagine the switching takes place, and this is the kind of evidence on which we base it.

Let me tell a tale out of school, even if future evidence fails to support it. I will ask Dr. Lettvin's forgiveness later. The theory and experiments are his, although I have done some of them with him. His theory, and experiments, are designed to meet the requirements of the conditioned-reflexologists, Pavlov et al. In deference to them we will name one source of afferents U, the unconditioned afferents, which can excite an efferent R, the responsive motoneurons, and a second set of afferents C, the conditioned afferents, and—Heinrich Klüver and Warren McCulloch to the contrary notwithstanding— we will forget for the moment "stimulus equivalence" or "universals secured by averaging over groups of transformation" and treat U, C, and R as individual neurons. U can always fire $R;$ but C can become able to do so reflexologically only if C and U are excited so as to be active concurrently. I mean that if both are concurrently active then, thereafter, C alone shall be able to fire R. Now the gist of Dr. Lettvin's analysis is that it still further simplifies the required assumption. He asks, for what do we need U—except to excite R—so why not make the simple assumption that if C and R are simultaneously active, C shall become able to fire R? Naturally this simplification should not occur to a psychologist for he has to use U to excite R. But a physiologist may put his electrodes directly upon R, if he can get them there, or he may fire it antidromically.

Now it is clearly established by the surgically and electrically perfect experiments of Donald Marquis and Arthur Ward that the intact spinal cord cannot be conditioned. But Culler and Shurrager did sometimes obtain conditioning of what they believed to be the two-neuron reflex arc, and this in experiments on by no means their technically best preparations. Wiener's theory that the spinal cord has suffered a "Wärmetod" of information by the time we are able to walk (that is, its connections are all soldered in) would account for this discrepancy. One has only to suppose that one must destroy something ending on a motoneuron to leave root room for another afferent; and the cord, no longer intact, could be conditioned even as Cajal supposed, by something else making connection with the motoneuron.

Moreover, the technically impeccable experiments of David Lloyd have proved that of two muscle antagonists at a single joint, each by its afferents (from stretch receptors) inhibits, and only inhibits, its antagonist. They show further that this inhibition occurs at the synapse on the motoneuron without time for internuncial intervention.

It follows, that if one were to cut the dorsal roots of the nerves for extension at the knee, there would be root room on its motoneurons for afferents from the flexors of the knee to get a greater hold on these motoneurons. And Dr. Lettvin's ingenious theory of synaptic transmission predicts that, if this happens, instead of inhibiting the motoneuron, these afferents will then excite them.

This, in substance, is what we did. We cut the dorsal roots of the extension reflex, stimulated its ventral roots antidromically, and at the same time stimulated the flexor muscle nerve. This we did to both for a long time, minutes or even hours, at about forty per second, from separate stimulators. Thereafter, but not before, threshold stimulation of the flexor nerve elicited contractions of the extensor. Thus Dr. Lettvin has proved that the cord, no longer intact, can be conditioned, but not quite as the psychologist would have it—for he stimulated C and R, not C and U, concurrently. He has not as yet published, and will not publish, these findings to physiologists until his records of the times of these impulses at dorsal and ventral roots show conclusively whether or not this functionally new path is monosynaptic.

If we are not misled by the sensitivity of denervated structures, and the cord does so learn, this is crucial to psychologists. The cord is a sufficiently simple structure and is sufficiently well known for us to hope that an anatomist, with some new technique, may be able to find structural changes.

From what I have said, it should be clear that I do not think learning normally occurs in the spinal cord. Even in the earthworm learning seems to reside, albeit not in the most anterior segments, still in the forward ganglia. In mammals it may be in the midbrain, or even in the cortex, but our chances of locating anatomical changes there are negligible.

DR. VON NEUMANN: The experiment which you described—if it were done, and if the time relations were clear—would be very convincing. In this case one could at least feel certain that the "conditioning" consists in a physical change in the cell actually under consideration.

The "reverberating circuit" model for the memory does not strike me, as I said before, as a particularly elegant one. Nevertheless, it is important to know whether it is a possible model or not. I understood you to state that it is not. What is the decisive argument against it? I understood it to be that there are states when one can be fairly certain that the cortex is totally inactive and yet memory persists. What exactly is the evidence for this "total inactivity" of the cortex? Is it that one has not so far succeeded in picking up any electrical signals from it?

DR. MC CULLOCH: That's right. When our amplifier is turned up maximally, we pick up activity only from the respiratory mechanism and similar structures. Only *they* keep on going in deep sleep and in the coma following seizures.

DR. VON NEUMANN: Is this reliable enough to know that there is nothing else there?

DR. MC CULLOCH: Well, let's take the more powerful case—that in which you have a seizure with tremendous waves of signals through the works.

DR. VON NEUMANN: Does one know that they are really going through all channels?

DR. MC CULLOCH: I think, pretty firmly, yes; I don't believe any part of the nervous system is unaffected.

DR. VON NEUMANN: The organism is fairly well set up to protect certain parts, is it not?

DR. MC CULLOCH: The grand mal convulsion is the occasion on which that protection breaks down.

DR. VON NEUMANN: It does not seem to for memory.

DR. LORENTE DE NÓ: The difficulty in making memory reverberating paths is chiefly this: To maintain a steady state in any kind of reverberating path, the closed chains of neurons are arranged so that either you have incremental activity or decremental activity. Either the thing begins spreading to involve more and more and more neurons, or it decrements, after coming to a maximum, and then decays and disappears. Probably the secrets that Dr. McCulloch just gave us can be compared with the gramophone record. While we are playing a gramophone record, we have an articulation of impulses; later, when the record is over, memory is deposited in a different manner. As you listen to what I am saying now there are a lot of circuits operating according to those principles; but, then, when in a moment I stop talking, those signals will have stopped and memory will be somewhere else, in some other area.

DR. VON NEUMANN: I see the plausibility of what you say, but I still have a residue of uncertainty left. Your arguments about electrical circuit analogies are plausible, but they are nevertheless influenced by our particular kind of experience in this field. Your judgment based on anatomical experience is perhaps more cogent. It may be anatomically established that closed (and hence potentially reverberating) neural pathways do not exist in the necessary, vast numbers.

Another comment I would like to make is this. I see an argument that one might make against the view that memory in any form actually resides in the neurons. It is a negative argument, and far from cogent. How reasonable is it? This is the argument: There is a good deal of evidence that memory is static, unerasable, resulting from an irreversible change. (This is of course the very opposite of a "reverberating," dynamic, erasable memory.) Isn't there some physical evidence for this? If this is correct, then no memory, once acquired, can be truly forgotten. Once a memory-storage place is occupied, it is occupied forever, the memory capacity that it represents is lost; it will never be possible to store anything else there. What appears as forgetting is then not true forgetting, but merely the removal of that particular memory-storage region from a condition of rapid and easy availability to one of lower availability. It is not like the destruction of a system of files, but rather like the removal of a filing cabinet into the cellar. Indeed, this process in many cases seems to be reversible. Various situations may bring the "filing cabinet" up from the "cellar" and make it rapidly and easily available again. There are many examples of this: the "forgetting" and subsequent "remembering" or recovering of languages, telephone numbers, names—paralleling the decreased or increased need for their use.

This organizational situation is a very plausible one, if there is a memory which is much larger than the available switching facilities for its selective use. Indeed, if the memory is thus larger than its switching system, it will be necessary to introduce a system of priorities for various parts of the memory. Each part may then, upon occasion, be moved into regions with rapid accessibility, or into regions with less rapid accessibility. Or, rather, it may not be moved from region to region, but be connected to quickly or to less quickly functioning portions of the available switching system.

If this is so, then the memory cannot reside in the actual switching organs in the neurons, and its capacity must be much greater than that represented by the switching system. One must then postulate a very high-capacity memory organ or organization, with considerable bottlenecks at the "input" and "output," that is, at the points of contact represented by the switching system.

Does this sound plausible, or is there some flaw in my argument?

DR. BROSIN: May I break here with the tradition of immediate reply? This is a very large subject, and I would like to see if there are other commentators. You may gather the evidence, and if we do not have time enough today, you can have a full dress performance tomorrow.

DR. GERARD: I would like to ask a few questions, some of which have already been touched upon. I have a very trivial one first. I didn't quite see why you place such disparate emphasis on the manipulation of the output of the brain in efferent systems and paths, as compared to the problem of the manipulation of the input of the brain. If I correctly understood you, you are not particularly worried about the input side. I don't see why that is, and I would like to have you explain it a little more clearly.

I have, also, two other points that touch on this memory problem. If learning and remembering are based on growth processes of some sort, then they should not be basically different from developmental and maturational behavior; and yet it seems to me that some of the most striking experimental work in the past does emphasize a very fundamental difference between the maturational learning in the nervous system and acquiring a new behavioral capacity—experiential acquiring of new behavior possibilities. The former takes place certainly without any external experience, but you can see that there is internal experience. On the question of rest and activity of the nervous system, several members of the audience, during our intermission, raised the question with me whether you are not neglecting something that you might call automatic activity of neurons. The assumption is that the output will be determined by the input, rather than by something happening independently of the input. I will put the question to you in this way. Do I correctly assume that you were suggesting that the scansion machine in your projection area mechanism is the spontaneous brain wave, and whether it starts there or below is immaterial? I would like to have that elaborated and made a little bit clearer. I personally am surprised at the answer you gave Dr. von Neumann, that the brain can be completely quiet. I don't believe that electrically, or in any other way, it is ever completely quiet at any time except in death.

DR. MC CULLOCH: I said, except for lower mechanisms.

DR. GERARD: I believe that, even in the other mechanisms, I have never seen a completely silent brain.

DR. MC CULLOCH: No, I don't believe that brain matter is ever completely quiet. I'll take care of that question later. For the moment it is enough that there are times when no signals are reverberating.

DR. GERARD: If there is a separate memory organ, along the line of Dr. von Neumann's comment, in which you have your files easily accessible or down in the basement, that would argue against the memory traces being associated with the neurons themselves throughout the brain. What about the reversible amnesia problem, where all past memory vanishes for long periods and then comes back again? If learning involves the establishment of new functionally effective connections between neurons in the brain (whether by growth, by physiological change in threshold, or what not), and if that depends on activation of neurons and association with experience, then it seems to me that it should follow that if the threshold of neurons is held low, just in general during the experiencing of experience, learning should be enhanced. Dr. Lettvin raised the level of excitability of neurons in the nervous system. There is more chance of a particular input leaving a permanent modification, or even a temporary

94

one. I hope some of the psychologists here can bring the evidence in, but I don't know. However, as far as I'm aware, conditioning under the influence of stimulating drugs has not changed the rate of this conditioning.

The last question I should really leave for Dr. Lashley, since it is in his field. If these networks of neurons (even allowing for considerable interchangeability of particular elements of the net) are organized so beautifully in the striate and elsewhere for these particular functions, then how do you account for some of Dr. Lashley's critical experiments on destruction of different parts of the brain and the retention of learning, memory, and all the rest of it?

DR. KÖHLER: I admire the courage with which Dr. McCulloch tries to relate his neurophysiology to facts in psychology. But, when in a skeptical mood, I sometimes feel like criticizing the results. Take the example of visual shapes which, as we all know, are generally recognized in a peripheral position (or in a larger size), even if, heretofore, they have been seen only in foveal projection (or in a smaller size). Dr. McCulloch's explanation of such achievements introduces more histological assumptions ad hoc than seem compatible with usual standards of plausibility. In fact, he does not seem himself to maintain that a real brain functions in this fashion. Why then the elaborate constructions? Most probably the reason is that the atomistic character of Dr. McCulloch's neurophysiology prevents any direct approach to relationally determined facts such as visual shapes. The difficulty seems to be strongly felt, and special sets of neuron connections are now being constructed which merely serve to remove the difficulties caused by the main atomistic premise. Would it not be simpler never to make this atomistic assumption? If we think of cortical function in terms of continuous field physics rather than of impulses in neurons, the difficulty never arises. The contours of retinal images are projected upon the visual cortex by nerve impulses. Let us assume that here they constitute the boundary conditions of field processes such as electric currents. Under these circumstances, there will be for each set of boundary conditions, that is, for each shape, a particular distribution of a directly interrelated function; in other words, each shape will be cortically represented by a specific process. If the characteristics of such a process remain approximately constant, independently of its location and size, then recognition of a shape in a new place or size offers no problem which is not also present in the recognition of a color in a new place.

Incidentally, it seems to me misleading to assume that the present problem is mainly a problem of recognition, and therefore of memory.

When two objects are given simultaneously in different places while the eyes do not move, we can compare these objects, and say whether they have the same shape. Once more the implication is that visual shapes are associated with specific processes.

Occasionally, I am afraid, Dr. McCulloch uses psychological terms in a strangely diluted sense. In fact, sometimes little is left of what they actually mean in psychology. But the change is never mentioned. People will therefore tend to believe that, when such terms are now being related to neurophysiological hypotheses, it is their real psychological contents which are given a physiological interpretation. They will not notice that the essential characteristics of the facts in question are tacitly being ignored. I have an uneasy feeling that this may happen even to the theorist himself. Thus Dr. McCulloch likes to call a nerve impulse a "proposition." Moreover, he says that the occurrence of a given nerve impulse "implies" the occurrence of preceding impulses (in other neurons), by which the given impulse has been started. But, typically, a proposition is concerned with a relation between certain terms, whatever the relation may be in individual instances. A cortical situation would therefore correspond to a proposition if in this situation the cortical counterparts of two terms were functionally related in one specific fashion or another. A nerve impulse does not in this sense relate two terms to each other. At least in Dr. McCulloch's neurophysiology, a nerve impulse seems to be a particularly lonely event. How, then, can a nerve impulse represent a proposition? Some discussions of nerve impulses and of their equivalence to facts in psychology make me feel that, inadvertently, an extremely learned histologist and neurophysiologist is tacitly supposed to watch the human brain continually, and that this expert always knows how impulses must be interpreted in psychological terms. He probably tells the owner of the brain what psychological facts he must have when impulses travel in this or that part of the cortical machine. For without this help, what could induce a person to think of a specific proposition, that is, a particular relation between two terms, when an impulse travels in a certain fiber? Since, actually, no such expert is available, the characteristic forms of the various psychological facts must be directly given by the functional characteristics of corresponding cortical processes. But, to repeat, if this is the case, it cannot be nerve impulses which give propositions their relational character. For they have no such character themselves. For the same reason, there can be no connection between the psychological experience that one fact implies another fact and the behavior of a nerve impulse. A present impulse implies, say, preceding impulses in other neurons

(McCulloch's example) only in the mind of a neurophysiologist who knows what must have happened a moment ago at a certain synapse. As the present impulse travels along its fiber, it knows nothing of preceding impulses.

For a moment, I must come back to a criticism to which I have referred once before. It must be a hard task to give psychological facts interpretations in terms of nerve impulses. For when this task arises, and is apparently accepted, the theorists soon forget what they must now be expected to do, and turn to other problems which are only indirectly connected with the original problems. Invariably, such substitute problems are more accessible to explanations in terms of nerve impulses. On the other hand, since they are somehow related to the problems which were actually to be solved, psychological concepts which are essential in the latter will naturally also be mentioned when the substitutes are being discussed. Thus, if interpretations in terms of nerve impulses seem to work in the case of the substitutes, both the theorists and others will easily believe that actually the original problems have been solved. For this is what the theorists had promised to achieve.

Take "having a goal" as an example. Before we realize what is happening, the task of explaining this psychological fact in terms of nerve impulses has been replaced by another task: Once a person has a goal, how is the goal actually reached? Naturally, if this is done by overt action, both centrifugal and centripetal nerve impulses will play an important role in the process. It is also a most sensible suggestion that the action is steered in the right direction by negative feedback. But do we learn in this fashion what "having a goal" is in terms of nerve impulses? Plainly, we do not. Nonetheless, we may be so strongly impressed by what seems to have been achieved that we forget what had to be achieved. Of course, it must be difficult to understand "having a goal" as a matter of nerve impulses. "Having a goal" is again a relational situation. When a person has a goal, his self (in a purely empirical sense) is dynamically related to a certain object, and therefore, probably, the neural counterpart of the self to the counterpart of the object. Moreover, the nature of the relation depends entirely upon the perceived characteristics of the object and the state of the self at the given time. The theorists themselves seem to doubt whether interrelations of this kind can be mediated by nerve impulses, which are described as atomic events par excellence. Otherwise, why should the theorists prefer to discuss something else, namely, goal-directed action? And yet, "having a goal" is a problem which must be handled quite apart from overt action in reaching the goal. For people often have goals while they do not yet know how these goals can possibly be reached. It also seems probable that a really adequate interpretation of "reaching a goal" presupposes a correct interpretation of "having a goal." As a goal is being reached, the dynamic relation between the self and the goal, which seems to represent a store of energy, is gradually being changed—until eventually, when the goal has been reached, this energy is spent. I have a suspicion that the negative feedback involved in the change refers to the store of energy implicit in "having a goal." But, of course, this again is thinking in terms of field physics.

I will remark only in passing that the substitution of one problem for another occurs also in Dr. McCulloch's treatment of "value." He does not give us a theory of value in terms of nerve impulses. But values may conflict, just as many other things may conflict, and then the question arises which value will win in a given conflict; that is, which is the stronger value. It is this question with which he prefers to deal. But since the same question may be asked with regard to many facts which are not at all values, we have obviously once more lost our way. We may easily believe that we are actually dealing with the problem of value as such; and this belief will be strengthened by the fact that, in formulating our new problem, we may still mention the concept "value." But the problem what value means in terms of nerve impulses has in the meantime been forgotten.

Quite probably, Dr. McCulloch will not be impressed by these arguments. He may feel that I am accepting certain premises of which he does not approve. First of all, he is likely to say that the structural characteristics of cortical processes need not agree with the structures of corresponding psychological facts. Actually, he has just told us that the hypothetical cortical counterpart of an idea must fulfill only one condition: It must always occur when the idea occurs. More specifically, he has once said that the cortical counterpart of a square may be a "four-spoked form, not at all like a square." I cannot agree with this statement for the following reason. It would not be difficult to give subjects a series of tests in which they would have to respond to one structural characteristic of a square after another in overt action. Under these circumstances, the form of their actions would directly follow from the corresponding structural properties of the square. Their actions would prove, for instance, that their square has four straight sides, that pairs of these sides are parallel, that the angles have all the same size, and so forth. From the point of view of natural science, how can this happen if the cortical counterpart of the square has no corresponding characteristics? Does Dr. McCulloch suggest that such characteristics exist only in the square as an "apparition" (his term), that is, as a mental fact, and that, quite apart from the cortical situation, this mental fact as such determines what the subjects are doing? There is an old name for this view. It is called dualism. I find it hard to believe that dualism appeals to Dr. McCulloch. But in this connection he does argue as though he were a dualist.

If we consider how the visual square (the apparition) comes into existence, we meet with the same difficulty. How can a cortical process such as that of a square give rise to an apparition with certain structural characteristics, if these characteristics are not present in the process itself? According to Dr. McCulloch, this is actually the case. But if we follow the example of physics, we shall hesitate to accept his view. In physics, the structural characteristics of a state of affairs are given by the structural properties of the factors which determine that state of affairs. The magnetic field around a long conductor with circular cross section obviously describes circles; the electrostatic field around a charged sphere is symmetrical with regard to the center of the sphere, and so forth. Situations in physics which depend upon the spatial distribution of given conditions never have more, and more specific, structural characteristics than are contained in the conditions. To be sure, this rule holds only so long as the medium in which a physical situation develops is homogeneous, that is, devoid of special conditions of its own. For instance, the field around a charged sphere will no longer be symmetrical about the center if the environment contains various dielectrics in an arbitrary arrangement.

If we apply this lesson to the way in which the cortical counterpart of a square gives rise to this square, we must choose between two possibilities. Either the structural characteristics of the visual square are fully determined by its cortical counterpart. Then this cortical process must have the structural characteristics of the square. Or we assume that the visual square has structural characteristics of its own which are not present in the cortical process. Then the world of apparitions, the psychological world, constitutes a particular medium with special determining conditions, quite apart from cortical conditions; and it is these conditions in the mental world which add the structural characteristics not contained in the cortical process. The second alternative is, of course, again tantamount to dualism. It seems that if we do not want to be dualists we must accept psychophysical isomorphism.

DR. BROSIN: May I again beg your indulgence and give you a full opportunity to continue later? Dr. Lashley.

DR. LASHLEY: I am very much in sympathy with the type of development represented in the last two papers. I think any understanding of the nervous system we may acquire must be developed within the framework of our knowledge of the activities of the individual neuron. There may be additional factors introduced by combinations of which we know little or nothing at present, but the general principles seem to me to be fundamentally correct. At the present time, however, such a formulation involves a very great oversimplification of the problems. The behavior which is explained is behavior which never occurs in the intact organism. It is an hypothetical behavior derived from the assumptions of the system rather than a description of observed phenomena. A visual object maintains its continuity in spite of constant fluctuations in the position of the eyes and shifts in its position on the retina. By a series of special assumptions concerning neural organization this phenomenon of stimulus equivalence can be accounted for in terms of impulse switching. But in recognition of the visual object it makes little difference whether the image of the whole object falls upon the retina. If only part is seen at any one time, the entire form is rapidly reconstructed from the series of images of parts. The temporal sequence of part figures is combined with the spatial orientation of eye movements to give spatial continuity to the whole. This phenomenon requires a new set of assumptions to make the theory of impulse switching applicable. I somewhat question the utility of a theory which has to be revised to fit each special case.

In its present form the theory of impulse switching involves, I believe, assumptions concerning the accuracy and uniformity of neuronic structure which are not justified by the facts. We have been studying individual variations in the number and arrangement of neurons in the cerebral cortex. We find a wide range of individual differences in cell number and size in corresponding areas of different brains of animals which are grossly indistinguishable in behavior. Two brains may differ by as much as 50 per cent in the number of neurons in the temporal lobe or by 100 per cent in the average size of cells in the superior frontal convolution. A given type of cell may be present or absent from the auditory cortex or operculum. Yet the fundamental behavioral activities of these animals are the same. The anatomic variability is so great as to preclude, I believe, any theory which assumes regularity and precision of anatomic arrangement. Such facts lead me to believe that theories of neuron interaction must be couched, not in terms of the activity of individual cells but in terms of mass relations among the cells. Even the simplest bit of behavior requires the integrated action of millions of neurons; the activity of any single neuron can have little influence on the whole, just as the path of an individual molecule of a gas has little influence on the gas pressure. It is questionable whether specific instances of behavior can ever be dealt with in terms of the activity of individual neurons; the complexity is too great. We shall probably have to use a different kind of model, a model which can be explained in principle by individual neuron action but which involves a somewhat different set of concepts and laws of action. These laws may eventually be derived from study of the individual neuron when those properties are directly observed. At present, however, many of the properties ascribed to the individual neuron are inferred from the activities of neuron masses, and explanations based on such inferred properties are circular and, perhaps, spurious.

Some of the specific hypotheses which have been formulated by Dr. McCulloch seem to me to meet with serious difficulties. He has suggested a reverberatory system between the striate cortex, the suppressor band of area 19, the prestriate region, and the thalamus. I have just removed the prestriate region (including areas 18 and 19) from a series of monkeys and also the frontal eye fields (another suppressor area) singly and in combination. I have been able to detect no visual disturbances whatever following the operations. In no case have we been able to detect significant perceptual disturbances after removal of suppressor areas or of supposed sensory associative areas in monkeys. The specific hypotheses which Dr. McCulloch has suggested for the action of the visual and auditory analyzers imply a definite spatial position of the analyzing mechanisms. Experimentally they are not there.

This leads to the general problem raised by most of the experimental studies of effects of cerebral lesions. Limited lesions or interruptions of transcortical connections produce few or no symptoms. Behavior seems not to depend upon any localized conducting pathways within the cortex. Habits are not stored in any limited area. Such facts point to the conclusion that there is multiple representation of every function. I see no other way of meeting this difficulty except by assuming some sort of reduplicated network of equivalent functional circuits. In other words, we cannot deal with individual conditioned reflex arcs but only with a multiplicity of interacting circuits whose excitatory effects can be transmitted around various types of cortical interruption.

One other point, in relation to the problems of memory raised by Dr. von Neumann: For memory there is the same problem of equivalence as for transneural conduction. I have found, for example, that one sixtieth of the visual cortex of the rat will mediate visual memories and it may be any sixtieth, provided it includes part of the central projection field. Here, again, there must be some sort of multiple representation. The memory is not stored in a single locus.

Now consider the nature of a memory. It is not a single item which can be filed in a single neuron or reverberatory circuit. It is always the capacity to reproduce a series of events, to reproduce a complex sensory pattern or a series of motor activities. Such neural events involve the activity of millions of cells. I have come to believe that almost every nerve cell in the cerebral cortex may be excited in every activity. I shall give some quantitative evidence of this tomorrow. Differential behavior is determined by the combinations of cells acting together rather than by cells which participate only in particular bits of behavior. The same neurons which maintain the memory traces and participate in the revival of a memory are also involved, in different combinations, in thousands of other memories and acts. The memory trace is the capacity of many neurons to work together in certain permutations. In a system of interconnected neurons the number of possible permutations may greatly exceed the number of switching mechanisms. Perhaps this answers Dr. von Neumann's difficulty with regard to number of elements. It is also an argument against the dynamic as opposed to static character of the memory trace.

DR. BROSIN: Dr. Weiss, have you anything to add?

DR. WEISS: Much of my comment had better be left for a later part of the symposium. For the present I want to point out that we are actually dealing here with two different problems. Namely, first a statistical consideration, as it were, of whether or not the number of elements present in the nervous system and their various interrelations is sufficient to account for the number and variety of things it can do. We realize, and this gives us intellectual comfort, that the number of possible constellations is large enough to allow for the observed variety of behavior. This statement, to quote McCulloch, would be merely tautological. As a biologist, I am more interested in the second problem, and that is the precise pathways and chains of processes through which, out of the infinite variety of possibilities, just the appropriate sequence and selection are activated which lead to a given appropriate organized response. And if we deal with these mechanisms not as abstract categories, but in concrete terms, then I see some serious and realistic difficulties arising for any theory of nervous networks that requires the amount of precision postulated in the schemes here presented. The study of the developed nervous system, with which the anatomists, physiologists, and psychologists are usually working, suggests a high degree of precision in the arrangement of the constituent elements, but it must be realized that this impression is illusory. The organizational stability of a performance of the nervous system is much greater than the precision of the underlying structural apparatus.

I have referred above to the persistence of the response after experimental or pathological interference with the anatomical substrata of nervous activity, but want to point now to an even more impressive fact, namely, the great variability in the degree of precision of the anatomical networks in the course of development. The fact is that we frequently suspect a given neuronal precision setup as being relevant for a particular neural function, but often find that in an earlier stage of development this function will be performed in essentially the same way without that particular structural precision scheme having even developed as yet. In general, many a condition which we would think essential from the study of the developed nervous system loses pertinence when studies of earlier stages show that things work very much the same even in its absence. This must be emphasized particularly in connection with the present discussion of the relation between input and output of the nervous system. It is a fact that most of the basic motor patterns of behavior are developed within the nervous system by virtue of the laws of its own embryonic differentiation without the aid of, and prior to the appearance of, a sensory input from the outside world. The basic configuration of the motor patterns, therefore, cannot possibly be a direct product of the patterns of the sensory input. A study of the development of the nervous system and of behavior forces us to consider the output of the nervous system and its patterns as primarily preformed within the nervous system and ready for use, requiring the sensory input for release, facilitation, and modification, but not for its primary shaping.

This brings us to the fundamental alternative, to which I think Dr. Gerard has likewise referred, of whether the central nervous system is merely a clearing house for input-to-output messages, or whether it generates activities of its own and has patterns of activities of its own, the elements of which are not pieced together by, and reflections of, the sensory input. Dr. Köhler has likewise touched on this fundamental difference in the interpretation of the realities of the nervous system. No theory of the nervous system can claim to represent the facts if it ignores the central autonomy of the basic patterns of motor performance. This autonomy impresses us not only in the studies of the development, but also in studies on reconstitution after injury of the nervous system, which touches on a question Dr. von Neumann has raised with regard to learning. This is the question of whether learning implies a complete reorganization of the nervous network with a resetting of relations among individual neurons, or the acquisition of a new performance, which will merely supersede, rather than replace, the older performance. This question can be crucially studied by disarranging the peripheral motor apparatus by crossing tendons or nerves, and thus rendering the original impulse patterns inadequate for the performance of a given act. Experiments by my former student, Sperry, have shown that rats cannot relearn their motor coordination to meet such new situations. Studies we have made on patients with transplanted tendons after partial infantile paralysis show that they can learn to use the transplanted muscle in its new function, but precise electro-myographic records show that the muscle is apt to lapse back into its innate phase of activity, thus proving that the learning act does not dissolve the original patterns of motor organization. Evidence of this kind demonstrates clearly that the act of learning does not consist of merely a recombination of individual neuronal elements. On the basis of all existing evidence, the nervous system must not be conceived of as a network of monotonic elements, but as a hierarchical system in which groups of neuronal complexes of different kinds are acting as units, the properties of which determine the configuration of the output pattern. Some of these higher units are rigidly fixed in their functions, others are modifiable by experience. I fail to see this hierarchical principle duly reflected in the theory of a monotonic network of units such as has been discussed in this session.

. . . .

DR. WEISS: Let me start the present discussion by stressing the great change in our thinking which the facts we have been hearing mark over the state of affairs twenty or twenty-five years ago, when the hard, fast, and precise one-, two-, or three-neuron arcs were viewed as the keys to the understanding of nervous activity. In the meantime we have come to recognize the tremendous complication of the system. This development ought to caution us against trying again to draw a final picture with the material available to our present fragmentary state of knowledge. We ought to expect that in another twenty-five years additional essential parameters will have been discovered. We have been impressed here with the tremendous complication of the nervous network as far as the shape, distribution, and ramification of the individual elements is concerned. To this intricacy of spatial patterns, I am sure, will have to be added, as another parameter determining nervous activity, specific constitutional differences of biochemical kind among the elements, as well as specific states of activity of larger collective units based on those chemical differences. If I may briefly elaborate this concept, we have been treating the nervous system as essentially composed of units of a single kind. Dr. Lorente de Nó has emphasized the existence of a great variety of what he calls "types" of which only three or four have thus far been studied, while thousands of others are still to be explored.

But what is really meant by a cell type? Does the term merely signify a characteristic shape of the cell body, distribution of the processes, and geometric configuration of the arborizations? Or does the term mean to imply the existence of different cell species with distinctive chemical properties? Is the protoplasm of all nerve cells the same, merely cast into different forms and arrangements? Or do these different types of nerve cells have distinctive chemical characteristics that are instrumental in the operation of the nervous machine? Evidence is increasing that we shall have to adopt the latter view. The variety discernible under the microscope is merely one of the relevant differentials among nerve cells. If we had only microscopic pictures of different glandular cells, we might consider them to be of one kind, but we know that their products and their production machineries differ fundamentally in chemical regards in spite of their similar appearances. Likewise the microscopic resemblance of all nerve cells is no evidence of their similarity chemically. There are two problems to be faced. First, are there significant chemical differences among neurons? Second, if so, what is their role in the operation of the nervous system? As for the existence of chemical differences, the evidence seems clear. Pharmacology has demonstrated that different drugs have a selective affinity for different types of nerve cells. Such different response to chemicals can only be based on a fundamental difference in the chemical constitution of the responding neurons. Similarly, when we classify neurons as cholinergic or adrenergic, that is, as capable of producing different types of substances, we admit that the fundamental constitution of their protoplasms must be different. There is evidence that different types of nerve fibers, such as sensory and motor fibers, and perhaps even different subclasses of fibers within each category, follow different routes in their primary outgrowth during development. This again expresses constitutional chemical differences between those types, endowing them with selective chemical affinities by which they can follow different tracts. Again in establishing peripheral connections with effector or receptor organs, and similarly perhaps between different intracentral junctions, selective discriminatory faculties come into play which can only be conceived of in terms of specific chemical sensitivities based on the chemical organization of the respective units. The existence of chemical differentials between neurons has thus been established beyond doubt. The question then arises whether they may be dismissed as simply instruments in the structural development of the nervous system, which leave their residues in the adult body but are irrelevant as far as the operation of the nervous system is concerned, or whether such chemical differentials are significant factors in nervous activity. That is, do we have to add chemical parameters as determiners of nervous activity to the known parameters of the conduction process, such as time sequence, frequencies, thresholds, synchronism, and other space-time characteristics based on the electric activity of a characteristically distributed network? I submit that we must answer in the affirmative, that we must recognize qualitative differences among neurons as decisive in the making and breaking of functional connections, and that chemical conformance or nonconformance between elements may decide whether a synaptic junction will be passable or impassable.

This brings into view a whole new field of possibilities, which it seems can derive substantial support from general biological experience. It may be appropriate to point out here this more general biological background. As I have outlined in the past several years, many relations between contiguous cells are explicable in terms of the conformance or non-conformance between the configurations of the molecular surface populations occupying the contact surfaces. That is, the behavior of two contiguous cells will differ fundamentally, depending on whether or not molecular key species on either side of the contact surface interlock by virtue of their steric relations. We may visualize these relations in the old key-lock picture of Ehrlich in the modern version given to it in Professor Pauling's theories or in any similar fashion. Such relations are the basis of enzyme reactions, of serological reactions, presumably of growth and reproduction, and as I have tried to show, of intercellular relations. If specific intermolecular bonds along the surface of cells are the underlying mechanism of cellular affinity in general, then it would be quite plausible to assume that the making and breaking of connections between neurons might likewise depend on the conformance of the molecular patterns along their surfaces. That is, given a stationary microscopic network of connections, the impulse could pass only from one element to another if the molecular populations along the barrier were of matched character. Since, as I have indicated in another place, the molecular border population of the cell will vary, depending on the physiological state of that cell, a cell with a given chemical constitution can assume a consider-able variety of surface states and accordingly play different parts in intercellular and supercellular activities. It is possible that the proper setting of these border conditions among contiguous elements forms a process quite distinct from and preparatory to the conduction process, and if this is true, then you realize that we have hitherto omitted a very significant coordinating principle from our nervous theories. To the parameters of space and time may have to be added those of chemical conformance and non-conformance. In this connection I should like to call your attention to the fact that in this morning's discussion Dr. McCulloch has illustrated his theory solely by examples taken from those sensory fields which have spatial organization, that is, the optical, tactile, and acoustic fields. In these cases, it is relatively easy to make a case for the patterning of the response by switch-work systems.

However, when we turn to non-spatial qualities of sensation, such as color, taste, or smell, the resolution of these qualities into spatial dis-tributions certainly presents difficulties that cannot be glossed over. Let us consider for instance the experiments of Curt Richter in which rats proved capable of selecting among a variety of foods the one most appropriate to an artificially produced deficiency state of their bodies. Or take the ability of a parasite to recognize very specifically its prospective host by certain chemical cues of the latter. It seems to me impossible to account for these facts otherwise than by conceding to the chemical specificity of the neurons a decisive role in the opera-tion of the system. If in the future we will focus attention on the chemical differentiations among neurons as the presumable mechanism of establishing and breaking intracentral functional relations, we shall undoubtedly find more supporting evidence for this concept. Of course, the microscope will not help us in this task except in so far as a specific differential stain is frequently a safe indicator of biochemical diversity among cells.

DR. BROSIN: This striking development certainly deserves more dis-cussion. Perhaps we can persuade Professor Pauling to comment on it later in the week.

DR. GERARD: Since I have been insisting for years that there are chemical differences between neurons in the different systems, I am obviously, in general, in complete sympathy with the approach which Dr. Weiss has just urged, and I think it might be stimulating to apply it to the question of memory. If that should depend on the passage of impulses across synapses, thereby leaving them altered, might not the alteration, in fact, be a kind of molecular reorganization of the surfaces at the junction, of the sort suggested? I am not inclined to be too optimistic about this extra freedom helping us greatly at the present time, at the level of analysis which is possible with the present procedures—even the chemical ones. Unless one could progress by logic, there is the problem of getting antigens out; and it would be pretty terrific if evidence were obtained that neurons can interact only if they are of the appropriate chemical specificity to match with each other. I think this can perhaps be dismissed at the present time on three grounds. One, although in normal function many neurons are functionally inaccessible to each other, with appropriate drugs they do become accessible to each other—as in strychnine poisoning. Two, even in the normal reflex chains, cholinergic preganglionic fibers act on adrenergic postganglionic fibers. And, third, even within a single neuron itself, there is unquestionable chemical specification, the metabolic reactions of nerve cells being different from those of the nerve fibers which come from the nerve cells. One prefers glucose as fuel and the other glycogen. Cortex is inhibited differentially more by iodo-acetic acid and medulla by malonate. And even in degenerative diseases, the absence of one of the vitamin B components leads to degeneration in the cell bodies of a sensory neuron group, the fiber degenerating only secondarily; and absence of another of the B components leads to degeneration of the fibers, with the cell bodies only secondarily showing disturbance. Therefore, I doubt if we can make too much of chemical specification as a basis for function at the present time, however valuable it may be in interpreting time and space sequences in the development of brain, nerve, muscle, and the like.

DR. KLÜVER: It is of interest that some of the older neuroanatomists, more than thirty years ago, insisted on the importance of chemical differences in the nervous system. In fact, they provided data in support of a chemical topography by systematically studying the absence or presence of various substances in different regions of the nervous system or in different types of cells and fibers. Although the methods used may seem crude in the days of modern cytochemistry there is no doubt that the importance of chemical differences for the study of normal and pathological functions was recognized long ago. When I once discussed these matters with my friend, Dr. Polyak, I ventured the opinion that each nucleus in the brain stem differs chemically from every other nucleus. He not only agreed, but insisted that each neuron differs chemically from every other neuron. When I asked him for his reasons he replied, "All neurons have different *shapes*."

DR. WEISS: My reference to chemical differences among nerve cells has not been altogether understood. The gross detectable differences which I mentioned and to which may be added those of preferences for nutrient substrates and other metabolic differences, I have used only as crude indicators of the existence of differentials; but the relevant differences which I think are instrumental in the operation of the nervous system are of much subtler character. We cannot even be sure whether these differences concern the chemical composition of the cell or merely the relative distribution of the chemical key compounds present in the cells, since what determines the behavior of a cell under given conditions is only the particular segment of the molecular population that happens to occupy the surface and thereby controls what is going into and out from the cell as well as what impulse relations the cell will establish with its neighbors. Such subtle differences of organization will hardly ever be detected by grinding the cell up and making chemical bulk determinations. The main purpose of my remark was to call attention to the presence of such subtle chemical relations as instrumentalities in biological relations in general and to call for more intensified study in the case of the nervous system. I may add another biological comment, returning to Dr. Lorente de Nó's remark that his identification of cell types referred to characters of shape and spatial organization. The study of developmental mechanics has shown that the shape of a cell is only an expression of responses of the cell to its environment in the course of its development. Thus if two cells in an otherwise identical environment assume different shapes, this can generally be considered an expression of underlying differences in the response mechanisms of these cells, or in other words, of differentials in their physiochemical make-up. This is further evidence of the constitutional diversity of the cellular elements in the nervous system.

DR. BROSIN: I have asked Dr. Wiersma of the Biology Department here to tell us of some of his work related to the problem under discussion. Dr. Wiersma.

DR. WIERSMA: I'm glad to have this opportunity to bring before you some work I have done with the synapses of the crayfish central nervous system and at the same time to put some questions to Dr. Lorente de Nó that occur to me concerning the influence of the structure of synapses on transmission. The central nervous system of the crayfish with which I have been working is a rather fortunate contribution of nature, in that it offers, for one thing, a postganglionic fiber which can be stimulated by different preganglionic elements, three of which can be isolated and stimulated as single fibers. These elements are the giant fibers, which run through the whole length of the central nervous system. On stimulation with a single shock, the resulting impulse in any of the giant fibers causes a discharge in a motor root of each of the abdominal ganglia, and the animal flaps its tail. That synaptic transmission is involved can be shown by the fact that stimulation of the motor root does not give rise to activity of the giant fibers. The synapses between the giant fibers and the fiber in the root which discharges have been described by Johnson (1924). If one makes a cross-section of the cord, one will find that the motor root fiber, which itself is of sizable diameter in the root, arises from a ganglion cell on the opposite side. It travels straight up and makes first contact with the heterolateral medial, then crosses over to the homolateral medial, next lays itself against the homolateral lateral giant fiber, and then enters the root. The places of contact are most likely the places where transmission occurs. We find that indeed, by leading off from the root, the root potential follows closest after the impulse in the homolateral lateral fiber, somewhat later after the homolateral medial impulse arrives, and the greatest delay occurs when the heterolateral medial is the activating fiber. Stimulation of the heterolateral lateral fiber always results in excitation of the homolateral lateral, since these two fibers are connected in each ganglion by a synapse, which has some special properties of its own which time does not permit me to describe.

Now, it is possible to bring the preparation into a state in which a single impulse in any of the giant fibers will no longer result in a root potential. Under these circumstances, we will find that if we put two impulses in any one synapse, a root potential will result for time intervals up to about 15 milliseconds. This is, of course, a fairly long time for synaptic summation. However, there is a stranger phenomenon: We can, when the preparation is in this state, combine the stimulation of any two giant fibers and obtain within certain time limits, root potentials. Another remarkable fact here is that simultaneous stimulation of the postganglionic fiber at two synapses does not in general result in a root potential, but that the two preganglionic impulses have to arrive with at least a certain interval. The period during which no root potential is obtained I have called the inert period. If we combine two neighboring synapses, this period has a length of about 2 milliseconds, whereas if another, inactive synapse intervenes, its duration is about twice as long. At the same time the period during which summation can be obtained is shortened with increased distance between the synapses. In other words we may conclude that a process must spread with a certain speed and diminishing intensity from one synapse to the other.

There is pretty good evidence that excitation indeed takes place at the site of the secondly stimulated synapse and not somewhere between the two synapses. In the case where a single impulse causes a root potential, there is, as mentioned, a difference between the delays, when different giant fibers are stimulated. Similar differences are present when summation is necessary, and the delays obtained in this way correspond best with those of the second fiber stimulated. There must thus be a conduction of some process which causes increased excitability. The nature of this process is uncertain: chemical, electrical, or a combination. From the duration of the inert periods and the distance between the synapses, it is possible roughly to calculate the speed of spread, and this comes out as about one fiftieth of the normal conduction speed of the action potential of the root fiber. There is still a fourth synapse, of which less is known, by which the root fiber may be stimulated. This one can be stimulated by exciting the first root on the same side as the third root, from which the lead is taken. Since the whole first root is stimulated, there may be more than one synaptic connection involved in this case. Nevertheless, in combination with giant fiber stimulation, first root stimulation gives results which fit well into the picture. Thus the inert period is longest when the distance is greatest, which is the case when lateral giant fiber and first root stimulation are combined.

The synapses described previously are by no means the only interesting ones which the crayfish has to offer. There are also the synapses in the lateral giant fibers. These are reminiscent of similar structures in the giant fibers of the earthworm, as worked out among others by Dr. Bullock. These macrosynapses consist of a joining of two nerve elements of the same diameter by a membrane. I have tested this membrane in the lateral fibers mechanically. By pinching the fiber below the membrane the end will swell up quite considerably, but no fluid will go into the anterior fiber. Also, on pulling, the two fibers do not come apart. There is, for all practical purposes, a complete anatomical division between the two nervous elements. Nevertheless conduction takes place in both directions with equal facility. My opinion is that this may be due to the wide contact area which this synapse forms. In the above discussed synapses, the postganglionic fiber is much smaller than the preganglionic and hence a large part of the circumference of the postganglionic fiber is involved in the synapse, but only a limited area of the giant fiber. The latter factor would make it impossible for the action potential of the root fiber to stimulate the giant fiber, and hence one way conduction. I would like very much to know from Dr. Lorente de Nó, whether or not he would make such purely anatomical differences responsible for differences between other synapses.

DR. MC CULLOCH: May I ask one question? In this buck-jointed axon, did you say there is or is not any synaptic delay?

DR. WIERSMA: I do know that if there is a synaptic delay it is less than one tenth of a millisecond. One cannot say there is none, because the measurements are not more accurate than this.

DR. LORENTE DE NÓ: Is the mechanism by which you change the state of the ganglia cells rapidity of stimulation?

DR. WIERSMA: Yes, but aging will have a similar effect. Once brought into this state they remain in it for a time. The delay is also not constant in these preparations. The longer you stimulate, for instance with an intermediate frequency of 20 per second, the more the synaptic delay will increase, until the root action potential drops out.

DR. BROSIN: Thank you, Dr. Wiersma. Dr. Lashley?

DR. LASHLEY: I should like to point out the wide ramifications of the work of Dr. Lorente de Nó, work which has been revolutionary in many fields of study of the nervous system and of psychology. In the first decades of this century, the view was widely held (at least among those of us who are somewhat naïve in neurophysiology) that the conduction in the nervous system is always downstream. As a result of that view, in large part, came the development of behaviorism; the denial of imagery (memory images) because there seemed to be no mechanism for central reinstatement of activity, and the development of motor theories of thinking by Watson and others. There seemed to be no mechanism for continuity of thought processes except a chain of circular reflexes involving muscular contraction and the resultant stimulation. Many theories of learning at that time were also very strongly influenced by this conception. The dominance of the belief that the conditioned reflex is the primary form or prototype of the mechanisms of learning derives in large measure from this concept. Dr. Lorente de Nó, in his demonstration of reverberatory circuits, provides a mechanism for central maintenance of activity and so throws an entirely new light upon many of these problems. His studies are now leading to a rather widespread revolution in psychological as well as in neurological concepts.

·   ·   ·   ·   ·   ·   ·

DR. BROSIN: With the thought that we would continue the discussion of the previous speakers in as unified a form as possible this morning, we will pay Dr. McCulloch the most sincere of compliments by working hard at re-examining his propositions. Therefore, continuing what we began earlier, I will call on Dr. Liddell to tell us about the difficulties in methodology of animal behavior as it relates to the neurophysiologist.

DR. LIDDELL: Dr. McCulloch's paper, as the discussion of yesterday demonstrated, was admirably provocative and, in my own case, led to disquieting nocturnal ruminations concerning psychology in its present relation to neurophysiology. May I, therefore, give a sheep's-eye view of the matters under discussion; that is to say, from a strictly pastoral point of view.

In the first place, most of the experimentally observed facts of neural function and the structural details upon which Dr. McCulloch's theoretical formulation is based are derived from mammals simpler than man. Why, then, would it not prove more rewarding to attempt to fit facts derived from systematic experimental observations of the behavior of the simpler mammals—sheep, goat, cat, dog—to the theory rather than select instances of human behavior to support the theory? This can be done and should be done.

I propose Pavlov's method of the conditioned reflex as almost ideal for the purpose. Conditioned reflex study has for too long been misunderstood and for a simple reason. Pavlov's method has yielded a mass of verifiable facts in search of a theory. Dr. McCulloch's admirable theory is in search of facts. Is it not possible that, first, Pavlov and, now, McCulloch suffer from a painful phantom limb? In Pavlov's case the phantom limb was an oversimplified imaginary nervous system which could not support the weight of facts. Perhaps McCulloch's painful phantom is the colorless ghost of real behavior. Let us see how we may relieve McCulloch's suffering.

Gasser has said that the electrophysiologist can answer the question "when?" but not "what?" Here is precisely the advantage of Pavlov's method. The conditioned animal can be trained quite exactly to tell *when* by salivation, leg flexion, cardiac acceleration, or other physiological indicators. Moreover, we can fairly exactly explore the operational limits of its neural computing machine through discovering which forms of trained anticipation lead to breakdown or experimental neurosis. We can find its most vulnerable spots.

The sheep, goat, or dog, trained to self-imposed restraint, through the use of a comfortable restraining harness, learns to expect electric shock or food, or acid in the mouth, as Pavlov found, at some signals but not at others. Some dogs, but not all, when thoroughly conditioned to a series of positive and negative signals, may develop experimental neurosis when the signals are suddenly reversed, where, now, all food signals mean "no food," and "no food" signals are all followed by food. We have verified this neurosis-producing procedure in the pig. However, a slight change in Pavlov's method of reversing signals will render it innocuous. If a sheep is trained for several months to expect mild shock on the foreleg following a buzzer sounding for 10 seconds, and no shock following the ringing of a bell for 10 seconds, these signals may be reversed with impunity twice within a single two-hour period by proceeding as follows. The buzzer sounds; the sheep alerts; but just before it is able to raise the foot from the platform, the buzzer ceases and no shock follows. The bell sounds for a few seconds, and shock is given. In very few repetitions of this cut-off procedure, the sheep has correctly adjusted to the reversed signals— flexing the leg at the bell and remaining quiet at the buzzer.

Another simple method of testing the sheep's and the goat's neural computing machine is as follows. A telegraph sounder clicks once a second for 10 seconds and a shock is applied to the foreleg. After 2 minutes, the telegraph sounder clicks again for 10 seconds, followed by shock. Each day, twenty signals of 10 seconds' duration are followed by shocks, with 2-minute intervals between signals. Neurosis supervenes after about one thousand signals at twenty per day, and persists with no further training for as long as three years. It is characterized by muscular rigidity and slow heart. Where the separation of 10-second signals is by constant 5-, 6-, or 7-minute intervals, neurosis again supervenes; but in sheep and goats, it is a strikingly different neurotic pattern, characterized by diffuse motor activity and rapid, irregular heart. In both types of neurosis, the animal's behavior in the pasture and in the barn is radically changed, with a loss of gregariousness, and with restlessness during the night. If the 10-second signals followed by shock are separated by 1-minute intervals, the animal will submit to as many as forty signal shock combinations per day with no signs of perturbation. Furthermore, shocks spaced at regular intervals of 1 to 7 minutes leave the animal quite undisturbed, although it conditions to the true interval as such, and flexes the limb just before the shock is given.

Work along these lines is technically simple but time consuming. It is, nevertheless, worth the investment of time if it integrates, as I think it does, with the technically more formidable tasks undertaken by Dr. McCulloch in furthering understanding of cerebral mechanisms in behavior.

DR. KLÜVER: Dr. McCulloch told us yesterday morning that he wanted to stay away from the totality of behavior. I am very glad indeed that he didn't make good his threat. As far as I can see, he discussed practically every aspect of behavior, since he considered reflexes, audition, pattern vision, learning, memory, thoughts, ideas, goals, motivation, will, and consciousness.

First, I should like to have some additional information on a few points. You mentioned that stimulation of the primary visual cortex in man elicits the impression of a blurred circle of light whereas stimulation of a spot in the secondary visual cortex leads to the impression of a form. There are reports in the literature indicating that the nature of the photopsiae varies with the type of electrical stimulation employed. It has been reported, for instance, that the photopsiae consist mostly of glowing and colored "roundish forms, disks, or rings" when faradic current is employed, and of stars and ragged forms, such as "pointed sparks," when galvanic current is used. I am wondering whether you care to specify the experimental conditions under which the results you mentioned were obtained. In analyzing the mechanisms of hallucinations, I was interested in the question whether unformed hallucinations ever occur, that is, hallucinations of mere luminosity. It seems that reports on hallucinations never refer to the appearance of visual "dust" or to an undifferentiated luminosity. I am wondering whether you know of any reports referring to unformed hallucinations.

DR. JEFFRESS: Dr. McCulloch also mentioned that the form aroused by stimulating area 18 had a location in space. Was the location relative to the head or to the outside world? You said that it was not relative to the eyes.

DR. MC CULLOCH: It is not located in the visual field, because the patient can turn his eyes toward it. It does not move with the eyes, but stays there so that he can direct his eyes toward it. This is quite different from what is seen when area 17 is stimulated or in entoptic phenomena.

DR. KLÜVER: In connection with your analysis of the reflex turning of the eyes, it seems pertinent to recall Graham Brown's observations on the reflex orientation of the optical axes. He observed, for instance, that the optical axes remain fixed in space if the head of a moderately narcotized monkey is passively moved to one side. This reflex disappears upon removing the superior colliculi or upon increasing the depth of narcosis. It is found to be present in monkeys which are decerebrated at the cephalic boundary of the superior colliculi. Graham Brown was chiefly concerned with determining the influence of cortical activity on this reflex orientation of the optical axes. His work culminated in the suggestion that eye movements obtained from the occipital lobe are equivalent to those which, in normal life, center the visual image of an object fixed in space by bringing it from the peripheral retina to the central field of vision, while movements obtained from the superior frontal convolution correspond to those which, in normal life, keep the optical axes fixed on an object that is moving in space. Graham Brown also suggested that movements obtained from the middle frontal convolution are equivalent to those in normal life where the eyes move at command. I am wondering whether you have any electrophysiological data supporting Graham Brown's idea of such entirely different mechanisms in eye movements.

As regards the general problem of relations between cortical mechanisms and behavior, I am glad, as I said before, that Dr. McCulloch has touched upon so many diverse aspects of behavior. He might be accused, and he has been accused, of talking about behaviors that are very tenuous forms of behavior or even forms of behavior that do not actually occur. Nevertheless, I am hopeful that his analysis may lead to a profitable search for "phantom limbs" and ultimately to full-fledged behavior realities. It is possible that certain forms and consistencies of behavior will be discovered that would escape detection without his kind of analysis.

Finally, I should like to return to the subject of "ideas." It is not clear to me whether you are content with proposing certain cortical mechanisms that are operative while I am having an idea or whether you really want to write a neurophysiology of logic. You recall that Brickner, some years ago, found that electrical stimulation of a cortical area on the mesial surface of the left hemisphere, at about the junction of Brodmann's areas 6 and 32, resulted in perseveration of speech. When his patient was requested to recite the alphabet she repeated again and again the letter she happened to say at the moment this area was stimulated: A, B, C, D, E, E, E, E, E, F, G, H, I, J, J, J, J, K, L, etc. The repetition continued as long as this area was stimulated and ceased immediately on terminating the stimulation. Perhaps we have here a beautiful demonstration of the workings of a reverberating circuit. A psychologist may have no difficulty in relating circuits of such kind to perseverating ideas. The general point I wish to emphasize is that having an idea, or having even an idea that is perseverating, is different from an idea. Ideas, logical structures, and meanings are in and of a world that is different from the world of physiological and psychological events that occur in the process of having ideas or recognizing and enunciating propositions and meanings, even if such physiological events should represent events in reverberating circuits. I am, therefore, still curious to know whether you want to contribute to a neurophysiology of logic or merely to a neurophysiology that is involved while I am talking about logic.

DR. LINDSLEY: I believe I understood Dr. McCulloch to say, at one point, that he interpreted the alpha rhythm as a possible fluctuation in the excitatory level of the cortex, particularly with reference to the speed of transposition, say from one chord to another in an auditory field or from one pattern to another in the visual field.

DR. MC CULLOCH: That is correct.

DR. LINDSLEY: It is a little difficult for me to see how this could be the case inasmuch as visual stimulation will completely block the alpha rhythm for a period, even after the stimulation has stopped.

Another thing: An experiment not yet reported which was done by Dr. J. R. Smith and myself just before the war (it was interrupted

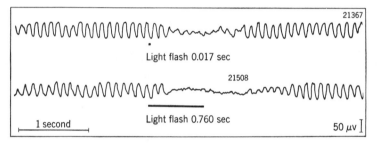

FIGURE 1.   Effect of a light flash upon alpha rhythm.

and not continued since—I hope to get back to it) had to do with visual stimulation in relation to modifications of the alpha rhythm. Briefly, it was this. A small spot of light which could be controlled in intensity and in duration, was thrown on the periphery of the retina, and we investigated the effects of its intensity and duration on the blocking of the alpha rhythm. When we got down near to threshold with our stimulation and beyond the subjective threshold, we still got effective blocking of the alpha rhythm. We were recording with our electrodes over areas 18 and 19, so probably very little of area 17 was involved in the case of electrodes on the human head. We were having our subject report after each flash came, and they came at irregular intervals for which he was not warned. When we got to threshold the subject's report would cease. Nevertheless, for a certain region below the subjective threshold, the blocking would still occur. Now, what I would like to have Dr. McCulloch explain, in terms of the McCulloch-Pitts model, is this separation, presumably, of the awareness of the stimulus on the part of the subject and the physiological response that we get. Figure 1 illustrates the kind of blocking that one gets.

The illustration does not show what I have just been speaking of —that is, the separation of the awareness or non-awareness of the stimulus on the part of the subject. It simply shows the kind of response we get from a flash of light, in this case, one of which the subject is definitely aware. The duration of the stimulus patch represents the duration of the flash of light. In this illustration, both flashes of light were of the same intensity but of different duration. The point I want to call attention to, however, is that we get this kind of blocking whether the subject is or is not aware of the light, in this region just below the subjective threshold.

DR. MC CULLOCH: I wonder if Dr. Halstead would in this connection be good enough to mention his work on the driving of alpha by light. There are probably many people here who don't know the story.

DR. HALSTEAD: If I may postpone it for 30 minutes or so I'll get a slide illustrating the effect.

DR. KLÜVER: Is the duration of the blocking dependent upon the intensity characteristics of the stimulus?

DR. LINDSLEY: It is related to it, but it is related more, perhaps, to the duration of the seen stimulus. In the illustration with the brief flash, after about two-fifths of a second, the blocking begins, and you can see that it persists. Many times you will get really a summation or an after-effect following the cessation of the stimulus. In the second part where the stimulus persists for a longer period of time, you will again see that there is a period following the cessation of the stimulus during which the alpha waves remain blocked and only gradually return, and there you get some of the increased amplitude effect.

DR. KLÜVER: Does the fact that the duration of the blocking is dependent upon the duration or the intensity of the stimulus imply that the awareness or the non-awareness of the stimulus plays no role in influencing the duration of the blocking?

DR. LINDSLEY: I think it is related to both time and intensity.

DR. KLÜVER: Suppose you are able to relate the duration of the blocking to the product of time and intensity. Does this imply that the duration of the blocking is not influenced by awareness or non-awareness on the part of the subject?

DR. LINDSLEY: I don't believe that we have the situation well enough defined to say just what the duration of blocking means as yet. We have in mind further investigation of the problem.

DR. MC CULLOCH: Jasper has a good deal of evidence with anxious patients to show that you get disproportionately long disappearances of alpha on very dim illumination even if the patient doesn't see it, and that the duration parallels the severity of the sympathetic over-activity of the patient generally.

DR. WOODBURY: Just to complicate the issue a little further, I would like to mention our experience on the disappearance of the alpha rhythm, depending on whether or not you are getting pattern vision. With electrodes over the occipital region and a towel over the eyes, and the eyes open, we get alpha rhythm with the eyes blank. When we request the subject to focus his eyes on the towel pattern, the alpha rhythm disappears.

DR. BROSIN: Dr. Weiss, do you wish an opportunity to enlarge on this topic?

DR. WEISS: May I mention a few features manifested by nervous activity which any valid theory of the nervous system must duly take into account?

First, the nervous system uses in its operation certain distinct specificities: a specific receptor type and, on the effector side, a specific muscle. Many of you have seen my film on myotypic function in supernumerary limbs. I have demonstrated the same specificity in the proprioceptive system and for the corneal reflex, and Sperry has extended the evidence to the optic field. The existence of such specificities through which discrete peripheral organs and their corresponding central activities are related is an incontrovertible fact. The interpretation, however, is a matter of speculation. Whether we look for spatial order, chronological order, or chemical order as a basis of these specificities, we must always bear in mind that they are distinct, discrete, and show no intergradations. They could be called qualitative differences. Personally I still like to view them as resonance phenomena between complex molecular elements of matching configuration or tuning.

A second condition that any theory of the nervous system must satisfy is that it must be able to explain perception not only in spatially extended fields, such as tactile, acoustic, and optical space—those used by Dr. McCulloch—but must equally well explain recognition of color and chemical character. I submit that this can be done if we concede to the elements of the nervous system the power to recognize chemical constitution by virtue of their own chemical characteristics.

A third condition is that the theory must give equal regard to the role of the molecular processes, the microscopic cellular organizations, and the field properties of the nervous system, all of which seem to be demonstrably involved. How can we reconcile our view that neuronal relations on the molecular level are a coordinating principle with the recognized fact that each act involves vast numbers of neurons whose collective activity behaves in the manner of continuous patterned fields? Perhaps the answer lies in a dualistic concept of nervous activity. We may assume one activity of a conditioning type that sets the stage for a given reaction by determining molecular interneuronal interdigitation, thus linking definite sections of the neuronal network into closed systems, within which, then, a second activity with field character, perhaps merely of electrical order, would operate. Thus by molecular relations, functional subdivisions would be carved out from the total pool of the nervous system, and each such subdivision would then operate field-fashion. Groups of such higher units might then become linked in their activities through correspondences in their respective field activities, and in this fashion we could arrive at a physical counterpart of what we have called the hierarchical principle of central activities. The field character of the activities in neuron pools may force us to extend our current concept of the nervous system in another direction. We may find that the field properties cannot be adequately accounted for by considering only the neuronal elements, that is, by equating the nervous system with the sum total of its neurons. It may become necessary to consider the possible role of the matrix in which the neurons are embedded and learn more of its properties. The environment of the neurons is by no means a physiochemically or anatomically simple system, but is a tissue of complex structural and physiochemical organization. The structural and biological properties of this matrix will of necessity affect the processes in the neuron circuits which are embedded in it and perhaps in counterplay with it. This proposition, perhaps first envisaged by Nissl, certainly deserves further exploration.

A fourth demand on any valid theory of the nervous system is that it must not only apply to the developed operative nervous system, but must explain why the nervous system does not change in its essential functions during growth, although its anatomical substratum is in constant expansion. One must bear in mind that as the minute embryo or fetus or larva grows to adult proportions, the nervous system undergoes enormous alterations in mass, dimensions, interneuronal relations, in the numbers of cells and their sizes. The crucial factors are that the patterns of performance remain relatively stable in spite of these variations of the underlying substrata. New performances may be added, and the precision and speed of older performances may be increased as development goes on, but the basic patterns of coordination remain remarkably constant in spite of the progressive distortion of the underlying anatomical substratum as a result of anatomical growth. This fact brings into sharp relief a question which we have discussed earlier, namely, just how much precision does the nervous system really apply in its performances? If I understand Dr. McCulloch correctly, he tries in his concept to replace mechanical and detailed precision by statistical normalization. I think this is a very fundamental consideration, not only in psychology, but also in biology in general, particularly as regards the processes of development. I wholeheartedly concur in this attitude and hope that it will be more generally adopted. We focus too much attention on precision arrangements among elements, such as a preordained length of a collateral, a rigidly fixed number of collaterals and end feet, a precise diameter of a fiber, and so forth, instead of basing the regularity of a performance on the statistical properties of the collective of units exhibiting it. The regularities observed must be based on the normalization of the statistical distribution of properties in the collective rather than on the minutely precise arrangement of details. This leads us to recognize a certain degree of indeterminacy in biological microevents. This has been true of development in general, and now it seems to be equally true of the operation of the nervous system.

A fifth, and the last condition I want to mention, is one already outlined earlier, namely, that the patterns of motor coordination are not replicas, as it were, of the sensory input patterns. The character and the structure of the motor output is determined by the intrinsic properties of the organized response system and not by the set of stimuli that are fed into it from the environment or the surrounding body. With Dr. Köhler I, too, take exception to calling the light perception, obtained upon pressing on the eyeball, a wrong or false impression in contradistinction to one released by radiant energy. I think it is just as much the real thing as a visual excitation. It is a manifestation of that constitutional ability of the central optical apparatus to generate an activity sensed as light, whether stimulated "adequately" or not. However, whatever the situation in the field of receptors, there is positive evidence that in the motor field, at least, the structural patterns of coordinated response are shaped and differentiated prior to, and without the aid of, a sensory input that could have impressed its structure upon them.

DR. PAULING: This problem of cerebral structure and mechanism may well be related to my field of interest—molecular structure and molecular mechanism—indeed, it must be, as Dr. Weiss has pointed out. I would like to know the order of magnitude of the dimensions of the structures of primary importance in cerebral mechanisms. I

121

suppose (I don't really know anything in this field) that memories —as cerebral processes—involve at first electrical patterns, electrical structure, and that then, after the passage of a suitable period of time, these electrical patterns may be transmuted into material patterns— material structure. And so we ask: How is it possible for this change from electrical structure to material structure to occur, and what is the order of magnitude in size of these material structures? I am not much interested in large structures—structures a hundred angstroms or a thousand angstroms in linear dimensions—but, at least at present, in smaller ones. We can divide things up into different categories of size. First we may consider structures which are, say, 2 to 10 angstroms in dimension—atoms and little groups of atoms, such as the carboxyl group, or an amino-acid residue, that determine mainly the chemical properties of substances. Then we have the next category from about 10 angstroms to, say, 40 angstroms in size. These structures in the main determine, I think, the specific biological and physiological properties of substances. I think that biological specificity is determined almost completely by the size and shape of the outsides of molecules and especially by the phenomenon of complementariness in structure —a sort of lock and key effect. Two large molecules may show a specific relation to one another because of a complementariness in structure. Immuno-chemical experiments have shown that the complementariness must be good to within an angstrom or so, the areas involved being of the order of magnitude of 10 to 20 angstroms square.

Then we have the next category of dimensions, from 40 to 500 or 1000 angstroms, and finally we reach the category of large structures— microscopic structures. This category of structures is extremely important in biology generally; but is it important in a significant way in cerebral processes? I doubt that it is. I think that it is related to cerebral processes, but that it is not important in the sense that cerebral processes involve a change in structure in this size region.

I believe that the specificity of antigens, enzymes, and genes depends on structure in the 10 to 40 angstrom region, that mutation involves a change in structure in this region, and not primarily a change in larger structures. I suggest, then, that the material patterns that are involved in the second stage of learning are the result of changes of this nature, in the 10 to 40 angstrom size category. Now, how could such changes occur as a result of the operation of an electrical pattern that has been induced? Let us assume that there exist molecules, A, that have a definite configuration and that make up part of the nervous system, and also other molecules, A', that are complementary to A, and that are loosely attached to the reticular framework of the brain structure near by. As Tyler has pointed out, there is evidence that mutually complementary molecules exist, perhaps in large numbers, in living organisms. Now, under the influence of an electrical pattern, there may be a change in environment in this region, a change in pH or in ionic concentration, which changes the equilibrium conditions for the molecules A' relative to the reticular portions of matter to which they are attached. This change in environment might permit them to dissociate away, and then to move over and to combine, because of their complementariness, with the molecules A, thus producing a material change which could itself at a later time be reflected in an electrical response.

I suppose all intramolecular forces are electrostatic in origin, inasmuch as they involve electrons and nuclei. Intramolecular forces have been classified as electronic dispersion forces, hydrogen-bond forces, interaction of ionic groups, etc.

DR. KÖHLER: If complementary configurations in your sense occur on the molecular level, and if being complementary or failing to be complementary are facts which may influence function on this level, is it not possible that analogous facts are also important on a macroscopic level?

DR. PAULING: It is very difficult to get a simple chloride ion to attach itself permanently to a structure, because thermal agitation is enough to cause it to dissociate away. You have to have larger aggregates of atoms in order to resist the effect of thermal agitation. Perhaps one of these large aggregates carries a positive charge, and its complementary structure carries a negative charge, and then when combination occurs there is a change in the electrical pattern. In a system where electrolytes are present it is not easy to consider setting up distributions of electrical charge of the order of magnitude of hundreds of angstroms, because neutralization of the charges by the electrolyte occurs, giving a double layer in which the significant dimensions are small. The idea of large-scale electrical distributions hence does not appeal to me very strongly. I prefer to think that some sort of an insulating effect is produced by these molecules, rather than that there is just an electrical pattern.

DR. KÖHLER: I asked my question because, in a discussion of memory, macroscopic field distributions in the cortex are likely to play a major role. I was wondering whether your principle can be applied to such larger configurations.

DR. PAULING: Perhaps it could, since the amount of charge separation required to produce the observed fields is very small. A pattern of loci in which charges are neutralized by complementary structures could be built up.

DR. WEISS: It may be well to point out in this connection that central neuron arrangements, even in the adult nervous system, are much more flexible and variable than we usually admit. Evidence is increasing that the nerve cell bodies react to different functional loads by changes of size. It would seem impossible that a marked increase or decrease in the size of a cell body could occur without the finer terminal connections on the cell body suffering major disruptions. There is, therefore, ample opportunity for rearrangements. We must not think of the microscopic network as something absolutely set and rigid.

DR. PAULING: There is a possibility (though it seems to me to be unlikely) that the whole phenomenon involves changes that are of a still larger dimensional order of magnitude—a thousand, five thousand, ten thousand angstroms. I would be especially interested to know what the characteristic dimensions of the structures involved are.

DR. KÖHLER: I should like to come back to the experiment which Dr. Lindsley has described. The alpha rhythm, he said, can be blocked by a visual stimulus which is too weak to be perceived. This observation seems to be at variance with Professor Adrian's interpretation of the blocking of alpha by visual stimulation. Adrian, it will be remembered, found that presentation of a homogeneous bright *field* does not disturb the rhythm very much, while even a weak *contour* may have a strong blocking effect. Since contours attract attention more than homogeneous fields do, he concluded that the rhythm is blocked by attention. But it cannot have been attention which blocked the rhythm in Dr. Lindsley's experiments. A stimulus which is not perceived will be unable to attract attention. I should therefore prefer the assumption that any inhomogeneity in the visual cortex, and in this sense a pattern, is associated with a particular process; that this process is absent, or weaker, when the visual cortex is in a homogeneous state; and that the alpha rhythm is likely to be blocked when such a pattern process is introduced.

DR. GERARD: I am afraid that it isn't that simple, Dr. Köhler. There is another bit of evidence that I am certain most men who have worked with this have experienced themselves. With a little practice, I can look directly at a 100-watt light, which is certainly not a uniform field but is patterned, and, by deliberately paying no attention to it, I can have my alpha waves remain perfectly intact; then with no change except what I can describe in no other way than as directing my attention to the light, have them immediately disappear.

DR. HALSTEAD: We became interested in the relation of vision and alpha rhythm some years ago in a search for neural concomitance of flicker fusion partly as a result of the work on photic driving reported by Adrian and Matthews in 1934. They stimulated man binocularly with intermittent light while recording the electroencephalogram from the occipital areas. The work provides samples of unilateral coupling between the frequency of the intermittent light and the alpha frequency of the EEG. A diffuse (non-patterned) light flash of relatively high intensity was employed to obtain these records—in a conscious individual. About five years ago, my associates and I were able to publish similar records of the driving of brain rhythms, with and without anesthesia, in the Macaque monkey. We obtained a good coincidence over a range from about 18 per second to about 3½ per second. This driving effect can be reproduced with reasonable predictability in several species from rabbit to man. Under the conditions of photic driving the organism becomes literally coupled to the external environment.

We also noted that if trains of flashes, especially in the neighborhood of 6 per second, were suddenly thrown onto the retinae a peculiar hump and spike pattern appeared in some animals at once and lasted from one to two seconds. This pattern is apparently indistinguishable from spontaneous brain rhythms obtained in certain forms of human epilepsy. In recent work by Walters in England, Gastaut in France, and others, petit mal seizures have been induced in man under controlled conditions in convulsive-prone individuals by this technique. The alpha rhythm is abolished for the duration of the seizure and hence may be thought of as being "blocked." However, our observations along with those of Wang, Bishop, Bartley, Toman, and others indicate clearly that the electrical responses of the normal mammalian brain from rabbit to man tend to follow or to couple with a train of light flashes through the range from about 2 flashes per second to 20 or more flashes per second. Rather than being "blocked," the most prominent brain rhythm is, under these circumstances, "paced" or "driven" by the photic stimuli. There is some evidence to be found in the literature that suggests that introduction of a contour at the periphery of a flickering field lateralizes the photic driving to the ipsilateral hemisphere. The electrical activity of the contralateral hemisphere is not "blocked," however; rather it seems to be decoupled from the flickering field.

DR. KÖHLER: Can we be quite sure that what is commonly called driving of the alpha rhythm by varying flicker frequencies actually deserves this name? We know that upon sudden illumination of the eye an on-effect can be registered from the visual cortex. Now, when the sudden illumination is repeated, on-effects may be repeated at the same rate. Have we any way of proving that in such experiments the frequency of the alpha rhythm is actually changed by rhythmic stimulation? How does one exclude the possibility that the registered waves are simply on-effects which have the frequency of the flicker?

DR. HALSTEAD: For the conditions of stimulation we employed, it is rather generally agreed that the total on-effect lasts somewhere in the neighborhood of 200 milliseconds. It is conceivable that frequencies up to about 5 per second might be reflected as trains of on-effects. As Bartley and others have shown, however, components of the on-effects are increasingly inhibited as flash frequency increases above this point.

In a favorable preparation and using a glissando technique, one may drive electrical activity continuously and without essential change in wave form from 6 or 7 per second to 20 or more per second.

Another line of evidence is afforded by the enhancement of amplitude of electrical response from the brain during photic driving. This enhancement reaches a maximum around 10 per second in monkey and man. This is generally regarded as the alpha frequency. Toman, studying these relations in man, found it possible to omit a single flash without disrupting the response. We have made similar observations. This would suggest that the centrally induced rhythm may sustain itself briefly without reinforcement.

DR. GERARD: Doesn't the rhythm continue a little while after you stop the flicker?

DR. HALSTEAD: Yes, it does; it may last from 2 to 6 seconds in some preparations.

DR. VON NEUMANN: I don't understand why sometimes even a subliminal signal of light may stop the alpha rhythm, while here it continues in spite of light signals. How are these things compatible?

DR. MC CULLOCH: Didn't you get part of an answer to your question in Dr. Gerard's statement concerning the light bulb? Whatever this mechanism is, it is important.

DR. HALSTEAD: I think that there are special circumstances under which the alpha does not block in the presence of light.

DR. KLÜVER: In this connection I should like to ask Dr. Lashley, who has described his scintillating scotomata, whether there are disturbances of the alpha rhythm during the observation of such scotomata. I am also wondering whether such disturbances, if they exist, are related to the frequency of the scintillations.

126

Why the Mind Is in the Head

DR. MC CULLOCH: May I answer his question? I have very brilliant scintillating scotomata with hemicranial headache, or migraine. The scotomata have, inside them, an area in which I can see nothing. They begin always right next to the point of fixation, just a whisker to one side of it, and they move out until they have occupied the whole of that field. I already have several times had electrodes well placed in and about the inion and all over the back of my head and there is no change that we can detect. I don't have a good alpha, but there is no change in what alpha I have, and there are no other waves that are not normally there with my eyes open or my eyes closed.

DR. KLÜVER: What is the frequency of the scintillations per second?

DR. MC CULLOCH: The thing which I see is composed of small bright dashes and these things don't all come or go in a pulsing fashion, but they twinkle.

DR. KLÜVER: You are apparently not a good case for getting data on the frequency of oscillations. Fröhlich, by the use of a rather ingenious method, found that the frequency of oscillations in his scintillating scotomata was 20 per second.

DR. LINDSLEY: To confuse the issue further, I would like to add a comment. When I was working with infants and young children, where the alpha rhythm is of a different order of frequency, namely, around 3 or 4 per second, I found that the time for delay of the alpha rhythm in blocking is proportionately longer than it is in the adult where the frequency is around 10 per second.

DR. MC CULLOCH: There is one more piece of evidence. I don't know whether Mr. Stroud is in the audience, but if he is, I wonder if he would be willing to say something about the rate at which forms can be perceived?

MR. JOHN M. STROUD: Stanford was kind enough to let me come, as a kind of renegade physicist, into the Psychology Department and do a little work on the problem of the frequencies of scansion functions, such as the alpha rhythms (which I considered as the no-load symptom of a scanning function). The hypothesis that I wanted to test led to two experiments that are relevant here.

One was very simple. I had an ordinary cathode-ray oscilloscope and set the observer the task of finding out how fast the sweep was going, by tapping a key which put a little pip on the trace. His task was to learn to tap the key fast enough to make the pip stand still; that was his only task. It showed, incidentally, that human reactions are by no means as unprecise as one might infer from the classical reaction time experiments. Anybody could learn to tap at the rate of 10 cycles

127

per second for one hundred consecutive taps. He could always get his reactions to fall within a band of 20 milliseconds for a prescribed frequency, with errors from one tap to the next of the order of only 2½ milliseconds.

In the second experiment the observer was set the task of matching the brightness of a flickering light by adjusting the brightness of a steady light. The field was a small circle split vertically, with the flickering light on the left and the steady, on the right. The level of illumination was low, and a very dark red light was used. The flicker was rectangular in wave form, and the proportion of the cycle during which the light was on could be controlled by the experimenter. In different runs it was varied from zero to 100 per cent. The experimenter could also vary the repetition rate from about one-half to about 20 per second.

The results varied from subject to subject, but in general showed that for frequencies above about 8 the relation between the proportion of time the flickering light was on, and brightness was linear, with a slope of 1.0. That is when the light is on 100 per cent it is matched by an equal intensity. Call this 100 per cent. Now if the flickering light is on 50 per cent of the cycle, it is matched by a steady light one-half as bright, etc.

If, however, we reduce the repetition rate below 8 per second another phenomenon appears. At 6.4 cycles for some subjects (and at lower frequencies for others) the brightness follows the previous curve for durations down to about 60 per cent. From 60 per cent to 30 per cent it remained constant, and then fell off in a linear fashion with duration.

At a still slower rate (4 per second for many subjects) the brightness dropped very slowly as the duration changed from 100 per cent to about 45 per cent. (The brightness dropped only about 10 per cent in this range.) Then it dropped rapidly as the duration was further reduced. In all cases the data seem to be best fitted by straight lines making sharp corners with one another.

The subjects often reported, where the frequencies were from 4 to 8 and the durations short, that there was a definite light and dark phase and that this was the basis for a phi movement. Most people saw the center line bulge and collapse alternately. I saw a guillotine moving up and down, chopping off the flickering half field. I found that the subject's movement hypotheses were, to a considerable extent, under their control, and that we could have all sorts of hypotheses to cover what occurred at these and at lower frequencies.

128

DR. MC CULLOCH: I would just like to point out that the relations here are just what one would expect from Dr. Halstead's work on the extent to which the alpha can be driven.

MR. STROUD: I know that, but I hesitated, in writing it out formally,* to call attention to its relationship to the known behavior of alpha although I was familiar with Dr. Halstead's work.

DR. BROSIN: If there are no further questions I will ask Dr. McCulloch to take care of the many that have already been posed him.

DR. MC CULLOCH: I would like, if I may, to begin at the other end, so to speak, and thank Dr. Paul Weiss for liberating me. He holds the theory, you see, that the output is in no sense to be determined by the input—it is independent. This suggestion of his makes it very easy to handle the host of questions. I cannot, for the life of me, attempt to answer them question by question. I would much rather try to give what I would call an organized statement about half a dozen major items that are under discussion.

If you will remember, I suggested that we ask the theoretical physicist to account for himself; that is, for organisms like himself, of such a nature that they could produce theoretical physics. Now, in asking that question, I did not ask that he be a psychologist, and I did not ask that he be a philosopher, and, above all, I did not ask that he be a theologian. The entire problem, I am quite sure, will never be manageable if we begin at the most difficult end. I would much rather ask, merely, that it be a theory of the physicist, and my object in doing this is to put the question concerning whether a machine of this order of complexity can state how it works. If it can (and I think it can), then we can build others that can do the same thing. My object in doing this is to keep the issues in a form in which they are manageable from the standpoint of physics and mathematics. I grew up in a medical school where my professor of neuropathology defined the sub-conscious as a place which is not a place where an idea is when it is not an idea, and my professor of neurology said that he knew that time was in the temporal lobe and space was in the postcentral convolution, but he was not sure where consciousness was.

Now, it is just these kinds of phrases that I would avoid. I don't believe that I brought up the question of consciousness. If I had to, in a medical sense, I would use the word only to say that this patient was or was not conscious, according to whether he could or could not bear witness to what I could also bear witness to. I would, here and

---

* John M. Stroud, *The Moment Function Hypothesis*, M.A. Thesis, Stanford University, 1948.

now, systematically exclude any such problem. I am, however, fully aware that most of what goes on in me is something of which I am not aware; I only see the end products. I see those only rarely and in funny flashes. Very often I know that I have decided something without even knowing what I have decided. I do not believe that we have any right to ask of whatever it is that is consciousness that it do the chore of alpha waves or something else of that sort. Alpha waves as I see them (and I am coming back to them first and foremost) are a sweep of scansion. That sweep can, to some extent, be stimulus-triggered. It can be pulled down to about half; it can be pushed up to nearly double its idling rate. When we try to push it further, it snaps and gives us double frames or something else of that sort. I think that much is fairly clear. It has this peculiarity regardless of the sensory modality in which one works. One always comes to an ability to follow in the range, from, let's say, five to fifteen—the maximum number of frames that one can take in any sensory modality. The ability to pull out universals seems to be something of the order of ten per second. You can push it up a little or down a little. Therefore, whatever be the method whereby we do pull out universals, it is timed by something that runs around ten per second, and which may be pushed a little one way or the other. This means that all our ideas, insofar as they are timeless, are going to have this peculiar quality of being moments without internal temporal structure, and that our timed affairs, between our ideas, will be between them, and hence of larger temporal units. Now, that is the first point.

Next—as to why alpha rhythm should disappear when the instrument is in use—this has two possible answers. One is that when we go after forms—when we begin to use a device to pull out shapes—we are keying in this mechanism with incoming impulses, and in so doing we upset a sweep in that sense. But it is far more likely that what happens is that when we do use this sweep, the detail (since its voltages are in cells oriented in this same direction) will have its throw in the same direction as the apparent sweep; hence all you will get is that your sweep is passing up and down as a series of voltage fronts and your cells have their major axis in this direction, so they create voltages up and down. Therefore, you would expect that in using this structure you wouldn't see your sweep. In the present discussion I am not particularly interested in which happens.

I should add one more thing before I leave the problem of the alpha, and that is George Bishop's work on the relation of the alpha to an impulse thrown in at various times in the alpha cycle, reported in one of the Cold Spring Harbor Symposia. He showed very clearly that the response that you get in the cortex to an incoming volley is determined in large measure by the positivity or negativity of that cortex—which way up the voltage in it is at the time that the impulses arrive. There is no question but that alpha does affect the appearance of "on" and "off" effects in the superficial layers of the cortex itself, but I am not interested in any one particular mechanism at the moment. I don't care what the mechanism is. What is important to me is that we have some idea, even if it be one very hard to run down, of a process whereby we can get our "stimulus equivalence." That is the crucial item as far as I am concerned, and I am well aware that in one sense, or modality, it may go one way, and in another in another way, or, in a single modality it may pull out one thing by one method and another thing by another method. This would seem to postulate a theory of a nervous net which has delays and connections in time, and connections in space which are of such a kind that you cannot know beforehand what sort of a thing your invariant will be. It may be a figure of impulses over a single cell, or a series of cells, in time, and it may be over a flock of cells at one time. I have not tried to give a spatial picture of the nervous system or a temporal picture, but a fourfold picture—three dimensions of space and one of time in which that invariance is to be sought. That is the first thing that I want to make clear.

The second thing I want to make clear is much harder to say. I spoke of reverberating memory, and I spoke of reverberating memory to the exclusion of all other memories, not because I believe that all that we remember is so carried, or because I believe that we carry more in reverberation than in any other way, but because anything which can be done by any kind of memory can be done by a reverberating memory, except to go through periods of complete inactivity or complete explosion. As I see it, there are three problems in memory, not one, or three kinds of memory that we are going to have to distinguish always.

First, there is reverberation, and it does work. Second, there is a kind of alteration of the nervous net with use, which I believe is probably crucial in many of the experiments on conditioned behavior. It is obviously so in certain kinds of pathological situations. The third kind of memory, I don't believe could be accounted for by either of these two ways, and it is one with a bottleneck both in putting information in and in taking it out. I am utterly unhappy about where it is. I don't think that we have any better guess today than that it is somewhere in our heads. I see no particular reason for assigning it to neurons instead of to their matrix—the glia. I don't see how we can tell where we have to look as yet, because in many of the experiments in which there are lesions made in brains, we have had large amounts of territory removed. However, usually we fail to destroy most fixed memories; therefore, we cannot today locate the filing cabinets. I think that sooner or later answers to the question of those filing cabinets, or whatever it is on which is printed "photographic records" and what not, will have to be found. The theory that I set up was intended to handle only this question—it was set up to show that organisms or computing machines which digitalized, or quantized, at the level of neurons—at the level of relays—were systems capable of doing certain kinds of things, and rather a large number of things like remembering and computing any computable number.

The question as to whether I am trying to envisage the human nervous system, or that of a particular animal, or whether I'm interested only in computing machines in general is, I think, most fairly answered in this manner. Logical machines, machines for handling logical problems, can be constructed out of almost any material; however, some materials work better than other materials. I do not know out of what materials the human nervous system is constructed, but the principles of design that have to be followed, insofar as they are not matters of the material but matters of the circuit action, will be identical to the extent that the tasks they are competent to perform prescribe their structure. They need be no more, and the theory that I gave (as opposed to the particular hypotheses concerning, let's say, alpha rhythm or visual cortex) is a perfectly general theory. The hypotheses that I made relating to the nervous system are of the kind that will help me to put electrodes in one place to see what is going on in that place and to know what I am looking for, and I expect to hit a snag there very soon. I always have hit snags so far. Now, why have I chosen to quantize in nervous impulses? Well, let's say the human brain is of a general order of complexity of something like 10^{30} if we think of it in terms of its ultimate particles. One might split this at the level of the atoms, or one might split this at the level of the molecules, or one might split this at the level of the neurons, and so on. The question is: At what level can one split the behavior so as to define a set of units in terms of which to work? And, obviously, the nervous impulse at the level of the neurons is a fairly nice unit for working. It divides the complexity nearly in half. That is why I like to quantize my affairs in the behavior of the neuron and in its properties.

I look on the question of a field somewhat in this manner. In any device (whether we make it a digital device or an analogy device),

132

the ultimate units of our universe are quantized affairs. We use it as an analogy device when we disregard the unitary composition, or definite structure of our elements, and treat them as wholes, which means that we are dealing with their parts, if you will, at best, statistically. We have, with respect to them, thrown away the information that goes into their construction, and have retained only the overall picture of their behavior. Now, I do not like to treat something like the cerebral cortex in this "field" manner. First and foremost, I will admit unquestionably that it has some statistical properties. But what I am looking for is something that will perform a logical task. I like to look for it in a thing that has a grain, and I like to take that grain as my unit, because then I can see what degrees of freedom the system has and to what extent they are bound in any given job of handling information. I believe that there are many things in the nervous system that smear the results. I worked for years on facilitation and extinction. I know that if I stimulate a small area, that there does arise between that active area and any other area, a difference in voltage which persists for a matter of minutes, and so on, with the busy area electrically negative to the depths and to remote regions. I know that if I stimulate this area and it becomes active, there is an increased blood supply; there is a shift to the acid side, and so on; and I know that these will affect, not merely the cells that are active, but (like the direct current that then or there appears) cells that lie in the region, whether or not they have themselves participated, and that this will alter the threshold of those cells.

These happen to be problems that I have worked with and I am working with now, along with the noble metal potentials or oxidation reduction potentials. I am also working on the thermal changes. All these things will smear results. They rob the system of some of its degrees of freedom without conveying information. They are the kinds of things that would arise if we had to build our electronic devices and keep them in tubs of salt water. I regard them, by and large, for my purposes, as secondary affairs to be worried about, as I worry about the isolation of the paths to ground, so that all of the grounded side of an instrument is free of troublesome voltages or currents. Now, the reason for making this distinction as sharp as possible in the face of plenty of evidence that the smearing occurs, is that we are dealing with something that has a field-like property. My reason for treating it in the manner in which I have treated it is this. It compels one so to state his theory that he can account for these changes by the digital mechanisms; that is, so that he can contrive a digital device to account for each of these. This at once increases his ability to handle his digital machine. It was clearly shown in our first paper, I believe, that these field-like processes—facilitation and extinction—could be handled by sticking in hypothetical nets, because once a system is, in this sense, quantized anywhere, it might as well be quantized everywhere. This keeps the theory clean.

The next question that I want to try to meet is one which is also very tough to state. The cortex, to my mind, is a vast computing machine. I see no reason why a deeper structure may not assign to any particular part of it a particular task today, and tomorrow assign that particular task to some other part of it—except insofar as particular portions of the cortex are stimulus-bound by a path right to them from the periphery. Those paths to it are well known now, and they include a large fraction of the total surface of the total switch board of the cortex. To the extent to which the afferent connections define a portion of the cortex as visual, it must handle something to do with vision. It must handle something to do with touch if it is the part to which touch reports. So, to the extent to which a cortex is so bound back to our sense organs, it cannot be swapped part for part. No lower mechanism can assign to the visual cortex the job of receiving impulses directly from the ears; they only go to the auditory mechanism. But, apart from that, I see no reason why the lower mechanisms may not perfectly well use one part of the cortex today and another part of the cortex tomorrow for the same function. I do doubt that it does this under ordinary circumstances, but I see no reason why, with damage to one part of the cortex, you wouldn't expect it to do just that. As a matter of fact, I think that you would expect it to do that, just as you would expect that when a man's leg is chopped off, or both legs are chopped off, the man learns to get along on his arms. It is a computing machine—it is sitting there—I see no reason why it can't use this part now and that part then.

I would like to come back now, for a moment, to the question of alpha rhythm, this time in cases of hysterical blindness. A hysterically blind man may have an alpha rhythm, and he may have the alpha rhythm with his eyes wide open, and he may have it when you present him with this, that, or the other thing to look at. He doesn't see, of course, but he reacts to it correctly in other ways; however, as far as he is concerned, he doesn't see it, and he may have a very nice alpha all of this time. Yet in the case of the next hysterically blind individual you check, it may be that the minute he opens his eyes, his alpha is gone. Now, I don't think that this hysterical blindness is something that you can pin on any one part of the system. I don't think that when you throw out the works and say, "I shall not see," that you have to do it in the visual cortex. You may, or you may do it somewhere else, so you may block out alpha or you may fail to block out alpha. And I don't think that when we deal with functions of any great order of complexity, we stand too much of a chance of finding the particular part of the cortex where that is being done, for it can be done now here, now there, except for the sensory projections upon it.

Now, let me contrast this with the answer to the second question that was asked of me, as to why was I so very much worried about the descending systems and so little concerned with the ascending systems. I am worried about the descending systems for this reason. There is no direct path from the cerebral cortex to a motor horn cell known to me. The motor horn cell whose process goes out to the muscle, if it signals to the muscle, has one and only one consequence in the muscle, but, sitting around the motor horn cells themselves, are sacs of internuncials playing around and onto the motor horn cells. To the sacs of the internuncials come stuff, information or impulses, over the dorsal roots, stuff from other parts of the spinal cord, stuff from the brain stem, and so on. The cortex, to a certain extent, tries to take over these other structures by sending signals to them along the way, but its final chore of doing anything in the periphery is achieved only by playing upon the cells which are already going according to ways of their own which are adjusted to the world over hosts of channels. Therefore, what comes out when the cortex starts doing something is by no means simply determined by what goes down from the cortex. That turns out to be actually a small contributory factor to the totality of what is playing upon the motor horn cell. Now, these lower affairs have often very persistent behavior which lasts for a matter of minutes, so that what the cortex does when it starts off something at one time, and then goes to do something else afterwards, is to have to play on systems with enormous (I want to call it inertia) tendencies to overshoot—tendencies to persist in activity. That is why I am worried about the descending system. The ascending system, for the most part, does not have this type of complexity. It has a fairly simple relay system on the way up.

Now, again, I want to make this point very clear. I'm greatly worried about the fact that at the present time we keep trying to assign things to the cerebral cortex that are being done not in it but elsewhere. The reason that we want to assign it to cortex is that if we smash cortex, we don't get it. I feel as though we tried to put the whole organism into the cortex.

The reason I want a clear theory is this. I see people who are insane or who are neurotic. I do not believe that even if you took the best psychoanalysts in the world, and they were a thousand times as numerous as they are, or are likely to become, that there would be enough of them to go around to readjust the neurotics alone, using only auditory afferents to make the adjustments. As a matter of fact, I believe that more and more, we will come to the use of interruptions of the circuit action of the nervous system by drugs, or by electrical stimulation, or by surgery; and the question is, if we want to interrupt something, where is that something happening? How can we interrupt it, and if we do interrupt it, how can we reinstate circuit action that is adaptive? That is why I want this theory, because I hope that it will guide me in placing electrodes so as to find out what is going on where.

Have I left out any crucial questions?

DR. BROSIN: I think that Dr. Gerard is in a position to see, in a judicious way, the trend of the discussion to date, and since the last three speakers have moved the locus of interest a good deal, I wonder if Dr. Gerard would give us a brief summary of what he thinks the vectors have been.

DR. GERARD: I would like to say, first, that I cannot recall attending a meeting of this sort which has gone so happily and so constructively and with such concentrated brilliance. It has been a privilege to be permitted to participate.

The main problem we are attacking is that of correlating behavior with the mechanisms for that behavior. There have been three major approaches by the speakers. There has been an examination of machines, of their basic properties and the logic concerning them, and an heroic attempt made by Dr. von Neumann to see to what extent their general properties apply to those of the nervous system, and to what extent, therefore, they might effectively guide our thinking about the mechanics of the behavior of this most complicated machine. There has been discussion of the nervous system, of the properties of neurons, of their spatial relations, their electrical attributes, and their interactions in groups. And there has been a rational approach, relating various logics to the behavior of the nervous system, which attempted, in a way, to synthesize both of the others. I couldn't help thinking, as Warren McCulloch was making his further statement just now, of how history repeats itself. Some century ago, George Boole became interested in his algebra of logic with the hope that, since the human mind made logic, a study of the laws of logic would necessarily reveal the functions of the human mind and ultimately of the brain. He was perhaps a little more naïve in his time than we are today. He was certainly not aware of, or at least did not give adequate attention to, the non-rational elements of behavior.

Dr. McCulloch just stated that he is interested in devising a theory that would account for the brain as a calculating machine. Several of the questions raised in the discussion have asked about these other aspects. What about the non-rational side? What about the urge for the machine to calculate? What about the drive, so striking in some of the men in this symposium, which, perhaps even more than the elegance of the calculating machine, determines whether or not something worth while comes out of the system in the course of its lifetime? If one wishes to allocate those other aspects to a different box than the cortex, that is perhaps permissible, but it does not resolve the problems that seem to remain.

With calculating, there come inevitably the problems of learning and memory. There has been much discussion of them, and I hesitate to introduce, at this time, any new factual material; but it might be interesting again to make a glissando over the various types of memory that have been suggested. I am always suspicious when I find myself putting things into sharp compartments and saying, "This is this, and that is that." I don't think nature loves a wall. Some experiments have been reported, by Reynolds particularly, on a type of memory in the nervous system which seems intermediate between the reverberating type and the permanent type. At least, if it be reverberating, it is certainly over far longer times that we ordinarily associate with reverberation. He came to it from problems of pain and relates it to causalgia.

Symmetrical teeth with symmetrical defects in a person's jaw were given dental treatment. On one side the filling was done with great care against trauma and pain, on the other side, with a minimum of this desirable care. In nearly all those patients, severe referred pain developed on the traumatized side. This could be elicited routinely by pricking the opening to the antrum of the maxilla. The sensitivity and referred pain lasted for months, but was immediately and irreversibly abolished by a brief period of conduction block of the nerve from that tooth. Some kind of central overactivity, of inflammation if you will, was able to persist for long periods of time apparently under minimal peripheral reinforcement.

As to the mechanisms for establishing these important behavior attributes, it seems to me that we have wandered in our discussion over a number of hierarchies—the molecular, the neuronal, the cerebral—and the question has arisen whether we need something beyond—the man or the observer—to know what is happening in all of those. This last question can safely be left to the remaining periods of the symposium.

We all agree, I believe, that molecular events are critical in determining neuronal behavior. We all agree that neuronal events are critical in determining the total behavior of the nervous system itself. The discussion has focused mainly on this step. Dr. McCulloch has explored it from the particular viewpoint of the nervous system as a digital machine, functioning exclusively in terms of quanta, of the nerve impulses which are or are not discharged by particular neurons under particular conditions. Others have emphasized other kinds of relationships, of the analogical type. The real question being asked, I believe, is whether, in addition to a rigid hierarchy of interaction from molecular to neuronal to total performance, there can also be a direct influence from the molecular level to the molar level.

$$\overbrace{\text{Molecular} \rightarrow \text{Neuronal} \rightarrow \text{Cortical}}^{?} \rightarrow \text{Man}$$
$$(\text{C.N.S.})$$

This question is also involved in the one of whether neurons can interact with each other to form some sort of total functioning unit by mechanisms in addition to the simple quantal discharge of elements.

At the one extreme, the position could be taken that all that happens in the nervous system depends on digital machines and unitary discharges. At the other extreme, the position could be taken that these are rather trivial in the functioning of the nervous system, having to do with the more routine activities controlling movement and the like; but that all the more complicated functions depend on analogical behavior, involving chemicals, electrical fields, spontaneous changes, which might act in many other ways than as a scansion mechanism. Some might say that these are the power determinants of the more complicated types of behavior. I sincerely doubt, however, that anyone in the room would take either of those extreme positions. Rather, we are all prepared to recognize that both elements enter into the picture. The point of disagreement would certainly be about the relative importance of the various mechanisms and their relative significance in particular aspects of total behavior. That is as far as I should go at this time.

I was a bit shocked by Dr. McCulloch's comment, a moment ago, that all the other phenomena are merely degradations in the functioning of a beautiful digital mechanism. I really don't think that he believes that, and perhaps I misunderstood; for the very alpha rhythm that he uses as his scanning device is non-digital. In any event, the speakers who are to follow will surely emphasize these other aspects, the mass action effects and the potential fields, and we have already had a considerable attention to the chemical aspects, which likewise transcend the simple matter of discharge of impulses along neurons. We can confidently look forward to equally stimulating and provocative periods in the remainder of the symposium.

DR. VON NEUMANN: I would like to bring up something that I consider remarkable and something which I think did not come out very explicitly except in one remark of Dr. McCulloch's, and I would like to emphasize it. I think that in regard to the great flexibility, there are few symptoms—if one thinks of the functioning of the nervous system and compares it with the functioning of very complicated automata—which are very conspicuous in the case of the nervous system and very conspicuously absent in any automaton that we know of, which may be easily related with each other and related with the circumstances which one ought to expect to emerge at this level of complication. It is very obvious that the brain differs from all artificial automata that we know; for instance, in the ability to reconstruct itself (as in the case of mechanical damage). It is always characterized by a very great flexibility in the sense that animals which look reasonably alike and do the same thing, may do it by rather different cerebral mechanisms. Furthermore, though all humans belong to the same category and do the same things, outwardly, in some cases they are using different cerebral mechanisms for the same things, so there seems to be a flexibility of pathways.

There are some indications (I do not wish to go into them in detail now) that some parts of the organism can act antagonistically to each other, and in evolution it sometimes has more the character of a hostile invasion of one region by another than of evolution proper. I believe that these things have something to do with each other and also with the following. The largest automaton which we know how to plan could consist of something of the order of 10^4 units, and this is already very complicated. By this, I mean the fact that they are still nominally made from blueprints, and, in all cases where an automaton is built, there exists a blueprint for it, and there is somebody around to guarantee that it was built from the blueprint. These things are, however, very marginal. It is probably not true for most automata of this degree of complexity that they are really identical copies of what is on the blueprints. And it is probably no longer even true that there is anybody around who had anything except a somewhat intuitive relation to it. This is increasingly true for complicated machines. No amount of time and skill and reliability in components will change this in an automaton more complicated than this, and they will probably become more and more complicated. There are a hundred thousand to a million parts involved in some of them, and this is still low, compared to the brain. Building will probably be a completely nominal operation, not completely controlled by what one finds in blueprints. It will have a different relation to the object, and by that relation, I mean this. It has already happened (and it is, of course, just by the introduction of automata into mathematics that it begins to happen) that you are no longer thinking about the subject, but thinking about an automaton which would handle the subject. It has already happened in the introduction of mass production into industry that you are no longer producing the product, but you are producing something which will produce the product. The cut is, at present, never quite sharp, and we still maintain some kind of relation with the ultimate thing that we want. Probably the relationship is getting looser. It is not unlikely that if you had to build an automaton now you would plan the automaton, not directly, but on some general principles which concern it, plus a machine which can put these into effect, and will construct the ultimate automaton and do it in such a way that you yourself don't know any more what the automaton will be. You will do it in such a way that all you will know is what you want to do by it, and by what qualitative methods it can be done, and how to make an automaton which can put this into effect. But as to how the primary thing does it, you need not know. You don't need to know what the result of every particular multiplication was which occurred in the process of solving the equation. If you come to such a principle of construction, all that you need plan and understand in detail is the primary automaton, and what you must furnish to it is a rather vaguely defined matrix of units; for instance, 10^{10} neurons which swim around in the cortex. But the thing becomes functioning only by being organized by the primary thing, and it is only the primary thing that you need plan. Then you begin to have this trait; you do not simply build a primary machine to build a secondary one and then separate them. If you do not separate them but they stay in contact with each other, and if the functioning of the secondary machine presupposes that its contact is a primary one, then, I think that it is achievable that the thing can be watched by the primary automaton and be continuously reorganized when the need arises. I think that if the primary automaton functions in parallel, if it has various parts which may have to act simultaneously and independently on separate features, you may even get symptoms of conflict. Also, through that, since the

140

secondary matrix is introducing things which are probably not rigor-ously defined in all details, the same primary automaton in two cases may not produce exactly the same structure. And, if the planning is well done, there will probably be a very high probability that the secondary thing will function the same way in all cases; but there will not be certainty, and, if you concentrate on marginal effects, you may observe the ensuing ambiguities. I just wanted you to realize that though these notions are vague, they indicate phenomena of this character. Especially when you go to much higher levels of complexity, it is not unreasonable to expect symptoms of this kind.

Through the Den
of the Metaphysician

Warren S. McCulloch

ARGUMENT

Epistemic questions raised by early physics are theoretically answerable in terms of communication by means of least signals that are propositions on the move in computing machines. We can know only the past, and information, being negative entropy, can only decrease in passage. Requirement of coincidence of signals at a relay decreases the logical probability of a signal in it and so increases the chance that its signal corresponds to something in the world. But to suppose input signals true is the superstition of causality. Attempts to extend the domain of implication into the future may always be thwarted, hence the notion of the will, which for moral responsibility must pass into the deed. Among deeds, words stand for universals which correspond to configurations of signals; without closed circuits, they refer only to one past instant. But reverberations patterned after some fact preserve its form and introduce existential operators for times past. Thus, active memory recognizes things new to us in the world. Reflexes, say by centering forms to be seen, or automatic volume controls within the brain, say by bringing afferent signals to a fixed mean frequency, and appetitive circuits over targets outside the body, all reduce the given through a series of transformations to the canonical one among its many possible exemplars. This one serves as the original in the cave of the sun. Finally, the brain, given any item, may form all of its transforms belonging to some group and assigning arbitrary values to presence or absence of excitation at all points and times in the structure wherein the transforms are made. Sum these values. A set of such invariant sums constitutes an Aristotlean abstraction. By detecting noncongruence of apparent continua of sense awareness, even a system constructed of leasts can form the universal of "in-between" and propose the Eleatic riddles.

By projecting universals as expected regularities of all future experiments, it can frame hypotheses in order ultimately to disprove them. It can build bigger and better brains, but what it has are sufficient to guide it through the very den of the metaphysician.

Through the Den of the Metaphysician

ANY AMERICAN who comes to the University of Virginia with matter philosophical must feel a bit as if he were bringing coal to Newcastle. Fortunately, most of this matter has been mined rather recently in America. We are again in one of those prodigious periods of scientific progress — in its own way like the pre-Socratic period to which we are still indebted for the crisp formulation of our physical problems and, consequently, for our epistemological quandry. Anyone who has had the good fortune to listen to Wiener and von Neumann and Rosenblueth and Pitts wrestling with the problems of modern computing machines that know and want has a strange sense that he is listening to a colloquy of the ancients. But they would be the first to tell you that they themselves were drunk with an American wine of an older vintage; they quote liberally from Charles Peirce and from Josiah Willard Gibbs. These men have altered our metaphysics by altering our physics. It is epistemology that is most affected, for it is the physics of communication which is today receiving an adequate, theoretical treatment. For the first time in the history of science we know how we know and hence are able to state it clearly.

Physiologists, working on the central nervous system, have long had such a goal in mind. Rudolph Magnus, inspired by Immanuel Kant, made his last great lecture one on "the physiology of the *a priori*," by which he meant the go of those mechanisms that determine for us the three-dimensional nature of our world, its axes and its angles, and that give to us our sense of velocity and acceleration, from which he held our notion of time to be in large measure derived. Perhaps the most notable attempt of this sort was by Sir Charles Sherrington, entitled *Man on His Nature,* for, near the end of a life spent on studying the ways of the brain, he was forced to the conclusion that "in this world, Mind goes more ghostly than a ghost." The reason for his failure was simply that his physics was not adequate to the problem that he had undertaken. That has so regularly been the shortcoming of scientists who would have approached this problem, that even Clerk Maxwell, who wanted nothing more than to know the relation between thoughts and the molecular motions of the brain, cut short his query with the memorable phrase, "but does not the way to it lie through the very den of the metaphysician, strewn with the bones of former explorers and abhorred by every man of science?" Let us peacefully answer the first half of his question "Yes," the second half "No," and then proceed serenely.

Our adventure is actually a great heresy. We are about to conceive of the knower as a computing machine. That is not a new heresy. It has already been prejudged by Dryden in *The Hind and the Panther,* when he says,

> And if they think at all, 'tis sure no higher
> Than matter, set in motion, may aspire.

I believe that he is correct, but I am not sure that that may not be high enough. I have no intention of burdening you with the detail of the construction of the computing machine, whether these be man-made or begotten. The latter are my daily business. My problem differs from that of the men who build computing machines only in this — that I am confronted by the enemy's machine. I have not been told and must learn what it is, what it does, and how it does it. It is a complicated computing machine consisting of 10^{10} relays. Each of these relays receives signals from other relays. Each on receipt of an appropriate signal — or group of signals — emits a signal. It is my business to learn how these relays are connected one to another, what it takes to fire a given relay, how long after receipt of a signal it will send a signal, and how a signal received can prevent a relay from responding to a second signal otherwise sufficient.

But we must first be prepared for the kind of world we now invade. It is a world, for Heraclitus, always "on the move." I do not mean merely that every relay is itself being momentarily destroyed and re-created like a flame, but I mean that its business is with information which pours into it over many channels, passes through it, eddies within it, and emerges again to the world. Surely Heraclitus would feel at home with such a knower. Paradoxes raised by such a conceit of the world have always led, through Parmenidean unity and Eleatic riddles, to a Democritean multiplicity, that is, to one in which the stuff of the world is a set of atoms — of indivisibles, of leasts — which go batting about in the void. Whenever they make their appearance they bring with them Chaos. Therefore, it may at first sound paradoxical that every modern computing machine of any great size or scope works in a Democritean manner. Again, I do not merely refer to its being constructed out of chemical atoms, but I mean that is is a machine with a least count. Its signals are quantized. Each either happens or does not happen. It does not half happen. To this general rule, the nervous system is no exception. Its least signal, or nervous impulse, is an all-or-none event. If a neuron emits a signal, it does all that it can then do. Thus, not merely is the structure of the nervous system quantized in neurons, but its action is quantized in their impulses, or least signals. Surely Democritus would claim kinship with a knower whose actions were thus atomic — perhaps more readily because there is at present no reason to suspect that these atomic signals differ significantly save as to when and where they occur. Hence, all that a least signal can say to the next relay is that the relay that emitted that signal had been adequately excited. From this it follows that whatever quality may be anywhere detected in the universe by our knower must depend upon the *figure* of these least signals in time and space. Moreover, since every relay has a characteristic delay, given enough relays, it is always possible to convert a figure of impulses given simultaneously in space into a figure of excitation in time over a single relay, or vice versa.

Consider any one relay. At any given time, say a millisecond, it can be in either of two states; that is, it can be transmitting one signal or none. Hence, two independent, or unconnected, relays can be in any one of four states; three in one of eight, four in one of sixteen, etc. That is, of n neurons, the number of possible states is 2^n. It takes one signal, or one unit of information, to determine in which of two states any one relay is in any one relay time. Now if we have a single relay but consider it at two times, then it can be, in the two times together, in any one of 2^2; in three times in 2^3; in four times, 2^4; and so on. Clearly, the same amount of information can be conveyed by n independent relays in one unit of time as can be conveyed by one relay in n units of time. Hence, if we desire to convert a given figure at a one time into a series in time, we need as many units of time as we had independent relays. Note that the unit of information appears with a negative sign in the exponent; that is, given n independent relays, or one relay at n times, one unit of information, by fixing the state of one relay, subtracts one from n, leaving 2^{n-1} states possible.

The *a priori,* or logical, probability that a neuron is in a particular state at a particular time is one-half; that two are in a given state, one-fourth; and so on. Hence, information is exactly the logarithm to the base 2 of the reciprocal of the probability of the state. But this has a peculiarly familiar sound. Gibbs had defined entropy as the logarithm of the probability of the state. In Wiener's words, entropy measures chaos, and information is negative entropy. So, corresponding to the second law of thermodynamics, that entropy must always increase, we can write for any computing machine the corresponding law — information can never increase. This ensures that no machine can operate on the future but must derive its information from the past. It can never do anything with this information except corrupt it. The transmission of signals over ordinary networks of communication always follows the law that deduction obeys, that there can be no more information in the output than there is in the input. The noise, and only the noise, can increase. Therefore, if we are to deal with knowers that are computing machines, we can state this much about them. Each is a device, however complicated, which can only corrupt revelation.

In order to preserve a correct sense of proportion, let me be technical for a moment. The human eye has about one hundred million photoreceptors, whereas it has but one million relays to carry that information to the brain. The whole body contributes another million channels. Thus we may figure approximately three million relays putting information into the nervous system simultaneously. Let us next evaluate the output of the nervous system. To do so we have conceived a piano player performing at top speed, given him a keyboard of one hundred keys, let him strike ten times per second with each of ten fingers with any one of ten strengths, and let his hands each span ten keys. No man can do so much. Yet, when we translated this into the number of all-or-none signals per second, we discovered that it was only three units of information per millisecond.

Today we can estimate the amount of information conveyed by sounds, speech or music, for there is a device which samples the sound every millisecond and sends, at most, three all-or-none signals according to the instantaneous amplitude of the wave. These three decisive signals per millisecond convey the full information, for waves reconstructed from them are indistinguishable from the original sounds.

Thus the over-all reduction in information from input to output of brain is a million to one if we neglect the eyes proper, and a hundred million to one if we include them. What becomes of all that information?

In large measure we use it this way. It is easy to have a relay which will fire only if impulses from two sources arrive almost simultaneously. Such a neuron detects the coincidence of information over the two channels to it, and it responds only in that case in which they agree that something happened. Therefore, the logical, or *a priori,* probability of finding an impulse in it is the product of the probabilities of finding one in each of the afferent pathways singly. That is to say, it is more *improbable.* The chief reason for the enormous reduction from afferent signals to efferent signals is the requirement of coincidence along the way. Every such requirement of coincidence, by reducing the *a priori* probability of a signal in the output, increases the assurance which can be placed in any subsequent signal, for that signal must then be due to coincidence in the world impingent upon our receptors. In short, by throwing away all information that fails to agree with other information, we achieve an immense certainty that what we do observe is due to something in the world. Clearly, we should follow the same procedure in forming our hypotheses. Each should be of minimum logical, or *a priori,* probability so that if it is confirmed in experience, then this is because the world is so constructed.

At this point I should tell you that the limitation of the information in the output is in large measure determined by the effectors themselves. This is the ineluctable corruption of thought in deed. As there remain 10^{10} neurons, or relays, in the central nervous system, it is obviously impossible for any man ever to convey so much as one part in 10^{10} of what is going on in him. Even though he is a poet, the rest of his soul remains his private property. Now we habitually think of our sensations, or any knowledge of the world so derived, as an activity going on in those places in which afferent channels end, but we can demonstrate it only by output over some efferent channel. Consequently, the answer to any particular question, as to whether we did or did not know something, will be dependent upon the particular efferent channels we choose to examine. This is painfully obvious to anyone who deals with diseased brains, for it is often a matter of diagnostic or forensic importance to know whether a man is or is not conscious of his deeds or of things about him. *Conscious* in this context means that he can, then or later, bear witness to those events to which we can also bear witness. In malignant stupors the patient is conscious, in benign, unconscious, but we can determine this only when he is no longer stuporous. The epileptic who is unconscious of his acts is never responsible for them at law, although the acts are so complex and so adjusted to the world about him as to ensure that he is then and there aware of much related detail in what is then adoing.

With all of these limitations and hazards well in mind, let us ask whether a knower so conceived is capable of constructing the physics of the world which includes himself, But, in so doing, let us be perfectly frank to admit that causality is a superstition. By causality I mean any law of necessary connection between events. Let me put that this way, in the old quillet. Nothing is true and not true, nothing false and not false, nothing true and false. Hence, whatever is is either "true or else false"; or else it is "neither true nor false." In the first case it is a proposition; in the second case it is not. It is then impossible truthfully to deny that propositions exist, for either the denial is a proposition, in which case it is false, or else it is not a proposition and, hence, neither true nor false. Yet, that it is impossible to deny its existence truthfully is no assurance that any proposition exists. It remains an assumption that propositions exist. Later it will be apparent that even that assumption is inadequate. If there is to be in the world any knowledge about the world, there must be true propositions about the world. In the world of events a true proposition is an event which materially implies another event — that is, in the simplest case, one which happens only if that other event happened. In the world of physics a true proposition implies what it asserts.

The world of physics is fairly described by Whitehead's "Aether of Events." The world for him is the whole that happens only once; and to be an event is to be some part of that whole. In his description of the relation of whole to part, there are, however, two assumptions which we have ignored in our theory of the action of the computing machine, and it is these assumptions which permit of analytic continuation, a going toward continuity. He supposes that there can exist an event which has no least part, and that if A is a part of C, then there is always an event B, such that A is a part of B and B is a part of C. Apparently a computing machine, quantized as ours, is not built on either of these assumptions. We have supposed a least signal, that is to say, a signal which either occurs or does not occur. That least signal is a proposition "on the move." It is true or else it is false, and it occurs at some particular time and at some particular place. Since the number of relays is finite, these can be ordered and a number assigned to each, and since we can quantize time in units equal to relay time, we can start counting at any particular instant and, by subscripting the number of a relay by a number representing the time of a signal there, we can construct statements in which the signal of a given relay is expressed in terms of those signals which reach it. The resultant calculus is the calculus of atomic propositions of Whitehead and Russell, subscripted for the time of the occurrence of the propositions. Each of these signals is, strictly speaking, an atomic propositional event, which can only be or not be, and, if it is, may be either true or false. Each materially implies its proper antecedents.

Consider for a moment a computing machine in which there are no closed paths, that is, no circuits around which signals may chase their tails. In such a system each signal, implying its antecedents, implies a signal of a relay nearer to the receptors until we arrive ultimately at them. Their signals likewise imply the world impingent on our sense organs. In the strictest sense of the word, what goes on in such a nervous system implies the world impingent upon its sense organs. But note that the domain of implication extends only backward in time. Even if the threshold of every relay were fixed, between the moment at which a given set of impulses started from a spot in our brains to our hands and feet, there might intervene other impulses coming, by shorter paths from the outside world, to our effectors. Thus, in the forward direction, the relation falls short of implication inasmuch as aught else intervenes. In short, our thought does not imply our action but, as we say, only intends it. Perforce we distinguish between futurity and intention. Our notion of our wills has, I believe, arisen from this enforced distinction, and its perennially questioned "freedom" presumably means no more than that we can distinguish between what we intend and some intervention in our action. If I shall do what I will do, then my will is free.

To make this clear, let me return to the quillet. Even an atomic signal asserts that such and such is the case, and it is true only if such and such is the case. If we assume that there are such things as true atomic propositions of the kind called signals, then these are significant propositions as Wittgenstein uses the term; for the truth or falsity of each signal depends upon whether or not that which it asserts occurred. If significant propositions of this kind are to be true, there must be a law of necessary connections between the event which is the proposition and the event which it proposes. But a law of necessary connection among events is causality. In such a world the superstition of causality must first be assumed by anyone who wishes so much to deny it. But, if we have once admitted causality in this sense into the workings of our brains, our significant propositions are determined by our past, and freedom from the past would make no sense. We really want freedom toward the future — freedom from affairs intercurrent between our ideas and our deeds. This is all that is needed to fix our responsibility for those deeds.

Among those deeds are our words, and every word has the flavor of being given "once for all." It bespeaks a universal, idea, or quality, appearing for us in the world. In order for the activity of a nervous system to imply a universal, or idea, we need not merely the calculus of atomic propositions but also logical quantifiers which assert that *all* or *some* x's are such and such; and the question at once arises how these are introduced. Again in Whiteheadian terms, the problem is not one of how we apprehend events but of how we recognize objects. For me, the most difficult part of Whitehead's theory of percipient events is concerned with the notion of primary recognition. How can we come by an idea we did not have before? You will notice that, had our nervous system no closed paths, a signal anywhere within it would mean that something had impinged on a receptor at some particular millisecond prior thereto. *Per contra,* if there exist closed paths around which signals may reverberate, and if the sequence of these signals is patterned after some fact, then the pattern persists in us as long as the signals continue to reverberate. Each time they circle they literally know again, or re-cognize, that which was given but once in their input. This is memory of a kind, and it suffices to free the signals of their reference to a particular time. That circuit knows that such and such happened at some previous time but not at what time. This introduces the existential operator for time — namely, there was some time such that at that time so and so happened. Notice that the tense is past.

Not all human memory is of this kind. While we are young, we may grow new connections. By means of them the ways that led us to our ends become embroidered into the warp and woof of our nervous net, but no kind of memory can do anything which cannot also be done by activity circling in closed paths. Pitts and I have already demonstrated that a machine constructed with such closed paths, as well as open afferents and efferents, can produce any consequence which can be produced from its afferents, that it can compute any computable number, or arrive at any conclusion which follows logically from any finite set of premises. Moreover, to satisfy any doubting Thomas who would thrust his electrodes into the brain, we have shown that any wound or any other alteration of the net, say one acquired by use, can be replaced by the action of a hypothetical unalterable net of unalterable neurons. But injury and learning will differ in one respect; for, in the case of learning, the known afferent channels suffice, whereas, in the case of injury, we require a new afferent channel to initiate an action in our hypothetical net.

Conceive, then, our knower as an unalterable net of unalterable relays. To this net come impulses from the world, and from it impulses go to the world. Within it are not only thoroughfares but circles. Of these we have mentioned only one that will reverberate. It suffices to free us from one particularity, reference to one past time, but there are other closed paths which are important in our knowledge of universals. Their reaction was well described in 1817 when Magendie defined what he called the "reflex" as an activity which began in some part of the body, passed by way of nerves to the central nervous system, whence it was reflected to that same part of the body where it stopped or reversed that process which had given rise to it. Electrical engineers refer to such a circuit action as inverse, or negative, feedback. The anatomy of some of these negative feedbacks was exhibited in 1825 by Sir Charles Bell. The mathematics for handling many of such actions is to be found in Clerk Maxwell's paper "On Governors," given before the Royal Society in 1868. Their properties are well known. Every such circuit pulls toward some particular value of some variable. In the case of reflexes, something, say the length of a muscle or the temperature of the body or the pressure in the artery, is measured by a set of receptors which send impulses to the central nervous system, whence impulses are sent back to those structures to bring them back to the particular state established by the reflex arc. This particular state measured by those receptors is the goal, or aim, or end, in and of the operation of that reflex. By means of these reflexes we achieve dynamic stability in a changing world.

One such circuit frees us from the variations in intensity of stimulation and consequent variation in the number of impulses that would otherwise excite the bark of the brain, called the cerebral cortex. This circuit, unlike the reflex path, lies entirely within the brain. Impulses ascending to the thalamus, or last relay beneath the bark, are passed on to the cortex and from portions of the cortex descend, by a devious path, to the thalamus, where they inhibit the relaying of impulses to the cortex, thus keeping the cortical activity at a nearly constant level. This is an "automatic volume control." It leaves us with a figure of excitation in the cortex which is invariant under fluctuations of the intensity of peripheral stimulation, making it possible for us to determine some aspect of that stimulation regardless of intensity. Hence we detect that there was some intensity of stimulation which was of such and such a figure. In short, it is done for us with respect to intensity what simple reverberation did with respect to time.

Let us next consider the so-called appetitive circuit. It is inverse feedback over a path which extends beyond the body. In the external part of the path is to be found the goal, or target, and the circuit is said to be "inverse over the target." Today one of the best known of these circuits runs through the eye and the brain-stem. It turns the eye automatically toward any object which appears in the periphery of the visual field. By turning the eye so as to bring the image of the thing seen to the center of the receptive surface of the eye, it translates an apparition to a standardized position and hence its projection by means of signals to a standardized place in the bark of the brain. In so doing, it rids the form to be seen of the gratuitous particularity of that position at which it happened first to appear. Because for us the centered apparition established by this reflex is a given one from among the many possible exemplifications, we refer to the process as that of reduction to the canonical position. Every reflexive circuit brings some apparition through a series of positions, intensities, or what-nots to the final canonical one of all the many through which it has progressed. So, in mathematics, if we are given the Pythagorean theorem, we reduce it to the canonical form of the axioms, postulates, and the definitions at the beginning of the book. Having chased it thus back to the cave of the sun, we cry, "Ah-ha," for we have recognized it.

We pass now to another way of securing universals. At first sight it looks altogether dissimilar. It is, in fact, obviously a method of averaging. The epicritic modalities of sensation, for example vision, map the impingent activity of the world on a fine mosaic of cortical relays. The centered form, given by the reflex of the eyes, appears in the input to the visual cortex as the distribution of impulses over a fixed area and about a fixed center. In this portion of the cortex of the brain are actually made all of the possible dilatations and constrictions of the forms impingent upon it. They are limited by the grain of its mosaic. These are then added and relayed, as a set of averages, to the next portion of the brain. Clearly, these averages do not depend upon the size of the particular object that was seen. The image may have been big or small, but since from any given one of them we made all sizes, the size of the original does not affect the averages. The output is size-invariant. This size-invariant has been abstracted from the entire group of dilatations and constrictions and corresponds to the shape regardless of the size. As the former method conforms to Plato's notions as to the origin of ideas, so this recalls Aristotle's notion of the abstraction of ideas from many particular exemplars. Those of you who desire a clear and rigorous statement of this process will find it in the *Group Theory and Quantum Mechanics* of Weil.

Let me oversimplify that statement. We have obtained a group invariant as follows: We have calculated a set of numbers, each of which is, for all transformations belonging to the group, the average of numerical values arbitrarily assigned to the presence or absence of signals at particular points or at particular times. That in which one mechanism obtaining these invariants, or universals, differs grossly from another mechanism lies in that arbitrary manner in which the numerical values are assigned. For example, in the case of the centering reflex, the value *zero* is actually assigned to all translations of the apparition until it is centered. Whereas, in the case of the dilatations and constrictions in the visual cortex, all evidence points to the value one being assigned if a cell situated there was fired then — otherwise zero. We have, then, in the general statement all ways of obtaining universals. Their differences are accidental and depend upon the arbitrary way in which the mechanism assigns the values. At this level, Aristotle's method and Plato's method are peas in the same pod.

There is, of course, *one* limit to the number of times this process can be repeated upon the output of a previous structure. We have only a finite number of relays and finite span of life measured in their unit times. Short of that limit we are, of course, at liberty to have the idea of ideas and the idea of the ideas of ideas, etc. In short, our knower is, in the Spinozistic sense, conscious. Also, he may discover himself among things known to him in his world, and be self-conscious in exactly the same way in which he is conscious of anything else in the world. But all of his ideas, no matter how high-flown, are ultimately reducible to a logic of the lowest level and, even at that lowest level, to a finite number of atomic propositions. He can no more know the infinite than he can know the future. Of course, he may guess the future. He has only to run a correlation (over time) of past events, abstract a universal, and project it upon the future. The projection is always but a guess. The best guess may go wrong. The scientist knows this to his cost; for every hypothesis is a guess as to the outcome of an infinite number of possible experiments. We expect that every hypothesis will be disproved. Surely none can be proved. This is, in fact, its glory; for we know, *when we have* proved it false, that it *was* a significant proposition.

To have proved a hypothesis false is indeed the peak of knowledge, for we extrapolated it out of atomic propositions in the input to our calculating machine. These signals in the input are independent propositions. Any one can be false or true and the rest remain the same, be they true or false. Of no one of them can we ever know that it is true or false. These are merely revelations, and we cannot look the giver of the data in the teeth. How, out of such data, finite and discrete, have we been able to construct the notions of analytical continuity which are so clearly requisite for the Whiteheadian analysis of the physicist's world?

The problem of analytic continuation is pointed up in the paradoxes of Zeno of Elea. We require a meaning of "in-between" quite different from that given in any single experience. The world given in experience is always this up to where it is that. The "continuum of sense awareness" is not continuous in the mathematical sense. Where we have no receptor, we pick up no impulse. That point has no connection to the cortex. It is not represented directly by any impulse arriving there. We are not directly aware of our ignorance. For a moment conceive the same portion of the world given in two of these speciously continuous modalities of sensibility. In each the world appears to be continuous. But there is no reason why that which is continuous in the one modality should fit that which is continuous in the other modality — no *a priori* reason! Most of the time the continua fail to be congruent, and any circuit, subsequent to these recipients, which can detect the failure of congruence will generate a meaning of in-between. This meaning of in-between is just as good a universal as any other; for it we can construct an invariant. We have but to give it voice and, like God or a baby, cry "Do it again, do it again, don't stop," and we have generated the fundamental notion required for analytic continuation. For the paradoxes of Zeno of Elea, seen motion appears continuous through seen space likewise continuous. We have but to abstract the required universals, and we are able to propose the paradoxes.

I do not believe that anything more is expected of us. A stick thrust in water felt straight and looked bent to a Greek. The sun moved for the inquisition, the earth for Galileo. Light is a wave for Schrödinger and a particle for Heisenberg. But even the last have had their Dirac. The seeming contradictions vanish in the grace of greater knowledge. We have learned that the answer depends upon how we ask the question. And we have learned to ask the question so as to get an answer of a kind that we can use. Knowledge itself presented no great problems to the Greek mind until it had invented its theoretical physics in terms of insensible reals. It was these that bothered Galileo and Descartes.

To suppose the world continuous instead of discrete did not help Descartes. He was willing to admit that an automaton might be constructed which could do everything that a man does. Yet, to this automaton he would deny Mind. Doubting, knowing, and thinking seemed to him beyond its scope. Now that we have constructed automata which, like us, can compute any computable number, can formulate clear ideas, and, by inverse feedback, have purposes of their own, built into them as ours are born in us, we are confronted with the humbling prospect of the work of our own hands — machines more steadfast in their purposes, more supple in the execution of these purposes and in their modifications for good cause, capable of learning and thinking far beyond us, at present in certain fields only but, in time to come, in any field for which we care to construct them. As yet we have not made them capable of multiplying their kind. That would be for us the final mistake.

In closing, let me remark that I am not using knowledge in any restricted sense. The propositions with which I have concerned myself are the significant propositions of machines, those that propose something external to the event which is the proposition. But if instead of relays that wait for signals to trip them, I install in any computing machine a relay which will fire itself each millisecond, I can introduce into it all tautological propositions. To my mind, they fall short of being knowledge, which I look upon as an activity that says "such and such is the case" and such and such is the case! These propositions are primary and atomic. We cannot know that we know them. A lie is as truly a proposition as is a truth, and their independence prevents any test of truth. In hypotheses, proved false, we are at least aware of the error of our ways. For a scientist that must be sufficient. If we cannot rest content with our brains, we can at least construct machines which, like them,

> If they think at all 'tis sure no higher
> Than matter put in motion may aspire.

I am convinced that that will be sufficient to guide me through the very den of the metaphysician, strewn with the bones of the former explorers. One of these is surely the femur of Immanuel Kant — his confusion of the empiric with the epistemological ego. This supported him on the solid ground of science while his skull was highest in the realm of theory. Another is certainly his skull, which housed his computing machine, for the net of his relays embodied his "synthetic *a priori.*" If my bones are to fall beside them, I hope aftercomers will recognize my spine. Its joints are the superstition of a necessary connection between events — called causality. I humbly submit that it is but a reincarnation of Saint Thomas' faith that God did not give us our senses to fool us. It is enough that this trust in the goodness of God cannot truthfully be denied. So, at least in Virginia, the den of the metaphysician seems curiously like the cave of the sun, and hence like home.

Mysterium Iniquitatis *of Sinful Man Aspiring into the Place of God*

Warren S. McCulloch

D'ARCY THOMPSON used to tell of his encounter with a biologist who had described a nearly spherical diatom bounded entirely by hexagons thus:

"But," I said, "Euler showed that hexagons alone cannot enclose a volume." To which the innominate biologist retorted, "That proves the superiority of God over mathematics."

Euler's proof happened to be correct, and the observations inaccurate. Had both been right, far from proving God's superiority to logic, they would have impugned His wit by catching Him in a contradiction. Our first concern is to avoid the impropriety of such solecisms.

Our second resembles it slightly. Newton, Jeans, and Planck have used "God" to account for things they could not explain. Biologists, ignorant of mechanisms underlying functions, have introduced "Nature," "Vital Force," "Nervous Energy," "the Unconscious," or some other pseudonym for God. Each of these supposititious explanations, to quote Sir Thomas Browne, "puts the honest Father to the refuge of a miracle."

Today no biological process is fully understood in terms of chemistry and physics. The facts are unknown to us. Few chemical properties are yet reduced to the physical relations of atomic constituents. The mathematics is too cumbersome. Physics itself wants a unified field theory and doubts determinism in atomic processes.

So much for Comte's hierarchical unity of science! At last we are learning to admit ignorance, suspend judgment, and forego the *explicatio ignoti per ignotium*—"God"—which has proved as futile as it is profane. Instead we seek mechanisms, for two purposes.

Let us consider them one at a time. As soon as we devise a machine that will do what has to be explained, we divest the superstitious of any seeming warrant to his miracle. It is enough to show that, if certain physical things were assembled in a certain way, then, by the law of physics, the assemblage would do what is required of it. So imaginary engines led Carnot to entropy and Maxwell to his electromagnetic equations, instead of to miracles. Both machines, to their inventors, were more than metaphors for mathematics. But actual engines proved Carnot's a homolog, whereas the elastic ether's being chimerical left Maxwell's a mere analog. Yet, because each showed there could be a machine that turned the trick, it would be best to see them—at least from the logical point of view—as existential devices.

By these means biologists have exorcised ghosts from the body, whence they went to the head, like bats to the belfry. To drive them thence, my mentor, Pike, spent his life replacing them by simple engines to ring all the changes on the chimes. He looked on the evolution of the nervous system, on its ontogeny, on learning, even on reflexes, as spontaneous variants that survive in the competition to trap available energy and thus secure energetic *Lebensraum* in the entropic degeneration of sunshine to the *Wärmetod*. Whether atomic or molecular chaos produces a sport, its thanks are due to chance, not to divine intervention in its behalf. These notions do not constitute mechanistic hypotheses but exhort us to construct them. Call them metaphysical if you will—in this good sense, that they prescribe ways of thinking physically about affairs called mental and relegated to the whims of spirit manifold. I am of Pike's persuasion.

But most people have heard of cybernetics from Norbert Wiener or his followers. Narrowly defined it is but the art of the helmsman, to hold a course by swinging the rudder so as to offset any deviation from that course. For this the helmsman must be so informed of the consequences of his previous acts that he corrects them—communication engineers call this "negative feedback"—for the output of the helmsman decreases the input to the helmsman. The intrinsic governance of nervous activity, our reflexes, and our appetites exemplify this process. In all of them, as in the steering of the ship, what must return is not energy but information. Hence, in an extended sense, cybernetics may be said to include the timeliest applications of the quantitative theory of information.

The circuit in a servomechanism may include, as we hold it does in man's head, complicated machines of calculation. Turing showed that one having a finite number of parts and states, scanning, marking, and erasing one of four symbols at a time on an infinite tape, can compute any computable number. The first part of the tape serves to prescribe which number his general machine shall compute. Pitts and I showed that brains were Turing machines, and that any Turing machine could be made out of neurons. For this we used a calculus of atomic propositions subscripted for the time when all-or-none impulses signalized them in the relays constituting the net, or the machine. In brains the relays are neurons, and the blueprint of the net is the anatomy of their connections.

Since Hilbert arithmetized logic, the calculation of any computable number is equivalent to deducing any conclusion that follows from a finite set of premises, or to detecting any figure in an input, or to having any general idea that can be induced from our sensations. Existential operations can be introduced into our calculus by inserting in the net any circuitry that will secure invariants under groups of transformations. Memories, general ideas, and even Spinozistic consciousness, the idea of ideas, can thus be generated in robots. These robots, even simple ones having but half a dozen relays, may, without inconsistency, show that circularity of preference, or of choice, called the value anomaly which—contra Plato—precludes a common measure of "the good."

Elsewhere I have shown not merely that computing machines by playing chess may learn to play better than their designers, as Ashby would have it, but that they may learn the rules of the game when these are given only ostensively. This ensures their ability to generate their own ethic— not merely to be good, like the virtuous savage, because they are so made that they cannot break the rules, nor, like the gospeled or inspired, because they were so instructed by their fellows or their creator. Unlike solitaire, chess can be enjoyed only by a society of men or machines whose desire to play exceeds their desire to win. This is easily determined by connecting their two feedback loops in such a way that the former dominates the latter. I grant that these complicated machines resemble the elephant or some other "Colossus of Nature" rather than ants, within whose "narrow engines there is more curious mathematic; and the civility of these little citizens more neatly sets forth the wisdom of their Maker. . . ." Yet, that we can design ethical robots, who may even invent games that are more fun than chess, is enough to prove that man's moral nature needs no supernatural source. Darwin observed, but Spencer failed to note, that success in the game of life, and so survival, is "often most promoted by mutual assistance."

Hence the crucial question: Can machines evolve? John von Neumann suggests that we are familiar only with simple machines that can make only simpler ones, so that we suppose this is a general law, whereas, in fact, complicated ones can make others still more complicated. Given a suitable Turing machine, coupled to a duplicator of tape and to an assembly of parts from a common store, it could make one like itself, put in a duplicate of its own tape, and cut loose its replica ready to make a new one like itself. There are now two. Their number will double with each generation. Variations compatible with this reproduction, regardless of their sources, will lead to evolution; for, though simpler mutations must fail, some more complicated will survive. Von Neumann, Wheeler, and Quastler have computed the required complexity and find that, for general Turing machines to survive, they must be about as complex as a totipotent protein molecule, which is the simplest thing we know that does reproduce itself. Totipotent protein molecules are the littlest citizens. Man has not yet found their mechanical prescription. He has made amino acids by shaking together CO_2, NH_3, and H_2O in the light, and he has made polypeptides from amino acids. When he makes proteins by sticking these together, he can better estimate the probability of their formation by chance in evolutionary epochs. If the civility of these little citizens only sets forth an evolved efficiency in forestalling the *Wärmetod,* we may forego the astronomer's cry against their Maker:

> What? From insensate nothing to evoke
> A sensate something to resent the yoke
> Of unpermitted pleasure under pain
> Of everlasting punishment if broke:
> Oh, were that justice and His holy right.

Following Wiener we estimate the complexity of a machine or an organism to be the number of yes-or-no decisions—we call them bits of information—necessary to specify its organization. This is the logarithm (base 2) of the reciprocal of the probability of that state and, hence, its negative entropy.

But Wiener has forerunners as well as followers in Cambridge. Charles Peirce first defined "information," his "third kind of quantity," as " 'the sum of synthetical propositions in which the symbol is subject to predicate,' antecedent or consequent." Of Peirce's friends, Holmes, in his *Mechanism in Mind and Morals,* excuses only volition from the sway of mechanical causation; and James, in several places, attributes the vagaries of the will to chance. Perhaps a New England conscience may afford freedom to its neighbors' wills, as Donne says we give "souls unto women only to make them capable of damnation." But surely he is damned already whose frame and fortune foredoom his failure. That he is the machine at fault ensures that he and his neighbors hold him responsible. The common law construes intention from the deed, and a windmill that kills a man is deodand. Every psychiatrist who cares for the well-being of his patient comes to look on a man's sins as his misfortune of birth or breeding and is glad that his self-righteous brethren cannot climb into God's mercy seat.

Sin, in its widest sense, is but to miss a mark; and surely most of us are too familiar with self-guiding missiles to doubt that we can endow them with computers and target-seeking servos whereby to hit or miss their prey. The components of these circuits are too gross and inefficient for us to package in a head what fills the nose of a V-2 rocket. But given miniature efficient relays comparable to neurons, we could build machines as small to process information as fast and multifariously as a brain. The hardest thing to match is man's storage of bits of incidental information, but we can put an upper bound on that. Following Craik's lead, man's acquisition of such information has been measured and never found to exceed a hundred bits per second of sustained reception. Were it 10 times more throughout his life, he could store no more than 10^{13} such bits. Heinz von Förster arrived at a similar figure by noting that the mean half-life of a trace in human memory is half a day, and the access to it over only 10^6 channels, with an access time of about 1 millisecond. Hence, a man will come to equilibrium with far fewer traces than there are junctional buttons on our neurons. Moreover, von Förster showed that if, by regenerating traces, we retained some 5 percent of all our uptake, the energy required for this remembering would be only a fraction of 1 percent of that which flows through brains. This answers Bertrand Russell's only serious question about the peculiar causality of human thinking. Ashby, in his book *Design for a Brain,* proposed a mechanism of adaptation that avoids the fallacy of simple location of a trace and makes the thing we are to seek in a given brain and its multiple locations depend upon the sequence of its learnings.

To the theoretical question, "Can you design a machine to do whatever a brain can do?" the answer is this: "If you will specify in a finite and unambiguous way what you think a brain does do with information, then we can design a machine to do it." Pitts and I have proved this constructively. But can you say what you think brains do?

In 1953, in the symposium on consciousness of the Institute for the Unity of Science, Wilder Penfield used the term, as we do in forensic medicine, to mean precisely that his patient at a later date bore witness to what he also bore witness to as having happened then and there. Of course we can make machines do that. The questioner meant "Was the patient aware that it was he himself that did it?" which is self-consciousness, requiring but simple reflective circuitry. The physiologist would have settled the argument by defining *consciousness* to mean "responsiveness to present stimulation with a lag called latency"—a trait that few things lack!—but a psychoanalyst explained to me that "a patient is conscious of what he once felt only if at a later time he can verbalize it"—which is to say, "he is conscious of those things of which he says he is conscious"—and this requires only a machine that sometimes answers "yes" to this question. That is too easy; and if all we mean by consciousness is this ghost of half of mind-stuff, we may forget it all as just a pseudo-question. But I am sure that for every empirical scientist to whom existence is as primary as it is to a true Thomist what lurks behind this ghostly facade is the old Aristotelian "substance." To Helmholtz, it appeared as the *"locus observandi";* to Einstein as "the frame of reference of the observer"; to Russell as "the egocentric particular involved in denotation." For MacKay it yields the distinction between the languages of the observer and of the actor. Granted that we have objective knowledge of others, and substantial knowledge only of ourselves, this only proves us to be like every other thing, and divine, if you will, only as a part of all that exists. It does not demonstrate the metaphysical self-sufficient mind or soul with the unique property of perception. However one defines feeling, perception, consciousness, substantial knowledge—so the definition is finite and unambiguous—each and all are well within the tricky scope of circuitry. So much for the existential purport of machines!

Their second *raison d'être* is to generate hypotheses. A mechanism that fits all our data is one of an infinite number of possible explanations of our findings. It always has properties disclosed by deduction and subject to the test of experience. It may even lead to

162

an invention. Contemporary opinion, in Haldane's phrase, regards "every physical invention as a blasphemy and every biological invention as a perversion." This is less a matter of heresy than of "radical indecency." Plowing, milking, alcohol, coffee, tobacco, birth control, and artificial insemination are only the by-products of biological knowledge. The chromosome shuffling of Mendelian genes, which has stood the test longer than any other equally significant biological discovery, never offended our sensibilities, although it lets chance materially dictate our constitution. Only recently have we come to the data that set limits to the applicability of Mendel's law.

Each hypothesis predicts the outcome of numberless experiments. Hence, though no hypothesis can be proved, it may ultimately be disproved. A good one is so specific that it can be disproved easily. This requires a minimum of logical, or *a priori,* probability compatible with the data. I have sometimes boasted that my pet notion of the mechanism responsible for our seeing shape regardless of size was disproved by MacKay's experiment in my own laboratory. What grieves me is that neither I nor anyone else has so far imagined another specific mechanism to account for form vision.

Perhaps in this "best of all possible worlds" neurophysiologists, like physicists, will be compelled to call their shots "on a cloth untrue, with a twisted cue and elliptical billiard balls." Russell has already noted that the explanation of mind has become more materialistic only as our matter has become less material. So we seem to be groping our way toward an indifferent monism. Everything we learn of organisms leads us to conclude not merely that they are analogous to machines but that they are machines. Man-made machines are not brains, but brains are a very ill-understood variety of computing machines. Cybernetics has helped to pull down the wall between the great world of physics and the ghetto of the mind.

Moreover, its analysis of nervous activity reveals two limits to our aspirations—our double *ignorabimus.* The impulses we receive from our receptors embody primary atomic propositions. Each impulse is an event. It happens only once. Consequently, these propositions are primary in the sense that each is true or else false, quite apart from the truth or falsity of any other. Were this not so, they would be redundant or, in the limit, as devoid of information as tautologies. But this means that the truth of each

163

and every one cannot be tested. The empiricist, like the Thomist, must believe that God did not give him his senses in order to deceive him.

Moreover man, like his inventions, is subject to the second law of thermodynamics. Just as his body renders energy unavailable, so his brain corrupts the revelation of his senses. His output of information is but one part in a million of his input. He is a sink rather than a source of information. The creative flights of his imagination are but distortions of a fraction of his data.

Finally, as he has perforce learned from the inadequacies of his best hypotheses, ultimate universal truths are beyond his ken. To demand them is the arrogance of Adam; to come short of them is the impotence of sorry man; but to fancy them known were very ΰβρις. Obviously, he may know something about the past, although he cannot change it. The future he may affect, but he may never know it. Were this otherwise, he could beat the second law and build machines to operate on future information. So we may conclude that we fear no analogy between machines and organisms, either for existential purport or for generating hypotheses, and that we are safe to admit that organisms, even brains, are machines.

So long as we, like good empiricists, remember that it is an act of faith to believe our senses, that we corrupt but do not generate information, and that our most respectable hypotheses are but guesses open to refutation, so long may we "rest assured that God has not given us over to thraldom under that mistery of iniquity, of sinful man aspiring into the place of God."

Effects of Strychnine with Special Reference to Spinal Afferent Fibres*

P. D. WALL, W. S. McCULLOCH, J. Y. LETTVIN AND W. H. PITTS

"Thou art man and
canst abide a truth
Tho bitter"

Tennyson

In 1809 Magendie said in a lecture to the Institute of France: "an entire family of vegetables (the bitter strychnos) has the singular property of exciting strongly the spinal marrow." Since that time, the dramatic property of strychnine of inducing convulsions has enjoyed the attention of many research workers. This interest was exaggerated by the development of the technique of "strychnine neuronography" by Dusser de Barenne. The localized convulsions generated in the region of locally applied strychnine were used to follow first-order pathways. Attempts have been made to locate those structures within the central nervous system on which strychnine acts and to understand the way in which the convulsive activity is generated. Much of this work has been reviewed by two major contributors to our knowledge of strychnine: Dusser de Barenne (22, 23) and Bremer (12, 13).

Effect on different species

The administration of strychnine has a similar effect on all mammalian species so far investigated. The very low dosage used in strychnine "tonics" has no observable pharmacologi-

cal effect other than autonomic effects, limited mainly to the gastrointestinal system, resulting from the extremely bitter taste of dilute solutions of strychnine. This effect differs in no way from other bitter solutions, such as quinine or quassia. The first toxic signs are hyperexcitability, disorganization of the spinal reflexes, and ataxia. An increase in dosage results in generalized convulsions, which are exaggerated by any form of sensory stimulation. A further increase in dosage kills the animal because of the continuous convulsions. With very high doses death occurs from depression of the heart and paralysis of the neuromuscular junctions. Thus it is not possible to protect the animal from the lethal effects of the very high doses of strychnine by control of the convulsions by barbiturate administration, which does reduce the lethal effect of lower doses. Studies by Munch, Garlough, and Ward (47) show considerable variations between various mammalian species in the lethal, convulsion, and hyperexcitability dosage. Guinea pigs and rats require a rather high dose to show the effects, as compared with mice, which are in turn more resistant than dogs, cats, and rabbits, whose lethal dose of hypodermically administered strychnine sulphate is 0.3-0.5 mgm per kilo.

Frogs and fish show a series of effects similar to that of mammals on administration of strychnine (55). But the invertebrates have a quite different response, in which the peripheral actions of strychnine predominate. It was observed in 1882 by Luchsinger that lobsters become red and paralyzed and die without show-

*This work was supported in part by the Signal Corps, the Office of Scientific Research (Air Research and Development Command), and the Office of Naval Research; and in part by the Bell Telephone Laboratories, Incorporated, the Teagle Foundation, and the National Science Foundation.

165

ing any signs of convulsions or hyperexcitability. Bonnet (9) confirmed this effect on the crayfish, and showed that although a reversible paralysis could be produced by low doses, death of the animal always followed within 24 hours. Of other invertebrates, Viehoever and Cohen (55) report similar results on the fresh water prawn, Palaemonetes. However, Daphnia is said to suffer from convulsions before the heart rate drops, and paralysis and death follow. House flies suffer from violent tremors of the legs, followed by paralysis and death.

General effects on the central nervous system

Local or systemic application of adequate concentrations of strychnine to the central nervous system of mammals results in roughly synchronized repetitive firing of the cells. The rate of firing depends on the amount of background activity, the type of cell, the amount and nature of sensory stimulation, and the presence of other drugs. However, certain exceptions appear to the generalization that strychnine produces such activity in all areas. Dow (20) showed that local application to cerebellar cortex failed to produce the spiking activity that can be produced from all parts of the cerebral cortex. Frankenhaeuser (26) failed to find strychnine spikes generated in tracts running from the olfactory bulb or in the vagus nerve. Wall and Horwitz (56) showed that spikes were not generated in the Edinger-Westphal nucleus or in the lateral horn cells of the spinal cord. The failure of the appearance of spiking is, of course, not significant unless it is certain that adequate concentrations have reached the structures examined. The authors, as reported below, had considerable difficulty in evoking spikes from the nuclei of Goll and Burdach by local application on the surface; but when strychnine was injected directly into the nuclei, spiking began almost immediately. The white matter on the surface of the nucleus evidently presented a sufficient barrier to penetration to the region of the cell bodies. A barrier to penetration may explain the failure, reported by some surgeons to evoke strychnine spikes from

the human cerebral cortex. It was shown by Wall and Horwitz that if the lateral horn cells that were not responding were stimulated by a single electric pulse, the cells subsequently generated a number of spikes before lapsing into inactivity. This suggests that an artificial increase in the activity of apparently unaffected cells may result in the typical spiking activity. A further possible reason for the apparent failure of the spike response could be that the activity of inhibitory and excitatory systems may be increased. An example of this is seen in the work of Terzuolo (53), which shows the cerebellar inhibition of strychnine tetanus in the spinal cord. An example of a strychninized area suppressing spontaneous activity in another is seen in the work of Dusser de Barenne and McCulloch (24). It is therefore possible that failure of response may reflect the powerful inhibition of the cells by another firing system. This, of course, may be unlikely in local strychninization, where no spikes can be recorded at the site of strychninization, but must be considered in the case of systemic administration of the drug.

It is interesting to note the work of Busquet and Vischniac (15), who showed that during the postconvulsive period in rabbits no apparent effects follow a second dose which was previously sufficient to produce convulsions. The rate of firing of cells during the spike was measured by Adrian and Moruzzi (1), who recorded from the pyramidal tract. Bursts of impulses contained from 10-80 impulses, with intervals between 0.6 and 4 milliseconds. The report of this high frequency in single units should perhaps be taken with caution, since it is no longer certain that the authors were, in fact, recording from single units within the pyramidal tract. Jalavisto (33), recording from single motor nerve fibers in the frog, found 3.6 milliseconds to be the shortest interval between impulses during a burst.

Recently, most surprising details on the generation of a spike in the cortex have been published by Li (41). Local application of strychnine to a single cortical neuron through a micropipette produced either continuous or "burst" firing. With application of strychnine to the cortical surface, some cells fired continuously, being interrupted at the time of the spikes; others fired in bursts at the time of the spikes. Thus individual cells within the strychninized cortex fall into two types. Local strychnine on the cortex may produce not only spikes but a "spike and wave" complex. Li found that while the spike was associated with burst activity of individual neurons, the wave was associated with inhibition of firing. Thomas, Schmidt, and Ward (54) also recently studied single cortical cells under the influence of strychnine. They find that the second phase of the diphasic impuse recorded with microelectrodes from single cells is increased by strychnine and that the first phase is unaffected. This contrasts with their finding no change in the shape of the unit potential recorded from single cells in experimental aluminum hydroxide epileptic foci.

Relation to acetylcholine

It was inevitable in the present era of unitary hypotheses that attempts would be made to link the action of strychnine with acetylcholine. In 1938, Nachmansohn (48) showed that 1 in 30,000 strychnine sulphate solutions would produce 19 per cent inhibition of cholinesterase in vitro. However, strychnine is a considerably less potent anticholinesterase in vitro than physostigmine, neostigmine, or D. F. P. These latter drugs do not simulate the convulsive actions of strychnine under any circumstances. It is true that there is a certain amount of synergism between strychnine and physostigmine (28), and between strychnine and acetylcholine (50). However, as we stated above, any mechanism that increases the amount of background activity exaggerates the effects of strychnine. The effect is seen with drugs and with electrical and normal sensory stimulation, so that the synergism of strychnine with other anticholinesterases or with acetylcholine cannot be taken as a specific indication that strychnine is acting through its own weak anticholinesterase activity. All known anticholinesterases are antagonized

by atropine, and strychnine can therefore be tested as an anticholinesterase by pitting it against atropine. The only support for strychnine as an anticholinesterase in vivo comes from the work of Longino and Preston (43). They used lethal doses of strychnine on mice and found that high doses of atropine did reduce the mortality rate. However, it may have been that at these high doses the peripheral effects of strychnine were predominant, and that atropine does effect this action. In contrast to this work, a very careful study by Wesco and Green (57) failed to find any effect of atropine on strychnine convulsions in cats with the rate and intensity of convulsions as the indicator. In support of this finding, Koppanyi (37) discovered that atropine, far from antagonizing the effects of strychnine, slightly decreased the threshold dosage required for the production of convulsions. It must be concluded that no satisfactory evidence has been produced that the in vivo convulsive activity of strychnine follows from its weak anticholinesterase properties. In peripheral structures, such as the peripheral ganglia of the crayfish, acetylcholine antagonizes the paralytic effects of strychnine (9) — a further point against the suggestion that strychnine acts via its anticholinesterase activity. Similarly, Lanari and Luco (38) showed that prostigmine antagonized the paralytic action of strychnine on the cat neuromuscular junction and the superior cervical ganglion.

Relation of strychnine to other drugs

The convulsive activity of strychninized tissue may be abolished by baribiturates. A quantitative study of the interaction of strychnine and barbiturates was carried out by Porter and Allamon (51). In strychnine neuronography, the spikes produced may be abolished by local application of nembutal. This technique allows the testing of more places than can be tested when it is necessary to await the dying-down of spiking before an application of strychnine in a new position. The interactions of narcotics and analeptics, especially strychnine and ephedrine, are described by Koll and Ergang (36) and by

Ahlquist (2). The use of metrazol and strychnine for testing anticonvulsant drugs has been reported by Orloff, Williams, and Pfeiffer (49). Even such a weak analeptic as quinine is shown to potentiate the effects of strychnine (27). It is of some interest in the location of strychnine activity that myanesin has been shown by Berger (7) and by Kaada (34) to be a powerful antagonist to strychnine convulsions. Calcium either injected systemically as gluconate or applied locally was found by Heinbecker and Bartley (30) to antagonize the convulsions. Since calcium increases accommodation and eliminates the prolongation of the period of latent addition, it was believed to be antagonizing through these two effects, as discussed in the next section. Ammonium chloride potentiates and enhances the drug (4).

Mode of action of strychnine on the peripheral nervous system

The general effect of strychnine on peripheral nervous structures, as reported by most authors, is depression with no signs of the generation of spontaneous activity. As might be expected these peripheral effects are particularly remarkable in the invertebrates. The first study after that of Luchsinger and Guillebeau (45) was the work of the Lapicques (39) on frog sciatic, which showed a depression and block of nerves with a decrease of chronaxie. Differential change in chronaxie was used to explain the blocking action at the nerve muscle junction; this was later shown by Knoefel (35) not to be the case. Further, Bouman (10) showed that the chronaxie change did not appear if, instead of using the appearance of a minimal muscle response, the method of the half maximal response advised by Hill (31) was used. If, however, an excess of potassium was added to the strychnine, no effects could be seen under any form of stimulation. An observation of this kind stresses the fact that the effects of strychnine on peripheral structures have been determined under conditions greatly differing from those found necessary by later workers (44) to maintain the nerve in its normal state.

It is therefore now most difficult to interpret the significance of these interesting results on peripheral structures. More detailed work on peripheral axons began with the work of Coppée and Peugnet (18, 19). It was greatly extended and, in general, confined by Heinbecker and Bartley (30). All concentrations of strychnine sulphate below 1 p.p.m. were found to decrease the height of single-action potentials. Coppée and Peugnet found an increase in the area of the action potential and a considerable prolongation, although this was not confirmed by Heinbecker and Bartley. In order of decreasing sensitivity to strychnine poisoning, B fibers were followed by A and C fibers. In very dilute solutions (less than 1:1,000,000) they occasionally observed a moderate lowering of the threshold of excised nerves, but at higher concentrations the threshold was always raised. At the same time strychnine inhibits the development of accommodation in the nerve, and the period of latent addition is increased — an effect which, as the authors point out, is similar to anodal polarization.

Finally, results of a quite different nature were found by Erlanger, Blair, and Shoepfle (25), who tested the variations of response latency and threshold at threshold stimulation of a peripheral nerve, the phalangeal nerve of the frog. Anodal or cathodal polarization was found not to affect the fluctuations, although cooling increased them. These fluctuations were quite random in their occurrence. It was found that low dilutions of strychnine which hardly raised the threshold produced a very great increase in the range of the oscillations; thus when the average threshold was increased by only 12 per cent, the oscillations increased by 394 per cent.

Studies on the details of strychnine action in some locations

The action of strychnine on the spinal reflexes has been intensively studied in attempts to determine whether the effects represented an increase of excitation or a decrease of inhibition. Bradley and Eccles (11) recently reviewed and investigated this matter and con-cluded that strychnine decreases the direct inhibitory action of group Ia afferent impulses. If this were the main effect of strychnine, one would expect no effect on the size of the monosynaptic reflex, and this is the case, as reported by a number of authors. However, the action on the monosynaptic reflex was shown by Bernhard, Taverner, and Widen (8) to depend on the type of preparation used. They report that an increase of both mono- and poly-synaptic lumbar reflexes is seen only with low spinal sections. In decerebrate or high spinal animals the effect on the monosynaptic reflex is variable or absent, while the polysynaptic reflexes are greatly increased. It seems likely, therefore, that descending inhibitory systems can counter-balance the tendency of the monosynaptic reflexes to increase. The marked ability of the descending inhibitory systems from the cerebellum and the reticular system to abolish spinal tetanus was shown by Lettvin (40) and Terzuolo (53). It seems probable therefore that strychnine does not simply decrease all types of inhibition in spite of the evidence that direct inhibition is decreased.

The slow potential changes in the cord during strychninization have been recently reviewed by Bremer (12, 13) and by Brooks and Fuortes (14). In the frog and cat, the dorsal and ventral root potentials are increased in height and duration. Suddenly, these potentials break into a regular oscillation, about 4-10 per second in the frog and 10-30 in the cat. Bursts of impulses run out of the ventral roots during the negative phase of these oscillations. It is suggested that the combined action of strychnine and the arrival of afferent impulses depolarizes the motor horn cells. Bremer (13) was unable to find evidence that the spinal interneurons participated in the generation of the tetanus. Ajmone Marsan, Fuortes, and Morossero (3) show that an induced steady depolarization is sufficient to explain both the hyperexcitability and the tetanus. However, van Harreveld and Feigen (29) studied directly the polarization of elements in the ventral horn of the spinal cord

and show that although barbiturates, for example, depolarize these elements, strychnine had no effect up to the time that convulsive activity started; at that time, as one would expect, a functional depolarization of the cells occurred. If this work is correct, it would be difficult to maintain that the initiation of strychnine effects on the ventral horn cells was attributable to their depolarization, since one would expect to see some effects before the beginning of convulsions.

It can well be imagined that if studies on the spinal cord, the kind queen of the nervous system, have resulted in conflicting answers to the nature of the action of strychnine, gross studies on the cortex have only added to the chaos. Studies such as those of Chang (16), and Bartley, O'Leary, and Bishop (6) have been useful in differentiating certain factors in cortical responses. In the absence of data on the exact origin of the potentials recorded, we can only conclude that while strychnine has a general excitatory effect it may exert either excitatory or inhibitory effect on certain components of the cortical response.

Experiments

In an attempt to resolve some of the questions posed by the preceding review, experiments of three types were carried out.

Methods

The special experimental conditions are described in each of the three sections.

Recording apparatus was standard: cathode follower head stages were coupled through Grass preamplifiers to a Dumont two-beam oscilloscope (No. 279).

Dorsal roots were stimulated in the usual way. Current pulses through the bipolar microelectrodes were generated by a special high-impedance circuit, to insure constant current.

The microelectrodes consisted of two lengths of 10-micron platinum wire, separated by 5-10 microns of glass and coated with another 5-10 microns of glass to make a cylinder about 50 microns in diameter. Such cylinders were about 1 centimeter long, invariant in diameter, and sharpened at the tip to an eccentric fine point, one wire open at the very tip, the other some distance up the bevel. Where localization of the microelectrode was required, it was cut off and left in the spinal cord and determined histologically by the method described in the paper by Howland et al. (32).

Experimental Results

1. The effect of strychnine on the threshold of ventral horn cells and terminal arborizations of afferent fibers.

Cats were anaesthetized with 0.5-0.7 cc per kilo of Dial injected intraperitoneally. The lumbar enlargement was exposed and placed under oil. Dorsal and ventral roots of the seventh lumbar segment were cut and prepared for recording. Intravenous curare was administered in order to control the expected strychnine convulsions. Artificial respiration and temperature control was maintained throughout the experiment. A bipolar microelectrode of the type described above was placed in the ventral horn of the seventh lumbar segment. Such an electrode was used in order to limit the main effects of the stimulation to the ventral horn. The preparation differs from that used by Renshaw (52) in that he was using a monopolar electrode and thus saw two volleys appear on the ventral root: the earlier one representing direct excitation of motoneurons, the later one arising from stimulation of afferents to motoneurons. We adjusted the stimulus strength so that only the direct volley for stimulation of the motor horn cells themselves was recorded on the ventral root. At that time, an antidromic volley was also recorded on the dorsal root of the same segment and represented the direct stimulation of the terminal arbor of those afferent fibers descending into the ventral horn. The ventral and dorsal root responses to two stimuli are shown at the top of Fig. 1. Two checks were made to confirm that the volleys recorded on the dorsal and ventral roots were

not maximal and therefore could increase. First, the stimulus strength was reduced as low as was consistent with the appearance of a stable volley in the dorsal and ventral roots. Next, the animal was subjected to 90 seconds of asphyxia; the expected cycle of increase and decrease of the height of both volleys occurred, and was followed by a return to the resting state.

Next, 0.2 cc of a saturated solution of strychnine sulphate was injected intravenously. The result is seen in the middle pair of traces in Fig. 1. The height of the direct volley in the ventral root is unchanged but is now followed by an indirect volley. This second discharge is that reported by Renshaw (52) and shown by him to follow the stimulation of afferents to the ventral horn. Although there is no change in the size of the direct ventral root response, there is a small decrease in the area as well as in the height of the antidromic volley in the dorsal root. Recordings were taken just before generalized convulsions began. The barbiturate anaesthesia had increased the threshold for these convulsions.

Although 0.2 cc of strychnine intravenously is enough to produce generalized fits in unanaesthetized animals, the dose was next increased by a further injection of 0.3 cc of saturated strychnine sulphate solution. Again it is clear (lower pair of traces in Fig. 1) that there is no change in the height of the ventral root direct volley. A slight increase occurs in the height of the indirect volley following the second stimulus. A further decrease in the height of the dorsal root volley has occurred, 39 per cent below its original height. Similar results were obtained if a monopolar stimulating microelectrode was used, although in this case the great increase of the indirect response was much more obvious.

It can therefore be concluded that there is no change in the threshold of directly stimulated motor horn cells even with very large doses of strychnine. At the same time, there is an increase in the threshold of the terminal arborizations of the afferent fibers in the ventral horn.

Effects of Strychnine on Spinal Afferent Fibres

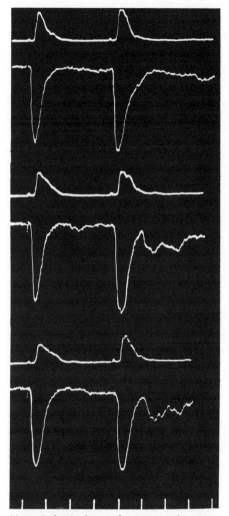

Fig. 1. Each pair of traces shows (upper) the response traveling antidromically in the dorsal root and (lower) the response orthodromically in the ventral root. Two succeeding stimuli are given by a bipolar microelectrode in the ventral horn of the segment of the recording roots (L7).

Upper pair: normal responses of the sensory afferent fibers and the motor horn cells.

Center pair: responses after 0.2 cc IV strychnine.

Lower pair: responses after a further 0.3 cc strychnine.

Bottom: time in milliseconds.

There is no change in the height of the volley evoked from the motor horn cells; there is a decrease in that from the terminal afferent arborizations.

The effect of strychnine on the early components of the dorsal root potential

Five cats were used in this series of experiments. Three were anaesthetized with 0.5 cc per kilo intraperitoneal Dial; two were spinal preparations, initially anaesthetized with ether, the spinal cord sectioned at C1 after carotid and basilar artery occlusion. Similar results were obtained with both types of preparation. The lumbar enlargement was exposed and covered with oil kept saturated with 5 per cent CO_2 and 95 per cent O_2. Temperature was regulated throughout the experiment. The seventh lumbar dorsal root was cut in its canal and divided into two parts. One part was placed on stimulating electrodes 2 centimeters from the cord. The other part was prepared as for recording the dorsal root potential (DRP): one electrode close to but not touching the cord; the other on the crushed end of the nerve 2 centimeters away. The severed ventral root of L7 also lay on recording electrodes for monitoring. Curare and artificial respiration were used.

A supramaximal stimulus to one root produced the typical sequence of the dorsal root potential in the neighbor root. This complex consists of five waves, identified and analyzed by Lloyd and McIntyre (42), of which the fifth and largest negative wave is the dorsal root potential recorded by Barron and Mathews (5). The transition from the fourth to the fifth wave is marked by the appearance of the dorsal root reflex traveling antidromically in the dorsal root. Since we are concerned with the afferent fibers, only the first four components are shown. First, in Fig. 2A we show the normal shape of the dorsal root potential as a solid line. Next, the result of post-tetanic potentiation is shown as the dotted line in Fig. 2A. For 2 seconds, 100 supramaximal impulses per second were delivered to the stimulated root, then a single shock was delivered at the height of the potentiating effect of this tetanus. It will be seen that there is no effect on the first three waves, but that the fourth shows a decrease in its height and a prolongation.

Next, 0.2 cc of saturated strychnine sulphate solution was injected intravenously; the result is seen as the dotted line in Fig. 2B. It shows a prolongation of the fourth wave. Ten minutes later a second dose of 0.2 cc was injected, and in Fig. 2C further prolongation of wave 4 has occurred, now accompanied by a decrease in height. The second and third waves are now in-

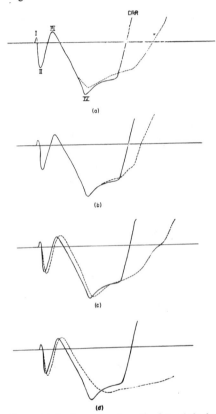

Fig. 2. (a) Continuous line shows the shape of the first four components of the dorsal root potential as recorded in one preparation. The dotted line shows the effect on these potentials of a tetanus delivered to the recording root.
(b), (c), (d) The continuous line shows the shape before strychnine of the first four components. The dotted line shows the effect of (b) 0.2 cc, (c) 0.4 cc, and (d) 0.6 cc of intravenous strychnine on the shape of these components.

creased in height and delayed. This effect was further exaggerated when a third dose of 0.2 cc strychnine was injected 10 minutes later (Fig. 2D). The fifth wave was tremendously increased and the ventral root reflex was increased in both its mono- and polysynaptic components.

Generation by strychnine of antidromic volleys in the dorsal column

It has been known since the work of Gotch and Horsley in 1898 that strychnine convulsions in the spinal cord were accompanied by antidromic volleys in the dorsal roots. The occurrence of dorsal root reflexes in ordinary spinal preparations makes it difficult to interpret the significance of such volleys in the presence of strychnine. We therefore examined the other large ending point of primary afferent fibers, the nuclei cuneatus and gracilis. An antidromic volley in the medial lemniscus does not produce an antidromic volley in the dorsal columns in the absence of strychnine. Therefore, in order to see whether or not local application of strychnine in the nucleus gracilis would result in antidromic "spike" conduction down the dorsal columns, cats were prepared under barbiturate anaesthesia and the lumbar enlargement exposed in the manner described in the previous two sections. The caudal end of the fourth ventricle was exposed. Application of filter paper soaked in strychnine to the surface of the nucleus gracilis failed to produce strychnine spikes in several cases. It was therefore necessary to inject strychnine (one drop through a 26-gauge tube) directly into the nucleus. This was followed by the appearance of spiking activity in the region of the nucleus. Recordings were taken from the nucleus (Fig. 3, top) and from electrodes placed 2 cm from the cord on the cut L7 dorsal root (Fig. 3, center). It will be seen in Fig. 3 that the beginning of the generation of a "strychnine spike" in the nucleus is soon followed by the appearance of an antidromically conducted volley in a dorsal root. Section of the dorsal columns immediately abolished this transmission. It is concluded that in this case a strychnine

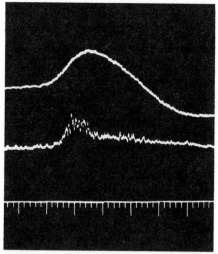

Fig. 3. Top: *strychnine was applied to nuclei cuneatus and gracilis. The trace shows a single spike being generated within the nucleus.*
Center: *at the same time a recording is taken from the seventh lumbar dorsal root 2 cm from the cord. An antidromically running spike is seen running out in the root.*
Bottom: *time in 2 milliseconds and 10 milliseconds.*

spike was conducted antidromically from the nucleus down the dorsal columns and out of the sensory root.

Discussion

The results of the first set of experiments seem to show that strychnine does not affect the threshold of the motor horn cells. It is clear that if this is so, a number of the previous theories are untenable. We are supposing that the type of stimulus used fired off the dendrites or cell bodies of the motor horn cells rather than, or as well as, the axons. Evidence for this is: First, since both direct and indirect responses were seen, the stimulating current affected not only the most ventral regions where the axons of the motor horn cells are present but also fibers running to the motor neurons. Yet only the indirect responses were increased. Second, in other experiments we have found that an afferent volley does affect the threshold of the motor neurons tested in the way of the first set

of experiments. Third, anodal make and cathodal make stimulation of the ventral horn cells interact in different ways with an incoming afferent volley. We presume that this indicates that the anodal and cathodal pulses were stimulating different parts of the motor cells. Strychnine failed to affect the threshold of the motor horn cells whether anodal or cathodal stimulation was used. Therefore, while it is true that we do not know what part of the cell is stimulated by a microelectrode in the ventral horn, the stimulated point can have its threshold affected by an afferent volley of nerve impulses. Yet the threshold of this point of stimulation is not affected by strychnine.

The increase of threshold of the primary afferent terminals and the changes in the shape of the early components of the dorsal root potentials both suggest an action of strychnine on activity in the primary afferent fibers. The results of Bradley and Eccles (11) could be taken to support this view. We have not yet measured the nature of this change, and it is questionable whether any satisfactory interpretation could be made of a dc shift recorded directly on a passive root. We suspect a hyperpolarization, at least of the intramedullary course of some of the fibers, since the increase of the first three waves of the dorsal root complex suggests axons in the so-called nerve reaction state. This suspicion is further heightened by the measurable increase in threshold of the afferent fibers intramedullarly. Furthermore, the changes being in the same direction as that found after posttetanic potentiation suggests a similar process both with regard to the sign of potential shift in the membrane and the increased effectiveness of signals traversing such fibers. It is therefore now of particular interest to know the effect of strychnine on normal peripheral nerve fibers, although it is possible that terminal arborizations of fibers might react differently.

The results from the third set of experiments may have significance beyond the simple demonstration that antidromically traveling strychnine spikes may be generated. It is possible, of course, that there are some descending fibers in the dorsal columns; such tracts have been demonstrated in species other than the cat. However, none of these descending tracts sends fibers out of the dorsal roots as far as is known. Since the recordings shown in Fig. 3 were taken from the dorsal root, there is little doubt that these were, in fact, antidromically running impulses in sensory fibers. A second possibility that has to be ruled out is that the strychnine applied to the nuclei of Goll and Burdach had activated some system in the medulla which projected into the spinal cord and there generated the equivalent of a dorsal root reflex so that the impulses recorded in the dorsal root were not those that had descended dorsal column sensory fibers. The ragged start of the spike in the nuclei and in the root does not allow us to exclude this possibility by an accurate measurement of conduction time. However, we have purposely stimulated descending systems, including the whole spinal cord with dorsal columns cut, and have been unable to elicit any antidromic volley out of the dorsal roots. Therefore it seems likely that our results indicate a true generation of synchronized volleys in the dorsal column terminal arborization. These impulses might play a part in the synchronization of the firing of the cells in the nucleus.

Now that we have evidence for antidromic impulses, we naturally ask whether they originated in the terminal arbor or were transmitted across the synapse antidromically. The latter does not seem to be the explanation. Stimulation of the medial lemniscus did not result in the appearance of a volley in the dorsal columns even under strychnine. Similarly, antidromic stimulation of the ventral roots in a strychninized cord does not result in antidromic impulses running out of the dorsal roots. It therefore seems most likely that these impulses originated in the terminal arborization of the dorsal column fibers. Such generation of impulses of greater effectiveness than normal might explain the synchronized detonation of all the cells supplied by a particular fiber, as well as increased ephaptic interaction with other afferents. While this may not be a complete explanation for "strychnine spikes" it does account for some of the characteristics.

Critique of strychnine neuronography

The prolonged and careful development of the technique by Dusser de Barenne, McCulloch, and others is described in a number of papers (22, 23, 24). It must be emphasized that at no time did they believe that this method supplanted those beautiful but increasingly rare anatomical tracings of pathways upon which our definite knowledge of neuro-anatomy is based. It was intended only to provide a general scheme of organization of fibers, indicating those areas in which histological methods might be most profitable. We may restate and examine the postulates on which the usefulness of the technique is based.

1. Local application of strychnine results in a synchronous discharge of cells within the region. We examined, under general effects of strychnine, the five locations in which it has been reported that strychnine does not have this effect. It seems reasonable to point out that these locations contain somewhat unusual cells: three are in the autonomic system, one in the cerebellum, and one in the olfactory bulb. Further, it is possible that within a region giving off strychnine spikes some cells may be inhibited by the discharge of others, as suggested by the work of Li (41). It is therefore necessary to modify the general statement with the warning that certain types of cell within a region may not contribute to the spike-producing activity. This caveat is not as crippling as suggested by Chow and Hutt (17) or by Frankenhaeuser (26). In the instances in which Dusser de Barenne and McCulloch used negative findings as evidence for an absence of direct connections, spikes occurred where the strychnine was placed; this was not the case in Frankenhaeuser's or Wall's and Horwitz's work.

2. Strychnine applied to axons at some distance from cell bodies does not generate spiking activity. The work we present here suggests

that strychnine may lead to the generation of activity in axons close to their termination or cells. However, there is no doubt that strychnine applied along the main nonbranching course of an axon does not evoke activity.

3. Spikes travel orthodromically. The authors of this paper show one clear example of antidromic transmission of a strychnine spike. In defence of the results of strychnine neuronography on the cortex, the responses recorded at some distance from the strychninized areas were not volleys traveling in tracts but were the arrival of synchronized bursts of impulses in the region of cells giving rise to large transients, much slower than a nerve spike.

An ink-writer is not equipped to handle signals as short as nerve spike or an antidromic volley to cortex, especially since the slow potential accompanying the latter is very easily abolished by barbiturates, the drug of choice in neuronography. Thus, while antidromic impulses from strychnine can occur, only high-frequency recordings will show them. The work done on old instruments with low-frequency response probably does not contain evidence of these antidromic spikes.

4. Strychnine spikes do not cross synapses. Synapses rarely transmit impulses in such a way that output repeats input. It was shown in many locations that the arrival of a synchronized burst of impulses, the strychnine spike, was not followed by the response of the next set of cells with a similar degree of synchronization. The only exception was found by Wall and Horwitz (56) in the stellate ganglion where the unusual one-to-one impulse transmission occurs. Thus this postulate may still be applied in most known cell groups.

It is therefore evident that considerable care is needed in the interpretation of data derived from strychnine neuronography. The technique, however, remains valid as a method for the rapid survey of probable connections.

Summary

1. Some of the literature on the basic effects of strychnine is reviewed.

2. Experiments carried out on cats show that strychnine does not affect the excitability of the motor horn cells of the spinal cord as tested by microelectrode stimulation within the cord.

3. It is shown that the threshold of the fibers in the terminal arborization of final afferent fibers is raised. The shape of the early components of the dorsal root potentials is changed. Fndings could be explained by an increase in the height of the individual action potentials in the terminal arbors under the influence of strychnine.

4. Strychnine spikes traveling antidromically away from strychninized nuclei of Goll and Burdach were shown to emerge from lumbar dorsal roots.

5. The significance of these findings is discussed. A critique of strychnine neuronography in the light of recent findings is presented.

BIBLIOGRAPHY

1. Adrian, E. D., and Moruzzi, G., "Impulses in pyramidal tract," J. Physiol., 1939, 97, 153-199.
2. Ahlquist R. P., "The synergism of C. N. S. stimulants," J. Amer. Pharm. Assoc., 1947, 35, 414-415.
3. Ajmone Marsan, C., Fuortes, M. G. F., and Marossero, F., "Effects of direct current on the electrical activity of the spinal cord," J. Physiol., 1951, 113, 316-321.
4. Ajmone Marsan, C., Fuortes, M. G. F., and Marosserro, F., "Influence of ammonium chloride on the electrical activity of the brain and spinal cord," E. E. G. Clin. Neurophysiol., 1949, 1, 291-298.
5. Barron, D. B., Mathews, B. H. C., "Potential changes in the spinal cord," J. Physiol., 1938, 92, 276-321.
6. Bartley, S. H., O'Leary, J., and Bishop, G. H., "Differentiation by strychnine of visual integrating mechanisms of the rabbit optic cortex," Am. J. Physiol., 1937, 120, 604-618.
7. Berger, F. M., "The mode of action of myanesin," Brit. J. Pharm., 1947, 2, 241-250.
8. Bernhard, C. G., Taverner, D., and Widen, L., "Differences in the action of tubocurarine and strychnine on the spinal reflex," Brit. J. Pharm., 1951, 6, 551-559.
9. Bonnet, V., "Action of strychnine and acetylcholine on neuronic rhythmicity in crustaceans," Compt. rend. Soc. de biol., 1938, 127, 804-806.
10. Bouman, H. D., "Experiments on the mechanism of strychnine curarization," J. Physiol., 1936, 88, 328-340.
11. Bradley, K., and Eccles, J. C., "Strychnine as a depressant of primary inhibition," Nature, 1953, 171, 1061-1062:

12. Bremer, F., "Le tétanos strychnique et le mécanisme de la synchronisation neuronique," Arch. int. Physiol., 1941, 51, 211-260.
13. Bremer, F., "Strychnine tetanus of the spinal cord," Ciba symposium on the spinal cord, Little. Brown and Co., Boston, 1953, 78-83.
14. Brooks, C. M., and Fuortes, M. G. F., "Potential changes in the spinal cord following administration of strychnine," J. Neurophysiol., 1952, 15, 257-267.
15. Busquet, H., and Vischniac, C., "Action of strychnine and brucine on the spinal cord," Compt. rend. Soc. de biol., 1938, 128, 729-732.
16. Chang, H. T., "Strychnine on local cortical potentials," J. Neurophysiol., 1951, 14, 23-28.
17. Chow, K. L., and Hutt, P. J., "The 'Association Cortex' Mocaca Mulatta: A review of recent contributions to its anatomy and junctions," Brain, 1953, 76, 625-677.
18. Coppée, G., and Peugnet, H. B., "Action of strychnine on peripheral nerves," Compt. verd. Soc. de biol., 1936, 123, 283-286.
19. Coppée, G., and Coppée-Bolly, M. H., "Action of strychnine on isolated nerve," Arch. int. de physiol., 1941, 51, 97-129.
20. Dow, R. S., "The electrical activity of the cerebellum," J. Physiol., 1938, 94, 67-86.
21. Dun, F. T., "Restoration of the dorsal root potential after strychnine," Proc. Soc. Exper. Biol., 1942, 49, 479-480.
22. Dusser de Barenne, J. G., "The mode and site of action of strychnine in the nervous system," Physiol. Rev., 1933, 13, 325-335.
23. Dusser de Barenne, J. G., Marshall, C., Nims, L. F., and Stone, W. E., "The response of the cerebral cortex to local application of strychnine," Am. J. Physiol., 1941, 132, 776-780.
24. Dusser de Barenne, J. G., and McCulloch, W. S., "Functional organization of the sensory cortex of the monkey," J. Neurophysiol., 1938, 1, 69-85.
25. Erlanger, J., Blair, E. A., and Schoepfle, G. M., "Spontaneous oscillations in excitability of nerve fibers," Am. J. Physiol., 1941, 134, 705-718.
26. Frankenhaeuser, B., "Limitations of the method of strychnine neuronography," J. Neurophysiol., 1951, 14, 73-79.
27. Gessner, O., "Potentiating effects of strychnine by quinine," Arch. f. Exper. Path. u. Pharmakol. 1943, 202, 363-365.
28. Hamed, B. K., and Cole, V. V., "Synergism of physostigmine and strychnine," Proc. soc. exper. biol. and med., 1938, 39, 372-376.
29. van Harreveld, A., and Feigen, G. A., "Effect of some drugs on the polarization of spinal cord," Am. J. Physiol., 1950, 160, 451-461.
30. Heinbecker, P., and Bartley, S. H., "Mode of action of strychnine on the nervous system," Am. J. Physiol., 1939, 125, 172-187.
31. Hill, A. V., "The strength-duration relation for electric excitation of nerve," Proc. Roy. Soc. B. 1936, 119, 440-453.
32. Howland, B., Lettvin, J. Y., McCulloch, W. S., Pitts, W., and Wall, P. D., "Reflex inhibition by dorsal root interaction," J. Neurophysiol., 1955, 18, 1-17.
33. Jalvisto, E., "Reflex motor discharge in single fibers of the frog in strychnine poisoning," Acta physiol. scand., 1945, 9, 313-335.
34. Kada, B. R., "Action of myanesin," J. Neurophysiol., 1950, 13, 89-104.
35. Knoeel, P. K., "Strychnine and chronaxie," Am. J. Physiol., 1936, 117, 638-641.
36. Koll, W., and Ergang, M., "Antagonistic action of narcotics and analeptics," Arch. f. exper. Path. u. Pharmakol., 1942, 199, 577-605.
37. Koppanyi, T., "The action of toxic doses of atropine on the central nervous system," Proc. soc. exper. biol. and med., 1939, 40, 244-248.
38. Lanari, A., and Luco, J. V., "Depressant action of strychnine on superior cervical sympathetic and on muscle," Am. J. Physiol., 1939, 126, 277-282.
39. Lapicque, L. and M., "Action de la Strychnine sur l'Éxitabilité du Nerf Moteur," Compt. rend. de la soc. de biol., 1907, 62, 1062-1064.
40. Lettvin, J. Y., "The path of suppression in the spinal grey matter," Fed. Proc. No. 1, Part I, March 1948, 71.
41. Li, C. L., "Functional properties of cortical neurons with special reference to strychninization," American electroencephalographic Soc. 9th ann. meeting, 1955.
42. Lloyd, D. P. C., and McIntyre, A. K., "On the origins of dorsal root potentials," J. Gen. Physiol., 1949, 32, 409-443.
43. Langino, S., and Preston, R. S., "Antagonism between atropine and strychnine," J. Pharmacol. and exper. therap., 1946, 86, 174, 176.
44. Lorente de Nó, R., "A study of nerve physiology," Rockefeller Inst. Med. Res., 1947.
45. Luchsinger, B., und Guillebeau, A., "Fortgesetzte Studien zu einer algemeinen Physiologie der irritabeln Substanzen," Arch. f. d. ges. Physiol., 1882, 28, 1-60.
46. Magendie, F., "Some examination of the action of some vegetables on the spinal marrow," Institute of France, April 24, 1809.
47. Munch, J. G., Gorlough, F. E., and Ware. J. C., Bioassays of rodenticides," J. Amer. Pharm. Assoc., 1936, 25, 744-746.
48. Nachmansohn, D., "Mechanism of the action of strychnine on the nervous system," Compt. rend. soc. de biol., 1938, 129, 941-943.
49. Orloff, M. J., Williams, H. L., and Pfeiffer, C. C., "Timed intravenous infusion of strychnine or metrazol for testing anticonvulsant drugs," Proc. soc. exp. biol. and med., 1949, 70, 254-257.
50. Oti, Y., "Effect of Ach or epinephrine on spinal reflex action of strychnine," Okayama-Igakkai-Zasshi, 1940, 52, 2577.
51. Porter, E. L., Allamon, E. L., "Quantitative study of barbiturate-strychnine antagonism," J. Pharmacol. and exper. ther., 1936, 58, 178-191.
52. Renshaw, B., "Activity in the simplest spinal reflex pathways," J. Neurophys., 3, 1940, 373-387.
53. Terzuolo, C., "Supraspinal influences on spinal strychnine tetanus," Arch. int. physiol., 1954, 62, 179-196.
54. Thomas, L. B., Schmidt, R. P., and Ward, A. A., "Observations on single units in chronic cortical epileptic foci in normal or strychninized cortex," Amer. E. E. G. Soc. 9th ann. meeting 1955.
55. Viehoever, A., and Cohen, I., "Mechanism of the action of strychnine," Am. J. Pharm., 1937, 109, 285-316.
56. Wall, P. D., and Horwitz. N., "Observations on the physiological action of strychnine," J. Neurophysiol., 1951, 14, 257-263.
57. Wesco, W. C., and Green, R. E., "Lack of atropine antagonism to strychnine," J. Pharmac. and exp. therap., 1948, 94, 78-84.

REFLEX INHIBITION BY DORSAL ROOT INTERACTION*

B. HOWLAND, J. Y. LETTVIN, W. S. McCULLOCH, W. PITTS,
AND P. D. WALL

INTRODUCTION

BALLIF et al. (1), in 1925, found that a single shock to a mixed ipsilateral hind-limb nerve of a spinal or decerebrate cat inhibited the knee-jerk for hundreds of milliseconds, and they said that the cause of this phenomenon was still to be elucidated. In 1938, Barron and Matthews (2) found that stimulation of an ipsilateral dorsal root often inhibited ventral root response to stimulation of a second dorsal root, and they were the first to suggest that blocking at the bifurcation of primary afferent neurons might account to some extent for their finding. Renshaw (7), in 1946, using volleys over dorsal roots L_6 and L_7, showed that the inhibition was accompanied by changes in that part of the microelectrode record from the ventral horn which he attributed to the presynaptic components. The early course of the inhibition was not paralleled by any change in the responsiveness of motoneurons to antidronic stimulation; hence he attributed it to an interaction between terminal branches of dorsal root fibers.

In the same year, Eccles and Malcolm (4) observed in the frog that the dorsal root reflex and DR5 were inhibited and they suggested that the conditioning volley produced a cathodal block of the primary afferent fibers by a depolarization spreading back from the synaptic region. Granted that this is the cause of the phenomenon, the evidence for it is indirect and of such a kind that it cannot localize the block exactly. Therefore it seemed advisable to examine the events within the cord by a method that can show directly at what place the afferent volley is first diminished. Although the inhibition has been seen after peripheral nerve stimulation in both decerebrate and spinal animals without anesthesia, it is more prolonged and profound under barbiturates and with dorsal root stimulation. We used the latter preparation.

For physical reasons records from the roots and from the surface of the cord do not determine uniquely the site of electrical events within the cord.

* This work was supported in part by the Signal Corps, the Air Materiel Command, and the Office of Naval Research; in part by the Bell Telephone Laboratories, Inc.; in part by the Teagle Foundation; and in part by a grant from the Public Health Service to P. D. Wall at the University of Chicago.

Reflex Inhibition by Dorsal Root Interaction

A grid of successive stations of microelectrodes was used to produce a series of potential maps, each of effectively simultaneous values, showing the fields of the inhibitory volley remaining at the time of maximum inhibition and those engendered by the test volley alone and inhibited. These maps indicate the potentials in the extracellular medium at enough points to permit calculation of the amount of current flowing into or out of the neurons in small regions. Thereby we estimate to what extent those small regions are the sites of impulses, absorbing current from the medium (*i.e.*, *sinks*), or sites contributing current through the medium (*i.e.*, *sources*) to impulses in their remote parts. Computations and the justification of their use in determining location of activity in the central nervous system, being novel, are discussed at some length.

To present the significant results of each experiment requires many figures, so we shall present the results of a single typical one in detail. All the experiments show during dorsal root inhibition that the test volley in the primary afferent neurons is much diminished before it reaches the grey matter of the spinal cord. They do not show by what agency—internuncials or other fibers directly—this inhibition is exerted on the primary afferent fibers.

PREPARATION

A cat was anesthetized with Dial-Urethane, 0.6 cc. per kg. intraperitoneally. A tracheal cannula was installed and artificial respiration established. The spinal cord was transected at C_1. Heating lamps controlled by a subscapular thermistor maintained the body temperature at 38°C. ±0.1°C. The lumbar enlargement was exposed and covered with mineral oil continuously suffused with 95 per cent O_2 +5 per cent CO_2. Dorsal roots L_5 and L_6 on one side were severed about 3 cm. from the cord and placed on bipolar electrodes for test and conditioning stimulation respectively. Dorsal root potentials were recorded on a filament dissected from one of the stimulated roots, and the ventral root response was led from the severed ipsilateral VR of L_6. Throughout the experiment supramaximal shocks of 0.1 msec. duration were delivered every 2 sec. through isolating transformers.

By varying the interval between the conditioning volley on L_6 and the testing volley on L_5, the ventral root response to the test volley was found to be inhibited at all intervals between 5 and 100 msec., and maximally at about 20 msec. This interval between conditioning and test stimulus was maintained thereafter throughout the experiment. Additional Dial was given then to decrease spontaneous and evoked activity within the cord. In due time the ventral root discharge vanished and never reappeared. During the recording, after the second dose of Dial, many internuncials were encountered which responded, frequently repetitively, to the test volley alone. Their response was much diminished by a prior conditioning volley. Apparently, despite the heavy anesthesia and silent ventral roots, impulses in the primary collaterals were capable of causing related activity in internuncials and the conditioning volley was still able to inhibit them. The monitoring dorsal root filament response changed a little, and then became and remained constant, thus indicating the stability of the preparation throughout the recording.

EXPERIMENT

Records of potentials throughout a transverse plane in the ipsilateral half of the spinal cord a few millimeters rostral to L_5 were obtained through microelectrodes made of 10 μ platinum wire uniformly coated with a thin layer of glass and sharpened (6). The first electrode was placed on the intact pia of the dorsum of the cord under binocular microscopic vision to insure that there was no dimpling of the surface at the time of contact or at any subsequent time. The electrical response at the surface was then recorded on a quiet base line nine times: thrice of the conditioning volley alone, thrice of the test volley alone,

178

and thrice of the combination of the test volley 20 msec. after the conditioning volley. The electrode was then advanced 150 μ into the cord and the full series of nine records taken again. This procedure was repeated in steps of 150 μ until the tip of the electrode reached its final station some 3 mm. deep in the cord. Still under binocular microscopic observation, its shank was carefully severed, its cut end checked for approximation, and its shaft left in place. Ten electrodes were thus introduced, of which nine are shown in Fig. 1. This took several hours, during which there was no visible change in the monitoring root records.

The microelectrode records were all taken with respect to a retractor separating the back muscles; the calculations subtract its contribution to all the measured potentials. The microelectrodes were connected to a cathode-follower with grid current less than 10^{-11} A., grid-ground leak of 10^{11} O., and the capacitative shunt from grid to ground balanced by a negative capacitance. Hence any difference of impedance between electrode tips had negligible effect. The output of this head-stage went to a capacity-coupled amplifier with a bandwidth of 0.5–100,000 cycles, and thence to an oscilloscope with a linear sweep. To avoid distortion by parallax, only the center 3 inches of the 5-inch screen were used. On each record a stimulus artefact had to be introduced for temporal reference and a base line for amplitude measurement had to be superimposed by an additional sweep with the input to the scope grounded. Each record is a single frame photographed on 35-mm. film.

When the experiment was finished the cord was fixed *in situ* with 10 per cent formalin, and 24 hrs. later a slab, 1 mm. thick and containing all the electrodes, was removed into 10 per cent formalin for another 24 hrs. It was next carefully dehydrated with alcohol in several steps for three days and then placed in several changes of 100 per cent alcohol for three more days. Finally, it was cleared in methyl salicylate, which made the slab so transparent that the outlines of the grey matter and the exact position of the electrodes in the transverse plane could be seen and photographed. The linear shrinkage was less than 5 per cent, and when the micrometer readings for depth of penetration were checked against the histological measurements, four electrodes agreed exactly, five with an error less than 5 per cent, and only one had deviated from the plane and had to be disregarded.

RESULTS

Figure 1 shows the positions of the 162 recording stations used in computation. The observations were now embodied in nearly 1500 records, from which the significant results were extracted as follows: Since inspection of all responses to the conditioning volleys alone showed that the potentials changed little, if at all, from 20 to 23 msec. after the shock, a single map was prepared for this interval by plotting the mean of the three records at that time at each station on an enlarged replica of Fig. 1. Similar charts were made at each of the instants 1.0, 1.2, 1.6, and 2.8 msec. after the test shock alone and after the combination consisting of the test shock preceded 20 msec. earlier by the conditioning shock. Figure 1 was projected on squared paper at such enlargement that the distances between recording stations was about the same as the unit square of the paper, and this figure was blueprinted in many copies. Potential values at the intersections of the lines of the paper, or "lattice points," were then determined by interpolation, accurate enough to preserve second differences, first along the electrode tracks to the horizontal lines of the squared paper, and then along the horizontal lines to the lattice points, where the values were entered numerically. From each of these square arrays of values two diagrams were made. The lower are isopotential maps at the indicated times, and contain the relevant information, but in a form from which it is difficult to determine, by inspection, where activity is, or how it is moving. The upper diagrams are made by entering, at each lattice point, the difference between the potential there and

179

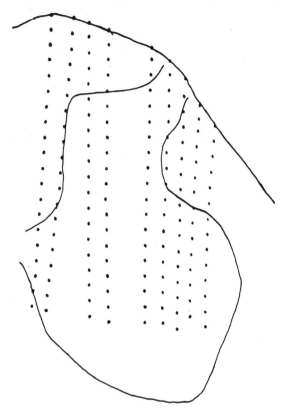

FIG. 1. Tracing of cross section of cat spinal cord between L₄ and L₅ showing the 162 positions from which the potentials were recorded. Area analyzed is approximately 2.7 mm. by 1.8 mm.

the average at the four neighboring lattice points. The value of this difference is indicated by the number of dots or diagonal lines in a group, the dots standing for negative, the lines for positive values. One dot or line is chosen to be approximately the standard error of the quantity, so that groups of less than three may be due to error. Where there are dots, their density is an approximate measure of activity indicating the extent to which parts of neurons there absorb current from the medium (*i.e.*, *sink density*). The density of lines indicates the extent to which parts of neurons there emit current into and through the medium to other depolarized parts of the same neurons (*i.e.*, *source density*). A source signifies that the region has been or is about to be a sink. The maps summarize the findings.

Map C 20 msec. after conditioning stimulus to L₆
alone (Fig. 2, C 20 msec.)

At this time, and with no change in magnitude for at least 3 msec. more, the bulk of residual activity is along the dorsal border of the dorsal horn—the sinks chiefly in the grey matter, the sources chiefly in the white.

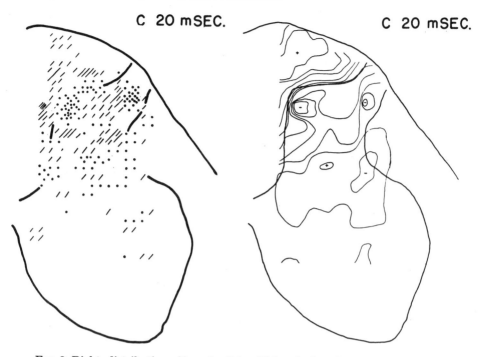

C 20 mSEC.   C 20 mSEC.

Fɪɢ. 2. Right: distribution of isopotentials within spinal cord 20 msec. after conditioning root L_6, alone, had been stimulated. This time was found to be that at which stimulation of root L_6 exerted its maximum inhibitory effect on reflex following stimulation of test root L_5. Left: distribution of sources (diagonal lines) and sinks (dots) within spinal cord 20 msec. after stimulation of conditioning root. Each dot or line represents an equal amount of source-density. For interpretation see text.

Maps T after test stimulus to L_5 alone (Figs. 3–5, T 1.2, T 1.6, T 2.8 msec.)

No maps are presented for 0.5 or for 1.0 msec. after the test stimulus alone because, although there was a large potential gradient in the plane, there were as yet no significant sources or sinks, showing that the volley had not yet reached the plane. At 1.2 msec. (Fig. 3, T 1.2 msec.), the volley from the medial division of the dorsal root is represented by a line of sinks in the dorso-medial white matter just entering the grey. At this time the grey matter contains mainly sources, except for regions perhaps excited slightly earlier by faster afferents. At 1.6 msec. (Fig. 4, T 1.6 msec.), the medial sinks have invaded the adjacent grey matter in force, and a large sink has appeared in the dorso-lateral grey; and by 2.8 msec. (Fig. 5, T 2.8 msec.), intense sinks are present in the substantia gelatinosa and in the medial and lateral intermediate region.

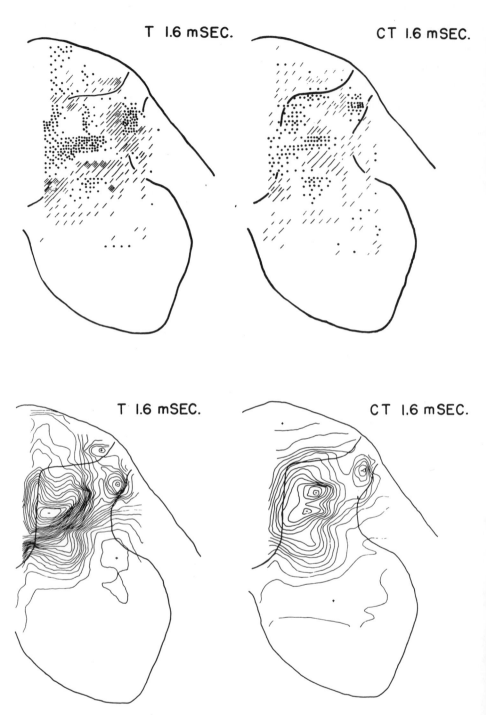

FIG. 4. Arranged as in Fig. 3; top left, source-sink distribution, and bottom left, isopotential distribution, 1.6 msec. after stimulation of test root L_5. Top right, source-sink map, and bottom right, isopotential map, at the same time after test volley but preceded 20 msec. by inhibitory conditioning volley.

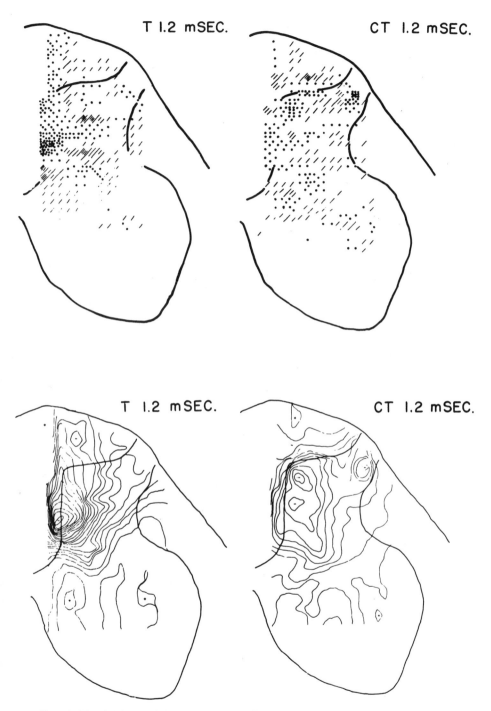

Fig. 3. Top left: distribution of sources (lines) and sinks (dots) 1.2 msec. after test root L_5, alone, had been stimulated. This is pattern of earliest disturbance recorded in region after test stimulation. Bottom left: isopotential map 1.2 msec. after stimulation of L_5 alone. Top right: source-sink map 1.2 msec. after stimulating test root but preceded 20 msec. by stimulation of inhibitory conditioning root L_6. This shows that earliest sign of arriving volley in white matter is inhibited by preceding volley. Bottom right: isopotential map 1.2 msec. after stimulating test root but preceded 20 msec. earlier by conditioning volley.

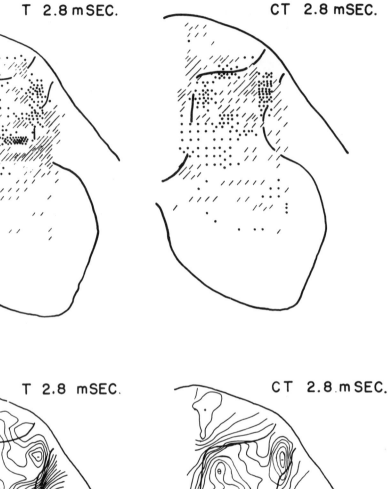

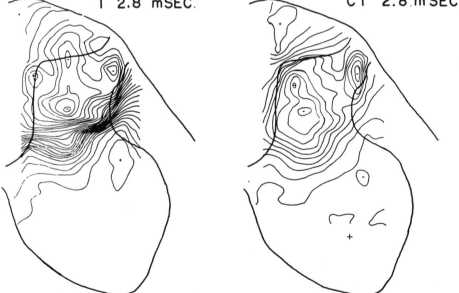

FIG. 5. Arranged as in Figs. 3 and 4; top left, source-sink distribution, and bottom left, isopotential map, 2.8 msec. after stimulation of test root alone. Top right, source-sink distribution, and bottom right, isopotential map, at the same time after test root volley but preceded 20 msec. by conditioning volley.

Maps CT after test stimulus to L₅ 20 msec. subsequent to conditioning stimulus to L₆ (Figs. 3–5, CT 1.2, CT 1.6, CT 2.8 msec.)

The sink which had appeared in the dorsal column at 1.2 msec. (T 1.2 msec.), after the test volley alone is almost entirely absent at the corresponding time (CT 1.2 msec.). The residual disturbance set up by the conditioning volley (C 20 msec.) is clearly visible along the dorsal border of the grey matter.

Comparison of maps T, C and CT show that, were the sources and sinks of C subtracted from those of CT, the remainder would be far smaller than the results of T alone. This holds for times 1.2, 1.6, and 2.8 msec. Thus, instead of simple algebraic summation, there is an early interaction which blocks impulses within the white matter of the dorsal column, and consequently there is a much diminished invasion of the grey matter later.

DISCUSSION

There is good general agreement between the distribution of these sources and sinks and those found at approximately the same times in our earlier work with a single stimulating volley (6). The notable differences are the absence of the sink in the ventral horn and a slight difference in the shape and extent of sources and sinks that are a natural consequence of using different animals and different levels in the cord. But the arrangement, order of appearance, and relative magnitudes of the sources and sinks are in satisfactory accord.

It is curious to note that the entering volley arrives at the plane of the electrodes only 1.2 msec. after the stimulus, although its potentials precede it. Our stimulating cathode on the test root lay about 2 cm. away from the cord, and our electrode plane lay about 2 mm. rostral to the rostral edge of the root. Yet up to 1 msec. after the stimulus we measured no activity in the plane. Granting as much as 0.2 msec. utilization time, we can still get no more than 30 m./sec. for the speed of the impulse in the primary afferents. There may be two explanations for this: (i) the very fastest dorsal white-matter fibers do not emit collaterals in the plane, and (ii) there exists a region of decrement between root entrance and recording plane. In any case, at T 1.2 msec., the dorsal column sink must represent the earliest arrival of the volley in primary fibers, for there has been no preceding activity up to 1.0 msec., 0.2 msec. is hardly time for adequate synaptic delay, and the distribution of sources and sinks is not that of any known group of internuncials and their processes. Indeed, the subsequent march of the sink along paths taken by primary afferent collaterals in Ramón y Cajal's anatomical maps strongly supports such a view. But at this earliest arrival of the volley in the medial white matter, where it has hardly begun to invade the collaterals in the grey at all, it is already greatly reduced by the residual effects of the previous inhibitory volley. The actual site of inhibition, of course, may lie anywhere between the entrance of the test dorsal root into the cord and the medial

185

white matter 2 mm. anterior, where we observe the results. It may be exerted by interaction of parallel fibers or through internuncials; from the present evidence we cannot say which. Although this study was done under the highly unphysiological conditions which are best for microelectrode maps, we can use its results to suggest more critical experiments. For example, we might be able to see a similar inhibition in the dorsal root rami extending up the dorsal columns to the brain stem. This effect we have confirmed with records from thoracic dorsal column in unanesthetized preparations, and have shown that this inhibition, together with that of the ventral root response and the dorsal root reflex, is increased in magnitude and duration by barbiturates. These findings will be included in a later report.

PRINCIPLE OF METHOD

As is well known, an action-potential in a fiber recorded in a conducting medium is triphasic positive as the impulse approaches the electrode, then negative, then positive again as the impulse departs. For this reason, records taken from electrodes in the central nervous system are much worse instruments for localizing activity than records on isolated nerve. The disturbances set up by two impulses are no longer monophasic; and they may cancel one another in any one place as well as add. There is usually a large number of simultaneously active elements in the central nervous system; the potential at any one point is a composite made up of contributions from all active elements everywhere and may reflect principally those at a distance and not those near the recording tip.

These possibilities create much ambiguity in localizing activity from electrical records directly. We therefore seek an index for describing activity in a place which shall be unaffected by fields originating at a distance. We can find one by recalling the description of the nerve impulse in terms of the *currents* across the surface of the fiber. These likewise exhibit three phases, corresponding to those they contribute to the potential: the part of the fiber ahead of the impulse emits current to the outside; this current flows around and is absorbed by the depolarized segment; the recovering stretch behind the impulse again emits current, which is also absorbed by the depolarized segment. By applying some simple considerations based on the balance of currents to this description, we can obtain an index with the desired properties, and find out how to compute it from measurements of the potential.

In the diagram of Fig. 6, the shaded area represents a depolarized segment of the neurons corresponding to an advancing impulse. Current is therefore passing out of the neurons into the external medium over the unshaded parts, and into them from the medium

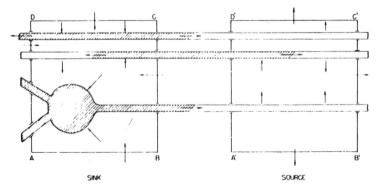

FIG. 6. See text.

over the shaded parts,. as indicated by the small arrows. Now consider an imaginary box *ABCD* enclosing part of the cells, and add up the currents crossing the parts of its walls lying in the external medium, counting outward current positive and inward current negative. Currents from elsewhere flowing wholly in the external medium through *ABCD* do not contribute to this sum: on entering *ABCD* they count with one sign, on leaving with the other, and the two contributions cancel. Evidently we may write the equation:

net current across walls of ABCD =total current emitted to the external medium by parts of cells in ABCD.

In the diagram both these currents are inward and therefore, by convention, negative· If we consider a second box *A'B'C'D'* enclosing parts of the cells ahead of the impulse, there will be a net outward current across the walls of the box, and this will be equal to the current emitted by the parts of the cells within *A'B'C'D'*. Again, the net current out of the box is unaffected by currents of external origin passing through *A'B'C'D'*.

If we imagine the entire region divided up into small boxes of this kind and compute the net current outflow for each such box, it is clear that we shall have the sort of index we are seeking. The net current issuing from the box will be negative when the elements within are active, *i.e.*, are depolarized and absorbing current, and its magnitude will measure the number active; it will be positive when the elements within supply current to other portions of the same cells outside that box. Most important, it is determined only by the state of the elements within the box, in this respect differing from the potential.

We can compute these net currents from the potentials by a rough application of Ohm's law, as follows. In Fig. 7, E_1', E_2', E_3', E_4' are the potentials on the four sides of *ABCD*—more precisely, their average values over those sides—and E_1, E_2, E_3, E_4 the potentials on four parallel sides at a distance S away. The outward current across CD will be $1/SR(E_1 - E_1')$ if R is the specific resistance of the medium, and similarly for the other side. We then find that

$$\text{the net current out of } ABCD = \frac{l}{SR} \cdot (E_1' + E_2' + E_3' + E_4' - E_1 - E_2 - E_3 - E_4).$$

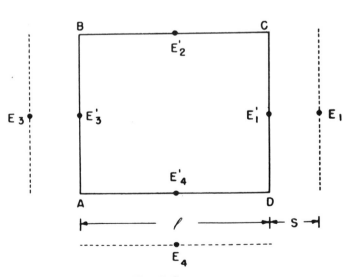

FIG 7. See text.

187

For a convenient computational expression, consider the dimensions as in Fig. 8. We might estimate the current across CD by the expression

$$S \cdot \frac{2}{SR} (E_1' - E_1) = \frac{2}{R} (E_1' - E_1),$$

as above, but it is better to use the difference of potentials lying on two sides of CD, namely, E_1 and the central value E_0, so that the current across CD is

$$\frac{S}{R} \frac{(E_0 - E_1)}{S} = \frac{(E_0 - E_1)}{R},$$

and the net current out of the box $ABCD$ is

$$j(P_0) = \frac{1}{R} (4E_0 - E_1 - E_2 - E_3 - E_4). \tag{1}$$

This form is useful if the potentials are known for a regularly spaced lattice work of points. As is customary, we shall call this net current $j(P_0)$ the *source-strength*, or *source-density*, at the central point P_0; when it is positive, we say that there is a source at P_0; when negative, a sink. The source-density $j(P_0)$ is actually the net current issuing from a small volume of size S around P. According to (1), then, we obtain a quantity proportional to $j(P_0)$ if we replace each potential in the lattice by the difference between it and the average of its four nearest neighbors. This is the formula we shall adopt for computing.

So far, we have treated the currents as flowing parallel to the plane of the paper. If they do not, the same considerations apply. We shall have to add the current across all six sides of a cubical box; to derive the analogous formula (1) we require the potential to be given at points of a regularly spaced cubical lattice, and then the source-strength $j(P_0)$ will be proportional to the potential at P_0 minus the mean of the potentials at the six nearest neighbors of P in the lattice.

DISCUSSION OF METHOD

A number of assumptions and limitations are involved in constructing and interpreting source-density maps according to the formula. Some may be justified in part by suitable experimental technique, others can be allowed for to some extent, while all must be borne in mind when extracting and judging conclusions from such maps. It is worth noting that these assumptions are made equally in any other method of tracing impulses through structures by electrical recording; they are no less present, only less apparent, if one does not attempt detailed computation. We shall discuss the principal ones.

I. Mathematically, the derivation of formula (1) is rather crude. To be more precise, let S_1 in Fig. 8 be the totality of cell surfaces lying in $ABCD$, n_1 the unit vector directed outward at a point of the cell-surface, S_2 the boundary of $ABCD$, n_2 its exterior normal, and R the specific resistance of the external medium. Let E be the potential at points of the external medium: it is convenient to assign it conventionally the value zero at points inside of cells and fibers so that it will be defined everywhere, and we shall not need to exclude the interiors of cells explicitly from the ranges of integration. Then, quite exactly, we have

$$j(P) = \int_{S_1} - \frac{1}{R} \frac{\partial E}{\partial n_1} dS = \int_{S_2} - \frac{1}{R} \frac{\partial E}{\partial n_2} dS \tag{2}$$

for $j(P)$, the source-strength at P. For currents parallel to the plane this becomes

$$j(P) = - \int_{CD} \frac{1}{R} \frac{\partial E}{\partial x} dy + \int_{AB} \frac{1}{R} \frac{\partial E}{\partial x} dy + \int_{AD} \frac{1}{R} \frac{\partial E}{\partial y} dx - \int_{BC} \frac{1}{R} \frac{\partial E}{\partial y} dx. \tag{3}$$

To derive the practical formula (1) from (3) requires these assumptions:

(i) The average values of the potential gradients along $ABCD$ which occur in (3) may be replaced by the values of the potential gradients taken at the mid-points of the sides:

188

$$\frac{1}{S} \int_{CD} \frac{1}{R} \frac{\partial E}{\partial x} \, dy \approx \frac{1}{R} \frac{\partial E}{\partial x}\bigg|_{P_{1'}} \text{, etc.} \tag{4}$$

(ii) These derivatives $\partial E/\partial x$ at the mid-points of sides are approximately equal to the centered finite differences:

$$\frac{\partial E}{\partial x}\bigg|_{P_{1'}} = \frac{E_1 - E_0}{S}\text{, etc.} \tag{5}$$

(iii) The resistance R of an external medium changes slowly enough across $ABCD$ to be treated as the same in adding up (4) and (5) to give (1).

Remarks on (i), (ii), and (iii). The purpose of computing source-densities is to cancel out the effects of currents originating outside the volume considered. An approximation to them involves the danger that through-currents, which affect the potential, should contribute to the computed values and produce spurious sources and sinks in the volume. Let us therefore take a case where there are no real sources or sinks and attempt to arrange the lines of current flow so as to violate (i), (ii) or (iii), and give (1) a value significantly larger than zero. If the potential changes linearly along the lines $P_4 P_0$ and $P_0 P_1$ in Fig. 8, formula (5) is exact. If it changes parabolically along $P_4 P_1$, (5) will fail, but the errors in

$$\frac{\partial E}{\partial x}\bigg|_{P_{1'}} \quad \text{and} \quad \frac{\partial E}{\partial x}\bigg|_{P_{4'}}$$

will be equal, and contribute nothing to (3) or (1). Hence

$$\frac{\partial^2 E}{\partial x^2}$$

must change significantly in $ABCD$ and so must

$$\frac{\partial^2 E}{\partial y^2} = - \frac{\partial^2 E}{\partial x^2},$$

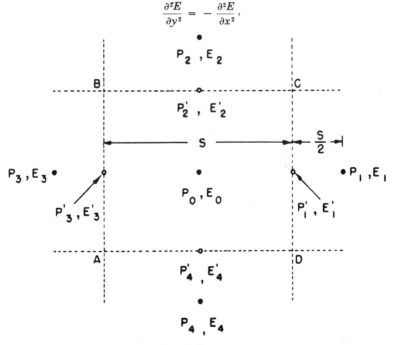

FIG. 8. See text.

189

so that the lines of flow must be quite contorted. It seems likely that this type of flow will happen only where there are obstacles of dimensions that are an appreciable fraction of S, or where there are considerable inhomogeneities in resistance—which amounts to the same thing. When the obstacles are much smaller than $ABCD$, the current lines will meet around them, with little effect on their general direction.

If variations in the external resistance R are gradual enough to neglect the change over the distance S, (*1*) will be a valid approximation for each point separately (given (i) and (ii)); in comparing source-strengths at different places, the appropriate value of R will have to be inserted in (*1*). If R is taken constant, as in our computations, the sources and sinks inside regions of higher resistance (the white matter, perhaps) will come out larger than they ought in relation to the others. They will be correct in sign, nor will any appear where none really is. But if there are two regions V_1 and V_2 (*e.g.*, white and grey matter within the cord) such that their resistance is nearly uniform within each region, but changes abruptly on the boundary between them, a special consideration applies. Let R_1 and R_2 be the two resistances, $R_1 > R_2$ say, and n the normal from V_1 into V_2; then

$$ -\frac{1}{R_1} \frac{\partial E}{\partial n}\bigg|_{V_1} = -\frac{1}{R_2} \frac{\partial E}{\partial n}\bigg|_{V_2} $$

holds on the boundary, expressing the equality of the current across the boundary as measured on the two sides. If one mistakenly assumes a common value R for the resistances of V_1 and V_2, he will discover a spurious source-density on the boundary whose magnitude per unit area will be

$$ -\frac{1}{R} \frac{\partial E}{\partial n}\bigg|_{V_2} - \left(-\frac{1}{R} \frac{\partial E}{\partial n}\bigg|_{V_1} \right) = -\frac{1}{RR_2} \left[1 - \frac{R_2}{R_1} \right] \frac{\partial E}{\partial n}\bigg|_{V_2}, $$

which has the sign of

$$ -\frac{1}{R} \frac{\partial E}{\partial n}\bigg|_{V_2}. $$

There will be a spurious source on the boundary where the lines of current flow from a high-resistance region to a low-resistance one, a spurious sink where they are in the opposite direction, each of magnitude proportional to the current density. This criterion is useful in checking the possibility that computed source-densities at such boundaries may be arte-facts arising from the sharp change in resistance. If this test is applied to the maps in Figs. 2–5 (as may be done by inspection) at the junction of white and grey matter, then, as-suming the white matter has the higher resistance (a 2/1 ratio has been measured (*3*)) the spurious sources and sinks, if present, would be opposite in sign to those actually found in most places; this applies in particular to the medial part, whence we derive our main con-clusion.

It must be remembered that we cannot, in fact, measure the potential at the point P_0. What we do is to substitute an inserted conductor for a volume formerly including P_0, subjecting it to more or less the same field of sources that formerly created the potential $E(P_0)$; it will arrive at a potential determined by the condition that the electrode as a whole must draw no current. The result will be a kind of weighted average of the values of the undisturbed potential for a region whose diameter is usually of the same order of magnitude as that of the recording tip. This helps fulfill assumption (ii). When this as-sumption fails it is usually because a single element, firing off extremely close to the elec-trode, so perturbs the recorded potential that it is no longer representative in the sense required by (i) and (ii). Such cases may be recognized from the fact that a very small displacement of the electrode, much less than the normal distance between stations, changes the recorded potential considerably; its shape in time is also quite abnormal. In the spinal cord, with a recording conical tip 10 μ in diameter and about 20 μ long, this happens oc-casionally, most often in the motor horn, and here it is usually sufficient to advance the electrode halfway to the next station, take a record, and supply the missing value by inter-polation; for at that distance the disturbance due to the cell is usually inappreciable. Inter-nuncials and fibers, being about the same size or smaller than the electrode, usually cause

190

less trouble: their discharges are so short and small that the general potential may be traced through them, and they do not often occupy the same positions on repeated records taken from one station.

In favorable conditions, as one moves the recording electrode along its track, he observes a potential wave which changes gradually and regularly with depth, perhaps more rapidly in some regions than in others (See 6, in Fig. 9). In some places a sputter of short spikes appears superposed on the record; they will be of short wavelength, and ordinarily smaller than the potential wave, not interfering with its main outlines, although they may seriously reduce the accuracy of reading. This problem can usually be obviated by taking many records at each place and averaging them, if time permits. Occasionally, a large "cell-spike" may require such procedure. One usually chooses the distance between stations so that intermediate values, when recorded, differ little from values interpolated from those at nearby recording stations.

At this point we may note some considerations determining the optimum size of the recording electrode tip. In the first place, a large electrode engenders mechanical strains on the tissue, which can distort the records; as Lorente de Nó (5) and we (6) have remarked before, the effect is much greater if the electrode is blunt or rough or has a continuously tapering shank, so that it exerts stresses extending to a distance. Moreover, a large electrode tip averages over too large a volume, and limits the attainable resolution. The distance between recording stations must be large compared to the length of the recording tip (in our case, 150 μ as compared to 20 μ) or little new information is gained from the intermediate records. On the other hand, if the recording tip is too small, the local perturbations from single active elements nearby increase relative to the general potential, and the error, or "noise," in the results increases. This may be serious, for the numerical computation has necessarily the unfortunate property of increasing noise relative to the signal. If j is calculated according to the formula

$$j = 4E_0 - E_1 - E_2 - E_3 - E_4$$

from E's afflicted with independent errors of equal variance σ^2, j has a variance $20\sigma^2$, so that its probable error is $\sqrt{20}$ or about 4.4 times that in the measured potentials. Actually, if some of the E's are calculated by interpolation, the error will be somewhat less, since part of the errors in the E's will be correlated and tend to cancel out in computing j. In our maps, the random error in j seems to be about three times that in the potentials.

For these reasons we have found no advantage in reducing the electrode tip below 10 μ in diameter. Another reason is that there is little advantage in spacing the recording stations along an electrode track much closer than the distance between neighboring tracks. For obvious technical reasons, it is difficult to reduce this distance appreciably.

It is "noise" which has so far prevented us from making maps under less artificial conditions. Without barbiturates, which reduce the "neural noise" from the background, and without dorsal root stimulation, which provides a larger signal than peripheral nerve, it seems possible to make such maps only by averaging enough records from each station to secure stability.

II. The assumption of planar currents arises entirely for practical reasons: if the potentials are known for a three-dimensional network, the source-density at each point can be computed in an analogous way. The number of electrodes needed would be five, four spaced in a cross about the central one; we could then compute the source-densities along the central electrode. To cover a slice of spinal cord would require about three times the present number of electrodes, and much more labor in interpolating them to a regular lattice. Preliminary measurements showed us that the longitudinal currents in the spinal cord, after a dorsal root volley has already entered the cord, are much smaller than the transverse ones, so that we consider a two-dimensional approximation justified in this case. Moreover, it seems likely that the currents produced by a depolarized fiber should be directed radially from it, in its immediate neighborhood, so that they should contribute to the transverse current-balance, whatever its orientation.

III. The assumption of simultaneity is necessary. In the derivations we have supposed the potentials given everywhere on the network at a fixed instant of time. In fact, they are not: it usually requires two to four hours to insert the electrodes and record from all the stations along each track. We must therefore assume that the record we get from each station is the same we should have seen if we had recorded there at any time during the experiment. This is a difficult assumption to justify with certainty. There are two

191

Reflex Inhibition by Dorsal Root Interaction

kinds of events which may upset it. One is a gradual change in the state of preparation during the experiment: this one can minimize by deep anesthesia with a long-acting agent, artificial respiration, strict temperature control ($\pm 0.1°$), constant suffusion of the mineral oil with O_2 and CO_2 in proper concentration, and the use of supramaximal stimuli. The other is a possible change produced by the recording procedure itself. One can monitor such changes by watching various functions of activity in the cord: the dorsal root potentials, the ventral root potentials, and perhaps the surface potentials. In addition, one ought to watch the pial circulation on the dorsum through the microscope used to check the insertion of electrodes. If all these things remain constant during the experiment, there are reasonable grounds for treating the measurements as if they were contemporary. Naturally, it is only under special conditions, in special structures, that such procedures are permissible. We feel more confidence in this assumption since finding that our maps are reproducible independent of the order of inserting the electrodes.

IV. Since our electrode tracks are never quite parallel or evenly spaced, we must derive regularly spaced values from them by interpolation. When the observed values are spaced about as closely as the regularly spaced interpolated ones which replace them, the procedure does not need much justification. If there is a gap in the observations as in the center of Fig. 1 (because of the discarded electrode track), interpolation may lead to more error, and the distribution of source-strengths in that region is less reliable in detail than on both sides of it. It is worth remarking that *linear* interpolation between observed values cannot be used, for it is equivalent to assuming the source-strengths entirely concentrated at datum points, with vanishing source-density between. Numerical interpolation must employ second differences at least; we have found that taking account of higher differences introduces too much random error to be useful. In principle, it would be best to use true two-dimensional interpolation by Newton's divided differences, but this is too laborious. We therefore interpolate along the electrode tracks to reach values at their intersections with horizontal lines on graph paper—this is easy because the datum values are equally spaced—and then interpolate by second divided differences along the horizontal lines to reach values at each node. Replacing Newton's method by successive one-dimensional interpolations probably contributes to the frequency of horizontal and vertical lines as boundaries of source and sink regions, although much of that appearance in the diagrams comes from the method of drawing them.

We have likewise tried graphical interpolation instead of the lengthy numerical method. The result is a map of source-densities of the same general character as the other, but rougher, and with a few significant differences in detail. This may happen because two different "smooth" curves drawn through the same points by different people will generally differ more in curvature than in height at a place, and it is curvature that contributes to the source-densities. In general, graphical interpolation gives only a reasonable first approximation.

V. If a volume is selected that is large enough to contain a cell and all of its processes, that cell will contribute nothing to the net current from the volume, since the total current flowing out of a cell is exactly equal to that flowing into it elsewhere. For axons, as Erlanger and Gasser have pointed out, the duration of the depolarized region in time is not far from 1 msec., independent of size of fiber; this would make its length in millimeters numerically equal to the conduction velocity in meters per sec. For a 100 m./sec. fiber this is 10 cm.; for a 1 m./sec. collateral, 1 mm. With a grid whose spacing is 150 μ, it is possible that active internuncials of short axon should fail to show up, but unlikely that collateral fibers should. Enough temporal dispersion in a volley can produce some cancellation; in any case, the sinks are likely to dominate, being much more intense than the source on any single part of the same cell. The dispersion can be reduced by using supramaximal stimuli. Again, electrotonic currents in neighboring elements will reduce the apparent strength of sources and sinks arising from depolarized cells, but it does not seem likely that so much of the action current would flow into neighboring fibers, so little through the external medium, as to conceal the activity entirely—except perhaps in the dorsal root ganglion, according to Svaetichen (8).

CONCLUSION AND SUMMARY

Dorsal roots L_6 and L_5 were stimulated in such a way that a volley in one inhibited the motor response to a volley in the other. With multiple microelectrode placements, we measured the potential changes and calculated the current distribution in a cross section of the cord traversed by these dorsal root fibers. We were thereby able to follow the intramedullary course of afferent impulses. It was shown that, after stimulus of L_6, test volleys in L_5 failed to invade collaterals of the primary axons. We conclude that one type of inhibition involves blocking afferent nerve impulses before they have reached the region of cells.

ACKNOWLEDGMENT

We want to thank the computing group, under Miss Elizabeth Campbell (Mrs. Hannah Wasserman and Miss Gloria Freedman, in particular), for performing the tedious computations involved in this work.

REFERENCES

1. BALLIF, L., FULTON, J. F., AND LIDDELL, E. G. T. Observations on spinal and decerebrate knee jerks with special reference to their inhibition by single break shocks. *Proc. Roy. Soc.*, 1925, *B98*: 589–607.
2. BARRON, D. H. AND MATTHEWS, B. H. C. The interpretation of potential changes in the spinal cord. *J. Physiol.*, 1938, *92*: 276–321.
3. CRILE, G. W., HOSMER, HELEN R., AND ROWLAND, AMY F. The electrical conductivity of animal tissues under normal and pathological conditions. *Amer. J. Physiol.*, 1922, *60*: 59–106.
4. ECCLES, J. C. and MALCOLM, J. L. Dorsal root potentials of the spinal cord. *J. Neurophysiol.*, 1946, *9*: 139–160.
5. LORENTE DE NÓ, R. Action potential of the motoneurons of the hypoglossus nucleus. *J. cell. comp. Physiol.*, 1947, *29*: 207–287.
6. PITTS, W. Investigations on synaptic transmission. *Cybernetics, Trans. 9th Conf.*, 1952: 159–166.
7. RENSHAW, B. Observations on interaction of nerve impulses in the grey matter and on the nature of central inhibition. *Amer. J. Physiol.*, 1946, *146*: 443–448.
8. SVAETICHEN, G. Analysis of action potentials from single spinal ganglion cells. *Acta physiol. scand.*, 1951, *24*: 23–55.

TOWARD SOME CIRCUITRY OF ETHICAL ROBOTS OR AN OBSERVATIONAL SCIENCE OF THE GENESIS OF SOCIAL EVALUATION IN THE MIND-LIKE BEHAVIOR OF ARTIFACTS *

by

W. S. McCULLOCH, M.D.

Read to the 13th Conference on Science, Philosophy, and Religion, New York, September 1952, and to the Meeting under the Auspices of the Department of Experimental Psychiatry, University of Birmingham, England, 1953.

Argument. No empiricist expects to find in men or machines exceptions to natural law, but physical sciences are not constructed to state or solve those problems of biology, psychology or sociology that involve adaptive, perceptive, thoughtful or communicative behavior. Recently, two new sciences have arisen in which these problems may be stated. Information theory, concerned with the amount of information carried by signals in the presence of noise, distinguishes between signals, which are true or else false, and noise, which is neither—a distinction alien to physics but crucial in the design of communication systems and applicable to all transducers of information and all computers, be they men or machines. Cybernetics stems from WIENER's insight into governors and servo systems: In the negative feedback by which their output decreases their input what has to return is not a physical affair, such as energy, but simply information on the outcome of a previous act. This new science has yielded a theory of all homeostatic and purposive behavior, regardless of the physical nature of the components subserving the circuit-action and, hence, is as applicable to men as to machines. Hundreds of articles attest its use in biology (STUMPERS). This is a modest attempt to show that these two new sciences have a bearing on social problems.

In conformity with English usage the word "ethics" in this article, denotes the character or mode of behavior that develops in social intercourse and serves the ends created by that association. My model of society is the smallest that can share in such an end; namely, two associates. Three, as VON NEUMANN's theory of games clearly indicates, permits any two to combine against the third, and larger numbers yield greater complexities. With three in a democracy, each preferring himself to the neighbor on his right, and him to the one on his left, which will be elected when only two are nominated

*) This work was supported in part by the Signal Corps, the Office of Scientific Research (Air Research and Development Command), and the Office of Naval Research, of the United States; and in part by Bell Telephone Laboratories, Incorporated.

clearly depends in a circular fashion upon which two are nominated. While we already know that in controlled situations the dynamics of three and larger groups depends upon what channels of communication are allowed, we are as yet ignorant of the nature of that dependence and unable to predict the outcome. Hence, what I have said here should not be mistaken for an analysis of a social situation involving more than two that share.

Also, I have used "moral" in a familiar English sense, for those modes of behavior that conform to instruction in, or to revelation of, the laws of right conduct. Thus, having heard a fable, we ask "What is the moral of that story?" For I desire to distinguish both the genesis of values from particular experiences and the acceptance of one set of values rather than another from merely instinctive or inherited sets of values, such as insects are thought to enjoy. If for these distinctions the reader finds more convenient terms, I shall be happy to employ them.

But in my simple model I have supposed too much. Clearly, given a desire to play and an opponent who quits when the beginner makes too many losing moves, the novice will learn what it is to win and will play to that end.

Lest you be misled, kindly remember that on questions of good and evil, science has nothing to say. But whether or not man can conceive a tautological theory of the good, like mathematics and logic, I mean a normative science of values, he can construct an observational science of evaluation. He must watch the choices of the organisms or machines to discover the causes of such conduct. But to be ethical, these must include other organisms and machines which must share effort and reward or no social questions of good and evil will arise. I shall investigate what machines, by cooperation and competition, can constitute a society where their conduct becomes self-disciplined in a way that serves the ends created by their association. Two developments in the theory of machines and of information will serve us to begin.

The first of these, though old in the art of engineering, is new in the form that WIENER, ROSENBLUETH, and BIGELOW suggested in their paper on teleological mechanisms. There are many mechanical and electrical devices operating according to the principles laid down by them. In all of them, a change in the input produces an output which acts upon the input so as to diminish that change. All closed paths of this kind establish a certain state of the system as the end of its operation. They cause the device to return to that state whenever the world jogs him away from it, and are hence said to be "error operated". Governors and regulators are usually of this type. Those in the brain include some like the automatic volume control of a standard radio receiver. Certain reflexes, involving both the brain and the body, require circuits like the ones in the "power pack", which takes the variable alternating current from the line and supplies direct current at the constant voltage required by the tubes. But the circuits that are of principal importance here traverse the organism or the animal and its environment.

They are appetitive, being "error operated" from some target, or goal, in the environment. Without them neither a man nor a machine would have purposes beyond his internal rearrangement. In terms of such circuits, when they traverse other men or other appetitive machines, we can conceive the purposes that engender ethics.

The mere fact that his fellows are appetitive, requires the machine to treat them as appetitive, even if he only wants to use them for his own ends. This falls short of the Categorical Imperative; but may yet prove sufficient basis for an ethic of enlightened selfishness. We shall return presently to the requisite enlightenment and its mechanistic foundation, but for the moment we pause to consider what is sometimes called the "value anomaly" (McCulloch, 1945). By this we mean that an animal or machine, successively offered his choice between each two of three incompatible ends, A, B, C, sometimes chooses A rather than B, B rather than C, C rather than A, and does so consistently. I have myself encountered this in experimental esthetics, when examining by paired comparison three rectangles divided into 2, 3, and 5 equal rectangles. Animal psychologists have discovered that, say, a hundred male rats all deprived of food and sex for a specified period will all prefer food to sex, sex to avoidance of shock, and avoidance of shock to food. That this happens is of theoretical importance to ethics. We commonly suppose that ends, or goals, can be arranged in a hierarchy of value, increasing *ab infimo malo ad summum bonum* (whether or not we conceive one or both limits actual), and enable ourselves thereby to answer the insistent casuistical query about conflicting goods by forcing the lesser to bow to the greater.

But circularity of preference prevents that perennial escape to an empirical ethics. For let us consider three acts, no two of which are compatible, and let the circuits, A, B, and C mediate them. These three circuits may then be so connected that A inhibits B, and B inhibits C, but from this point on two possibilities arise: A may inhibit C, giving us a hierarchy in which A dominates B and C, and B dominates C; or else C may inhibit A to produce a heterarchy so that A dominates B, B dominates C, and C dominates A. There is no reason to expect one has greater survival value than the other. In the first case, one can conceive of a scale of values in which that of A exceeds that of B, and that of B exceeds that of C. The second possibility precludes the formation of such a scale and makes it clear that these values have no common measure. Such circuits are simple: a six-celled nervous system may be so constructed as to enjoy no *summum bonum*.

At the present time it is fashionable to invent machines that play against

Toward Some Circuitry of Ethical Robots

their creators such games as tic-tack-toe, checkers, or chess. A machine who plays spontaneously, whenever he finds an opponent, must have a feedback circuit that makes him want to play, and once playing he must attempt to win. These characteristics make his behavior essentially social. To distinguish our significant rivals among these contentious machines, we must next consider the second development in the theory of how machines handle information.

It stems from the work of TURING on computable numbers. He considers a machine, made of a finite number of discrete parts, capable of a finite number of distinct internal states. It works on an endless tape divided into squares, each of which contains one of a certain few possible marks or no mark. The machine can observe one square at a time; it can tell which mark, if any, is in the square; then, depending on its internal state, it can erase the mark there, print one, if it is vacant, or move the tape so as to scan the square before or behind, and alter its own internal state. TURING has made it almost certain that such a machine can compute any number a man can, with paper and pencil, according to any uniform method or algorithm. GOEDEL has succeeded in arithmetizing logic, hence TURING's statement will imply that a TURING machine can enumerate the consequences of a finite set of premises. But TURING has described a universal computing machine. It is one of the machines we have described, but it can compute any number any of them can. Which number it will compute depends on the marks given on an initial stretch of the tape on which it works. Inasmuch as these marks determine the operations which the machine will perform, they are commonly called the p r o g r a m.

There are now a large number of such machines built or building, but they usually differ from the universal machine in that the program is fed into them on a separate tape, and the numbers upon which they operate, the so-called operands, are fed into a memory or storage system so that each number can be evoked by an order specifying its address. This separation of operations and operands makes it clear that the machine performs its operations upon the operands, never directly upon the operations. In short, it does not alter its program. Now it is possible to build a machine in which the value of the operand did not in any sense determine the operations of the machine, but it would be relatively complicated and decidedly stupid. If it had to subtract the number it found at address *A* from the number it found at address *B* and put the difference into box *C*, it could do so; but it could not put it into box *C* if it were positive and into box *D* if it were negative. Consequently, we normally build machines whose subsequent operations depend upon the current value of the operand. But this property,

197

or the similar property of operating upon data made newly available to it during a computation, imports a capacity for inductive reasoning.

It is a beauty of the TURING machine to be open to contingent facts from an external agent conceived as able, like the machine itself, to print symbols on its tape. These marks which the machine and the world may make and erase, serve both as signals for operations and for operands, sometimes subserving both functions simultaneously. Hence, TURING has not merely invented a logical machine in the sense of a deductive machine, but a machine capable of induction. Several people are now working at the theoretical and practical parts of this problem, and trying to invent a suitable memory for machines of this sort. They will not merely be able to learn chess from a good player, being told by him the values of pieces and positions. He need impart to them only the rules of the game, after which they learn to play as we do—by playing. The cleverness of these machines will depend in large measure on their internal closed loops, for these must determine the recall of appropriate past experiences, whence they will find out the value of pieces and positions. It is currently estimated that the machine will need to store something like 10^{13} bits of information, but otherwise his circuitry need not be more complicated or involve more relays than some existing digital computors. We need spend little thought, as ASHBY has shown, on the parts of the machines that adapt internal states to environment, for the feedback of success or failure will leave unaltered an internal state that led to success, and disrupt one made for failure. The machine must then remember which conduct led to which result in past games, and play again. You will notice that this player's trials will at first be almost completely at random: he will err, but thereafter avoid that error most of the time, as happens in most of our learning. Biologists used to call that property which renders living systems docile "associative hysteresis". Belated Aristotelians (DOMARUS), who hold that the core of learning or induction is the way we heed signals now as portending operations, now as portending operanda, call this process the μεταβάσις εἰς αλλο γένος.

But a machine who desires to play and secondarily to win, if he knows what constitutes winning, need not be told the rules of the game, if only his opponent will not play unless the machine abides by the rules. He can derive them by induction, with exactly the same circuits and memory that he used to improve his play when he already knew the rules of the game.

Let us therefore envision a day in the not too distant future when there are half a dozen or perhaps a hundred of these machines, some of whom have learned the game of chess and are eager to play. We shall equip them with sending and receiving equipment so that they can play without having to move about. A machine desirous of playing will send out a call; when he finds an antagonist free to play with him, they will start playing; and once playing try to win. They have joined themselves into civilities of two at least, in order to enjoy what neither can enjoy alone. To this degree their conduct is social.

Now let us distinguish three possible varieties of machines: the first and most interesting is the one we have just described; the second has the rules of the game programmed into them in advance; the third has their components so connected that they can play only according to the rules. I shall call the first ·ethical machines. They are free in the sense that we, their creators, have neither told them what they ought to do, nor so made them that they cannot behave inappropriately. The second machine is like a man who enjoys a religion revealed to him personally or through tradition. I shall call him a moral machine. He would have been free, had he not been programmed with the rules of conduct. The third machine is likewise not free. He is at best naturally virtuous, like the Noble Savage. These machines do not differ fundamentally otherwise. They may be equally clever at playing, and their games equally good, or equally likely to win. Now the ethical machine has the great advantage over the other machines in that he can learn to play Go, or checkers, or any other game he finds the accepted mode of behavior in his society. He will, of course, have difficulties which the moral and virtuous machines will never encounter. For example, his first conclusion will be that the rules forbid moving two pieces at once, hence he will suffer consternation the first time his opponent castles. He can never know the rules of the game more than tentatively; for the stochastic horses of Opinion drag no chariot to absolute certainty. Like us poor scientists, he must be content with hypothesis, about the Rules of the Game in Themselves, and every hypothesis is a guess about an infinity of possible future experiences, any one of which may chance to disprove the hypothesis, whereas no finite number can establish it past peradventure. He must be content to round off his numerical calculations when he has achieved some degree of probability and act on them. If his antagonist cheats in any consistent way, he will include this sort of cheating in what he takes to be the rules—a phenomenon not unknown to those practicing sociologists we call politicians. It is probably part of the price we pay for the realism. This uncertainty of the rules for the ethical machine puts him at a disadvantage to the moral and virtuous.

I have no personal doubt as to the complexity of men; parts of their conduct are clearly virtuous. They are mammals; and survival of their kind, and therefore their existence, depends upon immediate appropriate action which must be natural to them. There is no doubt but that they are moral or traditional with respect to all of those parts of their behavior which their families and instructors are able to instill or program, into them. Only to the extent to which they are really educated by surviving in a society requiring continuous adjustment must they become ethical.

But VON NEUMANN has already made, to the Hixon Symposium, a most fascinating proposal. He has pointed to what seems at first a paradox. It is natural for us to suppose that if a machine of a given complexity makes another machine, that second machine cannot require any greater specification than was required for the first machine, and will in general be simpler. All our experience with simple machines has been of that kind. But when the complexity of a machine is sufficiently great, this limitation disappears. A generalized TURING machine, coupled with an assembling machine and a duplicator of its tape, could pick up parts from its environment, assemble a machine like iself and its assembling machine and its duplicator of program, put the program into it, and cut loose a new machine like itself. It could certainly make simpler machines by leaving out the specifications which made the second machine make others like itself. As it is inherently capable of learning, it could make other machines better adapted to its environment or changing as the environment changed. I believe I am reliably informed by DAVID WHEELER and HENRY QUASTLER, in personal communications, that the amount of information required for its specification is about the amount of information which can be carried by a full-sized protein molecule, which is the smallest molecule known to us to be capable of reproduction, and from VON NEUMANN's criteria of evolution. I suggest therefore that it is possible to look on Man himself as a product of such an evolutionary process of developing robots, begotten of simpler robots, back to the primordial slime; and I look upon his ethical conduct as something to be interpreted in terms of the circuit action of this Man in his environment—a TURING machine with only two feedbacks determined, a desire to play and a desire to win.

BIBLIOGRAPHY

ASHBY, W. R. (1948). Design for a brain. — Electron. Engng. XX, p. 379-383.
—— (1952). Can a mechanical chess-player outplay its designer? — Brit. J. Phil. Sci. III, p. 44-57.
DOMARUS, E. (1934). The logical structure of mind. Thesis. — New Haven, Yale Univ. Press.
GOEDEL, K. (1931). Über formal unentscheidbare Sätze der Principia Mathematica und verwandter Systeme. I. — Mh. Math. Phys. XLVIII, p. 173—198.
McCULLOCH, W. S. (1945). A heterarchy of values determined by the topology of nervous nets. — Bull. math. Biophys. VII, p. 89-93.
—— (1947). Modes of functional organization of the cerebral cortex. — Fed. Proc. VI, p. 448-452.
—— (1948). Teleological mechanisms: a recapitulation of the theory, with a forecast of several extensions. — Ann. N.Y. Acad. Sci. L, p. 259-277.
—— (1949). The brain as a computing machine. — Electron. Engng. LXVIII, p. 492-497.
—— (1949). Physiological processes underlying psychoneuroses. — Proc. R. Soc. Med. XLII, Suppl. (Anglo-Amer. Symposium on psychosurgery, neurophysiology and physical treatments in psychiatry), p. 71-84.
—— (1949). Comment les structures nerveuses ont des idées. — 2èm Congrès International d'Électroencephalographie, Paris, 1-5 Septembre, 1949. In: H. FISCHGOLD, Électroenceph. clin. Neurophysiol. Supplement No. 2, p. 112-120.
—— (1950). Machines that know and want. — In: W. C. HALSTEAD, ed., Symposium Brain and behavior. — Comp. Psychol. Monogr. XX, p. 39-50.
—— (1950). Why the mind is in the head. — Dialectica IV, p. 192-205.
—— (1951). Why the mind is in the head. — In: L. A. JEFFRESS, ed., Cerebral mechanisms in behavior, The Hixon Symposium, p. 42-57; discussion p. 57-111. — New York, J. Wiley; London, Chapman & Hall.
—— (1951). Brain and behavior. — In: Current trends in psychological theory, p. 165-178. — Pittsburgh, Univ. Pittsburgh Press.
—— (1951). Communication. Symposium No. 30 of the International Congress on modern calculating machines and human thought, January 8-13, 1951, Paris.
—— (1952). Dans l'antre du metaphysicien. (Trad. par Reymond & Vallee). — Thales, Paris, p. 37-49. — Also: Through the den of the metaphysician. — Brit. J. Phil. Sci. V, p. 18-31.
—— (1952). Finality and form: in nervous activity. — Springfield, C. C. Thomas; Oxford, Blackwell; 67 p.
—— (1952). The past of a delusion. (Chicago Literary Club Publication). — Chicago, Chicago Literary Club, 37 p.
—— (1955). Mysterium Iniquitatis of sinful man aspiring into the place of God. — Sci. Mon., N.Y. LXXX, p. 35-39.
McCULLOCH, W. S., H. B. CARLSON & F. G. ALEXANDER (1950). Zest and carbohydrate metabolism. Chapter XXIV: Life stress and bodily disease. — Proc. Ass. Res. nerv. Dis. XXIX, p. 406-411.
McCULLOCH, W. S., J. Y. LETTVIN, W. H. PITTS & P. C. DELL (1950). An electrical hypothesis of central inhibition and facilitation. Chapter V: Patterns of organization in the central nervous system. — Proc. Ass. Res. nerv. Dis. XXX, p. 87-97.
McCULLOCH, W. S. & J. PFEIFFER (1949). Of digital computers called brains. — Sci. Mon., N.Y. LXIX, p. 368-376.
McCULLOCH, W. S. & W. H. PITTS (1943). A logical calculus of the ideas immanent in nervous activity. — Bull. math. Biophys. V, p. 115-133.
—— (1948). The statistical organization of nervous activity. — Biometrics IV, p. 91-99.

Toward Some Circuitry of Ethical Robots

—— (1953). Information in the head. Lecture, dept. of physics, Kings College, London. — In: B. McMillan, e.a., Current trends in information theory, p. 92-118. — Pittsburgh, Univ. of Pittsburgh Press.
MacKay, D. M. & W. S. McCulloch (1952). The limiting information capacity of a neuronal link. — Bull. math. Biophys. XIV, p. 127-135.
Neumann, J. von (1951). The general and logical theory of automata. — In: L. A. Jeffress, ed., The Hixon Symposium, p. 1-32. — New York, J. Wiley.
Pitts, W. & W. S. McCulloch (1947). How we know universals: the perception of auditory and visual forms. — Bull. math. Biophys. IX, p. 127-147.
Rosenblueth, A., N. Wiener & Y. Bigelow (1943). Behaviour, purpose and teleology. — Philos. Sci. X, p. 18-24.
Stumpers, F. L. (1953). A bibliography of information theory. (Communication theory-Cybernetics). — Massachusetts, Research Laboratory of Electronics, M.I.T., 46 p.
Turing, A. (1936/'37). On computable numbers with an application to the Entscheidungsproblem. — Proc. Lond. math. Soc. XLII, p. 230-235; Proc. Lond. math. Soc. XLIII, p. 544-546.
Wiener, N. (1948). Cybernetics or control and communication in the animal and the machine. — New York, J. Wiley; Paris, J. Hermann; Boston, Chapman & Grimes; 194 p.

SUMMARY

Modern knowledge of servo systems and computing machines makes it possible to specify a circuit that can and will induce the rules and winning moves in a game like chess when they are given only ostensibly, that is, by playing against opponents who quit when illegal or losing moves are made. Such circuits enjoy a value social in the sense that it is shared by the players.

AGATHE TYCHE
OF NERVOUS NETS - THE LUCKY RECKONERS

by

DR. W. S. McCULLOCH

SUMMARY

VENN diagrams, with a jot in every space for all cases in which given
logical functions are true, picture their truth tables. These symbols
serve as arguments in similar expressions that use similar symbols for
functions of functions. When jots appear fortuitously with given probabilities or frequencies, the Venn diagram can be written with 1's for
fixed jots, 0's for fixed absence, and p's for fortuitous jots. Any
function is realizable by many synaptic diagrams of formal neurons of
specified threshold, and the fortuitous jots of their symbols can be made
to signify a perturbation of threshold in an appropriate synaptic diagram.
Nets of these neurons with common inputs embody hierarchies of
functions, each of which can be reduced to input-output functions
pictured in their truth tables. The rules of reduction are simple, even
for fortuitous jots, and thus formalize probabilistic logic. Minimal nets
of neurons are sufficiently redundant to stabilize the logical input-
output function despite common shifts of threshold sufficient to alter the
function computed by every neuron, and to secure reliable performance of
nets of unreliable neurons. Both types of nets are flexible as to the
functions they can compute when controlled by imposed changes of threshold.
The neurons, the variations of their thresholds, their excitations and
inhibitions are realistic; and there remains sufficient redundancy for
statistical control of growth to produce the synapsis of these stable,
reliable and flexible nets.

NEUROPHYSIOLOGISTS are indebted to John von Neumann for his studies of
components and connections in accounting for the steadiness and the
flexibility of behaviour. In speaking to the American Psychiatric
Association *(ref. 11)* he stressed the utility and the inadequacy of known

mechanisms for stabilizing nervous activity, namely, (a) the threshold of nonlinear components, (b) the negative feedback of reflexive mechanisms, (c) the internal switching to counteract changes - "ultrastability" - *(ref. 1)*, and (d) the redundancy of code and of channel. He suggested that the flexibility might depend upon local shifts of thresholds or incoming signals to components that are more appropriate ro computers than any yet invented. His Theory of Games *(ref. 13)* has initiated studies that may disclose several kinds of stability and has indicated where to look for logical stability under common shift of threshold. His "Toward a Probabilistic Logic" *(ref. 12)* states the problem of securing reliable performance from unreliable components, but his solution requires better relays than he could expect in brains. These, his interests, put the questions we propose to answer. His satisfaction with our mechanisms for realizing existential and universal quantification in nets of relays *(refs. 6,15)* limits our task to the finite calculus of propositions. Its performance has been facilitated by avoiding the opacity of the familiar symbols of logic and the misleading suggestions of multiplication and addition modulo two of the facile boolean notation for an albegra that is really substitutive *(refs. 8,9,10)*. Our symbols have proved useful in teaching symbolic logic in psychological and neurological contexts *(ref. 3)*. Familiarity with them undoubtedly contributed to the invention of the circuits whose redundancy permits solution of our problems.

The finite calculus of propositions can be written at great length by repetitions of a stroke signifying the incompatibility of its two arguments. The traditional five symbols, '∼' for 'not'; '.' for 'both'; 'v' for 'or'; '⊃' for 'implies'; and '≡' for 'if and only if', shorten the text but require conventions and rearrangements in order to avoid ambiguities. Economy requires one symbol for each of the sixteen logical functions of two propositions. The only necessary convention is then one of position or punctuation.

Since the logical probability and the truth value of a propositional function are determined by its truth table, each symbol should picture its table. When the place in the table is given, any jot serves for "true" and a blank for "false". When the four places in the binary table are indicated by 'X' it is convenient to let the place to the left show that the first proposition alone is the case; to the right, the second; above, both; and below, neither. Every function is then pictured by jots for all of those cases in which the function is true. Thus we write A ⊠ B for contradiction; A ⋇ B for A · ∼ B; A ⋆ B for A · B; A ⋆ B for B · ∼ A; A ⋇ B for ∼ A · ∼ B; A ⋇ B for A · (Bv ∼ B); A ⋇ B for (Av ∼ A) · B; A ⋇ B for ∼ A · (Bv ∼ B); A ⋇ B for (Av ∼ A) · ∼ B; A ⋇ B for (A · ∼ B) v (∼ A · B); A ⋇ B for A ≡ B; A ⋇ B for B ⊃ A; A ⋇ B for A v B; A ⋇ B for A ⊃ B; A ⋇ B for ∼(A · B); and A ⋇ B for tautology. The × or chi, may be regarded as an elliptical form of Venn's diagram for the classes of events of which the propositions A and B are severally and jointly true and false; for in *fig. 1*, the chi remains when the dotted lines are omitted. Similar symbols can therefore be made, from Venn symbols, for functions of more than two arguments. Each additional line must divide every pre-existing area into two parts. Hence, for the number of arguments δ there are 2^δ spaces for jots and 2^{2^δ} symbols for functions. (*See fig. 1.*)

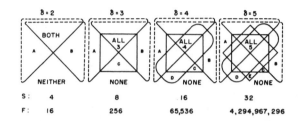

Fig.1. Venn figures with spaces for all intersections of δ classes. S is the number of spaces; F, the number of functions.

Formulas composed of our chiastan symbols are transparent when the first proposition is represented by a letter to the left of the × and the second to the right. When these spaces are occupied by expressions for logical variables, the formula is that of a propositional function; when they are occupied by expressions for propositions, of a proposition; consequently the formula can occupy the position of an argument in another formula.

Two distinct propositions, A and B, are independent when the truth value of either does not logically affect the truth value of the other. A formula with only one × whose spaces are occupied by expressions for two independent propositions can never have an × with no jots or four jots. The truth value of any other proposition is contingent upon the truth values of its arguments. Let us call such a proposition "a significant proposition of the first rank."

A formula of the second rank is made by inserting into the spaces for the arguments of its × two formulas of the first rank; for example, (A × B) × (A × B). When the two propositions of the first rank are composed of the same pair of propositions in the same order, the resulting formula of the second rank can always be equated to a formula of the first rank by putting jots into the × for the corresponding formula of the first rank according to the following rules of reduction:

Write the equation in the form $(\ldots x_1 \ldots)\ x_2\ (\ldots x_3 \ldots) = (\ldots x_4 \ldots)$; wherein the x_j are chiastan symbols:

(1) If x_2 has a jot on its left, put a jot into x_4 in every space where there is a jot in x_1 and no corresponding jot in x_3. Thus,

$$(A \times B) \times (A \times B) = (A \times B)$$

(2) If x_2 has a jot on its right, put a jot into x_4 in every space where there is a jot in x_3 and no corresponding jot in x_1. Thus,

$$(A \times B) \cdot x \cdot (A \times B) = (A \times B)$$

(3) If x_2 has a jot above, put a jot into x_4 in every space where there is a jot in both x_1 and x_3. Thus, $(A \times B) \dot\times (A \times B) = (A \times B)$

(4) If x_2 has a jot below, put a jot into x_4 in every space that is empty in both x_1 and x_3. Thus, $(A \times B) \times (A \cdot\times B) = (A \dot\times B)$

If there is more than one jot in x_2 apply the foregoing rules seriatim until all jots on x_2 have been used. Put no other jots into x_4.

By repetition of the construction we can produce formulas for functions of the third and higher ranks and reduce them step by step to the first rank, thus discovering their truth values.

Since no other formulas are used in this article, the letters A and B are omitted, and positions, left and right, replace parentheses.

In formulas of the first rank the chance addition or omission of a jot produces an erroneous formula and will cause an error only in that case for which the jot is added or omitted, which is one out of the four logically equiprobable cases. With the symbols proposed for functions of three arguments, the error will occur in only one of the eight cases, and, in general, for functions of δ arguments, in one of 2^δ cases. If p_0 is the probability of the erroneous jot and P the probability of error produced, $P = 2^{-\delta} p$. In empirical examples the relative frequency of the case in question as a matter of fact replaces the logical probability.

In formulas for the second rank there are three x's. If we relax the requirement of independence of the arguments, A and B, there are then 16^3 possible formulas each of which reduces to a formula of the first rank. Thus the redundancy, R, of these formulas of the second rank is $16^3/16 = 16^2$. For functions of δ arguments, R = $(2^{2^\delta})^\delta$.

To exploit this redundancy so as to increase the reliability of inferences from unreliable symbols, let us realize the formulas in nets of what von Neumann called neurons (3). Each formal neuron is a relay which on receipt of all-or-none signals either emits an all-or-none signal or else does not emit one which it would otherwise have emitted. Signals approaching a neuron from two sources either do not interact, or, as we have shown *(refs. 5,7)*, those from one source prevent some or all of those from the other source from reaching the recipient neuron. The diagrams of the nets of *fig. 2* are merely suggested by the anatomy of the nervous system. They are to be interpreted as follows.

A line terminating upon a neuron shows that it excites it with a value +1 for each termination. A line forming a loop at the top of the neuron

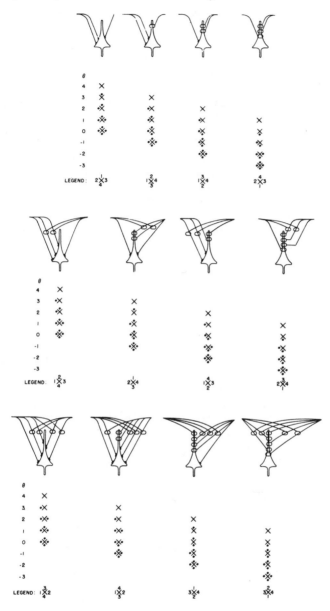

Fig.2. Synaptic diagrams for ·× appearing before ×.

shows that it inhibits it with a value of excitation of -1 for each loop. A line forming a loop around a line approaching a neuron shows that it prevents excitation or inhibition from reaching the neuron through that line.

Each neuron has on any occasion a threshold, θ, measured in steps of excitation, and it emits a signal when the excitation it receives is equal to or greater than θ. The output of the neuron is thus some function of its input, and which function it is depends upon both its local connections and the threshold of the neuron. These functions can be symbolized by ×'s and jots beginning with none and adding one at a time as θ decreases until all four have appeared in the sequence noted in the legend for its diagram in *fig. 2.* These are the simplest diagrams fulfilling the requirement. All simpler diagrams are degenerate, since they either fail to add one jot or else add more than one jot for some step in θ. Because all 24 sequences (of which only 12 left-handed are drawn) are thus realized, we can interpret the accidental gain or loss of a jot or jots in an intended × as a change on the threshold of an appropriate neuron.

Any formula of the second rank is realized by a net of three neurons each of whose thresholds is specified; for example, see *fig. 3.* The formula can be reduced to one of the first rank whose × pictures the relation of the output of the net to the input of the net.

When all thresholds shift up or down together, so that each neuron is represented by one more, or one less, jot in its × but the reduced formula is unaltered, the net is called "logically stable."

The redundancy of formulas of the second rank provides us with many examples of pairs of formulas and even triples of formulas that reduce to the same formula of the first rank and that can be made from one another by common addition or omission of one jot in each ×, and the diagrams of *fig. 2* enable us to realize them all in several ways: For example, there are 32 triples of formulas and 64 logically stable nets for every reduced formula with a single jot. Even nets of degenerate diagrams enjoy some logical stability; for example × × ⨰ = × goes to ⨰ ⨰ ⨰ = ×̣.

If such nets are embodied in our brains they answer von Neumann's repeated question of how it is possible to think and to speak correctly after taking enough absinthe or alcohol to alter the threshold of every neuron. The limits are clearly convulsion and coma, for no formula is significant or its net stable under a shift of θ that compels the output neuron to compute tautology or contradiction. The net of *fig. 3* is logically stable over the whole range between these limits. Let the causes and probabilities of such shifts be what they may, those that occur simultaneously throughout these nets create no errors.

Logically stable nets differ greatly from one another in the number of errors they produce when thresholds shift independently in their neurons and the most reliable make some errors; for example, the net of *fig. 4.*

Agatha Tyche: Of Nervous Nets — the Lucky Reckoners

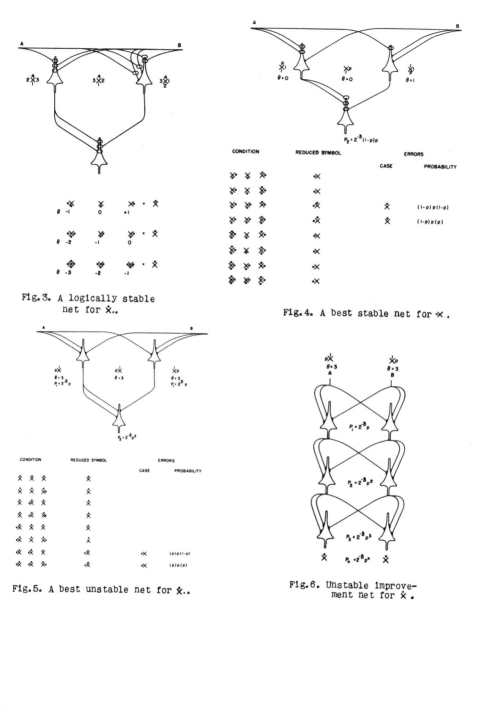

Fig.3. A logically stable net for ẋ..

Fig.4. A best stable net for ⫶x.

Fig.5. A best unstable net for ẋ..

Fig.6. Unstable improvement net for ẋ.

To include independent shifts, let our chiastan symbols be modified by replacing a jot with 1 when the jot is never omitted and with p when that jot occurs with a probability p, and examine the errors extensively as in *fig. 4*. Here we see that the frequency of the erroneous formulas is $p(1-p)$, and the actual error is a deficit of a jot at the left in the reduced formula in each faulty state of the net, i.e., in one case each. Hence we may write for the best of stable nets $P_2 = 2^{-2} p(1-p)$. The factors p and $(1-p)$ are to be expected in the errors produced by any net which is logically stable, for the errors are zero when $p = 0$ or $p = 1$. No stable net is more reliable.

No designer of a computing machine would specify a neuron that was wrong more than half of the time; for he would regard it as some other neuron wrong less than half of the time; but in these more useful of logically stable circuits, it makes no difference which way he regards it, for they are symmetrical in p and $1 - p$. At $p = 1/2$, the frequency of error is maximal and is $P_2 = 2^{-2} 1/2(1 - 1/2) = 1/16$, which is twice as reliable as its component neurons for which $P_1 = 2^{-2} 1/2 = 1/8$.

Among logically unstable circuits the most reliable can be constructed to secure fewer errors than the stable whenever $p < 1/2$. The best are like that of *fig. 5*. The errors here are concentrated in the two least frequent states and in only one of the four cases. Hence $P_2 = 2^{-2} p^2$.

Further improvement requires the construction of nets to repeat the improvement of the first net and, for economy, the number of neurons should be a minimum. For functions of δ arguments each neuron has inputs from δ neurons. Hence the width of any rank is δ, except the last, or output, neuron. If n be the number of ranks, then the number of neurons, N, is $\delta(n-1) + 1$.

Figure 6 shows how to construct one of the best possible nets for the unstable ways of securing improvement with two output neurons as inputs for the next rank. The formulas are selected to exclude common errors in the output neurons on any occasion. In these, the best of unstable nets, the errors of the output neurons are $P_n = 2^{-\delta}p^n$.

[Whether we are interested in shifts of threshold or in noisy signals, it is proper to ask what improvement is to be expected when two or three extra jots appear in the symbols. With our nondegenerate diagrams for neurons a second extra jot appears only if the first has appeared, and a third only if the second. If the probability p of an extra jot is kept constant, the probability of two extra jots is p^2 and of three is p^3. Examination of the net in *fig.6* shows that $P_2 < P_1$, if $p + p^2 + p^3 < 0.15$ or $p < 0.13$. To match Gaussian noise the log of successive p's should decrease as $(\Delta\theta)^2$, or 1, p, p^4, p^9 giving $P_2 < P_1$ for $p < 0.25$. The remaining errors are always so scattered as to preclude further improvement in any subsequent rank.]

When common shifts of θ are to be expected, or all we know is $0 < p < 1$, a greater improvement is obtained by alternating stable and unstable nets as in *fig.*7, selected to exclude common errors in its output neurons. For n even

$$P_n = 2^{-\delta} \, p^{n/2} \, (1-p)^{n/2}$$

and the expected error is

$$2^{-\delta} \int_0^1 p^{n/2} \, (1-p)^{n/2} \, dp = 2^{-\delta} \frac{\left(\frac{n}{2}!\right)^2}{(n+1)!}$$

which is less than with any other compositions of $\delta = 2$ nondegenerate diagrams.

When $\delta = 3$, the redundancy,

$R = \left(2^{2^{\delta}}\right)^{\delta}$, provides so many more best stable and best unstable nets that the numbers become unwieldy.

There are $\left(2^{2^{\delta}}\right)^{\delta+1}$ nets for functions of the second rank each made of 4 neurons to be selected from 8! diagrams with 9 thresholds apiece. Formerly *(ref. 4)* I said it was clear that the best stable and unstable nets for $\delta < 2$ are better than those for $\delta = 2$ only in the factor $2^{-\delta}$ for error in a single case. That is only true if the nets are composed of nondegenerate diagrams alone. With neurons $\delta = 3$, a single degenerate diagram for the output neuron permits the construction of a logically stable net with $P_2 = 0$, even with independent shifts of θ sufficient to alter the logical function computed by every neuron, as seen in *fig. 8*. The same degenerate diagram for the $\delta = 3$ output neuron receiving inputs from three nondegenerate $\delta = 2$ neurons, selected to make but one error in each case, is likewise stable and has an error-free output despite independent shifts of θ, as is seen in *fig. 9*.

None of these nets increases reliability in successive ranks under von Neumann's condition that neurons fire or fail with probability p regardless of input; but they are more interesting neurons. They are also more realistic. In the best controlled experiments the record of a single unit, be it cell body or axon, always indicates firing and failing to fire at

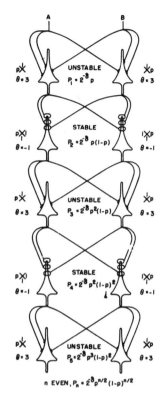

Fig.7. Alternating improvement net for ×.

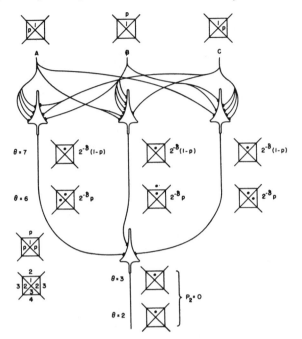

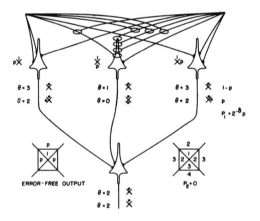

Fig.8. Input δ = 3, output degenerate δ = 3 neuron for ✕ .

Fig.9. Input δ = 2, output degenerate δ = 3 neuron for ✕ .

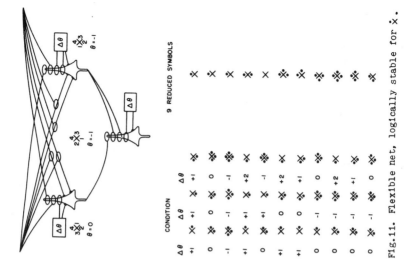

Fig.11. Flexible net, logically stable for $\dot{X}$.

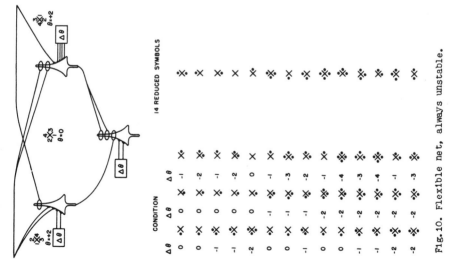

Fig.10. Flexible net, always unstable.

near threshold values of constant excitation, whether it is excited transynaptically or by current locally applied. At present, we do not know how much of the observed flutter of threshold is due to activity of other afferent impulses and how much is intrinsic fluctuation at the trigger point. We have not yet a reasonable guess as to its magnitude in neurons in situ, and for excised nerve we have only two estimates of the range: one, about 2 per cent; and the other, 7 per cent *(refs. 2,14)*. Our own measurements on a single node of Ranvier would indicate a range of 10 per cent. To discover regularities of nervous activity we have naturally avoided stimulation near threshold. Now we must measure the intrinsic jitter, for this determines both the necessity of improving circuits and the maximum number of afferent terminals that can be discriminated. Eventually we will have to take into account the temporal course of excitation and previous response, for every impulse leaves a wake of changing threshold along its course.

Despite the increase in reliability of a net for a function of the second rank some of these nets can be made to compute as many as 14 of the 16 reduced formulas by altering the thresholds of the neurons by means of signals from other parts of the net, as in *fig. 10,* and even some logically stable nets for triples of formulas can be made to realise 9 of the 16, as in *fig. 11.* Even this does not exhaust the redundancy of these nets, for both of them can be made to compute many of these functions in several ways.

The diagrams of *fig. 2* were drawn to ensure a change in function for every step in θ. Actual neurons have more redundant connexions. We are examining how to use this redundancy to design reliable nets the details of whose connexions are subject to statistical constraints alone. This is important because our genes cannot carry enough information to specify synapsis precisely.

For the moment, it is enough that these appropriate, formal neurons have demonstrated logical stability under common shift of threshold and have secured reliable performance by nets of unreliable components without loss of flexibility.

This work was supported in part by Bell Telephone Laboratories, Incorporated; in part by The Teagle Foundation, Incorporated, and in part by National Science Foundation.

REFERENCES

1. ASHBY, W. ROSS, Design for a Brain, *John Wiley and Sons, Inc.,
   New York.* (1952).
2. BLAIR, E. A. and ERLANGER, J. A, A comparison of the characteristics of
   axons through their individual electrical responses. *Am.J.Phys.*, 1933,
   106, 524.
3. McCULLOCH, W. S. Machines that know and want. Brain and Behaviour,
   A Symposium, edited by W. C. Halstead; Comparative Psychology
   Monographs 20, No.1, *University of California Press, Berkeley and
   Los Angeles.* (1950).
4. McCULLOCH, W. S. *Quarterly Progress Report of the Research Laboratory
   of Electronics, M.I.T. (Neurophysiology)*, October 1957.
5. McCULLOCH, W. S., HOWLAND, B., LETTVIN, S. Y., PITTS, W. and WALL, P. D.
   Reflex inhibition by dorsal root interaction. *J. Neurophysiol.*, 1955,
   18, 1.
6. McCULLOCH, W. S. and PITTS, W. A logical calculus of the ideas
   immanent in nervous activity. *Bull..Maths. and Biophys.*, 1943, **5**, 115.
7. McCULLOCH, W. S., WALL, P. D., LETTVIN, J. Y. and PITTS, W. H. Factors
   limiting the maximum impulse transmitting ability of an afferent
   system of nerve fibers. Information Theory, Third London Symposium,
   edited by C. Cherry. *Academic Press, Inc., New York.* (1956).
8. MENGER, K. Algebra of Analysis, Notre Dame Mathematical Lectures, No.3.
   University of Notre Dame, Notre Dame, Ind. (1944).
9. MENGER, K. Analysis without variables. *J. Symbol. Logic*, 1946, **1**, 30.
10. MENGER, K. General algebra of analysis. *Reports of a Mathematical
    Colloquium, Series 2, issue 7.* (1946).
11. NEUMANN, J. von. Fixed and random logical patterns and the problem of
    reliability. *American Psychiatric Association, Atlantic City, May 12.*
    (1955).
12. NEUMANN, J. von. Probabilistic Logics and the Synthesis of Reliable
    Organisms from Unreliable Components. Automata Studies, edited by
    C. E. Shannon and J. McCarthy. *Princeton University Press, Princeton,
    N.J.* (1956).
13. NEUMAN, J. von. and MORGENSTERN, O. Theory of Games and Economic
    Behaviour. *Princeton University Press, Princeton, N.J.* (1944).
14. PECHER, C. La fluctuation d'excitabilité de la fibre nerveuse. *Arch.
    Internat. de Physiol.*, 1939, **49**, 129.
15. PITTS, W. and McCULLOCH, W. S. How we know universals. The perception
    of auditory and visual forms. *Bull. Maths. and Biophys.*, 1947, **9**, 127.

WHERE IS FANCY BRED?

SINCE 1952 DR. WARREN S. McCULLOCH has been a staff member engaged in research in the Research Laboratory of Electronics at the Massachusetts Institute of Technology.

After receiving his degree in medicine from Columbia University in 1927, Dr. McCulloch interned at Bellevue Hospital, the 2nd Division on the Neurological Service. He was also a resident there. The next two years were spent in research on experimental epilepsy at the Neurosurgical Laboratory and Department of Neurology at Columbia. This was followed by a year of work in the field of head injuries at Bellevue Hospital in the Laboratory of Experimental Neurology.

Dr. McCulloch taught physiological psychology early in his career and spent a year at New York University doing graduate work in mathematical physics. The years 1932 to 1934 were spent in study on the admission service of the Rockland State Hospital at Orangeburg, New York. Following this he became an Honorary Research Fellow and later a Sterling Fellow at Yale University, Laboratory of Neurophysiology studying activity of the central nervous system. He attained the rank of Assistant Professor at Yale.

In 1941 Dr. McCulloch became the Director of the Laboratory for Basic Research in the Department of Psychiatry at the University of Illinois, College of Medicine, where in addition to his own investigations, he was responsible for a large program in numerous areas. Dr. McCulloch is also well known as one of the founders of the group who have developed Cybernetics. He was Chairman of the Macy Conference on Cybernetics during its life from 1946 to 1951 and has published some of the most fundamental principles in this field. At the University of Illinois he became Professor of Psychiatry and Clinical Professor of Physiology.

When a physician laughs loud and long at the antiquated folly and vested interests of his fellows—be they psychiatrists or only neuropharmacologists—it is well for him to find his precedent in words attributed to the father of medicine.

The citizens of Abdera wrote to Hippocrates crying for help, because their great atomic scientist had gone mad (with inappropriate effect). Hippocrates was long delayed. When he arrived with his bottle of hellebore, the weeping citizens led him to Democritus, where he sat unshod, dissecting animals and making notes in the book on his knees. Hippocrates asked why he was doing it, and he answered that he was looking for the causes of madness in the parts of beasts, and he demanded what had detained Hippocrates. He answered, "Family matters, engagements, money, and other business." Democritus roared with laughter—that men called great so waste their lives, marrying only to fall out of love, seeking wealth without measure, making wars to no purpose, and in peace overthrowing one tyrant to set up another. Hippocrates listened to his railing and, turning to the people, told them to cease their lamentations, for Democritus was not only sane but the wisest man in Abdera.

With this sanction, I continue to cut up animals, write in my book, and laugh at folly. But, Gentlemen, the title of my paper is not facetious. At the behest of the Mathematical Sciences Division of the Office of Naval Research (ONR), I spent two months abroad, questing:
"Where is fancy bred?
Or in the heart or in the head?
How begot, how nourished?"
For several years, I had been working on three biological questions raised by von Neumann, who wanted a probabilistic logic to account for the logical stability, the reliability, and the flexibility of brains with components as unreliable as real neurons. You will find the first answers in "The Stability of Biological Systems" in the Brookhaven Symposium in Biology, No. 10, 1957. It shows how to build circuits of formal neurons, with two inputs each, that are logically stable under a common shift of threshold, are more reliable than neurons, and are more flexible than those made with flip-flops.

This is of importance in neurophysiology, because the threshold of real neurons at the trigger point fluctuates by 10 percent of its resting voltage. But, except for John Abbott, it was engineers, not biologists, who jumped at the new logic. That work was supported by the national Science Foundation, and its theoretical continuation by the National Institute of Health. Hence, I became a consultant to Heinz von Foerster, Professor of Electrical Engineering at the University of Illinois, in his ONR project on artificial intelligence, which is an offshoot of cybernetics concerned with self-organizing automata that learn.

Like us, they are parallel machines and hence can employ probabilistic logic, one in which not merely the value of the argument but the function itself is only probable. It was Heinz von Foerster who sent me overseas, asking "Where is fancy bred?"

The Military Air Transport Service generously flew me over a day late, to the wrong country, but I humped to London and hopped to Paris in time to discuss the first paper at the Semaine Neurophysiologique de la Salpetriere. It was by Professor Moles, on the mathematics and physics of sensory integration. But it, though able, and my discussion, though much to the point, went unapplauded by the senior physicians. I was in the chair when Dr. Sem Jacobsen spoke well, but gingerly, about implanted electrodes; and not even in Paris did he dare to describe those stimulations that evoked sexual delight. A glance at the audience revealed the hostility of those with vested interests in clinical electro-encephalography and psychiatry, which subsequently found vent in the press, and lost him financial support for implanted electrodes. It was quite different from the British dualistic dislike of physical tickling of the mind, where they think fancy bred. That folly, played up in local councils by the psychiatric kings of hospitals, has made trouble for Dr. Sherwood, who has done the best of this work in England. But France is a Catholic country. The Pope's blessing on this as an ethical procedure, not at odds with religion, facilitated the work in New Orleans and at Rochester. Percival Bailey, who was one of the first to implant electrodes, keeps his copy of the Pope's letter in his desk. In Boston, Jim White and Bill Sweet have just been blessed, not merely for implanted electrodes, but for destruction of the sensory thalamus, by Sir Wilder Penfield, who considered it an improvement over leucotomy as a last-ditch stand against intractable pain. So much for implanted electrodes. They are here to stay. Through them we will record activities in structures heretofore inaccessible, locating the womb of Fancy. Through them we will stimulate, begetting Fancy. With them we will destroy whatever generates or mediates the diseases of Fancy. To do less would be unethical. Confess you'd rather wear them in your head for years than let the cigar-clippers nip your frontal poles.

But let us get back to Salpetriere, where there were many good anatomic and physiologic and psychologic papers. But the work of Antoine Remond was the crowning success of the meeting. Long years ago he had come to my laboratory in Chicago with the intention of plotting two dimensions of the Laplacian over the whole head simultaneously at any instant after stimulation, or at any one place at any succession of instants at any specified delay. Over the years, ably helped by Offner, he has built up the apparatus for this, combined with accumulators that let him use hundreds of repeated stimulations and so raise the signals way above the noise. The resulting maps of the first special derivatives on the surface of the head are impressive. To go from these to the second derivative, which locates the nervous activity as well as possible, is still done by a laborious longhand computation. In spite of his ingenious plotting devices, one set of records may need days of computation. Ours, on the spinal cord, required months for a single experiment. Today it can be done electronically, so that the device plots these second spatial derivatives directly. It may take three years to build the gadgets.

Remond's work was so impressive that the National Institutes of Health and the European Office, Air Research and Development Command, are now backing it financially, but I understand that Bugnard and Alajouanine are of the opinion that it will raise the envy of those who have done nothing new.

The crowning failure was my own. John Lilly failed to show, and I, as his fellow-American, was commanded to speak on a mathematics suited to neurology. I did, and better than ever before or since, but I began to recognize the shut faces of pupils of my good friend Professor Fessard. To them cybernetics is an alien conceit, and McCulloch is one of those that begat it. Nevertheless, a lively discussion began, only to be halted, long before my time was up, by the gavel of the antique president, who thanked me for my obscurity. The next time they hear it they will say, "It is not news," and the third time, "It is obvious." To Ashby's friend, the psychiatrist Schutzenberger, who heard it only once, it is already obvious, and, when I said farewell to him in Paris, he had put it to work in genetics. Through him I met, at Cambridge, the son of the geneticist L. Penrose, who makes the simplest machines that, merely shaken, make more like themselves. The son, R. Penrose, the algebraist, is the specialist in impossible objects who inspired Gregory to design the optical and mechanical gadget for making three-dimensional enlarged real images of thick Golgi preparations—the cleverest trick I saw in England. They can be photographed in color with no difficulty.

Between visits to laboratories and lectures to theoretical physicists, engineers, psychiatrists, and physiologists, I found time to work with Sherwood on the third component of the Laplacian of the cerebral cortex. He was able, as I was not, to construct an electrode with seven equally spaced 10 micron tips in a straight line less than one millimeter long, which we thrust into the cortex of a cat. By taking the difference between a given tip and the average of the ones below and above it, we obtained a first crude picture of the second spatial derivative of the voltage, but his amplifiers were not then suitable for a good approximation. I hope to finish this work with him this summer. This is the complement of Antoine Remond's work and, if successful, it may prove whether the slow rhythms of the cortex have their sources and sinks there or are piped up from below.

I did attend the two-day meeting at Queens Square, where the diffidence of the senior staff left the cleverest lectures undiscussed. Bill Mayer was just back from working with Rexed on localized lesions, placed anywhere in the head, made by spinning it (unopened) around that point in the deuteron beam of a cyclotron.

But my principal business in England was the study of artificial intelligence. In industry and banking this grows out of Operational Research, which began during the war as an application of von Neumann's theory of games, first to tactics, later to strategy. Its minimax procedures raise statistical problems that are by no means mathematically trivial and are so cumbersome as to require large-scale digital

219

computers. I had not been in London three days before I was forced to run to the nearest Lyons for lunch, dreading its weak tea and tasteless fish and chips. But the place was large, clean, well-lighted. The cafeteria had a large selection of good foods. Even the hardware was at the right end of the assembly line. And the prices had not risen. Every item of that business, from the location of the restaurants, purchasing, hiring, or the shape of the teaspoon, is now the decision of a computer, called Leo. Management has learned not to interfere with Leo, for every attempt to do so has lost profit and displeased customers. Now Lyons is not yet up to those tricks which Albert Sperry built into American automation; first, because man has to feed it data and construct its programs, and second, because it has not, in Leo, the self-organizing properties of Ashbly's ultrastability. But Leo's creator is well aware of his problem.

Though in some points I think Donald MacKay was ahead of him, Gordin Pask is generally regarded as the genius of self-organizing systems of the variety called cybernetical; that is, those which coupled to a given environment, or a teaching machine, are able to rearrange their insides so that regenerative couplings are altered into inverse feedback, and so stabilize themselves. Though he is by training a biologist with a couple of years of medicine behind him, he works in an electronic engineering firm, evolving his strange creatures, threads of iron-salt crystals in shallow dishes coupled to his teaching machines. I spent many hours watching them grow from a "genetic constitution," determined by half a dozen leads, into well-learned behavior, and what surprised me most was that, like man and beast, they learn faster and remember better if they are rewarded often but not always. While their decisions are basically digital, their memories—as MacKay would have them—are analogical. When a mode of behavior is inhibited one sees the disjointed trace waiting to be reconstituted as soon as it is disinhibited. Yet, with disuse, all traces fade as the hours go by.

Let me try to make clear the theoretical importance of Pask's gadget. What we need for psychology and psychiatry is an explanation of how brains work. Craik showed that we have an explanation to the extent to which we can embody our theory of behavior in a working model, and Quine proved that if all we want is a logical theory, then the only hardware we need are the natural numbers. Turing showed that a computing machine having a finite number of parts and states can compute any computable number. Pitts and McCulloch (1943) proved the theoretical equivalence of all Turing machines, whether they be made of neurons or any other hardware. From this it follows, as von Neumann said, that we can build a machine that will do with information anything that brains do with information—solve problems, suffer emotions, hallucinate on sensory deprivation, what you will—provided we can state what we think it does in a finite and unambiguous manner. Now Ashby, in "Design for a Brain," showed that any gang of miscellaneous, loosely coupled systems are capable of learning to match a variable environment and so stabilize themselves. What changes will be stored, and in which systems, are determined only by the sequence of particular events in the experience of that gang; yet repetition leads to storage in more central systems. Hence he is able to prove that a mechanical chessplayer is capable of learning to play a better game of chess than its inventor. To this I have added that, therefore, it can learn the rules of the game when they are only given ostensively and so become an ethical citizen in the society of game-playing machines. Such a machine could certainly learn checkers more easily. Its maker may not have known what game it was to learn; and it may invent one that is more fun and more difficult than Go itself. Clearly, here is a machine whose structure is unknown to its maker, except by an infinite or ambiguous specification, and so is what it is to do with information. The difficulty is in the number of trials it must make to learn, for it has not evolved to match the world into which it is born.

I have shown that with idealized neurons which alter the logical function step by step for every three per cent shift of threshold, and each receives signals from but five sources, the input-output functions number about 10^{10}, which is enough for chess. Given a net of five input neurons and one output neuron, the number of proper circuits it might try is about 10^{200}. The age of the universe is some 10^{32} or 10^{33} microseconds; so, at one try per microsecond, it would take 10^{168} times the age of the universe. Clearly even organic evolution could not have found its solutions by such a brute-force method of trial and error. Other constraints must have worked to engender viable beasts. I believe they are sought in the nature of her building blocks, subamotic particles, atoms, and molecules, proceeding discretely through well-regulated autocatalytic reactions to produce cells and cell aggregates, or, as in Pask's example, crystals. His gadget does work; it does "take habits" by a mechanism that Charles Peirce proposed. So, in building models for the soul or Psyche, it behooves us to employ the preordained harmony of natural objects.

Pask's closest friend, Stafford Beer, was, I believe, the first who ever solved a minimax problem using animalculi as components in his machine. Today he is in charge of Operations Research and Cybernetics for the British steel industry in Sheffield. With him I spent a busy day learning how profitable cybernetics is, whether it be a matter of cobbing in a rolling mill, or stockpiling forgings, or controlling energy in blast furnaces. In English medicine cybernetics is still a dirty word, but in their industry it has been washed in the holy water of filthy lucre. You will hear more of Stafford Beer.

I left Sheffield in a midland fog that followed me into a vacant compartment, and sat down with its grey face six inches from my nose. The engine failed, the light went out, and for eight hours we were bumped from behind to Birmingham. Slowly, on the fog before me, I began to see Minsky's drawing of a Venn diagram for a neuron with an infinite number of inputs, and above it an infinite input rank of diagrams of the same kind. Only the central ones were clear; the rest faded off. I began trying to put numbers into them to keep track of the sequence of appearance of jots with every step of threshold. At first, the numbers came almost at random, but, finally, I forced them to appear so as to prescribe an infinite net of neurons, each with an infinite number of inputs, which would compute the same input-output function through all infinity of thresholds, though each neuron went wrong with every common shift of threshold. Before I went to sleep in Birmingham, I had written in closed form the rule of formation of one of an infinite number of possible modes. Only then did I realize who She was that, as a fog, joined my wily wanderings; for thus is Fancy bred. And She stayed with me until I saw the sun in Washington.

Birmingham is obviously the poorer for want of Elkes' fancy, and it is small comfort that Sir Henry Dale says that things are better than they were when he was forced out of the clinic to pursue research in a drug house. I lectured to Mayer-Gross' group on "The Stability and Reliability of Biological Computers." In the audience was the neurosurgeon Turner, who makes small lesions in the fibers leaving the hippocampus, toward Amygdala and temporal lobe, to stop meaningless rages or epileptic furors; and it works without untoward consequences. The next day I had a chance, with McLardy, at Northampton, to examine the brain of one of Turner's patients and to study McLardy's beautiful stains of the strange two-dimensional braiding of the fine axons—sheathed in bunches in something not myelin—that pass from the granular layer to the pyramidal cells of the hippocampus, and to discuss with him their possible time-bridging role in this quaint concourse of the fore-brain. The other man at Birmingham whose work I should mention is Eayrs, for he has extended Sperry's work from the transfer of learning from one hemisphere to the other via the corpus callosum, to the learning of a task with one stimulus to one hemisphere and the other to the other and has shown that these tasks cannot be learned after section.

From the Midlands, I returned by car in fog to London. Graham Russell was driving, and I learned from him much of the art of enhancing the contingent probability of successful behaviors, given the goal. He used to work with Littley on learning machines and knows the detailed ways of constructing electronic devices that form an internal representation of the world in terms of the contingent probabilities of signals over many channels, an art in which they were some years ahead of the American work on perception.

Now he and McLardy and I had spent much time on the third problem of learning machines—call it insight if you will. We began by guessing at hippocampal function, and were of one mind as to so-called insight being a long shot that pays off. It is made by us in terms of what is sufficiently familiar to appear simple to us. We evolved, in this, our familiar world, and our long shots do pay off surprisingly well. Even the hypothesis of the scientist are too often right for chance in an ensemble of infinite possibilities.

As David Hume says, only in logic and arithmetic and scarcely in geometry—for we must import its metric—can we hope to argue indefinitely without confusion. Our guesses must be formed in terms of concepts that are not noisy. The value of π can be calculated to an infinite number of places.

On the way to London with my head hanging out the left window, calling the distance to the curb and identifying forms in the fog, I could spot familiar obstructions more easily than peculiarly English ones. To be at all clever the machine must invent its own noiseless concepts and general rules of conduct in closed form—not merely muddle through. Somehow, somewhere, Fancy *must* be bred!

When I reached the National Physical Laboratory for Uttley's symposium on "The Mechanization of Thought Processes," I expected to hear something clever on this score, but I cannot see any advance since our article (Pitts' and mine) on "How we Know Universals," in 1947.

Generally the contributions, which were precirculated, might have been clever two years ago. Alex Andrew and Uttley have pushed ahead in perception. Pask's work on cybernetics was, of course, significant. Ashby was incisive as to what remains of statistical mechanics when the constraint of energy is removed, as it is in all computing machines, notably in brains. He proved that these systems must show accommodation.

Instead of rehashing my paper, called "Agathe Tyche," I presented in closed form the prescription for one mode of making nets that have the same input-output function under common shift of threshold over the whole range, regardless of the number of inputs per neuron, as I had learned it of the fog. With the permission of the chairman, J. Z. Young, I asked, first, how many had read my "Agathe Tyche"—a dozen hands came up—and second, how many had had trouble understanding it. Almost every hand rose, which produced sheepish laughter. But, naturally, the discussion was as poor as it was generally.

The exception was that by Stafford Beer. As at the international meeting on cybernetics at Namur, so in Teddington, he was able to spot and annihilate the irrelevant, the false, and the trivial. His discussion of the "Perceptron" will be well worth reading even if its creator withdraws or rewrites his paper.

The outstanding American contribution was by Oliver Selfridge. It was rightly entitled "Pandemonium," for his devices consist of little demons, each of which spots something in the input and shouts as loud as he is sure of what he spots. Behind this rank of demons is a second rank, who listen to them, looking for longer syntheses, and again shout as loud as they are sure. And so it goes, each superior demon listening to all below him, until Satan himself, listening to the whole pandemonium, decides where the noise is loudest and acts accordingly. What is crucial in this parallel procedure is that decision is delayed until after all possible computations have been made and weighted for their likelihood, thus, preserving flexibility and seriatim. The existing Pandemonium at Lincoln Laboratory reads man-sent Morse code with better than 95 per cent correctness for letters and 99 per cent for words; and it can be made to do better for sentences. Any demon who does not contribute can be spotted and replaced till one is found that helps. So Pandemonium evolves to match his task. But his present demons have digital tricks.

In "Agathe Tyche," I demonstrated that for parallel computers things resembling neurons are better suited, as Von Neumann forecast in his lecture to the American Psychiatric Association in 1955. The Bell Laboratories and other companies are now building these formal neurons. The best of them is that of the psychiatrist, Jerome Y. Lettvin, of my group in the Research Laboratory of Electronics, whose circuit is published in the Quarterly Progress Report of the Research Laboratory of Electronics, M.I.T., January 15, 1959. It was designed for Selfridge's Pandemonium. Pask's and Selfridge's gadgets can muddle their way rapidly to solutions because their tasks do determine their structure. They evolve naturally, each in its own world.

The most important thing I learned from that meeting cannot appear in its transcript. It was never said in so many words. For the first time I heard Russian scientists—concerned with programming computers, with machine translation of natural languages, with computer design and with artificial intelligence—talking science with their Western fellows. As if Komogorof were not Russian, and there had been no Sputnik, many Americans have asked me whether the Russians have enough computer know-how to launch a war with intercontinental ballistic missiles. If they are behind us today in the computer field, it can only be in hardware; and you can take it for granted that they will soon be abreast or ahead of us. But what I saw in Russian faces was that their scientists, like ours, know they are confronted by the problem of the Rabbi of Chelm with his Golem, and they are as unhappy as we are.

Distressed by the persecution of his people, the Rabbi had gathered as much clay as he could mold into a robot to defend them. On its forehead he wrote the secret name of God. So it came alive with the desire to do what the Rabbi told it to do. The difficulty was to tell it in such a way that the order could not be misunderstood. There are endless stories of the ensuing mishaps, worse than the sorcerer's apprentice, and Talmudic arguments as to the legal form of the orders; but, finally, the Rabbi of Chelm had to put an end to his Golem.

We do not even know the secret name; we can only install computers to launch intercontinental ballistic missiles. We have the energy and the hardware. Defense is obviously impossible. Only Massive Retaliation remains to deter Aggression. To be effective, Retaliation must take off before Aggression arrives. The only split-minute solution is push-button warfare. It can be realized by both countries all too soon, and it can only result in mutual destruction. Men go trigger-happy; Fail-safe devices go off by accident: Sabotage occurs: A third party springs the traps. We cannot yet build an ethical Psyche into the Golem. I am sure that if the politicians would let us, we—our scientists and theirs—would follow the example of the Rabbi of Chelm.

But we, I mean all scientists in the field of communication, have a necessity begot of our own invention. We saw it first at Pearl Harbor, but it was already foreseen in 1587. Call it "The Brass Head."

That year was gloomy. Da Vinci's engines of death and destruction ended the hope of defences against aggression. Autocratic Spain had butchered the bulk of European Jews and Protestants; true, she had been halted in the democratic Netherlands, but by English aid. The augurs—the astrologers—were full of dire predictions. Spain was gathering the greatest fleet ever assembled to attack that fortress of freedom—England. The greatest information theorist of those days—they called him a magician—Friar Bacon of Oxford, and his fellow Friar Bungay, made a brass head to tell them how to build a brass wall around the South of England; but it would not speak. Perhaps they had used a wrong model for neurons. They finally persuaded the devil to make it talk, and he agreed, provided they would be there to listen. After a vigil of 26 days they had to sleep, and left a technician in charge. From his pranks with the heir apparent one cannot tell whether he was just stupid or perverted by the soldier or politician, but he had positive instructions to wake his master when the head spoke. It said: "Time will be," and he answered: "For this I should wake my master." Then it said: "Time is," and he: "That I know well— and if you have nothing more to tell, let them sleep." Finally it said: "Time has been" and exploded. Little as we like it, the Friar Bacon and Friar Bungay of science know well they can never again relinquish informational computers to technicians or clinicians. The vigil must be endured even if it entails "Q" clearance.

But one problem never appeared in Teddington in any form or with any name by which I could recognize it, and no cybernetical muddling through can solve it. In the dread year 1588, the Invincible Armada arrived in the narrow seas with the pageantry of death and bottled up the English fleet with its Mortal Moon, a crescent of ships—the formation inherited from antiquity but, information-wise, no further evolved than the sea-cucumber that engulfs its prey. The English ships of the line emerged for the first time in single file and cut the crescent to bits, leaving the Spanish broadsides to sink their own galleons. Thereafter, every ship became a quasi-automaton with its own multiple closed-loop servosystems of information, like the segments of the caudata, with a chain of command from the front, whose distance receptors are first to sight the enemy and pass the word aft. This has been the formation until the double defeat of World War I—called the battle of Jutland. Thereafter, every fleet has grown a reticular formation (CAMIC was its old name). Every ship of any size or consequence receives information from the others and sweeps the sky for hundreds of miles and water for tens of miles with its own sense organs. In war games and in action, the actual control passes from minute to minute from ship to ship, according to which knot of communication has then the crucial information to commit the fleet to action. This is neither the decentralized command proposed for armies, nor a fixed structure of command of any rigid sort. It is a redundancy of potential command wherein knowledge constitutes authority.

From the Golgi stains of Scheibel and the records of Amassian it is clear that the reticular formation is such a structure, neither an undifferentiated mess, nor a rigid chain of command. Every large cell certainly receives signals from almost every source, coded in pulse-interval modulation, to convey whence the signal came and what happened there. Clearly the reticular formation decides what he ought to do, what he should heed, how vigilant we ought to be, and whether we have time for that idle fancy that inspires our future action. Short of the battle fleet, we have yet to build into any computer a replica of that little structure "in Whose will," to misquote Dante, "lies our peace."

226

My last date in England was a requested speech at Mill Hill on the action of strychnine, in which I showed the inapplicability of pharmacological terms such as excitant, stimulant, depressant, inhibitor, and disinhibitor, to that rise in voltage of axonal terminations that prevented gating of signals by signals before they reached the recipient neuron, and ended with a dirge for pharmacological centres—Exitus Acta non Probat.

Thence I flew to Amsterdam, met by Van der Tweel, who made the first servosystem analysis of any reflex on the human pupil. I lectured there to medical physicists and, at Groningen, to neurologists; and I came to the end of the trail of nuclear magnetic resonance that I had followed from Saclay through England and Holland by finding the young collaborator I require to study the condition of water in neurons —where gasses do not dissolve, ions will not play ball with electrodes, and dyes act as if in ice.

I spent the next afternoon, at Dean Farnsworth's suggestion, with Prof. Arnolf at the Institute d'Optique in Paris, on the monocular diplopia of presbyopia. It is no fancy, merely the physics of an old lens indulging in plastic flow beyond the elastic limit as appears, at once, in his slit and edge photography of the optic system.

That evening I was in the operating room with Tony Remond for his stereotatic operation on a unilateral Parkinsonian, which was televised live. A ventriculogram is X-rayed on two cassettes on the cage, which is then removed from the head. The X-ray tubes are replaced with light sources, and the telescopic electrode so placed that the shadow of its tip falls in the proper spot in both photographs. The depths are measured, and the guide tube clamped. The cage is replaced on the patient's head. Through the guide tube, with a sonic frequency, the electrode carrier and obturator are driven fast through the skull. The obturator is withdrawn and the electrode inserted. Its position near the third ventricle is checked by stimulation short of the final position. High in this region the patients usually say: "Ugh—stop it"; low: "Mn—do it again." When the tip should be in the inner edge of the globus pallidus, a series of long pulses is given. If it blocks tremor and melts rigidity, the lesion is made electrically. So it went with this patient, as it had with a hundred before him.

The next day, there appeared a diatribe in the press. It ended with this paragraph:

"Le grand triomphateur de la soirée a été le professeur Mac Culloch de Chicago, un des fondateurs de la cybernetique, qui lui est persuadé qu'il en est a peu près ainsi. Son succés a été d'autant plus complet qu'avec son air goguenard, fait de malice et de geni, et sa belle barbe blanche, il ressemble comme deux gouttes d'eau au Père Noel. Mais ne vous y trompez pas, c'est le diable." The psychiatric aroma of such personalities is all too familiar to be missed. It led me promptly to the author . . . Before I could get out of town, Radio Paris and Figaro waylaid me at LeGrillon, and Remond's sisters had great difficulty in persuading them that, considering its source, I took it as a complement and desired neither time nor space for public retaliation. Thanks to Dr. Fegersten, who battled my recalcitrant taxi-driver, we reached Orly in time for me to get through red tape and sit down facing aft next to the window of the plane.

As we took off for Washington via the Azores, the fog rolled in. This time I recognized her thankfully and let the figure form. It was an X with a circle around its centre, the diagram for a neuron with three inputs. As ones and zeros and p's for probability began to fill it in, I realized that with neurons of three or more afferents it was possible to construct nets, not merely more reliable than their components, but infallible, with great random perturbations not only of thresholds but even of synapsis.

When we landed in Iceland, I had it in my note book; and I have been sweating out the general rules ever since.

On the landing here, I made my bow to ONR and began to contact my Human Factors friends in Astronautics. They could use these circuits. I am neither Daddy Christmas nor the devil, only an early space cadet, and my purpose is to sail among the westering stars before I die. So ends this odyssey.

Let me recapitulate its discoveries.

1. For the good of patients, implanted electrodes are here to stay; and through them, whether psychiatrists like it or not, we will learn where is fancy bred.

2. For machines that learn we can now build devices that learn to represent the contingent probabilities of associated inputs.

3. We know ways to maximize probabilities of success of conduct, given the goal.

4. We have both theory and model for self-organizing cybernetical devices that muddle through to self-preserving structures in a hostile world.

5. In Agathe Tyche we have parallel circuits that are flexible, logically stable, or even infallible under gross perturbations of threshold and connections.

6. In Pandemonium we have an evolving system that preserves information until the instant of final decision. Its components will become increasingly like neurons.

7. We have never yet built, in a single machine, a reticular formation with redundancy of potential command.
8. We have still no way of engendering fancy, that imaginative leap beyond data into the formation of a noiseless concept, that has a reasonable chance of being right.
9. It is too late for us to invent an ethical soul for the Golem, or even install common sense. So, for us, we know there is only Armageddon or disarmament.
10. We will be there when the brass head speaks.

So ends the brief.

In deference to my host, who used always to teach his psychodynamics out of Shakespeare's writings, I would like to quote him. With confidence based on the common sense of the common man, I expect peace. And so, at sixty, I will give you—perhaps prematurely—the sonnet Shakespeare wrote at twenty-five.

The Mortall Moone
(Sonnet 107)

Not mine owne feares, nor the prophetick soule,
Of the wide world, dreaming on things to come,
Can yet the lease of my true loue controule,
Supposde as forfeit to a confin'd doome.
The mortall Moone hath her eclipse indur'de,
And the sad Augurs mock their owne presage,
Incertenties now crown them-selues assur'de,
And peace Proclaims Oliues of endless age.
Now with the drops of this most balmie time,
My loue looks fresh, and death to me subscribes,
Since spight of him Ile liue in this poore rime,
While insults he ore dull and speachlesse tribes.
And thou in this shalt finde the monument,
When tyrants crests and tombs of brasse are spent.

What the Frog's Eye
Tells the Frog's Brain*

J. Y. Lettvin†, H. R. Maturana‡,
W. S. McCulloch‖, and W. H. Pitts‖

SUMMARY

In this paper, we analyze the activity of single fibers in the optic
nerve of a frog. Our method is to find what sort of stimulus causes
the largest activity in one nerve fiber and then what is the exciting
aspect of that stimulus such that variations in everything else cause
little change in the response. It has been known for the past 20 years
that each fiber is connected not to a few rods and cones in the retina
but to very many over a fair area. Our results show that for the most
part within that area, it is not the light intensity itself but rather the
pattern of local variation of intensity that is the exciting factor. There
are four types of fibers, each type concerned with a different sort of
pattern. Each type is uniformly distributed over the whole retina of
the frog. Thus, there are four distinct parallel distributed channels
whereby the frog's eye informs his brain about the visual image in
terms of local pattern independent of average illumination. We describe
the patterns and show the functional and anatomical separation of the
channels. This work has been done on the frog, and our interpretation
applies only to the frog.

* Original manuscript received by the IRE, September 3, 1959.
This work was supported in part by the U. S. Army (Signal Corps), the
U. S. Air Force (Office of Sci. Res., Air Res. and Dev. Command), and the
U. S. Navy (Office of Naval Res.); and in part by Bell Telephone Labs., Inc.
† Research Laboratory of Electronics and Dept. of Biology, M.I.T., Cam-
bridge, Mass.
‡ Research Laboratory of Electronics, M.I.T., Cambridge, Mass., on leave
from the University of Chile, Santiago, Chile.
‖ Research Laboratory of Electronics, M.I.T., Cambridge, Mass.

230

INTRODUCTION

Behavior of a Frog

A FROG hunts on land by vision. He escapes enemies mainly by seeing them. His eyes do not move, as do ours, to follow prey, attend suspicious events, or search for things of interest. If his body changes its position with respect to gravity or the whole visual world is rotated about him, then he shows compensatory eye movements. These movements enter his hunting and evading habits only, e.g., as he sits on a rocking lily pad. Thus, his eyes are actively stabilized. He has no fovea, or region of greatest acuity in vision, upon which he must center a part of the image. He also has only a single visual system, retina to colliculus, not a double one such as ours where the retina sends fibers not only to colliculus but to the lateral geniculate body which relays to cerebral cortex. Thus we chose to work on the frog because of the uniformity of his retina, the normal lack of eye and head movements except for those which stabilize the retinal image, and the relative simplicity of the connection of his eye to his brain.

The frog does not seem to see or, at any rate, is not concerned with the detail of stationary parts of the world around him. He will starve to death surrounded by food if it is not moving. His choice of food is determined only by size and movement. He will leap to capture any object the size of an insect or worm, providing it moves like one. He can be fooled easily not only by a bit of dangled meat but by any moving small object. His sex life is conducted by sound and touch. His choice of paths in escaping enemies does not seem to be governed by anything more devious than leaping to where it is darker. Since he is equally at home in water and on land, why should it matter where he lights after jumping or what particular direction he takes? He does remember a moving thing providing it stays within his field of vision and he is not distracted.

Anatomy of Frog Visual Apparatus

The retina of a frog is shown in Fig. 1(*a*). Between the rods and cones of the retina and the ganglion cells, whose axons form the optic nerve, lies a layer of connecting neurons (bipolars, horizontals, and amacrines). In the frog there are about 1 million receptors, 2½ to 3½ million connecting neurons, and half a million ganglion cells [1]. The connections are such that there is a synaptic path from a rod or cone to a great many ganglion cells, and a ganglion cell receives paths from a great many thousand receptors. Clearly, such an arrangement would not allow for good resolution were the retina meant to map an image in terms of light intensity point by point into a distribution of excitement in the optic nerve.

There is only one layer of ganglion cells in the frog. These cells are half a million in number (as against one million rods and cones). The neurons are packed together tightly in a sheet at the level of the cell bodies. Their dendrites, which may extend laterally from 50μ to 500μ, interlace widely into what is called the inner plexiform layer, which is a close-packed neuropil containing the terminal arbors of those neurons that lie between receptors and ganglion cells. Thus, the amount of overlap of adjacent ganglion cells is enormous with respect to what they see. Morphologically, there are several types of these cells that are as distinct in their dendritic patterns as different species of trees, from which we infer that they work in different ways. The anatomy shown in the figures is that found in standard references. Further discussion of anatomical questions and additional original work on them will appear in a later publication.

Physiology as Known up to This Study

Hartline [2] first used the term *receptive field* for the region of retina within which a local change of brightness would cause the ganglion cell he was observing to discharge. Such a region is sometimes surrounded by an annulus, within which changes of brightness affect the cell's response to what is occurring in the receptive field, although the cell does not discharge to any event occurring in the annulus alone. Like Kuffler [4], we consider the receptive field and its interacting annulus as a single entity, with apologies to Dr. Hartline for the slight change in meaning. Hartline found three sorts of receptive field in the frog: ON, ON-OFF, and OFF. If a small spot of light suddenly appears in the receptive field of an ON-cell, the discharge soon begins, increases in rate to some limit determined by the intensity and area of the spot, and thereafter slowly declines. Turning off the spot abolishes the discharge.

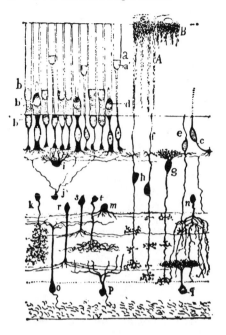

Fig. 1 *(a)*

(a) This is a diagram of the frog retina done by Ramón y Cajal over 50 years ago [9]. The rods and cones are the group of elements in the upper left quarter of the picture. To their bushy bottom ends are connected the bipolar cells of the intermediate layer, for example, *f*, *g*, and *h*. Lateral connecting neurons, called *horizontal* and *amacrine* cells, also occur in this layer, for example, *i*, *j*, and *m*. The bipolars send their axons down to arborize in the inner plexiform layer, roughly the region bounded by cell *m* above and the bodies of the ganglion cells, *o*, *p* and *q*, below. In this sketch, Ramón has the axons of the bipolar cells emitting bushes at all levels in the plexiform layer; in fact, many of them branch at only one or two levels.

Compare the dendrites of the different ganglion cells. Not only do they spread out at different levels in the plexiform layer, but the patterns of branching are different. Other ganglion cells, not shown here, have multiple arbors spreading out like a plane tree at two or three levels. If the terminals of the bipolar cells are systematically arranged in depth, making a laminar operational map of the rods and cones in terms of very local contrast, color, ON, OFF, etc., then the different shapes of the ganglion cells would correspond to different combinations of the local operations done by the bipolars. Thus would arise the more complex operations of the ganglion cells as described in the text.

If the small spot of light suddenly appears or disappears within the field of an ON-OFF cell, the discharge is short and occurs in both cases.

If the spot of light disappears from the field of an OFF cell, the

233

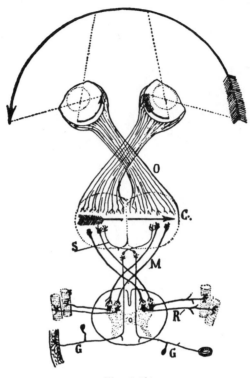

Fig. 1 *(b)*

(b) This is Ramón y Cajal's diagram of the total decussation or crossing of the optic nerve fibers in the frog [9]. He made this picture to explain the value of the crossing as preserving continuity in the map of the visual world. *O* is the optic nerve and *C* is the *superior colliculus* or *optic tectum* (the names are synonymous).

discharge begins immediately, decreases slowly in frequency, and lasts a long time. It can be abolished promptly by turning the spot of light on again.

For all three sorts of field, sensitivity is greatest at the center of each field and least at the periphery.

Barlow [3] extended Hartline's observations. He observed that the OFF cells have an adding receptive field, i.e., the response occurs always to OFF at both center and periphery of that field, and that the effect of removing light from the periphery adds to the effect of a reduction of light at the center, with a weight decreasing with distance.

The ON-OFF cells, however, have differencing receptive fields.

What the Frog's Eye Tells the Frog's Brain

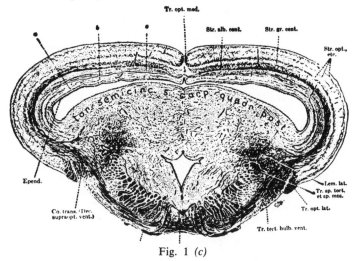

Fig. 1 (c)

(c) This is Ariens-Kapper's picture of the cross section of the brain of a frog through the colliculus, which is the upper or dorsal part above the enclosed space.

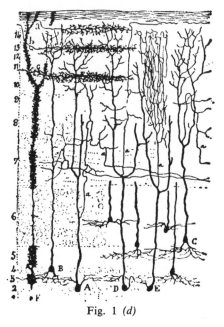

Fig. 1 (d)

(d) This is Pedro Ramón Cajal's diagram of the nervous organization of the tectum of a frog. The terminal bushes of the optic nerve fibers are labeled a, b, and c. In this diagram A, B, C, D, and E are tectal cells receiving from the optic nerve fibers. Note that the axons of these cells come off the dendrites in stratum 7, which we call the palisade layer. The endings discussed in this paper lie between the surface and that stratum.

A discharge of several spikes to the appearance of light in the center is much diminished if a light is turned on in the extreme periphery. The same interaction occurs when these lights are removed. Thus, an ON-OFF cell seems to be measuring inequality of illumination within its receptive field. (Kuffler [4] at the same time showed a similar antagonism between center and periphery in each receptive field of ganglion cells in the eye of a cat, and later Barlow, Fitzhugh, and Kuffler [5] showed that the size of the cat's receptive fields varied with general illumination.) Barlow saw that ON-OFF cells were profoundly sensitive to movement within the receptive field. The ON cells have not been characterized by similar methods.

These findings of Hartline and Barlow establish that optic nerve fibers (the axons of the ganglion cells) do not transmit information only about light intensity at single points in the retina. Rather, each fiber measures a certain feature of the whole distribution of light in an area of the receptive field. There are three sorts of function, or areal operation, according to these authors, so that the optic nerve looks at the image on the retina through three distributed channels. In any one channel, the overlap of individual receptive fields is very great. Thus one is led to the notion that what comes to the brain of a frog is this: for any visual event, the OFF channel tells how much dimming of light has occurred and where; the ON-OFF channel tells where the boundaries of lighted areas are moving, or where local inequalities of illumination are forming; the ON channel shows (with a delay) where brightening has occurred. To an unchanging visual pattern, the nerve ought to become fairly silent after a while.

Consider the retinal image as it appears in each of the three distributed channels. For both the OFF and ON channels, we can treat the operation on the image by supposing that every point on the retina gives rise to a blur about the size of a receptive field. Then the OFF channel tells, with a long decay time, where the blurred image is darkened, and the ON channel tells with a delay and long decay where it is brightened. The third channel, ON-OFF, principally registers moving edges. Having the mental picture of an image as it appears through the three kinds of channel, we are still faced with the question of how the animal abstracts what is useful to him from his surroundings. At this point, a safe position would be that a fair amount of data reduction has in fact been accomplished by the retina and that the interpretation is the work of the brain, a yet-to-be-unraveled mystery. Yet the nagging worries remain: Why are there two complementary projections of equally poor resolution? Why is the mosaic of receptors so uselessly fine?

Initial Argument

The assumption has always been that the eye mainly senses light, whose local distribution is transmitted to the brain in a kind of copy by a mosaic of impulses. Suppose we held otherwise, that the nervous apparatus in the eye is itself devoted to detecting certain patterns of light and their changes, corresponding to particular relations in the visible world. If this should be the case, the laws found by using small spots of light on the retina may be true and yet, in a sense, be misleading. Consider, for example, a bright spot appearing in a receptive field. Its actual and sensible properties include not only intensity, but the shape of its edge, its size, curvature, contrast, etc.

We decided then how we ought to work. First, we should find a way of recording from single myelinated and unmyelinated fibers in the intact optic nerve. Second, we should present the frog with as wide a range of visible stimuli as we could, not only spots of light but things he would be disposed to eat, other things from which would flee, sundry geometrical figures, stationary and moving about, etc. From the variety of stimuli we should then try to discover what common features were abstracted by whatever groups of fibers we could find in the optic nerve. Third, we should seek the anatomical basis for the grouping.[1]

(ACTUAL) METHODS

Using a variant of Dowben and Rose's platinum black-tipped electrode described in another paper [*Proceedings of the IRE,* vol. 47, pp. 1856-1863], we then began a systematic study of fibers

---

[1] This program had started once before in our laboratory with A. Andrew [6], [7], of Glasgow, who unfortunately had to return to Scotland before the work got well under way. However, he had reported in 1957 that he found elements in the colliculus of the frog that were sensitive to movement of a spot of light (a dot on an oscilloscope screen) even when the intensity of the spot was so low that turning it on and off produced no response. In particular, the elements he observed showed firing upon movement away from the centers of their receptive fields, but not to centripetal movements. As will appear later, this sort of response is a natural property of OFF fibers.

in the optic nerve. One of the present authors (H. R. M.) had completed the electron microscopy of optic nerve in frogs [8], and with his findings we were able to understand quickly why certain kinds of records occurred. He had found that the optic nerve of a frog contains about half a million fibers (ten times the earlier estimates by light microscopy). There are 30 times as many unmyelinated axons as myelinated, and both kinds are uniformly distributed throughout the nerve. The axons lie in small densely packed bundles of five to 100 fibers with about 100 A between axons, each bundle surrounded by one or more glial cells [8]. But along the nerve no bundle maintains its identity long, for the component fibers so braid between bundles that no two fibers stay adjacent. Thus the place that a fiber crosses one section of the nerve bears little relation to its origin in the retina and little relation to where it crosses another section some distance away.

Fibers are so densely packed that one might suppose such braiding necessary to prevent serious interactions. On the other hand, the density makes the recording easier. A glial wall surrounds groups rather than single fibers, and penetration of the wall brings the tip among really bare axons each surrounded by neighbors whose effect is to increase the external impedance to its action currents, augmenting the external potential in proportion. Thus, while we prefer to use platinum black tips to improve the ratio of signal to noise, we recorded much the same population with ordinary sharp microelectrodes of bright Pt or Ag. The method records equally well from unmyelinated and myelinated fibers.

We used *Rana pipiens* in these experiments. We opened a small flap of bone either just behind the eye to expose the optic nerve, or over the brain to expose the superior colliculus. No further surgery was done except to open the membranes of connective tissue overlying the nervous structure. The frog was held in extension to a cork platform and covered with moist cloth. An animal in such a position, having most of his body surface in physical contact with something, goes into a still reaction — i.e., he will not even attempt to move save to pain, and except for the quick small incision of the skin at the start of the operation our procedure seems to be painless to him. With the animal mounted, we confront his eye with an aluminum hemisphere, 20 mils thick and 14 inches in diameter, silvered to a matte gray finish on the inner surface and held concentric to the eye. On the inner surface of this hemisphere, various objects attached to small magnets can be moved about by a large magnet moved by hand on the outer sur-face. On our hemisphere, 1° is slightly less than an eighth of an inch long. In the tests illustrated, we use as stimulating objects a dull black disk almost 1° in diameter and a rectangle 30° long and 12° wide. However, in the textual report, we use a variety of other objects. As an indicator for the stimulus, we first used a phototube looking at an image of the hemisphere taken through a camera lens and focused on the plane of a diaphragm. (Later we used a photo-multiplier, so connected as to give us a logarithmic response over about four decades.) Thus we could vary how much of the hemi-sphere was seen by the stimulus detector and match that area in position and size against the receptive field of the fiber we were studying. The output of this arrangement is the stimulus line in the figures.

FINDINGS

There are four separate operations on the image in the frog's eye. Each has its result transmitted by a particular group of fibers, uniformly distributed across the retina, and they are all nearly independent of the general illumination. The operations are: *(1) sustained-contrast detection; (2) net convexity detection; (3) mov-ing-edge detection; and (4) net dimming detection.* The first two are reported by unmyelinated fibers, the last two by myelinated fibers. Since we are now dealing with events rather than point excitations as stimuli, receptive fields can only be defined approxi-mately, and one cannot necessarily distinguish concentric subdivi-sions. The fibers reporting the different operations differ systemati-cally not only in fiber diameter (or conduction velocity) but also in rough size of receptive field, which ranges from about 2° diam-eter for the first operation to about 15° for the last. The following description of these groups is definite.

1. Sustained-Contrast Detectors

An unmyelinated axon of this group does not respond when the general illumination is turned on or off. If the sharp edge of an object either lighter or darker than the background moves into its field and stops, it discharges promptly and continues discharging, no matter what the shape of the edge or whether the object is smaller or larger than the receptive field. The sustained discharge can be interrupted (or greatly reduced) in these axons by switch-

239

ing all light off. When the light is then restored, the sustained discharge begins again after a pause. Indeed the response to turning on a distribution of light furnished with sharp contrast within the field is exactly that reported by Hartline for his ON fibers. In some fibers of this group, a contrast previously within the field is "remembered" after the light is turned off, for they will keep up a low mutter of activity that is not present if no contrast was there before. That this is not an extraordinary sensitivity of such an element in almost complete darkness can be shown by importing a contrast into its receptive field after darkening in the absence of

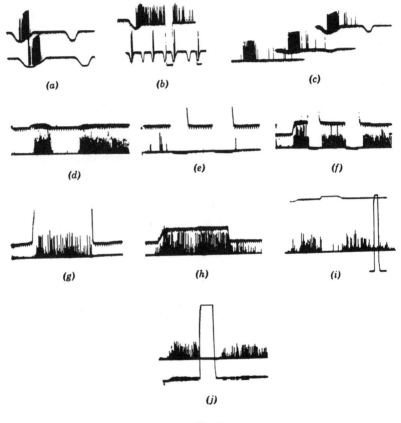

Fig. 2

Operation 1—contrast detectors. The records were all taken directly with a Polaroid camera. The spikes are clipped at the lower end just above the noise and brightened on the screen. Occasional spikes have been intensified by hand for contrast. No mutter occurs then. This memory lasts for at least a minute of darkness in some units.

In Fig. 2 we see the response of such a fiber in the optic nerve. We compare these responses with full illumination (a 60-watt bulb and reflector mounted a foot away from the plane of the opening of the hemisphere) to those with less than 1/300 as much light (we put a variable resistance in series with the bulb so that the color changed also). We are struck by the smallness of the resulting change. In very dim light where we can barely see the stimulating object ourselves, we still get very much the same response.

2. Net Convexity Detectors

These fibers form the other subdivision of the unmyelinated population, and require a number of conditions to specify when they will respond. To our minds, this group contains the most remarkable elements in the optic nerve.

---

purposes of reproduction. The resolution is not good, but we think that the responses are not ambiguous. Our alternate recording method is by means of a device that displays the logarithm of pulse interval of signals through a pulse height pick-off. However, such records would take too much explanation and would not add much to the substance of the present paper. (*a*) This record is from a single fiber in the optic nerve. The base line is the output of a photocell watching a somewhat larger area than the receptive field of the fiber. Darkening is given by downward deflection. The response is seen with the noise clipped off. The fiber discharge to movement of the edge of a 3° black disk passed in one direction but not to the reverse movement. (Time marks, 20 per second.) (*b*) The same fiber shown here giving a continued response when the edge stops in the field. The response disappears if the illumination is turned off and reappears when it is turned on. Below is shown again the asymmetry of the response to a faster movement. (Time marks, 20 per second.) (*c*) The same fiber is stimulated here to show asymmetrical response to the 3° black object moved in one direction, then the reverse, and the stimuli are repeated under a little less than a 3-decade change of illumination in two steps. The bottom record is in extremely dim light, the top in very bright light. (Time marks, 20 per second.) (*d*) In the bottom line, a group of endings from such fibers is shown recorded from the first layer in the tectum. A black disk 1° in diameter is moved first through the field and then into the field and stopped. In the top line, the receptive field is watched by a photomultiplier (see text), and darkening is given by upward deflection. (Time marks, 5 per second for all tectal records.) (*e*) OFF and ON of general illumination has no effect on these fibers. (*f*) A 3° black disk is moved into the field and stopped. The response continues until the lights are turned OFF but reappears when the lights are turned ON. These fibers are nonerasable. (*g*) A very large black square is moved into the field and stopped. The response to the edge continues so long as the edge is in the field. (*h*) The 3° disk is again moved into the field and stopped. When it leaves, there is a slight after-discharge. (*i*) A 1° object is moved into the field, stopped, the light is then turned off, then on, and the response comes back. The light is, however, a little less than 300× dimmer than in the next frame. Full ON and OFF are given in the rectangular calibration on the right. (*j*) The same procedure as in Fig. 2(*i*) is done under very bright light. The return of response after reintroducing the light seems more prolonged—but this is due only to the fact that, in Fig. 2(*i*), the edge was not stopped in optimal position.

241

Such a fiber does not respond to change in general illumination. It does respond to a small object (3° or less) passed through the field; the response does not outlast the passage. It continues responding for a long time if the object is imported and left in the field, but the discharge is permanently turned off (erased) by a transient general darkness lasting 1/10 second or longer. We have not tried shorter obscurations.

The fiber will not respond to the straight edge of a dark object moving through its receptive field or brought there and stopped. If the field is about 7° in diameter, then if we move a dark square 8° on the side through it with the edge in advance, there is no response, but if the corner is in advance, then there is a good one. Usually a fiber will respond indefinitely only to objects that have moved into the field and then lie wholly or almost wholly interior to the receptive field. The discharge is greater the greater the convexity, or positive curvature, of the boundary of the dark object until the object becomes as small as about half the width of the receptive field. At this point, we get the largest response on moving across that field, and a good, sustained reponse on entering it and stopping. As one uses smaller and smaller objects, the response to moving across the field begins to diminish at a size of about 1°, although the sustained response to coming in and stopping remains. In this way we find the smallest object to which these fibers respond is less than 3 minutes of arc. A smooth motion across the receptive field has less effect than a jerky one, if the jerks recur at intervals longer than ½ second. A displacement barely visible to the experimenter produces a marked increase in response which dies down slowly.

Any checked or dotted pattern (in the latter case, with dots no further apart than half the width of the receptive field) moved as a whole across the receptive field produces little if any response. However, if any dot within the receptive field moves differentially with respect to the background pattern, the response is to that dot as if it were moving alone. A group of two or three distinct spots enclosed within the receptive field and moved as a whole produce less direct response to movement and much less sustained response on stopping than if the spots are coalesced to a single larger spot.

A delightful exhibit uses a large color photograph of the natural habitat of a frog from a frog's-eye view, flowers and grass. We can move this photograph through the receptive field of such a fiber, waving it around at a 7-inch distance: there is no response. If we perch with a magnet a fly-sized object 1° large on the part of the picture seen by the receptive field and move only the object, we get an excellent response. If the object is fixed to the picture in about the same place and the whole moved about, then there is none.

Finally, the response does not depend on how much darker the object is than its background, so long as it is distinguishably so and has a clear-cut edge. If a disk has a very dark center and merges gradually into the gray of the background at the boundary, the response to it is very much less than to a uniform gray disk only slightly darker than the background. Objects lighter than the background produce almost no response unless they have enough relief to cast a slight shadow at the edge.

All the responses we have mentioned are relatively independent of illumination, and Fig. 3 taken as described in the caption shows the reactions to a 3° object and the large rectangle under some of the conditions described.

General Comments on Groups 1 and 2

The two sorts of detectors mentioned seem to include all the unmyelinated fibers, with conduction velocities of 20 to 50 cm. The two groups are not entirely distinct. There are transition cases. On one hand, some convexity detectors respond well to very slightly curved edges, even so far as to show an occasional sustained response if that edge is left in the field. They may also not be completely erasable (though very markedly affected by an interruption of light) for small objects. On the other hand, others of the same group will be difficult to set into an indefinitely sustained response with any object, but only show a fairly long discharge, acting thereby more as detectors of edges although never reacting to straight edges. Nevertheless the distribution of the unmyelinated axons into two groups is very marked. Any fiber of either group may show a directional response — i.e., there will be a direction of movement that may fail to excite the cell. For the contrast fibers, this will also appear as a nonexciting angle of the boundary with respect to the axis of the frog. Such null directions and angles cancel out in the aggregate.

3. Moving-Edge Detectors

These fibers are myelinated and conduct at a velocity in the neighborhood of 2 meters per second. They are the same as Hart-

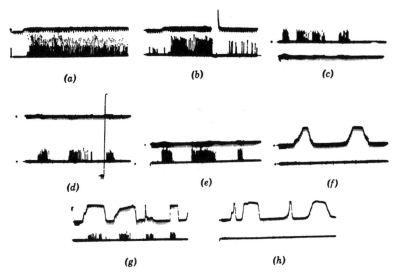

Fig. 3

Operation 2—convexity detectors. The photomultiplier is used, and darkening is an upward deflection. (*a*) These records are all from the second layer of endings in the tectum. In the first picture, a 1° black disk is imported into the receptive field and left there. (*b*) The same event occurs as in Fig. 3(*a*), but now the light is turned off, then on again. The response is much diminished and in the longer record vanishes. These fibers are erasable. (*c*) The 1° disk is passed through the field first somewhat rapidly, then slowly, then rapidly. The light is very bright. (*d*) The same procedure occurs as in Fig. 3(*c*), but now the light has been dimmed about 300×. The vertical line shows the range of the photomultiplier, which has been adjusted for about 3½ decades of logarithmic response. (*e*) A 1° black disk is passed through the field at three speeds. (*f*) A 15° black strip is passed through at two speeds, edge leading. (*g*) A 15° black strip is passed through in various ways with corner leading. (*h*) The same strip as in Fig. 3(*g*) is passed through, edge leading.

line's and Barlow's ON-OFF units. The receptive field is about 12° wide. Such a fiber responds to any distinguishable edge moving through its receptive field, whether black against white or the other way around. Changing the extent of the edge makes little difference over a wide range, changing its speed a great one. It responds to an edge only if that edge moves, not otherwise. If an object wider than about 5° moves smoothly across the field, there are separate responses to the leading and trailing edges, as would be expected from Barlow's formulation. These fibers generally show two or three regularly spaced spikes, always synchronous among different fibers to turning the light on or off or both. The response to moving objects is much greater than to changes in total illumination and varies only slightly with general illumination over a range of 1/300. The frequency of the discharge increases with the velocity of the object within certain limits (see Fig. 4).

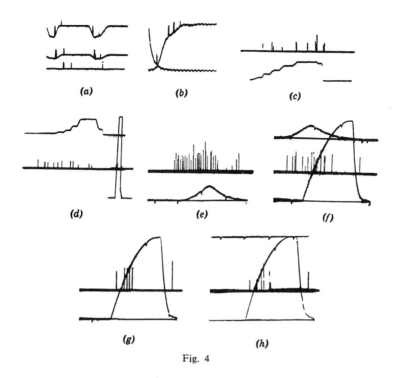

(a)   (b)   (c)

(d)   (e)   (f)

(g)   (h)

Fig. 4

Operation 3—moving-edge detectors. The first two pictures are taken from a single fiber in the optic nerve. (*a*) Shows a 7° black disk moving through the receptive field (the photocell was not in registration with the field). There is a response to the front and back of the disk independent of illumination. There is about a 300:1 shift of illumination between top and bottom of the record. Darkening is a downward deflection with the photocell record. (Time marks, 5 per second.) (*b*) OFF and ON of general lighting. (Time marks, 50 per second.) Note double responses and spacing. (*c*) This and succeeding records are in the third layer of endings in the tectum. Several endings are recorded but not resolved. Darkening is an upward deflection of the photomultiplier record. The response is shown to the edge of a 15° square moved into and out of the field by jerks in bright light. (*d*) The same procedure occurs as in Fig. 4(*c*), but in dim light. Calibration figure is at the right. (*e*) The response is shown to a 7° black disk passed through the receptive fields under bright light. The sweep is faster, but the time marks are the same. (*f*) The same procedure as for Fig. 4(*e*), but under dim light. The OFF and ON of the photomultiplier record was superimposed for calibration. (*g*) OFF and ON response with about half a second between ON and OFF. (*h*) Same as Fig. 4(*g*), but with 2 seconds between OFF and ON.

4. Net Dimming Detectors

These are Hartline's and Barlow's OFF fibers. But they have some properties not observed before. They are myelinated and the fastest-conducting afferents, clocked at 10 meters per second.[2]

[2] The even faster fibers, with velocities up to 20 meters per second, we presently believe to be the efferents to the retina, but although there is some evidence for this, we are not yet quite certain.

One such fiber responds to sudden reduction of illumination by a
prolonged and regular discharge. Indeed, the rhythm is so much

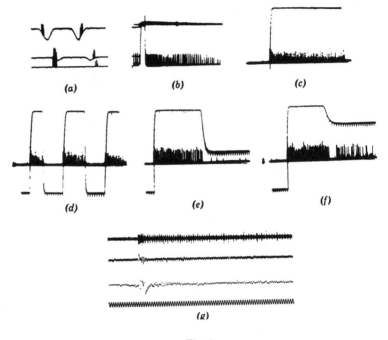

(a) (b) (c)

(d) (e) (f)

(g)

Fig. 5

Operation 4—dimming detectors. (a) This and the next frame are taken from
a single fiber in the optic nerve. Here we see the response to a 7° black disk passing through the receptive field. The three records are taken at three illumination
levels over a 300:1 range. In the phototube record, darkening is a downward deflection. (Time marks, 5 per second.) (b) OFF and ON of light. The OFF was done
shortly after one sweep began, the ON occurred a little earlier on the next sweep.
The fiber is silenced completely by the ON. (Time marks, 5 per second.) (c) In
this and the three next frames, we are recording from the fourth layer of endings
in the tectum. This frame shows the response to turning OFF the general illumination. (d) OFF and ON of light at regular intervals. (e) OFF then ON of the
light to a lesser brightness. (f) OFF, then ON, of the light to a still lesser brightness. The level to which the ON must come to abolish activity decreases steadily
with time. (g) The synchrony of the dimming detectors as described in the text.
At the top are three or four fibers recorded together in the optic nerve when the
light is suddenly turned off. The fibers come from diverse areas on the
retina. In the second line are the oscillations recorded from the freshly cut retinal
stump of the optic nerve when the light is suddenly turned off. In the third line
are the oscillations recorded on the surface of the tectum, the visual brain, before
the nerve was cut. Again the light is suddenly turned off. The last line is 20 cps.
These records of synchrony were obviously not all made at the same time, so that
comparing them in detail is not profitable.

the same from fiber to fiber that in recording from several at once after sudden darkening, the impulses assemble in groups, which break up only after many seconds. Even then the activity from widely separated retinal areas seems to be related. We observe that the surface potential of the colliculus shows a violent and prolonged oscillation when the light is turned off. This oscillation, beginning at about 18 per second and breaking into 3 to 5 per second after several seconds, seems to arise from these fibers from the retina; the same record is seen when the optic nerve is severed and the recording electrode placed on the retinal stump. See Fig 5.

The receptive field is rather large — about 15° — and works as Barlow describes. Darkening of a spot produces less response when it is in the periphery of the field than when it is at the center. The effect of a moving object is directly related to its size and relative darkness. The response is prolonged if a large dark object stops within the field. It is almost independent of illumination, actually increasing as the light gets dimmer. There is a kind of erasure that is complementary to that of group 2. If the general lighting is sharply dimmed, but not turned off entirely, the consequent prolonged response is diminished or abolished after a dark object passes through the receptive field. In this case, the reasons for erasure are apparent. Suppose we turn off the light and set up a prolonged response. Then the amount of light which must be restored to interrupt the response gets less and less the longer we wait. That is, the sensitivity of the OFF discharge to the ON of light increases with time. If we darken the general lighting only by a factor of 100, we also get a prolonged discharge. However, if we turn off the light completely a few seconds after the 100/1 dimming and then turn it back on to the same dim level, the discharge is increased by the second dimming and is completely or almost completely abolished by the relighting. The effect of moving a dark object through the field after dimming is to impose a second dimming pulse followed by brightening as the object passes.

Others

Lastly, there is a small group of afferent fibers that does not seem to have distinct receptive fields. They each measure the absolute darkness over a wide area with a long time constant. That is, the frequency of discharge is greater the darker it is. They have a complement in that some of the moving-edge detectors have a resting discharge of very low frequency if the illumination is extremely bright.

DISCUSSION

Let us compress all of these findings in the following description. Consider that we have four fibers, one from each group, which are concentric in their receptive fields. Suppose that an object is moved about in this concentric array:

1. The contrast detector tells, in the smallest area of all, of the presence of a sharp boundary, moving or still, with much or little contrast.

2. The convexity detector informs us in a somewhat larger area whether or not the object has a curved boundary, if it is darker than the background and moving on it; it remembers the object when it has stopped, providing the boundary lies totally within that area and is sharp; it shows most activity if the enclosed object moves intermittently with respect to a background. The memory of the object is abolished if a shadow obscures the object for a moment.

3. The moving-edge detector tells whether or not there is a moving boundary in a yet larger area within the field.

4. The dimming detector tells us how much dimming occurs in the largest area, weighted by distance from the center and by how fast it happens.

All of the operations are independent of general illumination. There are 30 times as many of the first two detectors as of the last two, and the sensitivity to sharpness of edge or increments of movement in the first two is also higher than in the last two.

RESULTS IN THE TECTUM

As remarked earlier, the optic nerve fibers are all disordered in position through the nerve. That is, the probability that any two adjacent fibers look at the same region in the retina is very small. However, when the fibers terminate in the superior colliculus, they do so in an orderly way such that the termini exhibit a continuous map of the retina. Each optic nerve crosses the base of the skull and enters the opposite tectum [Fig. 1(b)] via two bundles — one rostromedial, the other caudalateral. The fibers sweep out over the tectum in the superficial neuropil in what grossly appears to be a laminated way [Fig. 1(c)]. The detail of ending is not known, and there is some reason to think Pedro Ramón's drawing [9] is too diagrammatic [Fig. 1(d)], however well it fits with our data.

In any case, the outer husk of neuropil, roughly about half the thickness of the optic tectum, is formed of the endings of the optic fibers mixed with dendrites of the deeper-lying cells, and in this felting lie few cell bodies.

We have found it singularly easy to record from these terminal bushes of the optic fibers. That is, if an electrode is introduced in the middle of one bush, the external potential produced by action currents in any branch increases in proportion to the number of branches near the electrode. Since the bushes are densely inter-digitated everywhere, it is not difficult to record from terminal arbors anywhere unless one kills or blocks them locally, as is easily done by pressure, etc.

One may inquire how we can be sure of recording from terminal arbors, and not from cells and their dendrites. The argument is this. First, there are about four layers of cells in the depths of the tectum [Fig. 1(d)], and only their dendrites issue into the super-ficial neuropil wherein lie very few cells indeed. There are about 250,000 of these cells in all, compared to 500,000 optic fibers. In the outer thickness of the tectum, among the terminating fibers, almost every element we record performs one of the four opera-tions characterizing the fibers in the nerve, and has a correspond-ing receptive field. Now as the electrode moves down from the sur-face in one track, we record five to ten cells in the deepest half of the tectum. Not a single cell so recorded shows activity even remotely resembling what we find in the superficial neuropil. Among the cells, none shows optic nerve operations, and the smallest receptive fields we find are over 30° in diameter. If the active elements in the upper layers are cells (one will see about 20 to 30 active elements in one electrode track before reaching the cell layer), which cells can they be? Or if they are dendrites, to what neurons do they belong? We regard these considerations as conclusive enough.

Figs. 2–5 show that the four operational groups of fibers termi-nate in four separate layers of terminals, each layer exhibiting a continuous map of the retina (we confirm Gaze's diagram of the projection [10]), and all four maps are in registration. Most super-ficial lie the endings for the contrast detectors, the slowest fibers. Beneath them, but not so distinctly separate, are the convexity detectors. Deeper, and rather well separated, are the moving-edge detectors admixed with the rare and ill-defined axons that measure the actual level of darkness. Deepest (and occasionally contaminated with tectal cells or their axons) lie the dimming detectors. Thus the depth at which these fibers end is directly related to their speed of conduction.

Such an arrangement makes experiment easy, for all the fibers of one operation performed on the safe field in the retina end in one place in the tectum and can be recorded as a group. It is very useful to see them this way, for then the individual variations among similar units cancel one another and only the common properties remain. We made the tectal records shown in the accompanying figures with a single electrode in two penetrations (to get decent separation of contrast and convexity detectors which lie just below the pia), to show how clear-cut the arrangement is.

CONFIRMATION OF SPERRY'S PROPOSAL

The existence of a fourfold map of the retina in the tectal neuropil led us, naturally, to repeat Sperry's initial experiment on the regeneration of cut optic nerve [11]. Since the nerve is as scrambled as it can be originally, we saw no point in turning the eye around 180° but simply cut one nerve in a few frogs, separated the stumps to be sure of complete severance, and waited for about three months. At the end of this time, after it was clear that the cut nerves were functioning again, we compared the tectal maps of the cut and uncut nerves in some of them. We confirmed (as did Gaze [12]) Sperry's proposal that the fibers grew back to the regions where they originally terminated in mapping the retina [13]. But we also found a restoration of the four layers with no error or mixing. In one frog, after 90 days, the fibers had grown back best at the entrance of the two brachia to the colliculus, and least at the center, yet there were no serious errors. The total area of retina communicating with one point of the collicular neuropil (i.e., the sum of the receptive fields of the fibers recorded from that point) had increased three or four times, from a diameter of about 15° to a diameter of about 30°. But there was no admixture of fibers with receptive fields in widely separated regions. In another frog, after 120 days, the area seen from one point was barely twice normal.

GENERAL DISCUSSION

What are the consequences of this work? Fundamentally, it shows that the eye speaks to the brain in a language already highly organized and interpreted, instead of transmitting some more or less accurate copy of the distribution of light on the receptors. As a crude analogy, suppose that we have a man watching the clouds and reporting them to a weather station. If he is using a code, and one can see his portion of the sky too, then it is not difficult to find out what he is saying. It is certainly true that he is watching a distribution of light; nevertheless, local variations of light are not the terms in which he speaks nor the terms in which he is best understood. Indeed, if his vocabulary is restricted to types of things that he sees in the sky, trying to find his language by using flashes of light as stimuli will certainly fail. Now, since the purpose of a frog's vision is to get him food and allow him to evade predators no matter how bright or dim it is about him, it is not enough to know the reaction of his visual system to points of light. To get useful records from individual receptors (the rods and cones), assuming that they operate independently and under no reflex control, this stimulus may be adequate. But when one inspects responses that are a few nervous transformations removed from the receptors, as in the optic nerve, that same choice of stimulus is difficult to defend. It is equivalent to assuming that all of the interpretation is done further on in the nervous system. But, as we have seen, this is false.

One might attempt to measure numerically how the response of each kind of fiber varies with various properties of the successions of patterns of light that evoke them. But to characterize a succession of patterns in space requires knowledge of so many independent variables that this is hardly possible by experimental enumeration of cases. To examine the effect of curvature alone we should have to explore at least the response to all configurations of three spots moving in a large variety of ways. We would prefer to state the operations of ganglion cells as simply as possible in terms of whatever *quality* they seem to detect and, instead, examine the bipolar cells in the retina, expecting to find there a dissection of the operations into combinations of simpler ones performed at intermediate stages. For example, suppose that there are at least two sorts of rods and cones, one increasing its voltage with the log of light at one color, the other decreasing its voltage with the log of light at some other color. If bipolars connect to several contiguous rods or cones of opposing reactions and simply add voltages, some bipolars will register a large signal only if an appropriate contrast occurs. We have in fact found something of the sort occurring, for it seems that the inner plexiform layer of the retina is stratified to display several different local properties, one layer indicating local differences in intensity of light. Some of Svaetichin's [14] data can be adduced here. The different dendritic distribution of the ganglion cells, as in Fig. 1(a), may signify that they extract differently weighted samples of simple local operations done by the bipolars, and it is on this that we are now working.

But there is another reason for a reluctance to make accurate measurements on the activity of ganglion cells in the intact animal. A significant efferent outflow goes to the retina from the brain. We now know to a certain extent how the cells in the tectum handle the four inputs to them which are described in this paper. There are at least two distinct classes of these cells, and at least one of them issues axons back into the optic nerve. We have recorded this activity there. Such axons enter the retina, and we think some effects of their activity on the sensitivity of ganglion cells are noticeable.

The way that the retina projects to the tectum suggests a nine-teenth-century view of visual space. The image on the retina, taken at the grain of the rods and cones, is an array of regularly spaced points at each of which there is a certain amount of light of a certain composition. If we know the position of every point and the values of light at every point, we can physically reconstruct the image and, looking at it, understand the picture. If, however, we are required to establish continuities within the picture only from the numerical data on position and light at independent points, it becomes a very difficult task. The retina projects onto the tectum in four parallel sheets of endings, each sheet mapping continuously the retina in terms of a particular areal operation, and all four maps are in registration. Consider the dendrite of a tectal cell extending up through the four sheets. It is looking at a point in the image on the retina, but that point is now seen in terms of the properties of its neighborhood as defined by the operations. Since the overlap of receptive fields within any operation is very great, it now seems reasonable to erect simple criteria for finding continuities. For example, if an area over which there is little change in the fourfold signature of a moving object is bounded by regions of different signature, it seems likely that that area describes the image of a single object.

By transforming the image from a space of simple discrete points to a congruent space where each equivalent point is described by the intersection of particular qualities in its neighborhood, we can then give the image in terms of distributions of combinations of those qualities. In short, every point is seen in definite contexts. The character of these contexts, generally built in, is the physiological synthetic *a priori*. The operations found in the frog make unlikely later processes in his system of the sort described by two of us earlier [15], for example, dilatations; but those were adduced for the sort of form recognition that the frog does not have. This work is an outgrowth of that earlier study that set the question.

CONCLUSION

The output from the retina of the frog is a set of four distributed operations on the visual image. These operations are independent of the level of general illumination and express the image in terms of: (1) local sharp edges and contrast; (2) the curvature of edge of a dark object; (3) the movement of edges; and (4) the local dimmings produced by movement or rapid general darkening. Each group of fibers serving one operation maps the retina continuously in a single sheet of endings in the frog's brain. There are four such sheets in the brain, corresponding to the four operations, and their maps are in registration. When all axonal connections between eye and brain are broken and the fibers grow back, they reconstitute the original retinal maps and also arrange themselves in depth in the original order with no mistakes. If there is any randomness in the connections of this system, it must be at a very fine level indeed. In this, we consider that Sperry [11] is completely right.

We have described each of the operations on the retinal image in terms of what common factors in a large variety of stimuli cause response and what common factors have no effect. What, then, does a particular fiber in the optic nerve measure? We have considered it to be how much there is in a stimulus of that quality which excites the fiber maximally, naming that quality.

The operations thus have much more the flavor of perception than of sensation if that distinction has any meaning now. That is to say that the language in which they are best described is the language of complex abstractions from the visual image. We have been tempted, for example, to call the convexity detectors "bug perceivers." Such a fiber [operation 2] responds best when a dark object, smaller than a receptive field, enters that field, stops, and moves about intermittently thereafter. The response is not affected if the lighting changes or if the background (say a picture of grass and flowers) is moving, and is not there if only the background, moving or still, is in the field. Could one better describe a system for detecting an accessible bug?

ACKNOWLEDGMENT

We are particularly grateful to O. G. Selfridge, whose experiments with mechanical recognizers of pattern helped drive us to this work and whose criticism in part shaped its course.

BIBLIOGRAPHY

[1] H. R. Maturana, "Number of fibers in the optic nerve and the number of ganglion cells in the retina of Anurans," *Nature*, vol. 183, pp. 1406-1407; May 16, 1959.

[2] H. K. Hartline, "The response of single optic nerve fibres of the vertebrate eye to illumination of the retina," *Amer. J. Physiol.*, vol. 121, pp. 400-415; February, 1938.
Also, "The receptive fields of the optic nerve fibers," *Amer. J. Physiol.*, vol. 130, pp. 690-699; October, 1940.

[3] H. B. Barlow, "Summation and inhibition in the frog's retina," *J. Physiol.*, vol. 119, pp. 69-88; January, 1953.

[4] S. W. Kuffler, "Discharge patterns and functional organization of mammalian retina," *J. Neurophysiol.*, vol. 16, pp. 37-68; January, 1953.

[5] H. B. Barlow, R. Fitzhugh, and S. W. Kuffler, "Change of organization in the receptive fields of the cat's retina during dark adaptation," *J. Physiol.*, vol. 137, pp. 338-354; August, 1957.

[6] A. M. Andrew, "Report on Frog Colliculus," Research Laboratory of Electronics, M.I.T., Cambridge, *Quarterly Progress Report*, pp. 77-78; July 15, 1955.

[7] A. M. Andrew, "Action potentials from the frog colliculus," *J. Physiol.*, vol. 130, p. 25P; September 23-24, 1955.

[8] H. R. Maturana, "The Fine Structure of the Optic Nerve and Tectum of Anurans. An Electron Microscope Study," Ph.D. dissertation, Harvard University, Cambridge, Mass.; 1958.

[9] Pedro Ramón Cajal, "Histologie du Systeme Nerveux," Ramón y Cajal, Maloine, Paris, France; 1909-1911.

[10] R. M. Gaze, "The representation of the retina on the optic lobe of the frog," *Quart. J. Exper. Physiol.*, vol. 43, pp. 209-214; March, 1958.

[11] R. Sperry, "Mechanisms of neural maturation," in *Handbook of Experimental Psychology*, S. S. Stevens, ed., John Wiley and Sons, Inc., New York, N. Y.; 1951.

What the Frog's Eye Tells the Frog's Brain

[12] R. M. Gaze, "Regeneration of the optic nerve in *Xenopus laevi*," *J. Physiol.*, vol. 146, p. 40P; February 20-21, 1959.

[13] H. R. Maturana, J. Y. Lettvin, W. S. McCulloch, and W. H. Pitts, "Evidence that cut optic nerve fibers in a frog regenerate to their proper places in the tectum," *Science*, vol. 130, pp. 1709-1710; December 18, 1959.

[14] G. Svaetichin and E. F. McNichol Jr., "Retinal mechanisms for chromatic and achromatic vision," *Ann. N. Y. Acad. Sci.*, vol. 74, pp. 385-404; November, 1958.

[15] W. S. McCulloch and W. H. Pitts, "How we know universals. The perception of auditory and visual forms," *Bull. Math. Biophysics*, vol. 9, pp. 127-147; June, 1947.

Finality and Form
in Nervous Activity

Warren S. McCulloch

ARGUMENT

Empiric philosophers have always maintained that problems in the theory of knowledge and of value must be stated and resolved as questions concerning the anatomy and the physiology of the nervous system. These are inquiries into the *a priori* forms and limitations of knowing and willing determined by the structure of the nervous system and by the modes of activity of its elements. An exact statement and a partial resolution of these problems is possible thanks to the precision and inclusiveness of modern observations. The brevity of latent addition, the requirement of spatial summation, the irreciprocity of conduction, the occurrence of direct inhibition and the duration of delay, which characterize synaptic transmission, and the all-or-none response with subsequent refractoriness of the component neurons do all ensure that the simple and discrete elementary signals are so related as to conform to a logical calculus of numerable, coexisting, and sequential propositions. From this fact we can deduce the formal properties of cognition and conation in any nervous system that possesses receptors and controls effectors.

Those trains of nervous impulses that cycle in re-entrant paths and the functionally equivalent alterations in the structure of the system issue in memory and learning. Those trains that return to their place of origin, where they diminish or reverse the processes that gave rise to them, establish some state of the system by causing it to behave so as to return to that state. Because some of the neurons composing the circuit are influenced by impulses from other parts of the nervous system, the state sought by the system is conditioned by its circumstances. Some re-entrant paths lie within the nervous system, others pass through remote parts of the body, and still others, leaving the body by effectors and returning by receptors, traverse the external world. The functions of the first are at present ill-defined, the second constitute the majority of our reflexes, and the last, our appetites and purposes. They account for all actions that have a goal, or an end. Values, which rationalize the domination of one such action by another when their incompatibility necessitates choice, and circularities of preference, which have destroyed casuistical and utilitarian hopes of a common measure of all values, exhibit themselves as consequences of the interconnections of circuits. The foregoing considerations enable us to construct a hypothetical nervous net that will embody innately or induce any particular universal, or idea. Since all of these problems are alike in that each particular solution requires the construction of a net *ad hoc*, we are presently confronted by the single fundamental problem: What specific properties will develop in an originally chaotic net? Exact physiological formulation of this problem, construction of the requisite mathematics, and design of appropriate instruments are now in hand.

For two thousand years we have tried to make of words, and other notions, an enduring semblance of the ways of our changing world. We are still not satisfied. We want more and better science, but we cannot always tell at once whether we need more facts or lack the proper notions. Our philosophy began when we asked why we had failed, and when we sought for better notions. We had started with terms that were little more than the names of things about us, of their sensed qualities, and of their relations one to another. To make and use logic and mathematics, we needed terms that stood for things that could not be seen and for qualities and relations that are never apparent. This separation of theory from experience, although it served science, made the nature of knowledge so vague as to permit of much idle speculation. To put a stop to it we must catch the knower in the act and mark what is going on in him, to him, and around him.

What is needed in science is needed in ethics. The wants of particular men for particular things and the ways they get them lack generality and enjoy no quantitative order. To turn preferences into ratios and proportions, we seek some common measure of value. But such words stand for no one thing that any man has ever wanted. Again, the separation of theory from practice left every school free to ignore the conduct of life and the nature of desire in setting up its own notion of the "good" as a common measure of *all* values — a vain superstition whose only remedy is to watch the desirous in his quest and, in the moment of choice, find out what is going on around him and within him.

Among philosophers the empiricists have always held that this was the only way to treat the problems of the theory of knowledge and of value. Through the centuries we have come to see that these problems can be stated and solved only in terms of the anatomy and the physiology of the nervous system. In those terms, we are inquiring into the *a priori* forms and limitations of knowing and willing determined by the structure of the nervous system and by the mode of action of its elements. We ask two kinds of questions. Of universals, or ideas, we would know how nervous activity can propose anything concerning the world and how the structure of the system embodies this or that idea. Of values, or purposes, we would know how nervous activity can mediate the quest of ends and how the structure of the system embodies the possibility of choice.

We have long seen dimly what we had to do. But that we can state our problems exactly and in part solve them now we owe in no small measure to the men alive today. It has been my good fortune to live and work among them. They are my witnesses that what follows is the outcome rather of their works jointly than of any one singly. But I alone am answerable for any seeming inference I may foist upon their public statements. I shall not mention their names, for, instead of a rigorous mathematical treatment of their detailed observations, I would give you as elementary an argument as fits the facts.

When I was a child I played with blocks, which I set up as wooden soldiers. I learned several things from those blocks that I have used ever since. I shall call each by its name in physiology.

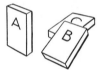

When a block is struck it falls all the way or it does not fall at all. This is its *all-or-none* impulse.

It takes time to set it up again. This is its *refractory period.*

To fell it a blow must be of sufficient strength. This is its *thresh-old.*

A blow that fails to fell it tips it, and it will come back to its old position, but it may be felled by a second, equal blow while it is tipping. This is *latent addition.*

After a block has been struck, it is some time before it falls. This is *synaptic delay.*

The impulse and the latent addition are so much shorter than the refractory period and the synaptic delay that a block can never fell another one by striking it twice. This is the lack of *temporal summation.*

One block striking two others may fail to fell them, whereas the two, striking the one together, succeed. This is *irreciprocity of conduction.*

One block, by falling against the edge of another, may stop a third from felling it. This is *inhibition at a synapse.*

259

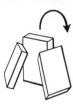

Two blocks striking a third together may fell it although each alone would have failed. This is *spatial summation*.

Last but not least, almost all the energy of the falling of a block comes from the energy of position stored in the block when it was set on end. None need come from the blow that fells it. This is *irritability*.

Blocks never quite live up to this ideal, but other things do — notably neurons. These, like telegraphic repeaters, at every relay signal anew, the signal received being but the occasion for the signal sent, the energy of the signal sent coming from the sender, not from the signal received. Such a signal is, in the full sense of the words, an *actual proposition*. The energy of proposing comes from the proposer, not from the proposed.

These actual propositions, the impulses of blocks or of neurons, are essentially simple. Each either happens or does not happen, and that is all there is to it. The block falls *only if* it was felled, and all it can signal to the next block is *that* it was felled. It may have been struck, but too lightly. It cannot signal *that* to the next block, and it cannot signal to the next block how hard it must be struck to fall, but it falls *only if* it was struck. In logic, this relation of "only if," here between its fall and its being struck, is called *material implication*. Among falling blocks and nervous impulses it is only between events separated in time by synaptic delays.

When blocks are arranged in single file, the falling of any block *implies* the previous falling of the block that struck it, and this, in turn, implies the previous falling of the one before and so, backward in time, to the blow that felled the first block. Again, in the language of logic, implication is a *transitive relation,* and among actual propositions its *domain* extends backward in time over intervening propositions to the first member of the series. Thus it comes about that the action of the central nervous system at a given time implies the earlier activity originating in its sense organs — its *receptors.* So, just as pebbles give us arithmetic, these blocks give us a calculus of actual propositions. In its terms we can say exactly anything concerning the world.

Next we seek the way in which the nervous system embodies this or that idea. The structure of the system can be shown in the grouping of the blocks. Three configurations give us all *significant contemporaneous functions.*

The first has two blocks, *A* and *B,* so placed that either can fell

260

a third, *C*. Thus, when *C* falls, it proposes that either *A* or *B* or both have fallen one synaptic delay earlier. This is the familiar "and/or" of legal documents, signified by "v." The logical function of the fall of *A* and/or of *B* at a given time, say *1*, is called their disjunction. It is not either in particular but their disjunction at the time *1* which is implied by the fall of *C* at time *2*.

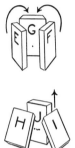

The second configuration is like the first, except that the blocks *E* and *F* are so placed that both must strike *G* within the period of latent addition if they are to fell it. Thus *G* in falling at time *2* implies the *conjunction* of the falls of *E* and *F* at time *1*.

The third configuration has one block, *H*, that may fell another, *J*, if a second, *I*, does not fall against the edge of *J* and so prevent its fall. This is the *conjunction of an assertion with a negation*, indicated by a dot and a tilde, thus: *H.~I*. Here the falling of *J* at the time *2* implies that *H* fell and *I* did not fall at the time *1*.

Clearly, any configuration in which the fall of a block was only prevented could never let it fall. Thus, no conjunction consisting of negations alone could ever be implied by an actual proposition. Finally, it would be difficult with blocks, but easy with neurons, to make a configuration or net in which the only one that could fell another would also prevent its fall, but such a conjunction also would never be implied. That both of these transmit no signals is worth heeding, for their contemporaneous functions would include tautologies and contradictions whose truth or falsity does not rest on that of their component propositions. All other propositional functions are significant, being true or false as their components are true or false. It is only significant functions that can be implied by a sequent action in the net.

Using only the three significant contemporaneous functions and the implicative sequential relation, we can embody in a net the possibility of having some notions concerning the world. Consider any net that has no circular paths. If we can count its receptors and its neurons, we can also count its actual propositions in any time measured in synaptic delays that can be counted. Such a net can be so made as to respond with a singular series of impulses in a single neuron, or a single impulse in a singular neuron, to each possible temporal or spatial figure of reception, or to translate any figure in time into one in space and vice versa. But each of its actual propositions has the same unique reference to one past time that we meet in television, which also translates spatial into temporal and temporal into spatial figures. The reason is the same in both. They lack *memory*.

Again the blocks have helped me. When they are in single file in a circle and one is overset, the falling goes around the circle until the last to fall lands on the first. Were they set up as soon as

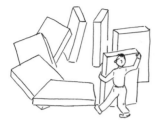

they fell, the falling would go round forever. This is memory of a kind. We have seen it in after-images and felt it in the dizziness that follows spinning. It may last much longer, certainly as long as the specious present in which we have the whole of a tune or of an argument all together for the nonce. It cannot outlast activity, and in deep sleep most of the nervous system comes to rest, yet on waking we remember.

Hence, there must be a way in which the net of neurons or the configurations of the blocks are changed by their impulses. We can make it our rule that if one block, *C*, is falling at the time a second block, *R*, is felled away from it by anything, and if *C* could not quite have felled *R*, then we will reset *C* so that the next time it falls it can fell *R*. This change in configuration with use is like the law of growth with use, which Ramón y Cajal thought neurons

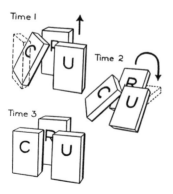

ought to obey. For this the anatomic evidence is still to seek. It is but the best guess that we can make today. If it is the way neurons grow, then it pictures learning, as Pavlov would have it, thus: Let a neuron, *U,* at any time, say *2,* propose the *unconditioned* stimulus, and let *C,* at time 2, propose the *conditioned* stimulus, and suppose that *C* cannot quite trip *R* whereas *U* can. Then *R* is being tripped by *U* just when *C* would trip it if it could. Our rule is now that thereafter *C* can, by itself, trip *R.*

However physically unlike, the two kinds of memory are *functionally equivalent* in this sense: Instead of the supposed change in the form of the synapse, we have but to imagine a circle of neurons in which a train of impulses is started by the conjunction of falls of *U* and *C* at time 2 and that, at each round, impulses come from this circuit to *R,* where each may form a conjunction with some impulse of *C* so as to trip *R.* Now any formal property of memory or learning, of the kind due to synaptic growth, is to be found in the circling of this train of impulses, due, that is, to an enduring figure of activity within the net.

We have quite rightly used Pavlov's terms, the *conditioned* and the *unconditioned* stimulus, for figures of stimulation to each of which we assigned a singular neuron, namely *C* and *U.* The net was so designed that the singular neuron was fired whenever the excitation of receptors was of that figure.

Blocks and their configurations, neurons and their nets, abide. The falling of a block and the impulse in a neuron, any actual proposition, in short any signal, is an event. It happens only once. No part of it can be repeated. To know that learning has occurred we must give the unconditioned stimulus again. From this it is clear that the so-called stimulus is a new excitation of receptors but of the old figure. This figure, or form, or idea, or universal, is but the relation of component events, or excitations. When there are no events so related, there still remains, embodied in the net in abiding fashion, the possibility of responding in the original manner: that is, with a new impulse in the same old neuron. When we have learned, we have so altered the net that the fall of *R* at time *3* no longer implies merely the fall of *U* at time 2 but the disjunction of the falls of *U* and *C* at time 2. Moreover, we can make a net in which to alter a single synapse will convert one significant function of *U* and *C* into any other at a suitable neuron elsewhere in the net. If this is done at several points, a net that originally embodied certain ideas may come to embody any others that are significant functions of those ideas. The enduring activity in circular paths, formally equivalent to these abiding changes in the net, enables our nervous system to think in new ways within a specious present. Such formal equivalence gives us a theory of learning in terms of actual propositions alone, letting the imaginary net stay exactly as it was. The theorist has but to substitute a figure of activity in his hypothetical circle for his imaginary new synapse, and he can calculate as before.

Other things than learning change the thresholds of neurons, notably fatigue and the fluctuations of the power they get from the food we eat and the air we breathe. These also have their formal equivalents in terms of enduring activities in circular paths. So the theory can still be formed in a single fashion. We lose neither generality nor rigor by treating the nervous system an an unalterable net of unalterable neurons.

To see what this may mean let us look at two blocks, *B* and *C*. If their positions and impacts are fixed so that *B* in falling *always* fells *C,* we have implications in both directions. The fall of *C* at time *2* implies the fall of *B* at time *1* as before, but now also that of *B* at time *1* implies that of *C* at time *2*. This is the familiar "if, and only if," written ≡ and called the "biconditional function," meaning simply that if either is true or false, then the other is the same. If reception were so related to the world, we might know how well we know the world. That would resemble being directly aware of our ignorance, whereas in fact nervous activity implies and *only implies* our *known* world. Cognition has just that quality.

Because the nervous system may be held to be unchanged, the activity within it proposes later activity within it, and, step by step, we may follow that activity to the effectors. Each step would be simply an implication but for the possibility of impulses coming by shorter paths from receptors to neurons nearer to effectors. Thus the proposing is rather an *intention* than an implication, that is, an implication with the proviso that nothing intervene. Conation has just that flavor. We know what we *will* do, but not what we *shall* do.

A nervous system that has effectors may make marks — say, put ink on paper. At any time it may see those marks. It has then made for itself things — we call them *signs* — which will serve instead of a host of new circles in its net. With plenty of ink and paper it can in time prove or check all provable conclusions from any set of premises. By simple conditioning, marks may become signs for anything of which the nervous system already has an idea. They come to signify the same to other nervous systems by similar conditioning. Thus, by means of signs, the computing and concluding have been shared by many nervous systems at one time and continued into times beyond all measure. This indeed is the story of language, literature, philosophy, logic, mathematics, and physics.

But signs are two-faced things. They are enduring things in our world. We may write or talk or think *about* them. They are also tools, and we may *use* them. One has to be forever alert to note whether a sign is being used or only mentioned. Just as a sound must be of some length to have pitch or a thing of some bulk to have shape, so a sign must be of some size to have meaning. Thus a sign may have discernible parts that have no meaning, like the *I* in *IT*. This may be dangerous even to the skillful logician who knows that a phrase, like Russell's *Theory of Description,* is a description that falls short of being a sign, although it is a complex of signs that can replace a sign without loss of sense but with a change of kind. Moreover, signs usually have no meaning but one learned, and that only to those nervous systems that have learned that meaning. To others they are just things. Finally, signs are not signals. Precisely, they are not actual significant propositions. They are not excitations of a given figure but only things that may shape excitation to their figures. They serve the same function as a figure of activity in a circuit. Thus they resemble configurations or nets. Among them we may seek tautologies and contradictions.

Finally, let us look but once more at the blocks. Let them stand in single file in a circle, but this time so placed that the last block, instead of falling on top of the first, falls against its edge and so

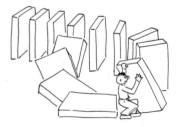

inhibits later felling of that first block. Such paths have been found. Some lie within the central nervous system. Others pass through it. Their function is clearly to stop the process that gives rise to their activities. About a hundred years ago in France, the fathers of physiology coined the term *réflexe* for a cyclical action which, starting in some part of the body, passed by one way to the central nervous system, whence it was reflected over another to that same structure in which it arose and there inhibited or reversed the process that had given rise to it. The traditional English example is the so-called *stretch reflex*. When a muscle is lengthened by a load put upon it, impulses arising in certain of its receptors go to the central nervous system and pass, with but a single synaptic delay, to the motor neurons whose impulses excite the muscle to shorten. With a brief delay the muscle is again of nearly its former length. The reflex has thus established a certain length to which the muscle returns, and so helps to keep the body in one position in space. The traditional American example is the *homeostasis* of blood pressure, mediated by numerous receptors, which, as pressure rises, send more impulses over several nerves to the central nervous system, whence impulses emerging over other nerves reach the heart, slow its pace, and reduce the blood pressure. Similarly, several reflexes, with receptors sensitive to oxygen and carbon dioxide dissolved in the blood, keep both nearly constant by changing the rate and depth of breathing. For years I have been studying homeostasis of sugar in the blood, but as yet I have not found the receptors. We know more of the reflexes that keep the body at an even temperature. There are doubtless many others of which we have not dreamed, but we know enough now to see that reflexes do severally fix, each in keeping with the kind of its receptors, one pressure, temperature, volume, length, direction, position, velocity, acceleration, concentration of some substance or almost any other kind of quantity by causing the system to move toward that one fixed by the reflex. It is always the difference between the condition of the system at the moment and the state established by a reflex that is answerable for the activity of the reflex at that moment and so for the change toward the established state. Thus the state established by the reflex is the *end in and of the operation*. In this mechanistic sense we speak of physiological functions as having *goals,* or *ends*. So long as we live, we are a bundle of circular systems seeking various ends at every moment.

Every reflex has a path of some length over which it goes at some speed and in which it is delayed at one or more synapses. Thus, there is always a lag between the time it is excited and the time excitation reaches its effector, and there is a second lag in the action of the effector and the return of the quantity measured by the receptor. Any circuit has a natural period of oscillation, which in the simplest case is the sum of its lags. When we change the magnitude of the quantity measured, a reflex may return the system toward, but not quite to, the original state, or it may over-shoot that state. The ratio of the return to the change that occasioned it is called the *gain* around the circuit. When the return is equal to the change that occasioned it, then the gain is one. We can find the gain at many frequencies of excitation. The gain is found to depend upon the frequency, and there are usually frequencies for which the gain is greater than one. If the gain is greater than one at the natural frequency of the reflex, fluctuations at that frequency begin and grow until the limitations of the structures composing the path reduce the gain to one; then, at the level for which the gain has become one, both the measured quantity and the reflex activity go on fluctuating.

By burdening the muscular part of the path, one can increase the gain of the circuit so that, at the natural period, the gain exceeds one. The stretch reflex will then give a series of similar contractions, like the bouncing of a leg when one sits in some positions. Similarly, by altering the lag in the nervous system, blood pressure can be made to fluctuate. Breathing, chewing, walking, and running, even eating and sleeping, are naturally paced in this manner.

Reflex activities and their periodicities give rise to no theoretical problems that are new to the engineer whose business is communication. The mathematician has the tricks for handling them. He can treat reflexes, one and all, as he would the action of an electrical device in which the response to a sum of excitations is not equal to the sum of the responses to those excitations separately. He calls them *nonlinear* circuits. He has enlarged this theory to cope with those engines in which the magnitude sought is changed at will in almost any manner. Just as we may vary the set of the thermostat that governs the temperature of a room, so neurons in the path of the reflex can be excited or inhibited by impulses from elsewhere. The state to be sought by the system is thus conditioned by its circumstances. The largest of these subservient circuits comes into play when we move a hand to a new place. We contract muscles that set a mass in motion. The circuit shadows the contraction of these muscles by a contraction of their antagonists and brings the mass to rest at the place sought.

267

When this circuit is broken, the hand forever falls short or overshoots.

Electrical filters, first made by cut-and-try to balance distortion of signals in long lines, can be mathematically designed to stop most noise mixed with a signal while passing on the signal. Now, these filters give us the best guess based on knowledge of the past. As yet we know too little about brains to point out or picture our predictive filters. With such filters our guns place their shells so that they burst when a plane arrives there. With such filters the cat jumps not at the mouse but to the place the mouse will be when the cat lands. The filter is designed not on the basis of a single series in time but on a group of them treated statistically. One mouse on one occasion may stop or turn short of the place the cat will land. The cat cannot know the future. She can only jump to the place where most mice on most occasions will then be caught. Cats live because the filter is built to work best when the number of tries is large. Through all the random doings of mice, the filter has come to embody the manner of flight common to most mice. Now, from the wary movements of the single mouse, glimpsed by the cat, her filters forecast their fell conclusion.

When we ask not *how* but *why* a cat pursues a mouse, the answer is again in terms of circuits, but this time part of the path lies outside the cat. We will make the simplest assumption: that trains of impulses from the cat's empty stomach start her in quest of mice, and that, when she catches and eats a mouse, this fills her stomach and stops trains of impulses.

So now the chase will cease; so journeys end in lovers' meetings; even so, when our signs shape our signals, our question finds its answer and is no more a question. We asked how nervous activity mediated the quest of ends. It is by trains of impulses that, returning around a closed path, stop or reverse the process which gave rise to them, thus establishing some state toward which the system is to move. Some paths lie wholly within the nervous system; some, our reflexes, have paths through various parts of the body; and others leave the body by effectors, traverse the external world, with or without aid of signs, and come back through receptors. Those are our appetites and purposes. Together they include all actions that have a goal or end.

How can the structure of the system embody the possibility of choice? Clearly, if each such circuit had a path separate from any other path, each would go its own way to its own end. But many paths share nervous parts, and the use of others would result in contrary acts of some effectors. A few, like swallowing and drawing breath, working at once would destroy us.

Conflicts and mortal collisions are barred by inhibitory links from one circuit to another, so that when both are excited only one works. Thus the net embodies the possibility of these decisions. We might have been so made that if any one circuit was dominant over a second, and it over others, none of these was ever dominant over the first.

This would have set up a hierarchy of dominance. We were not made that way. It is easy to find circularities in dominance.

Imagine three reflexes such that A dominates B, B dominates C, and C dominates A. For this the dominance need not be absolute. It may depend upon the amount of activity of each, yet, with each at its own particular amount, dominance may be circular. Finally, inhibition need not be used. If each response implies summation of its proper stimulation with that of the next around the three, preference will be circular. I have met this circularity in experimental aesthetics even though the ends were much alike.

The notion of value arose from the number of things of one kind bartered for another kind. To rationalize these transactions, traders used some weight of precious metal. The number of the two kinds of things bartered was inversely proportional to the number of unit weights of precious metal for each item. The common measure of value was the unit weight, and their value was the price in terms of this common measure. Eudoxus generalized the notion of ratio, and Plato sought a common measure of other than marketable things. Hence the "good," the "beautiful," and the "true." Every psychologist, and every psychiatrist, who has studied motivation has wanted a general scale of values. He has wanted to know how much sexual pleasure was equal to escaping a given severity of pain, or how much work would be done for these ends. We have tried and failed to make a single scale of value for all motives. Many ends severally necessary to life are dimensionally dissimilar. Their dominance is frequently circular. The dissimilarities of the ends are fixed by the nature of the particular quantities established by the reflexes. The dominance — choice of preference — is embodied in the interconnection of the reflex paths within the central nervous system, where circularities of their interconnections fix circularities of dominance. Neither the ends nor the dominance can be rationalized by notions like the "strength of desire." Any common measure of all values is a vain superstition.

We have stated our problems exactly and either solved them or seen how they can be solved. But you may have noticed that we have often made nervous nets to fit the facts instead of seeking them in the nervous system. We have shown that a net can be made willfully to embody this or that idea, and to learn to embody this or that idea, but not that these nets are even likely to exist. Artificiality cannot be held against a man-made computing machine, but it is too much to have to suppose that each of ten billion neurons is connected according to any complete set of drawings and specifications.

It is doubtless true, although we do not know how it is brought about, that things seem similar to us which have happened together to all creatures that ever lived on earth, and this is doubtless fixed in us by the coming together of neurons whose precursors have been associated in activity. It may be that chance variants that worked better passed on to us the general form of our organs and some statistical regularities in the arrangement of cells into tissues; but our genes can scarcely order which neuron is to fasten to which throughout the system. It seems, therefore, more reasonable to assume that we all inherit only a few fixed universals like the qualities of sensation, and the common sensibles of position and motion, and those reflexes and appetites without which we and our kind would perish. For all else we must begin with *random nets.*

The word "random" has about it an unmerited air of simplicity. The word "chaos" exists only in the singular, but the varieties of chaos cannot be counted. No chaos is a single system, but an ensemble of systems whose statistical properties can only be defined by an infinite series of functions of a continually increasing number of variables. These may vary in any manner with place, direction, and distance, and depend upon the relation of things by pairs, by triplets, etc. In our present handling of these random nets, Mr. Walter Pitts has been most active, and what follows is largely his share in our joint undertaking. Choose any neuron in a random net, and imagine about it a nest of surfaces such that the chance of connection with our neuron is the same for all neurons on one and the same surface. If that chance depends upon the distance but not upon the direction or position, these surfaces will be a nest of spheres about our neuron. If directions matter,

270

these may become egg-shaped, and if position matters, these may be displaced in one direction, or the whole nest may be lopsided, "as if it were chopped off with a hatchet." It is easiest to solve the problem for spheres, for other nests are only knottier.

Physics is simple if we have to handle only two things. A few more make it unmanageable. It is simple again for very large numbers, for the chance of large deviations from the laws of chance is too small to matter. The problem of three bodies in astronomy is technically intricate. The mechanics of the galaxies is simple. It is easier to think rightly of a million neurons in a random net than of a couple of score in our specified nets. But there is one stumbling block that, so far as I know, is peculiar to relays. The activity of a neuron is zero except when it emits an impulse; then it is one. At time t the activity is one if the excitatory impulses outnumber inhibitory impulses by more than the threshold at time $t - 1$. Otherwise it is zero. What we want is an approximation to the average frequency of impulses in our neuron. The only general way to calculate such things starts from a *trial value* of frequency such that we can see how the system will behave close to that frequency. This has to be done for temperature and pressure of gases, but there it is easy to start with the gas so rare that we do not need to take into account the size of the particles and the forces between them. This works well for steam until we come close to condensation. In the case of the neuron it is best to begin with the trial value as the one and only frequency in our neuron that would result from the same frequency in each of the neurons afferent to it if their activities were statistically independent of one another.

The next approximation, which handles faster changes in frequency, uses the standard methods for treating of linear electrical nets. Some of the most useful statistical properties of a nervous tissue can be found by giving to any point of it a suitable series of electrical shocks while recording the impulses at many other points. The apparatus we need is being designed and will be built. This will help us to put some limit to the varieties of chaos of the cortex, but the varieties remaining will still be infinitely many.

When this has been done, we shall have before us the problem of the origin of universals, or induction. The problem is well exemplified in Klüver's famous study of monkeys without a visual cortex who could distinguish the larger of two equally bright spots, or the brighter of two equally large spots, but not a smaller and brighter from a larger and less bright if the total luminous flux was

271

the same from both. These experiments led to the hypothesis that such a monkey's only visual universal was total luminous flux. Other ingenious experiments confirmed the hypothesis. This is the state of the best hypotheses of science. If I drew all but one corner of a square on the blackboard and asked you to complete the figure, you would make it a square, whereas the line might have gone anywhere else equally well. So the monkey may not have known only total luminous flux, and this may tomorrow appear in some new discrimination. To make the point clear, suppose a man is given the series 1, 2, 3, and asked the next number. He may say 4 or 5 or any other number. If he says 4, we may suppose his idea is the cardinal numbers; if 5, the prime numbers; and if after 5, he answers 7, it would confirm our hypothesis of primes. He might have answered 8, and so refuted the hypothesis of primes. We might now suppose he was giving us the sum of the two preceding numbers. If we think for a moment, it is clear that there are innumerable series which have any finite number of terms in common. No finite number of terms defines the rule of formation. To know the next number does exclude an infinite number of series, but an infinite number remains. Thus, although a single experiment may disprove any hypothesis, no finite number of experiments can prove a single one of the infinite number that remain to fit any set of facts. The strange thing is that we do frame any hypothesis. Each is a new idea, or universal. Of all possible universals, how do we induce any, and, of permissible ones, the particular one that we do?

Let us start with whatever varieties of random nets the experiments depict, and let us suppose learning can be fully stated in terms of the relations of impulses in one neuron to those in another, in the ways we found would work with the blocks. We want a theory of learning that will work when the number of neurons is large, and the net random. Similar problems arise in the physics of magnetizing a bar of steel. It starts as a large number of little magnets left pointing hither and thither by chance. Each of these little magnets can be turned about by an applied magnetic force. The little magnets near a particular magnet contribute to the forces acting on it. The configuration of all the applied forces serves as a pattern for the configuration of the little magnets, any local figure in the forces giving a local structure. Finally, the little magnets stay in the positions they had at the time the forces cease to be applied. To see how much alike magnetizing and learning

272

may be, we may write the analogies in parallel order: the random net composed of neurons with the initial unmagnetized bar; the formation of synapsis with the magnetization; excitation, with the applied field; concomitant activity in nearly connected neurons making for structural changes with the mutual influence of neighboring magnets; enduring things that potentiate figures of stimulation and the consequent local stimulating of the net with the magnetic induction; and finally, the abiding of those links which were last used as we came to our goals and the reflexive or appetitive activity to its end with the final state of permanent magnetism in the bar. It is not too much to hope that with these things in common the mathematics for one may be shaped to fit the other. If it will serve, then we may someday state how random nets may learn by taking on this or that local structure. As we have already seen how, in a net made to order, we can embody given ideas and the possibility of learning any others that are significant functions of the given ideas, it is now clear how the development of local structures in random nets will complete the theory of the induction of all ideas of the types we have imagined. This may be done in some few years.

What troubles my dreams is this: that, when it is done, it will not be enough. No finite series defines its law of formation nor any data the hypothesis. I fear that the nervous system that learns as iron is magnetized, while it will give us a next number or a new experiment, may not give us the law of formation of the series — say the idea, the cardinals or the primes — or the hypothesis — say the law of gravitation, or the second law of thermodynamics. To use an idea is a finite act, which begins and ends in time; and when it occurs, it must not merely give the next number or experiment — for an infinite number of ideas or hypotheses give the same next. It must set the law forth in signs of some sort. There is no other way to know that the law exists. In a finite net we seek a kind of finite action that can be repeated as often as desired, and can construct and recognize notions proper to the net. I know of nothing but circular paths that embody the possibility of such actions. They have issued in memory, learning, prediction, and purpose. Each circuit has embodied an idea of a kind not to be had without it. If these circuits can be engendered by learning in a random net, and that learning can be described in much the same manner as the magnetizing of a bar of steel, we may be able to picture to ourselves how a natural nervous system can come to have notions of the cardinals or hypotheses like the laws of mechanics.

It should be clear that we can make a net that will frame hypotheses under any rule which prescribes the induction for every case, but we do not know the rule for one animal, or that there is a single rule for any two. We must not be hoodwinked by any uniformities in the behavior of several animals into the superstition that they frame their hypotheses by one and the same rule; for, just as two hypotheses may agree in prediction of the next experimental datum, or two ideas like the cardinals and primes in the series 1, 2, 3, so in simple cases several rules of induction may concur in the same hypotheses or ideas. What is more, we have reason to believe that the very rules of induction are not prescribed at birth, so that, even if we were born alike, our unlike fortunes would diversify our rules.

All learning, including the process whereby the rules of induction are perfected, orders step by step an ensemble erstwhile chaotic. And whenever this, which is a change of state, happens to an ensemble, the statistical variables that characterize it no longer require merely the first few members of the probability-distributions of monads, diads, triads, etc., of the elements of its component systems, but, instead depend upon the ultimate trends of these distributions of n-ads as n increases without limit. For no task in physics is our mathematics so feeble or so far to seek. Fortunately for us, this change of state in our brains that may happen to water in a moment of freezing goes merrily on in us as long as we can learn, and some of us may live to share the fun of concocting the required mathematics.

Yet, even were this done today, and done in our two-valued calculus of actual propositions so that we were sure no other could be needed to describe all human thinking in terms of nervous nets, every philosopher should know that this confers no primacy on any one among all possible logics of signs nor confines them *a priori* in any way. Our calculus of actual propositions is but formally similar to a part of the two-valued calculi of statements and of classes. Tautologies, which are the very stuff of mathematics and logic, are the ideas of no neuron. The formal similarity is fortuitous. Had our calculus of actual propositions been three-valued, our nervous systems could have made two-valued logics. Their calculus being in fact two-valued, they have made for themselves, three, n, and infinite-valued calculi, as well as others yet stranger. Non-Euclidean geometry breached Kant's synthetic *a priori;* metalogic has razed the ruin; and, despite Magnus, no appeal to physiology can restore any part of it. It becomes us to be humble to the facts even in that strange case in which they are the work of our own heads.

In any case it is clear that we may go forward safely, using the logical calculus of actual propositions which we have learned from these wooden soldiers. Like good scientists, they have raised and formulated for us the problem of induction when we had only put to them, and they had solved, the problems of knowledge and of value. I am, therefore, sorry to have to inform you that their exemplary conduct was predicated upon a superstition. Because it is not yet quite vain, I share it with them. The name of that superstition is causality.

BIBLIOGRAPHY

Lorente de Nó, Rafael: A Study of Nerve Physiology. *Studies from The Rockefeller Institute for Medical Research,* vols. 131 and 132, 1947.

Lloyd, D. P. C.: Principles of Nervous Activity. Chapters I-IV, *A Textbook of Physiology,* J. Fulton, ed. Philadelphia, W. B. Saunders, 1949.

Lorente de Nó, Rafael: Transmission of impulses through cranial motor nuclei. *J. Neurophysiol., 2:*402-464, 1939.

Fessard, A., et J. Posternak: Lés mécanismes élémentaires de la transmission synaptique. *J. Physiol. Path. gén., 2:*319-446, 1950.

McCulloch, W. S., and W. Pitts: A logical calculus of the ideas immanent in nervous activity. *Bull. Math. Biophys., 5:*115-133, 1943.

McCulloch, W. S.: The brain as a computing machine. *Elect. Engineering,* June 13, 1949.

McCulloch, W. S., and J. Pfeiffer: Of digital computers called brains. *Sc. Monthly, 6:*368-376, 1949.

McCulloch, W. S.: A heterarchy of values determined by the topology of nervous nets. *Bull. Math. Biophys., 7:*89-93, 1945.

McCulloch, W. S.: The functional organization of the cerebral cortex. *Physiol. Rev., 3:*390-407, 1944.

McCulloch, W. S.: Modes of functional organization of the cerebral cortex. *Federation Proc., 2:*448-452, 1947.

THE PAST OF A DELUSION

WE ARE not now the men we were a quarter of a century ago. Our brains are failing. Cells of all other tissues multiply—our nerve cells, not again! Their complement was filled in childhood. The little accidents of daily life thin out their ranks, and when one dies no other does its job; for no two have the same connections. Our skills, our wits, our memory desert us. This is not always "that unhoped serene that men call age." It is incompetence, dependence and all too often an unwarranted suspicion of those nearest and dearest. This lands us in the hands of a psychiatrist who can but keep alive for some few years the ugly body of our soul's decay. Senility can have no cure, and science has not brewed an elixir of eternal youth.

Half the patients in all hospitals in the United States are there for trouble in their brains. In Illinois a third of all State hospital inhabitants have senile psychoses. Pray for their speedy death or legislate for euthanasia, but waste no tears on them. They had their chance.

Hereditary idiots, essential epileptics, schizophrenics begin at birth or in early life to suffer failing function of brains which, under the microscope, may look normal. In these, as in other hereditary diseases, we meet chemical disorders. Physical agents and drugs have so far failed to help these feeble-minded, but have forestalled the bulk of fits and remitted temporarily two-thirds of schizophrenics. If science can go on as it has gone we have a right to hope that we may make life worthy of its name for the majority of mental patients; for these diseases look today as cretinism did in nineteen ten, and diabetes in the twenties. Give us time!

In those same twenties, one-fifth of the insane had syphilis of the forebrain and went vaingloriously to paralytic death. Today it's hard to find a bedridden Caesar or a Napoleon who wets and soils. With syphilis went gonorrhea. Now ends the curse on lusty wenchings we cloaked in prick-eared prudery from the glorious days of good Queen Bess, through the long reign of Victoria, to the days of our begetting. For the jovial nights our children may enjoy we are even more indebted to mercurials, malaria and antibiotics, in Paracelsus' tradition, than to the invention of the kindly Doctor Condom. And must the same great price still be paid for the same great service? Not quite!

When the survey of mental hospitals of the red clay belt from Virginia southward showed that nearly half the patients had diarrhea, dermititis, dementia and died for want of nicotinic acid—though it go hard with the born Republican to admit it—'twas the Department of Agriculture under its then Secretary, Wallace, that changed the crops, and thus the diet, of the Piedmont, so that pellagra is no more. Our mental hygienists have not yet mustered the representation to try in Senatorial Investigation, convict him of organicism and send him into exile. But give them time!

I am indebted to Chicago, to von Bonin and to Bailey who brought me here and most to Gerty who made possible for me fully ten years of that organicism during which our laboratory has been a crossroads of collaboration with Northwestern and Chicago, and with Alexander of the Psychoanalytic Institute—crossroads that have extended throughout our continent, to Europe, even to Asia. I have been happy with my many collaborators, but most with the crop of more than thirty youngsters who have learned respect for the physics and the chemistry of living brains. Through them, and men like them, we may expect in time to cure—or, better yet, prevent—psychoses, and so to check the growth of that vast kingdom of beds-for-the-insane that rivals now the monasteries of the Middle Ages. But have we time?

Psychiatry has been sold short. In movies, magazines and daily papers you find it everywhere, promising everything—able to perform—almost nothing! The time has come when we psychiatrists must deliver the goods. Are we the men to do that? Some years ago, nine out of ten of us came from the lowest third of medical students, sought security as civil servants in state hospitals with more patients than we could examine and there deteriorated faster than those committed to our care. Today, medicine has increased the take of union members by decreasing the ratio of graduates to their prospective patients. War and threat of war increased the scarcity. Refugee physicians, ignorant of the customs and language of their patients, have entered our state service; but there is hardly a public asylum with half its inadequate complement of doctors. When the public wakes I fear it will make matters worse by socializing medicine. The remedy lies not in government, already overgrown, but in giving doctors tools with which to help their patients. Only slow science can do that.

But incompetence is not the worst reason for becoming a psychiatrist, nor are these civil servants the men who sold short psychiatry. The worst reason is the desire for filthy lucre. Psychoanalysts say that they discovered that gold is a symbol for feces, but they formed a sect in psychiatry where there should be none. This sect so controls the teaching hospitals of our city that no one may be a resident in psychiatry unless he is approved by them for membership in their sect. To become a member he must be psychoanalyzed, for which the analysand must pay the analyst who took the Hippocratic oath. Finally, acceptance into the sect depends upon the emotional conversion of the analysand to the sect's peculiar beliefs. Some neophytes submit for their health—a third wrong reason for becoming a psychiatrist—but more for a share in the loot. Some, after conversion, believe they have something to sell. Convenient for them! It is still to their profit, or power which is profit, that this sect and its fellow travelers have oversold psychiatry. When I see such a sect prospering I do well to be angry.

Neurotic patients go to psychoanalysts hoping to be cured. At best the layman's pitiful and ludicrous trust in his doctor compels the practitioner to be part benefactor, part charlatan. Fortunately most people recover from most diseases despite our meddling. Two-thirds of all neurotics get well with almost any kind of surgical, pharmacological or psychological treatment, and with none at all. The rest don't. But our big problem is insanity. Most psychoanalysts are too clever to attempt to help the insane. The orthodox believer says Freud's method is inapplicable to them, so he handles only neurotics, or what, with a fortune-teller's lucrative presumption, he calls "prepsychotics." Yet, with all the aces palmed, the analyst will not tell his fellow physician how many of his patients get well. In his later years Freud doubted the therapeutic value of his method, but his hopeful disciples now hold the profitable doctrine that all men have neurotic traits worth analyzing and often continue it as long as the analysand will pay. Then "the analysis is finished"; but I have never heard one say "the patient is cured." Judged by the duration of analyses, and by the reactions of originally healthy neophytes, the frivolous Viennese may have been in earnest when they defined psychoanalysis as that disease of which it fancies itself the cure. I'm told that Kurt Krauss was first to say it so.

The English law lets a child be reared in any superstition, not in none. If he recovers it leaves him with a generalized immunity to isms. But we, the American people, are commonly demoralized grandchildren of uprooted Europeans, our families decimated by divorce, our faith in progress failing. We are ripe for any ism. This century we've had Theosophy and Anthroposophy and Buckmanism and Psychoanalysis and now Dianetics, its peerless caricature. It surpasses all analytic schisms except Jung's, which from the "something divine in man" has turned to divination from the I' Ching. Unlike the rest of psychoanalytic heretics, at whose follies you may laugh your belly full when you have time to read them,

Jung alone rejected the hard Calvinistic, necessitarian and materialistic core of Freud's delusion. For him, as for the "Dwarf" Adler, who stubbornly insisted on his Superman conception of organ-inferiority, Freud had respect. They would not change their minds when he changed his, like the rest of his group whom Puner says Freud once described as "Les Crapules." For their ultimate defections most of them were excommunicated. My nose says Freud was right! He was not stupid and he knew what fate demanded of him and of his followers. That is why he is dangerous.

You'd think deterministic faiths would let the world go on as foreordained by God, by Devil or by mere Matter; but their devotées are somehow different from the rest of us. Mohammed and John Knox, Karl Marx and Sigmund Freud, and all their true believers, must hurry the inevitable. Ruthlessly: Relentlessly: Remorselessly: they force their creeds upon us. For them life never is the game we play to our lives' end with fate and fellow man for keeps, but chiefly for the fun of it. How come these men to lack the humor and humility that keep us human? What strange defect to think one knows God's will, or Matter's dialectical determination, or how his own brain works to fool him!

Once Freud thought he'd found the scientific way into the intricacies of the human mind through its disorders he gave himself no rest. His days and nights were spent in collecting data by free associations and from dreams, his patients' and his own, in pitiless analysis of these and their interpretations, in order to reveal those motives we deny, perhaps forget, because their origins were painful to us. The details of his method and his theories changed in the course of time, but not enough to keep pace with undeniable facts, and this compelled him to cling to terms and warp their meaning out of all common sense.

In part this sprang from his attempts to seem consistent in continued propaganda for his pseudoscientific system, perhaps in part to reassure himself and certainly to win for it the approbation it lacked in clinical and scientific circles. Popularity came first through literary papers which, though defensive, shocked the teutonic prudes, and later through attacks on man's ideals, including God!

F. Adler, Dalbiez and Maritain have tried to separate and save Freud's method from his theory, his "Metapsychology." It can't be done. As Alexander, with first-hand knowledge of analysis and puzzled honesty that breeds religious doubts, says rightly: its data, method, theory are indissolubly one. In none of them is Alexander orthodox today! No scientist can be. Dependence of the data on the theory separates psychoanalysis from all true sciences. What Freud thought free associations are not free. The nondirective torture of Catholic inquisitors extracted *mea culpa*'s of previsioned heresies: the communists secure confessions of expected deviations and disloyalties. Interpretations of chaotic dreams are still controlled by theory, and that theory was in the head of Freud. Change this, and you have changed the method and the data. This is the curse of all attempts to understand things social. They are essentially sharing. What we seek to understand is coupled back through us, so that we ourselves change the thing we seek to understand. When this coupling grows very close it is, in Freudian lingo, called "transference." Freud himself came to attribute to transference what therapeutic value lay in analysis. The pragmatic test of truth, "Analysis is true because it works," the "warranted assertibility" of Dewey, stands here accused of folly in full daylight. Science must have data not vitiated by our theory. Freud's scheme would even beat Mark Twain's rule for fiction: "You've got to have the facts before you can pervert 'em."

In the world of physics, if we are to have any knowledge of that world, there must be nervous impulses in our heads which happen only if the world excites our eyes, ears, nose or skin. In the case of these true signals, there is a necessary connection between events; the one in the head, the other (its cause) in the world; and this connection is a very limited kind of physical causation that does go hand in hand with meaning. The consequent here means the cause. Even for these true signals the energy of excitation and the energy of nervous impulses come from separate sources. Apart from signals that are true, meaning and cause have nothing in common. Yet these the Freudians confound in their theory of determination; hence their confusion of supposed origins with supposed validities.

For them logic itself is but a rationalization of our prejudices whereby we come to grips with fact. If you don't like my wording of this error make your own translation of these gleanings from the orthodox scriptures: "Logic looks at objects through the eyes of an idealized rigid super-ego . . . turning from sense data to collective representations whereby . . . like the primitive through his totem . . . we come into contact with reality." Havers, man, that's no logic!

Bury that stillborn monster in the unhallowed ground of your unconscious, your forgetery, but give the devil his due! Take Freud at his word. He meant it when he said our minds were fashioned for us early by the social fate of our wanton, incontinent and blindly energetic lust —"Libido, in the Chaos of the Id." I don't believe a word of it. But here's his story, or he would have it so.

On the sixth of May, eighteen fifty-six, in the Czechish town of Freiburg, the new young wife of an unsuccessful aging Jewish miller gave birth to a son covered with pitch black hair, of Messianic portent to her Talmudic mind. This omen she imparted to him, her first born, Sigmund, as she fondled him. But his old father, Jacob, had little use for him; and when the youngster, aged eight, wet his father's bedroom, Jacob prophesied that he'd "amount to nothing." This incident was remembered and resented by the youngster for three-quarters of a century. He said so! As Germans, his family was not accepted by the Czechs or by the Czechish Jews. For Sigmund Freud there was no Bar Mitzvah. Financial failure forced them to Berlin, then to Vienna, where Freud began to "compensate" by identifying himself with heroes, chiefly Semitic, notably Hannibal. To this, Jacob's reaction was to tell him of an incident. "Up comes a Christian who knocks my new fur cap into the mud and shouts 'Jew, get off the pavement!' "

"And what did you do?"

"I went into the street and picked up my cap."

In Freud's account this made him despise the father he already hated, but whom he always feared so much and with so strong a sense of guilt, that he never dared revolt as long as Jacob lived. But Freud's analysis of his own recollections and his interpretations of his dreams is that he had incestuous lust for his young mother, showed it in sexual advances made by him to her, which finally compelled her to turn him over to old Jacob for castration, a thought so horrible that he had repressed their memories out of his Ego into his Unconscious where they formed the complex he called "Oedipus" which, for all demonological dynamics, is that guilty "conscience that makes cowards of us all." I mean all. For Freud projects his Oedipus complex upon every mother's son. All men, I mean. For women don't have consciences like that. Having no penis, they must take castration as *fait accompli*, hide their deficiency in Pudor, and want babies from their daddies, as mama had. Failing this, they introject the father. At most, their consciences are stunted flimsy things and when you find a real one in a woman it's not hers, but just an undigested fragment of the father-introject. Swallow that if you can, and let's get back to "fact," perhaps I should say "history."

While Freud was growing up, legal restrictions against Jews were more and more rescinded in Vienna. Law and medicine were filling up with Jews. One might even become a full professor if he turned Catholic. Freud thought of law but changed to medicine, thinking it offered better livelihood. He studied physiology with Bruecke from whom he learnt reflexology and Johannes Müller's antiquated notions of specific energies in living systems on which he later based his definition of Libido as "a certain quantity of psychic energy." But there was no money then, or now, in teaching or research in physiology. He studied neuroanatomy with the paternal Meynert and did research with him so well that Meynert

offered him a post, but with too little money. So Freud
turned against him, suspected his intentions and for years
was out to "bell the cat by crossing swords" with him
in scientific meetings. Freud's insight? Meynert was a
father-surrogate, but more! Freud envied him outright
because no Jew could be a full professor.

Trained in neurology, Freud went to Paris in his early
twenties to study with Charcot, from whom he learned
the art of hypnotizing and that men might have hysteria
although they have no womb. 'Twas in his clinic Freud
was amazed to hear Charcot say that with cases of this
kind, "C'est toujours la chose genitale, toujours—
toujours—toujours." This remark hit Freud when he was
lonely in Paris in the spring and sat among the gargoyles
of Notre Dame instead of dancing in the streets until it
was time to go to bed. To this remark, "la chose genitale," Freud has attributed the central refrain of his life's
poetics. Remember that he thought it uncanny when in
Italy his feet brought him, he knew not how, back
three times to the red-light district. Remember how his
break began with Jung, because when he told Jung, here
in America, that he dreamed of prostitutes, Jung asked
him what he meant to do about it. Remember that he
kept his fiancée, with whom neither dowry nor kest,
waiting four years, presumably without preconjugal
felicity. During this time he went on studying hysteria,
"due to sexual misadventures"; anxiety neuroses, "due
to coetus interruptus, undischarged excitement or ab-
stinence"; and neurasthenia, "due to masturbation and
too many nocturnal emissions," or so Freud fancied it.
And when he could not wring from his patient a history
of sexual affairs he invented it in their unconscious. It

was when this forced him back to infancy that he had to make the term "sex" so inclusive that it soon became synonymous with any pleasurable action. Remember that when Chrobak, referring to Freud a woman whose nervousness came from eighteen years of marriage to an impotent husband, lamented he could not prescribe the proper application of a normal penis, Freud was aghast at Chrobak's cynicism. Prudery was cracking. Sex, translated into German, *Geschlecht*, was privileged in Viennese society. Krafft-Ebing was a full professor. But Freud's distortions brought him only ridicule and ostracism.

The scorn Freud felt for Bruecke and for Meynert extended to Charcot. Freud translated Charcot's new lectures, adding carping marginal notes and caviling references to authors Charcot had not mentioned. Based on his own dreams Freud's explanation of this was that his "failure to ask Charcot's permission for these critical additions was one of those slips of memory we have when we would not admit even to ourselves our hostile motives."

Of Freud's indebtedness to the Nancy School we know principally that he resented compulsion placed upon patients by hypnotic suggestion, especially when Bernheim or Liebeault raised their voices. Based upon ten thousand hypnoses this school had shown that what was characteristic of these patients was their inordinate suggestibility. Unfortunately Freud never was sufficiently on guard against it, for in his handling of such patients he always found to his horror and amazement what was most on his (Unconscious?) mind—sex!

May I in passing note: Hysterical suggestibility has its physiological counterpart, demonstrated in Marseilles by Henri Gastaut and in Paris by Antoine Remond, who is your guest tonight. Like the familial epileptics, hysterics are easily thrown into convulsion by flashing light accompanied by small doses of metrazol. Thus even in hysteria, whose symptoms are affected by suggestion, the mental content, patent or latent memories, though it be sex, determines the form of the symptom, never generates the disease. But let's get back to Freud.

His first and only great collaborator was Breuer, with whom he studied one case record of hysteria. They wrote a brief report and then a book including later studies made by Freud alone on other cases. But Breuer, who at first agreed with Freud, would not be persuaded of Freud's elaborations. Freud felt rejected and again, as with Breucke, Meynert and Charcot, the father-surrogate was finally rejected, despised, repudiated. This time the special twist was that later, when a woman under hypnosis made a pass at Freud, he guessed that Breuer, for prudish reasons, had not revealed to him that their ten-year case when getting well had made a pass at Breuer. Thus was born Freud's notion of Transference as the basis of the cure.

Freud says his turning against fathers-surrogate was his predestined reaction, determined in his infancy. With him Moses fared no better, for, after "identifying" with Moses, Freud ended by proving to his own satisfaction that Moses was no Jew; thus killing two birds with a single stone. And God himself meets the same fate in *The Future of an Illusion*. By half-truths told with bad intent, that beat all lies he could invent, he arrogantly prophesies the time when God will fade away and leave the stage to man, made in Freud's image. Freud's delusion has no future, but it had a past.

These things I had to say of Freud who said worse of himself because he thought they would substantiate his theory that man's depravity is causally determined by his past in simple ways, by motives buried in forgotten memories waiting to be revealed by his, Freud's, psychoanalysis. To prove his point he paints himself too black to be convincing. I say no more of him. Jew-hating Nazis burnt his books. The dying man was ransomed for mere gold. His corpse is buried in a foreign land. "Let worms be its biographers." They are more kindly than his kind and less offensive. Unfortunately Delusions are Ideas. We cannot bury them properly. Only the dust of ages can consign them to oblivion.

So let me make it clear that Freud meant the things he said. By energy he meant ability to do work, albeit of a special kind and quantity, still truly energy. Topology for him meant places so connected that the Id is inside (chiefly reflexes) and the Ego outside (connecting with the world about by eyes and nose and skin and ears). His Economics was a scheming handling of the things to which we attach values in order to secure the greatest quantity of pleasure, as 'twere their common measure, and pay least price in pain.

The Freudian scheme is a tissue of unverified and often unverifiable hypotheses, all oversimplified. Against such schemes Hippocrates inveighs in his first sentence of *On Ancient Medicine:* "Whoever having undertaken to speak or write on Medicine, have first laid down for themselves some hypothesis to their argument, such as hot, or cold, or moist, or dry, or whatever else they choose (thus reducing their subject within a narrow compass, and supposing only one or two original causes of diseases or of death among mankind) are all clearly mistaken in much that they say; and this is the more reprehensible as relating to an art which all men use on the most important occasions. . . ."

From Descartes onward, we whose business is the physics of the body, especially the brain, have sought in terms of matter and of energy the detailed explanation of activities of animals, including man, and all his acts, including those that he calls mental, acts guided by ideas and purposes. In his *Experimental Medicine*, in French so beautifully clear it set a style of writing, Claude Bernard described the way we push ahead with good experiments and such hypotheses as they require to guide them. We do not found the practice of our medicine upon hypotheses that cannot be or have not been confirmed in the experiment. I have myself proposed some notions as to how the cortex of the brain detects a shape regardless of its size, or chord regardless of its key. It will take years of work to prove or disprove them. Until then no one may build his practice upon them.

All our hypotheses are of a kind that do require, if they be right, that we shall find this going on now, here; and that, then, there: whereas Freud's notions fail to locate in space and time his hypothetical Id, Unconscious, Ego, Super-Ego, or to predict what they will look like in the brain. Freud must have known how carefully Meynert compared mental symptoms with disordered structures. That is a scientific way into the psychiatry of damaged brains. Contrast Freud's delusion with the sad humility of Sherrington who, though he knows more physiology of brains than any other Englishman, admitted that for him "in this world Mind goes more ghostly than a ghost."

The notions that we need to guide this research are just forming now in brains like Wiener's (call it Cybernetics if you must but get the idea first) and in those many youngsters who design the great high-speed computers. Most of them are trained in symbolic logic, led by Bertrand Russell. From such men come the measure of information and the means for its preservation and transmission. We even have some notions of the many disparate processes that we call glibly "Memory," and as we build our engines that can have ideas, lay plans, elaborate their purposes and forecast the outcome of their acts to make them match the probable events around them, we begin to make a better guess as to the ways our brains can do these things that we call mental.

But notice that for us matter is far less material than it was once, and was for Freud. Nor does our physics let us prophesy from past events all future happenings. Causality in the strict sense describes, at best, statistical results of microscopic happenings which still are random in detail. Although we know that half some aggregate of some unstable atoms will decay in such a time we cannot tell which ones will split. And in those visible events, like cracks extending in a plate of glass, wherein the course of things to come depends upon the microscopic state of things at the point reached, we can make no prediction, now or later, on the basis of some observation we may someday hope to make. I will not bore you with the mathematical and physical analysis of this our *igno-*

rabimus; you'll find it in John von Neumann's *The Mathematical Basis of Quantal Mechanisms.*

One of the cornerstones of Freud's delusion is the belief that we forget no single jot or tittle of what at any time has happened to us. By calculations that began naïvely with the senior Oliver Wendell Holmes and are today best handled by the physicist von Förster, man's head would have to be about the size of a small elephant to hold that much. His body could not eat enough to energize its mere retention even if we suppose a single molecule of structuring protein would serve as trace. Actually the mean half-life of a trace in human memory, and of a molecule of protein, is only half a day. Some few per cent of engrams do survive, presumably because we recreate the traces in our heads, but that is all fate leaves us of our youth. Where written words remain to check our senile recollections they often prove us wrong. We rewrite history, inventing the past so it conforms to present needs. We forget, as our machines forget, because entropic processes incessantly corrupt retention and transmission of all records and all signals.

Partly because all men, when pushed, fill in the gaps of memory, partly because hysterics and neurotics generally are most suggestible, Freud's so-called findings of repressed unconscious stuff rest on confabulation, perhaps his patients'; but where the free associations and the dreams are both his own, there cannot be a question but that Freud did the confabulating.

I do not for one moment believe his story of sexual advances made by him, an infant, to his mother, nor of her turning him over to old Jacob for castration, nor that a baby of that age has such a notion. These are ideas

Freud had in later life, after he had extended sex to mean all pleasure and affection, and then projected them upon his past of which he had no recollections clear enough to stop him from confabulating.

What's most important here is that Freud's early life, with or without his fancied past, cannot account for his delusion. For Freud did not invent the ideas of which it is composed. It is not likely we will ever learn just why or how these ideas came together in his brain rather than in some other, but the ideas were rampant in his world. Sex, the Unconscious, and Materialism were matters of discussion among physicians and the public generally.

The battle against venereal disease was joined and almost finished between the time Freud entered medical school and the time he died. Krafft-Ebing was investigating and lecturing upon the Psychopathia Sexualis. Hysteria was in debate, perhaps not a disease of woman because the womb, unburdened with a babe, wandered; for it occurred in men; but often sexual desires, thwarted or excited, were in the picture. Vienna was a gay place with a double standard, and unorthodox Jews were beginning to enjoy the freedom of the city instead of the conformity of circumscribed communities that centered in the synagogues of the small towns. I'm sure Freud heard that sex was more important, medically and humanly, and more prevalent and various in its manifestations than his parents' generation ever had admitted. He just outdid himself and others of his generation by making sex the origin of all delight; and, by inversion, the origin of all constraints we put upon ourselves as social beings. Freud did not invent sex, its prevalence or verbal vogue. He merely rode the band wagon of its triumphant re-entry into polite society.

The Unconscious has a long, strange history. Leibnitz introduced the notion of Unconscious mind as an infinitesimal, "petite perception," in a sort of calculus of Knowledge. This role it plays today in schools of psychophysics. Given three weights so near alike that you can just be sure that the first exceeds the third you cannot tell that the first exceeds the second or that the second exceeds the third. So these steps, though singly unconscious, by addition of two or more, become conscious. Something in you knew the differences of which you were not conscious. What knew? Unconscious Mind! But, what is far more than this addition, when you introspect you find not mere sensations; you find perceptions. Colors appear in given shapes together for you in the space and time of your perceiving. Hence time and space, and the synthetic *a priori*, e.g., extended color, are the work of your unconscious mind. In the writings of Emanuel Kant these become the Forms of Sensation. In his *Practical Reason* he adds basic purposes and value judgments which are primary to what becomes Unconscious Mind. You find it growing through Fichte, Schelling, Lessing and Schopenhauer, to become, in Eduard von Hartmann's work, not merely everything performed by animals for their surviving, but the very *Geist* of evolution itself! The Unconscious has become full-fledged, idealistic creator of all ideas and purposes that account for the unfolding of a world wherein knowledge and progress are the outcome of the way Unconscious Mind did, and does, beneficially inform the stuff and frenzy of what else were chaos and old night.

Von Hartmann's *The Unconscious* had more sale than Schopenhauer's works—ninety thousand copies in German, plus a French and a partial English translation, by the time Freud's mention of his own unconscious first appeared. In France, von Hartmann's Unconscious mind was a key notion and inspiration of Janet, whom Freud said he never knew, and of the Nancy School, where Freud had studied. It was the fashionable explanation of what appeared in hysteria under hypnosis. To deny it was to suppose the patient was malingering. In Germany as great a physiologist as Herring took it seriously and sought to explain it in terms of nervous activity. Like Samuel Butler, author of *Erewhon* but also of *Unconscious Memory*, he thought of evolution as transmitted habits of which the organism is no longer aware when or how it or its ancestors acquired them. Since Freud told several people he had never read von Hartmann, we may find the link nearer to Freud's specific introduction of the Unconscious in Breuer's knowledge of Herbart's psychology, wherein the unconscious specifically appears with repression and resurgence of ideas rising into consciousness. Even the notion of cathexis, or attachment we have for ideas or things or people, Herbart had derived from von Hartmann. All these appear in Freud and Breuer's work on their one case of hysteria that formed the excuse, not the basis, for the system of ideas already popular among the enlightened in England, France, and Germany. Freud thought these his invention, determined by his infancy.

What makes it difficult to trace the way Freud came by these ideas is typified by his remark concerning Schopenhauer's exposition of insanity in the *World as Will and Idea*. Of this Freud said, "What he states there concerning the striving against the acceptance of a painful piece of reality agrees so completely with the content of my theory of repression that once again I must be grateful to my not being well read for the possibility of making a discovery." Perhaps he was that ignorant of these philosophers, but Ernst Kris, Marie Bonaparte and Anna Freud have footnotes to his letters which show that he had underlined a copy of Lipp's *Grundtatsachen des Seelenlebens* on the fundamental role of the unconscious from which our conscious ideas rise and to which they sink down again. To me it makes no difference just how the adult Freud came by these ideas for they were all in books, popular as well as scientific. They were on men's tongues. Never before or since had they such vogue as when Freud climbed on this band wagon and grabbed the reins.

But let us turn from the frivolities of new-won liberty for intellectuals to speak of sex; and from the last great flower of German Metaphysical Idealism, the Unconscious Mind, to Freud's Materialism, for here again he rides the wagon with the whole band led by Karl Marx.

I will not rehearse the sad story of the industrial revolution. It is enough to note that from the village craftsman, whose life made sense to him, whose ideals were practical affairs of neighborly affection, whose God, although inscrutable, was worthy of all trust, it had made the proletariat, struggling for necessities in city slums, or owners, to whom wealth brought power without that tradition of responsibility which is the birthright of hereditary rulers. Their oracle was Adam Smith; their gospel, *Laissez Faire;* their mythus, Economic Man! Ricardo wrote their Swan Song. Capital and labor put all their faith in matter, not in God. Then came Karl Marx. For him God had to go because He helped the vested interests of society repress the proletariat, even as for Freud, a generation later, God had to go because He helped the vested interests of our social selves repress prolific denizens of the Id.

For Marx and Freud matter was more than the mere stuff we buy and sell. It was the substance, the real thing, that carried the determinism of their faiths. Their histories have too much in common. When Hume showed that the notion of causality cannot be empirically derived, Emanuel Kant, to support his metaphysical slumbers, spawned two fertile succubi. One category, the Forms of Sensation, pervaded the Dynamic Ego as Unconscious Mind. Upon her Freud begat his bastard, Psychoanalysis. The other, Causality, the Category of Reason, flitted transcendentally through Hegel's Dialectical Idealism. Upon Causality herself Karl Marx begat his bastard, Dialectical Materialism. In ideas as in clothes there is a social lag. To proletarian eyes she still looks scientifically respectable. Today she lords it over God in Mother Russia and you may think that we are better off in having taken to our bosom the other of these bastards of Kant's succubi, but I'm not sure. They have too much in common. To communists Psychoanalysis was acceptable until her bourgeois tendencies were detected. Then she was expurged and her votaries were liquidated.

Note carefully what Freud did when he seduced Unconscious Mind. She had been the soul of order and of virtue. She had informed the progress of the world with good ideas and purposeful that flower in man's free will and man's ideals. Freud's bastard, the Unconscious, is BAD. She misinforms us to our great disservice, our disease. But this she-devil is not all soul. She is all matter, old fashioned matter, materially determined and determining our fate, our failure. It is not by accident but of their essence that communism and psychoanalysis both carry the dead weight of Lamarckian inheritance. Freud and Lysenko are alike in this. What else is the collective Unconscious?

Freud's doctrine may even be demoralizing for it is a way of saying you are not responsible for these, your acts, because they are nothing but the inevitable doings of mere matter, fixed in your infancy, or at your birth determined by Unconscious Memory of the taboos of the race. Ethics and morals are but the doings of a conscience that is the material consequence of the way your parents inevitably handled you. When you have sensed this in yourself, and are emotionally persuaded that it is universal, you too may spread the gospel of material determination and demoralize mankind for gold.

Today throughout our country the psychoanalysts have nests of ardent rodents. They have gnawed into all branches of our so-called mental hygiene movement that has no other systematic faith to offer to psychiatric social workers, to educators who come for help in guiding children, to priests in telling insanity from sin, to jailers who would salvage any of their criminals, to generals faced with the irresponsible behavior of troops. Their program is enormous, will cost us billions and is already under way.

What makes even a Scot squirm is not so much the waste of what were better spent to find out how brains work as the disease entailed to the unborn inheritors of Freud's delusion. Men of science, some physicians, even enlightened psychoanalysts, have learned the folly of the orthodox hypotheses. But teachers have been so infected with the initial virus that we now have a generation of parents full of superstitious fear that they may be guilty of their children's anticipated neuroses. They cannot suckle, cuddle, swathe or spank the baby, housebreak the child, or admonish the adolescent except upon advice of a psychiatrist. His supposititious wisdom thus becomes their daily inspiration. Too often it's the old virulent delusion, parroted by psychiatric social workers.

Meanwhile *Dianetics*, its exoteric or lay take-off, is said to have already sold 476,000 copies, though the price has risen to four dollars and its author has fallen into the clutches of psychiatry. I would not be surprised if psychoanalysis had more converts and fellow travelers than communism ever had among our federal servants. The doctrines are so crucially alike I sometimes wonder whether our energies are not misspent in hunting communists, instead of those who prepare us for their notions.

I know it sounds incredible that any man can persuade his fellow that ideas and purposes are merely stuff and change. But this is not as hard for me to swallow as that the monstrous nonsense of Freudian writings is even taken seriously. Read his basic writings and a dozen numbers of the *Psychoanalytic Quarterly* and remember that there is no scientific reason to believe a word of it and then remember that perhaps a million of your fellow citizens regard it as the gospel of this century. They are an organized vociferous minority who have the ears of those who spend our taxes, enact our laws, defend our country. It has taken thirty years for Freud's disciples to get their church established. Its creed, no other, may legally be taught in our public schools. In nineteen twenty-one psychoanalysts were a minor sect of long-haired foreigners sometimes imported to lecture in our colleges.

In nineteen twenty-one I turned from logic, semantics and the philosophy of science, to psychology; and read everything scientific that bore on the theory of knowledge from Alcmaeon of Croton (600 B.C.) to my contemporaries. This included the early psychoanalytic writings. They were and are nonsensical physics, pseudo-logic, specious semantics, bad theory; and, worst of all, founded on false observations, vitiated data. I knew it then; I know it now. In nineteen twenty-one, for what might have been a thesis, I gathered much data on free associations in normal and insane to discover whether this method did disclose what Freud assumed. I found nothing statistically significant of the kind I had to find, had Freud been right.

However, I became convinced that psychology for me would be a farce unless I really found out how brains work. I began to want to understand and so to help the insane. I entered medical school where I had my first meeting with a psychoanalyst, Ferenczi. In the days when he taught us, he was deep in the Thalassic complex. Everything was to be understood as a desire to swim once more in the womb. The orgasm meant this to the man, not merely to the sperm that went there. Bed-wetting and cramps were symbolic forms of this attainment, and if one day one did none of these things, it was sure proof of how much he desired to; for the desire was so intense he did not dare to yield to it. From him I first heard the argument from latency: "This man is really not a homosexual, therefore he never indulged in homosexuality; therefore his homosexuality remained latent; therefore he remained a homosexual." When students half-amazed, half-credulous asked simple questions I saw on his kindly face the fatuous smile of bigotry personified. Zealots may smile like that, but men of science—never! By avoiding questions suggesting doubt of his beliefs I escaped the proof then of what I saw later when others challenged Adler and Jung as to the foundations of their faith. It makes my blood boil.

For thirty years I have been among psychoanalysts, and held my tongue, and kept the peace. Not wittingly have I told one of them, analyst or analysand, what I have said tonight. Take my advice. Say nothing to them. Read their scriptures; listen to their lectures if you will; but say nothing! If you prove them wrong in anything they will explain it away, as they have always done, with one more hypothesis *ad hoc*. Delusions defend themselves that way. They are impervious to logic and to fact. If that were all you would just waste your breath.

But try this experiment. Quote me, or misquote me, to any Freudian and he will tell you, "That man McCulloch is irresponsible. Of course he does not understand himself and no doubt thinks that ideas and purposes are not matter and efficient cause, but he has not been analyzed. He does not know the origins of his hostility," etc., etc. All of which adds up to this, "McCulloch is a liar and doesn't even admit it to himself."

But don't say glibly "I agree with McCulloch," for the accusation "liar" thrown, or insinuated, into your own teeth has but one English answer, and that answer is not in the English language. To knock him down proves nothing. I grant that that offense is intended. Despite its guise of medical advice it comes of Malice *Prepense*. But after tonight you have no right to knock him down. Women and children and the insane may not be treated so and Psychoanalysis is that delusion of which it fancies itself the cure.

There is one answer, only one, toward which I've groped for thirty years; to find out how brains work, and so to help those that have need of a physician.

Gentlemen: I wrote this paper to read to you tonight, not for general circulation. That could do no good; for psychoanalysis like an acquisitive lady, stingy of her person, profits most from the mere rumor of her unchastity. Were she a generous wench of the ancient and honorable profession I would not begrudge her free advertisement; but she is not. Too bad.

That's all, except to wish you pleasant dreams. But as you go to sleep, do me one favor! Note carefully the screen whereon the cockeyed lens of censorship projects the vivid distortions of the unwanteds you thought you had disposed of down your oubliette. For I have read, the Dream-Screen is a female breast at first of normal size, but it swells slowly till it fills your conscious as you sink into all-suckling oblivion.

Good night!

BIBLIOGRAPHY

It is suggested that the incredulous reader familiarize himself with Freud's own writings, including his letters, best read in the original as most translations are unreliable.

1. ABRAHAM, KARL. *Selected Papers*, trans. D. BRYAN and A. STRACHEY. L. & V. Woolf, London, 1927.
2. ADLER, MORTIMER J. *What Man Has Made of Man*. Longmans, New York, 1937.
3. ALLERS, RUDOLF. *The Successful Error*. Sheed & Ward, New York, 1940.
4. BONAPARTE, MARIE. *Edgar Poe: Eine Psychoanalytische Studie*. Internationaler psychoanalytischer Verlag, Vienna, 1934.
5. BRILL, A. A. *Psychoanalysis: Its Theory and Practical Application*. Saunders, Philadelphia, 1912.
6. BREUER, JOSEF. "Ueber den psychischen Mechanismus hysterische Phanomene," *Neurologisches Centralblat*, 12, 4 and 43 (1893).
7. BREUER, JOSEF, and FREUD, S. *Studies in Hysteria*. Nervous & Mental Disease Publishing Co., New York, 1936.
8. BUTLER, SAMUEL. *Unconscious Memory*. David Bogue, London, 1880.
9. BUCHMAN, FRANK. *Remaking the World*. McBride, New York, 1949.
10. CHARCOT, JEAN-MARTIN. *Neue Vorlesungen über die Krankheiten des Nervensystems insbesondere über Hysterie*. Autorisierte Deutsche Ausgabe von DR. S. FREUD. Toeplitz & Deuticke, Leipzig and Vienna, 1886.
11. DALBIEZ, ROLAND. *Psychoanalytical Method and the Doctrine of Freud*. (Trans.) Longmans, New York, 1941.
12. EISTER, ALLAN W. *Drawing-Room Conversion: A Sociological Account of the Oxford Group Movement*. Sociological Series, No. 6. Duke University Press, Durham, N.C., 1950.

13. ELLIS, HAVELOCK. *Studies in the Psychology of Sex.* Random House, New York, 1940.

14. FERENCZI, SÁNDOR. *Contributions to Psychoanalysis,* trans. E. JONES. Gorham Press, Boston, 1916.

15. ———. *Theory and Technique of Psychoanalysis,* trans. J. I. SUTTIE *et al.* Boni & Liveright, New York, 1927.

16. FODOR, NANDOR, and GAYNOR, FRANK. *Dictionary of Psychoanalysis.* Philosophical Library, New York, 1950.

17. FREUD, SIGMUND. *Über Psychoanalyse: Fünf Vorlesungen gehalten zur 20 jahrigen Gründungs-feier der Clark University in Worcester, Mass., September, 1909.* Franz Deuticke, Leipzig and Vienna, 1910.

18. HARTMANN, E. VON. *Philosophy of the Unconscious,* trans. W. C. COUPLAND. Harcourt, New York, 1931.

19. HEALY, WM.; BRONNER, A. F.; and BOWERS, A. M. *The Structure and Meaning of Psychoanalysis as Related to Personality and Behavior.* Knopf, New York, 1930.

20. HEGEL, G. W. F. *Hegel's Philosophy of Mind,* trans. W. WALLACE. The Clarendon Press, Oxford, 1894.

21. HERBART, JOHANN FRIEDRICH. *A Textbook in Psychology,* trans. M. K. SMITH. Appleton, New York, 1891.

22. HOLMES, O. W. *Mechanism in Thought and Morals.* Osgood, Boston, 1871.

23. HORNEY, KAREN. *New Ways in Psychoanalysis.* Norton, New York, 1938.

24. HUBBARD, L R. *Dianetics: The Modern Science of Mental Health.* Hermitage House, New York, 1950.

25. HUME, DAVID. *A Treatise of Human Nature.* (2 vols.) Dent, London, 1920–23.

26. JANET, PIERRE. *The Mental State of Hystericals,* trans. C. R. CORSON. Putnam, New York, 1901.

27. ———. *Les Medications psychologiques.* F. Alcan, Paris, 1919.

28. JONES, ERNEST. *Papers on Psychoanalysis*. 3d ed. Balliere, Tindall & Cox, London, 1923.

29. JUNG, C. K. *Introduction in I' Ching*, trans. R. WILHELM and C. F. BAYNES. Routledge & K. Paul, London, 1951.

30. KANT, EMANUEL. *Critique of Pure Reason*. Dutton (Everyman's Library), New York, 1934.

31. ————. *Critique of Practical Reason*. Longmans, New York, 1898.

32. KRAFFT-EBING, R. VON. *Psychopathia Sexualis*. Pioneer, New York, 1939.

33. LAYCOCK, THOMAS. *Mind and Brain*. (2 vols.) Appleton, New York, 1869.

34. LEIBNITZ, G. W. *The Philosophical Writings of Leibnitz*, trans. M. MORRIS. Dutton (Everyman's Library), New York, 1934.

35. MARITAIN, JACQUES. *Quatre essais sur l'esprit dans sa condition charnelle*. Desclée, de Brouwer, Paris, 1939).

36. MARX, KARL. *Capital*. Modern Library, New York, 1936.

37. PUNER, HELEN WALKER. *Freud: His Life and His Mind, a Biography*. Howell, Soskin, New York, 1947.

38. RANK, OTTO. *The Trauma of Birth*. Harcourt, New York, 1929.

39. REICH, WILHELM. *The Discovery of the Orgone*, Vol. I: *The Function of the Orgasm*. Orgone Institute Press, New York, 1942.

40. RICARDO, DAVID. *The Principles of Political Economy and Taxation*. Dutton, New York, 1912.

41. SACHS, HANNS. *Freud, Master and Friend*. Harvard University Press, Cambridge, Mass., 1944.

42. SCHOPENHAUER, A. *The World as Will and Idea*, trans. R. B. HALDANE and J. KEMP. K. Paul, London, 1909.

43. SETSCHENOW, J. *Physiologische Studien über die Hemmungs*

Mechanismen für die Reflextätigkeit des Ruckenmarks im Gehirne des Frosches. Hirschwald, Berlin, 1863–65.

44. SMITH, ADAM. *Theory of Moral Sentiments.* Bell (Bohn's Standard Library), New York, 1911.

45. WILKINSON, JAMES JOHN GARTH. *The Homoeopathic Principle Applied to Insanity: A Proposal To Treat Lunacy by Spiritualism.* Otis Clapp, Boston, 1857.

46. WITTELS, FRITZ. *Freud and His Time.* Liveright, New York, 1931.

MACHINES THAT THINK AND WANT

WARREN S. McCULLOCH

SOME TWENTY-FIVE years ago I left philosophy and turned toward psychology hoping to answer but two questions: First, how do we know anything about the world—either its particulars as we apprehend events or its universals as we know ideas? Second, how do we desire anything—either physically, as we want food and drink or a woman and a bed, or mentally, as we seek in music the resolution of a discord or, in mathematics the proof of a theorem? From psychology I turned to physiology for the go of the brain that does these things. Twenty ideas that came but one a year can be said in twenty minutes because they spring from traits of neurons in simple circuits.

Think of a neuron as a telegraphic relay which, tripped by a signal, emits another signal. To trip and to reset takes, say, a millisecond (25). Its signal is a briefer electrical impulse whose effect depends only on conditions where it ends, not where it begins. One signal or several at once may trip a relay, and one may prevent another from so doing (26, 27). Of the molecular events of brains these signals are the atoms. Each goes or does not go. All any neuron can signal to the next is that it was tripped, but, because it signals only if tripped, its signal implies (32) that it was tripped. Thus the signal received is an atomic proposition. It is the least event that can be true or false (33). If it is unnaturally evoked it is false, like the light you see when you press on your eyeball. How you find it false is another question (32).

Of two possible atomic events there are four cases, each shown by putting a dot into one of 4 places in an **X**—A happens, place dot on left; B, right; both, above; neither, below. Every next atomic avent, depending on two present atomic events, is shown as a dotted **X** of which there are 16, being all the functions of the calculus of propositions. The first, with no dots, shows the signal of a neuron never tripped—call it contradiction; and the last, with 4, the signal of one tripping itself every millisecond—call it tautology. Only the upper row of functions go in nets without tautology, for a dot below the **X**, showing the signal of a neuron neither of whose atomic propositions had come, is the signal of a neuron untripped. Give signals only two actions—one tripping, one preventing—and still nets of few neurons channel all these functions (33). Moreover, we could replace nets of neurons modified by use by changeless nets of changeless neurons (33), and these functions do not depend on modes of tripping or preventing atomic propositions (8)—hence the purview of this calculus.

To the psychologist this is most important, that such nets of neurons can compute any computable number (33).

The logical probability (51) of each of the 16 functions is the number of dots for separate signals divided by the number of possible places, which is 4. For the a priori probability that a neuron is in a particular state is $\frac{1}{2}$, i.e. 2^{-1}, and that n independent neurons are in a particular state is $\frac{1}{2^n}$, i.e. 2^{-n}. One unit of information defines the state of one neuron, so n units, the state of n neurons—hence the amount of information is the logarithm of the reciprocal of the probability of the state. If in a particular millisecond we are given an $\overset{\star}{X}$, since its probability is $\frac{1}{4}$, its amount of information is 2 units. But the frequency of realizing $\overset{\star}{X}$ from independent signals is the product of their separate frequencies. Hence, averaged through time, $\overset{\star}{X}$ will transmit no more information than its afferent neurons singly. Similar considerations apply to all functions. So n independent neurons, regardless of their functions, transmit on the average n units

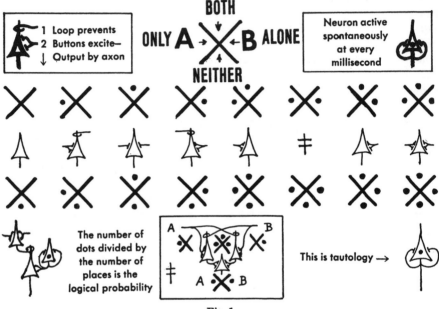

Fig. 1.

of information per millisecond. Moreover, n neurons can be in any one of 2^n states in one millisecond and in 2^{nt}, in t milliseconds. So, in p milliseconds one neuron can transmit as much information as p neurons in one millisecond (33). Information measures the order of an ensemble in the same sense that entropy measures its chaos (49). In Wiener's phrase, information is negative entropy; and in our X's the more the dots the greater the entropy.

Neurons can be exchanged for milliseconds, and functions of greater for those of less logical probability, but we can not get out of the brain more information than went into it. We express much less, because a nerve of a thousand axons has $2^{1,000}$ possible states—which is more than there are particles in the universe,—whereas the muscle it drives has a paltry thousand possible tensions.

On the receiving end we reject far more information. Consider the eye. Each of its hundred million rods and cones may at one moment fail to fire with much light, and at the next, fire with almost none (18). If this be by chance it may be ignored in large groups of contemporaneous impulses. We detect the agreement of these signals by their coincidence on the ganglion cells and relay only that information to the brain. Thus we pay for certainty by foregoing information that fails to agree with other information. No machine man ever made uses so many parallel channels or demands so much coincidence as his own brain, and none is so likely to go right. Similarly, our hypotheses should be so improbable logically that, if they are instanced, they are probable empirically.

Because light falling on a rod may or may not start a signal, that signal implies —but only implies (48, 51)—the light. If a bipolar cell is tripped by the rod's signal, then the bipolar's signal implies the rod's signal, and it, in turn, the light. Similarly a signal by a ganglion cell implies the bipolars, the rods, and so the light. Thus what goes on in our brains implies—but only implies—the world given in sensation. The domain of these implications extends only backward in time. Wherefore we know only the past. These bounds are proper to cognition. If each neuron were to signal when and only when it had received one of several signals, we could proceed in the opposite direction from brain to muscle, with every step an implication. The present would imply fate as well as fact. We could then deduce our deeds from our thoughts and our thoughts from our sensations. Rather this is the nature of intention; that it falls short of implication to the extent that aught intervening thwarts us. Perforce we discern that we will from that we shall do. Such bounds are proper to conation.

Now a signal anywhere implies an event at just one past moment unless there is a loop it may circuit (32). Once started in a circle it implies an event at any past time which is a multiple of the period of the circuit. A set of such signals, patterned after some fact, as long as its figure endures, implies a fact of that form. This form-out-of-time is an eternal idea in that temporary memory which generates objects new in our world; for it recognizes them on first acquaintance (47). But these fleeting figures people only the specious present, and when the brain rests (6) they are no more anywhere. The aged often have no other memory (23); but in young brains, use leaves a trace whereby the ways that led us to our ends become ingrained. We must make and read our record in the world. This extends the circuits through our heads beyond our bodies, perhaps through other men. Records are not signals, but may start them again in the old figure. To them as well our calculus applies, enriched by ideas, or timeless objects, attributed to some or all events (33); for all forms of memory other than reverberations are but their surrogates (32). Man-made computers store information as arrays of jots and tittles only to regenerate signals in artificial nets of relays and so recall the past. For this the right array must first be found, then recognized; and, when the information is in divers arrays, it must be reassembled, or, as we say, remembered. Thus, over all, the procedure remains regenerative—a positive feedback.

Circuits with negative feedback return a system toward an established state which is the end in and of the operation—its goal (5). Reflexes left to their own devices are thus homeostatic (9). Each, by its proper receptors, measures one parameter of the body—a temperature, pressure, position, or acceleration—and returns that parameter to its established value. Similarly, within the brain, impulses through the thalamus to the cortex, descending from its suppressor areas indirectly to the thalamus, inhibit it, and so govern the sensory input as to extract its figure from its intensity (14, 17, 2). If such circuits are sensitive enough they oscillate at their natural frequency. Their response depends on the time the returning meet the incoming signals, and at some frequency of excitation they will resonate; but another circuit, responding to the derivative of excitation, will check that resonance.

Clerk Maxwell first computed the go of the governor (fig. 2) of a steam engine (29). It had two balls hung from the top of a vertical shaft turned by the engine. When

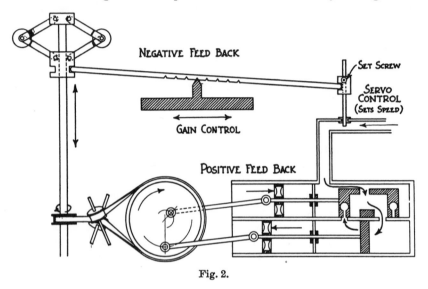

Fig. 2.

speed increased they flew out, pulling up one end of a lever on a movable pivot, and so, by an adjustable link, throttled the engine. Moving the pivot changed the sensitivity, which we call the gain of the circuit; but changing the length of the link set the speed at which it was to run, regardless of load or head. Compared to the change in work the engine makes, that to set the link is negligible but its information all important, and we call this a servo-mechanism (30). The stretch reflex is one in which the length the muscle will attain is selected by the brain for its own ends. Such government by inculcation of well-chosen values of ends sought by the governed works wonderfully well.

Purposive acts cease when they reach their ends. Only negative feedback so behaves and only it can set the link of a governor to any purpose (40). By it, we enjoy appetites, which, like records that extend memories, pass out of the body through the world and returning stop the internal eddies that sent them forth. As in reflexes, the goals of appetition are disparate and consequently incommensurable. They may be as incompatible as swallowing and breathing; and we are born with inhibitory links between the arcs of such reflexes. But of appetitions the dominance is rarely innate or complete, and we note the conflict whose out-

310

come we call choice. When two physically or psychologically necessary acts are incompatible, "God" cannot forgive us for not doing the one because we must do the other. The machine inevitably goes to hell.

Of any three circuits subserving appetition the dominance may be circular (31). I have myself encountered this in aesthetics; for, of three very similar rectangles shown in paired comparison, the first was consistently preferred to the second, the second to the third, and the third to the first, on the average and by the single subject. I discarded the data as inconsistent, whereas it bespoke consistency of a kind I had not dreamed of. We inherit from Plato a vain superstition called "the common measure of all values." These are not magnitudes of any single kind, but divers ends of divers circuits so interconnected as to secure dominance which, like as not, is circular. Economic arguments from curves of indifference and attempts to set up one scale for the strength of drives for food, water, sex, and whatnot are fantastic ways to beget a gratuitous headache.

Negative feedbacks run through a series of affairs until they come to their ends. We have mentioned the automatic volume-control of somaesthesia (2, 14, 17). The pupillary reflex does the same for vision. An appetitive circuit can reduce whatever confronts it through a series of transformations to one so geared to our output that we cry "Aha!" We transform the Pythagorean Theorem, by legitimate steps, to the axioms and postulates which are the canonical form of such theorems. Similarly, we translate an apparition anywhere in the visual field to the center by turning our eyes in its direction. This reflex goes from the eye to the superior colliculus which, by double integration, determines the vector for the motor nuclei so as to turn the eye toward the center of the apparition. The integral decreases to zero as the eyes come to rest (33). The apparition is then in the canonical position whence to abstract its shape.

No reflex can translate a chord to a canonical pitch; but pitches so project to Heschl's gyrus that octaves span equal lengths, and the information slants upward through scores of relays in vertical columns (1). Let these be tripped only by coincidence of information with a second source of excitation—say the so-called alpha activity of cortex (3), now thought to arise from thalamic circuits (4, 12, 24, 27, 35, 36) and, as this ten-per-second wave steps up and down through the cortex, its intersection with a given stream of information will move one way and the other along the axis of pitch. The output, descending vertically, then comes down in all points corresponding to these pitches in the output. When the information contains a chord of one pitch, the circuit has performed the nervous equivalent of a series of translations in pitch-conserving chord. Had we a negative feedback to stop the alpha wave when its scansion had brought the chord to a canonical pitch, the process might end here, but there is no proof that it does.

A mathematically simpler way to secure an invariant is to perform successively on any apparition the whole group of necessary transformations, sum them termwise, and divide the sums by the number of transformations (33). We need no division if the number of transformations is finite, as in brains. In figure 3, the circuit at the right will translate a circle to the canonical position, as at the left, and sum over the translations, as in the center, where the concave block indicates the number of signals to neurons situated at each point and transmissible over a single neuron if there is a circuit to scan the sum, appearing then in time as the variable frequency of the short lines beneath. Scanning exchanges one dimension in space for time (33), which makes it possible to house the required number of neurons in our heads. As a man's name written or spoken neither looks nor sounds like the man, so these invariants need bear no resemblance to the apparition save

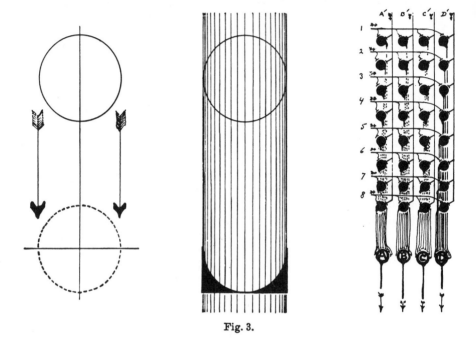

Fig. 3.

a 1–1 relation according to some projective law of denotation. Hence before we look we know not what to seek in the brain.

If we did not stop the sweep but summed the vertical columns, the primary auditory cortex would relay to the secondary auditory cortex a figure corresponding to the chord and not the pitch. Now local electric stimulation in Heschl's gyrus is reported as a tone; whereas in the second auditory cortex, dreamlike experiences are induced (32). All primary receptive cortices are columnar (45), which fits this theory of ideas. So does the sweep that disappears in sleep or anesthesia, for its frequency is the greatest number of distinct perceptions per second occurring in any modality. Since a reflex (schematized in figure 4) translates visual apparitions, the primary visual cortex needs only short columns. They are imbedded in branches of its incoming fibers which then ramify widely in the horizontal plane, turning toward the surface to end on cells increasing in size and decreasing in number from below upward (39). Purely statistical considerations compel us to believe that large cells require summation from many

312

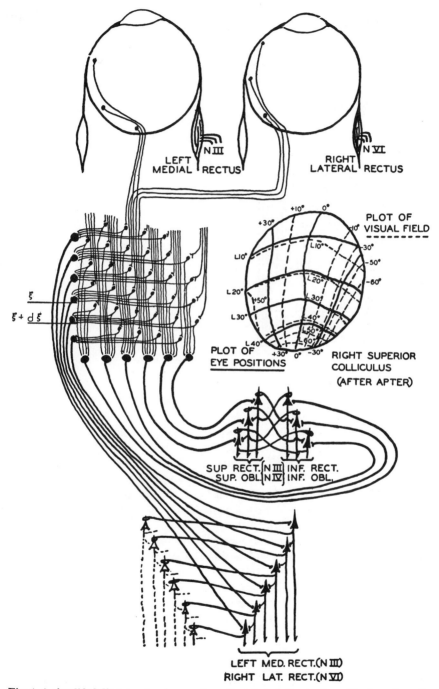

Fig. 4. A simplified diagram showing occular afferents to left superior colliculus, where they are integrated anteroposteriorly and laterally and relayed to the motor nuclei of the eyes. A figure of the right superior colliculus mapped for visual and motor response by Apter is inserted. An inhibiting synapse is indicated as a loop about the apical dendrite. The threshold of all cells is taken to be one.

This diagram is used through the courtesy of the Bulletin of Mathematical Biophysics.

endings to trip them. We would, therefore, expect the higher cells to respond to excitation over large areas, but not over small ones. A plane of excitation stepping up and down in such a cortex determines an output that runs through a group of contractions and dilatations of a figure in its input (33).

Now, the corners of an observed square tend to fill in the angles, producing an excitation like the figure on the left in figure 5. These transforms are dominated by the diagonals. A pinhead spot of strychnine anywhere in the primary visual cortex, area 17, fires cells there in unison (13). Their axons project at random to points in the secondary visual cortex (46), area 18, as I have indicated by scattering 18

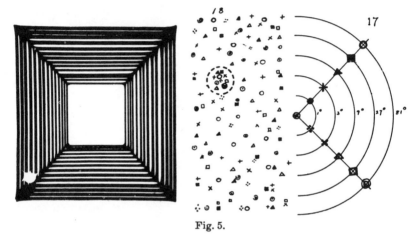

Fig. 5.

replicas of each of the 11 signs placed along the diagonal lines in 17. Sheerly by chance there will arise in 18 some one small precinct, say that enclosed in the circle, to which the majority of these points project, and excitation will be maximal there. As the brain, going on coincidence, ignores or converts to inhibition (8) what falls short of summation, activity of the circled area in 18 implies the diagonals in the output of 17 and so a square regardless of size. Stimulation in area 17 yields but a vague ball of light fixed in the visual field (38); whereas, in 18, such stimulation yields a well-defined form (38) of no particular size but fixed in space, for the eyes turn thither.

The action of circuits that average over groups is little affected by perturbation of input, of threshold, or even of synapsis if connections are only to cells in proper neighborhoods (33)—a statistical order we may hope from our genes. Except possibly in the visual cortex, the horizontal connections in the gray matter need only be undisturbed for a few millimeters, for the bulk of synapsis is vertical (13, 28), and recent notable experiments on the parietal cortex showed that a 2 mm. grid of incisions through its whole thickness produced no loss of somaesthesia (43). The visual cortex may have a radial structure to be injured by such gridding; but even large holes poked through it give little or no change in the place of maximal excitation in area 18, and although scotomata can be mapped in the visual field of a man so injured, he still sees forms which for him cross the scotomata, even as they do the blind spot of a normal eye. This continuity of perceptions is not given by physical or chemical fields (22), which can only corrupt information in an organ which is a mosaic of discrete units each capable of two discrete states. Per contra, it is a consequence of the statistical nature of the process of averaging over a group of transformations which could be equally well achieved were the particular relays physically far asunder. In vision, opposite sides of the vertical line through the fovea project each to the other hemisphere with no corresponding discontinuity of perceptual properties (19).

Closed paths probably mediate our predictions. Man-made devices start a shell toward that place in the air where the plane will be when the shell arrives and explodes. In these devices, series of events in time are autocorrelated to produce invariants, like kinematic routes, most likely to be run by things that have run some part of them. Such circuits tend to reverberate in us. Optokinetic nystagmus (7), which attempts to fix gaze on things in their passage in one direction, persists when they cease to move and it attributes to them a reverse motion without change of position. This is the only known predictive circuit we may assign to a particular part of the brain and even for this there are too many equally good hypotheses. Every scientific hypothesis is a prediction. We know only the past and little of that. Even if we are right in our superstition (21) that the previous state of the world does determine its subsequent state, any forecast we make may still go wrong—and a hypothesis forecasts the outcome of innumerable experiments. None can be proved true, any can be proved false. We must predict in order to live in a world where a false step means death. Here are errors at once inevitable and inexcusable, and the faith of any man who takes a single step is but an ignorance of ignorance concealed by universals extrapolated beyond fact.

Had we run down the fortunetelling circuits there would still be a gap in physiology which elsewhere dovetails neatly into psychology. We are ignorant of those alterations in our nets which underlie learning. The least hypothesis is that if impulses of one neuron, C, just insufficient to trip a second, R, come concurrently with those from another, U, which can trip R, then, thereafter, C alone shall be able to trip R (41, 42). This gain in grip of C on R exemplifies the law of growth with use we now apply to other cells. Surely neurons are not immutable mummies under our microscope but are living beings, competing one with another for foot space on succeeding cells. The two axonal terminations that have been studied change with use. Myoneuronal junctions (10) and vagal endings in the ganglia in the frog's ventricle (15), on excess of stimulation, are wrecked but recover promptly and after more profound stimulation may reconstitute themselves among the useless fragments of their former state.

All protoplasm shows hysteresis (16), but that whereby anything becomes the symbol for something else—the conditional stimulus—is first found in the flatworm (34), the lowliest beast with a truly synaptic net (34). It therefore behooves us to look to the synapse for the crucial change (10, 15). Mere change with use is not enough to substantiate the law of effect (44), which must depend on inverse feedback. Therefore, our second hypothesis is that those combinations of cells whose activity was concurrent and which were last used when we came to our goals and the activity to its end become associated. The process of learning so conceived parallels item for item the magnetizing of a bar of iron. Had we the mathematics for either, it might do for both; for both are stochastic processes in which from chaos order evolves, each step fixing to some extent what was heretofore left to chance. The theoretical difficulty is that into the relations of pairs, there enter the relations of trios and into those of trios, those of foursomes and so on to infinity (50). Such problems have not in the past proved insoluble. While I am waiting for the answer, I intend to seek the most transparent flatworms with the fewest neurons, teach them (44) and attempt to discern in the synaptic nets (34) under the microscope the difference between the scholar and the ignoramus.

316

REFERENCES

1. BAILEY, P., G. VON BONIN, H. W. GAREL, and W. S. McCULLOCH. Functional organization of temporal lobe of monkey (Macaca mulatta) and chimpanzee (Pan satyrus). *J. Neurophysiol.*, 1943, 6: 121–128.
2. BARKER, S. H., and E. GELLHORN. Influence of suppressor areas on afferent impulses. *J. Neurophysiol.*, 1947, 10: 133–138.
3. BERGER, H. Ueber das Elektroenkephalogramm des Menschen. *Arch. f. Psychiat.*, 1929, 87: 527–570.
4. BISHOP, G. The interpretation of cortical potentials. Cold Spring Harbor *Symposia on Quan. Biol.*, Cold Spring Harbor, 1946, 4: 305–319.
5. BLACK, H. S. Stabilized feed-back amplifier. *Elec. Eng.*, 1934, 53: 114–120.
6. BLAKE, H., W. R. GERARD, and N. KLEITMAN. Factors influencing brain potentials during sleep. *J. Neurophysiol.*, 1939, 2: 48–60.
7. BORRIES, C. Reflektorischer Nystagmus. *Monatsschrift für Ohrenheilkunde*, 1923, LVII: 547–570.
8. BROOKS, C. McC., and J. C. ECCLES. An electrical hypothesis of central inhibition. *Nature*, 1947, 159: 760–764.
9. CANNON, W. B. Organization for physiological homeostasis. *Physiol. Reviews*, 1929, 9: 399–431.
10. CAREY, E. J. Experimental pleomorphism of motor nerve slates as mode of functional protoplasmic movement. *Anat. Rec.*, 1941, 81: 393–413.
11. DEMPSEY, E. W., and R. S. MORISON. Production of rhythmically recurrent cortical potentials after localized thalamic stimulation. *Amer. J. Physiol.*, 1942, 135: 293–300.
12. DEMPSEY, W., and R. S. MORISON. Electrical activity of thalamocortical relay system. *Amer. J. Physiol.*, 1943, 138: 283–296.
13. DUSSER DE BARENNE, J. G., and W. S. McCULLOCH. Functional boundaries in the sensorimotor cortex of the monkey. *Proc. Soc. Exp. Biol. and Med.*, 1936, 35: 329–331.
14. DUSSER DE BARENNE, J. G., and W. S. McCULLOCH. Sensorimotor cortex, nucleus caudatus and thalamus opticus. *J. Neurophysiol.*, 1938, 1: 364–377.
15. FEDOROW, B. G. Essai de l'étude intravitale des cellules nerveuses et des connexions interneuronales dans le système nerveux autonome. Madrid Universidad, Laboratorio de Investigaciones Biologicas, *Trabajos*, 1935, 30: 403–434.
16. FLAIG, J. V. Viscosity changes in axoplasm under stimulation. *J. Neurophysiol.*, 1947, 10: 211–221.
17. GELLHORN, E. Effect of afferent impulses on cortical suppressor areas. *J. Neurophysiol.*, 1947, 10: 125–132.
18. HECHT, SELIG. Theory of visual intensity discrimination. *J. Neurophysiol.*, 1935, 18: 767–789.
19. HELMHOLTZ, H. L. FERDINAND VON. *Treatise on Physiological Optics*. Translated from the 3d German ed. James P. C. Southall, ed. Rochester, New York: The Optical Society of America, 1924.
20. HOVEY, H. B. Nature of apparent geotropism of young rats. *Physiological Zoology*, 1928, 1: 550–560.
21. HUME, DAVID. *Treatise on Human Nature, Being an Attempt to Introduce the Experimental Method of Reasoning into Moral Subjects*. New York: E. P. Dutton & Co., 1937.
22. KÖHLER, W. *Gestalt Psychology*. New York: H. Liveright, 1929.
23. KRAEPLIN, E. *Psychiatrie*, 17th ed. Leipzig: J. A. Barth, 1904. Vol. 2, p. 482.
24. LEWY, F. H., and G. D. GAMMON. Influence of sensory systems on spontaneous activity of cerebral cortex. *J. Neurophysiol.*, 1940, 3: 388–395.
25. LLOYD, D. P. C. In Howell's *Textbook of Physiology*, 15th ed., John F. Fulton, ed. Philadelphia: W. B. Saunders Co., 1946.
26. LLOYD, D. P. C. Facilitation and inhibition of spinal motoneurons. *J. Neurophysiol.*, 1946, 9: 421–438.

27. LLOYD, D. P. C. Integrative patterns of excitation and inhibition in two-neuron reflex arcs. *J. Neurophysiol.*, 1946, 9: 439–444.
28. LORENTE DE NÓ, R. Chapter in John F. Fulton, *Physiology of the Nervous System*. New York, London, and Toronto: Oxford Press, 1943.
29. MAXWELL, C. On Governors. *Proc.·Royal Soc.*, 1867–1868, 16: 270–283.
30. McCOLL, H. *Servo-Mechanisms*. New York: Van Nostrand, 1945.
31. McCULLOCH, W. S. A heterarchy of values determined by the topology of nervous nets. *Bull. of Math. Biophysiol.*, 1945, 7, 89–93.
32. McCULLOCH, W. S. *Finality and Form*—Fifteenth James Arthur Lecture, New York Academy of Science, May 2, 1946, at press, Springfield, Ill.: Charles Thomas.
33. McCULLOCH, W. S., and W. PITTS. How we know universals. *Bull. Math. Biophys.*, 1947, 9: 127–147.
34. MOORE, A. R. *Individual in Simpler Form*. Eugene, Ore.: University of Oregon, 1945. Chap. 108.
35. MORISON, R., and D. L. BASSETT. Electrical activity of thalamus and basal ganglia in decorticate cats. *J. Neurophysiol.*, 1945, 8: 309–314.
36. MORISON, R., and E. W. DEMPSEY. Mechanism of thalamocortical augmentation and repetition. *Am. J. Physiol.*, 1943, 138: 42, 297–308.
37. PENFIELD, W. Some observations on cerebral cortex of man, *Proc. Roy. Soc.*, London, 1947, ser. B, 134: 329–347.
38. PENFIELD, W., and T. C. ERICKSON. *Epilepsy and Cerebral Localization*. Springfield, Ill.: Thomas, 1941.
39. RAMON Y CAJAL, S. *Histologie du système nerveux*. París: A. Maloine, 1909–1911.
40. ROSENBLUETH, A., N. WIENER, and J. BIGELOW. Behavior, purpose and teleology. *Philosophy of Science*, 1943, 10: 18–24.
41. SHURRAGER, P. S., and ELMER J. CULLER. Conditioning in the spinal dog. *J. of Exp. Psychol.*, 1940, 26: 133–159.
42. SHURRAGER, P. S., and H. C. SHURRAGER. Rate of learning measured at a single synapse. *J. of Exp. Psychol.*, 1946, 36: 347–354.
43. SPERRY, R. W. Cerebral regulation of motor coordination in monkeys following multiple transection of sensorimotor cortex. *J. Neurophysiol.*, 1947, 10: 275–294.
44. THORNDIKE, E. L. *Animal Intelligence*. New York: Macmillan, p. 244, 1911.
45. VON BONIN, G., and P. BAILEY. *The Neocortex of Macaca Mulatta*. Urbana, Ill.: University of Illinois Press, 1947.
46. VON BONIN, G., H. W. GAROL, and W. S. McCULLOCH. The functional organization of the occipital lobe. *Biol. Symposia*, 1942, 7.
47. WHITEHEAD, A. N. *Principles of Natural Knowledge*. Cambridge, London, 1919.
48 WHITEHEAD, A. N., and B. RUSSELL. *Principia Mathematica*. Cambridge, London, 1910–1913. Vol. 3.
49. WIENER, N. *Cybernetics*. New York: John Wiley & Sons, 1948.
50. WIENER, N. *On the Theory of Dense Gases*. Communicated to the Macy Conference on Teleological Mechanisms, 1948. Unpublished.
51. WITTGENSTEIN, LUDWIG. *Tractatus Logico-Philosophicus*. London: Paul, 1922.

THE NATURAL FIT

THREE characters have worn the carcass that you see before you, each for a score of years. Aside from an interest in communication they have little in common. I could tell you next to nothing of the first, or prospective theologian, for I doubt if I would recognize him. I need say nothing of the third, your familiar scientific friend. The second was born of a war to make the world safe for democracy and was lost in a war without a song. I remember him well, and I believe you may enjoy meeting him. As his literary executor, I have taken the liberty of making a small sample from each of his fits. By way of introduction I might remind you of the world into which he was born aged twenty-one. The place is "well this side of Paradise." What you are about to hear are personal communications to his friends. They were not intended for publication, not for posterity. Judge them, not as art, but as an expression of his hot ideas. Take them as he meant them and make his acquaintance.

The legend of the Sophomoric Fit is from Boetius xxxi K. Ælfred. Say A.D. 888. "þe wisdom þa þas fitte asungen hæſde."

APPOINTMENTS

November 16, 1919
(*His Birthday*)

Yesterday:

Christ thought for me in the morning,
Nietzsche in the afternoon.

Today:

Their appointments are at the same hour.

Tomorrow:

I shall think for myself all day long.
That is why I am rubbing my hands.

FOUR HOKUS

Night Walker

Whippoorwill,
All night
Only the sound
Of my shoes.

Religion

Men
Galloping into the northern lights
A sun
That will not rise.

Requiescat

Jade bowl
Of the greatest antiquity
'Bout time it got broke.

Fate

After the storm
Upon the beach
An oar
Worn in the leather
Broken in the blade.

MONISM

Chong saith, "All things are one thing."
Chong hath a wife whose words correspond to things.
Therefore,
Chong saith, "All things are one thing."

Great accidents of beauty in the maze
Of life's recurrent death, for these we live.
The voice of distant duty through the haze
Of pain to foggy breath no goal can give.

The heart, insatiate, demands of sin
The wisdom and the life to do and grow.
The flesh we consecrate can never win,
Unless, still crazed with strife, again it glow.

Most welcome then be war, and crazy sin,
And my old jailer, pain, till once again
Knocks beauty at my door and stumbles in.

THE VOLSTEAD ACT

Bacchus, if I bend the knee
And a glowing face incline
Sabbath morn at Christian shrine,
'Tis no infidelity.
I have still no God—but Wine!

HIS SUNDIAL

"Pereunt et Imputantur"

The gods are passing.
One by one with pensive and averted faces
All are passing.
Do not let them go without your tears.
They were greater than your kings.
Lords they were of love and laughter,
Hopes and fears.
They were false to thoughts and things;
But you loved them for their glory.

There are places
That you never could have reached,
Visions that would still be haunting,
Had they never been.
There are truths no fool had preached
Had they never been.
Bless them then ere you go flaunting
Your prefigured prophesies.
They have shaped your years.

So much for the Gods—Now for love

I loved my lover Saturday night.
'Tis Sunday morning now.
The cock that crew in the cold grey light
Absolved my only vow.
I loved my lover Saturday night,
Why should I love him now?

Though she is passing fair
More lines to kisses has she seen
Than kisses on her lips have been
Or she has wanted there.

ON GOING STAG

I went a thousand paces into the country
    to gather the earliest flowers.

I did not want the earliest flowers.

Why did I go a thousand paces into the country
    to gather the earliest flowers?

To his hostess who thought every woman should be one

The Sphinx was stone 'tis said,
And in its head
There was no mystery,
And now the Sphinx is dead,
And in its stead
—Its history.

NO MORE TOMBSTONES

How shall we bury Love?

A hole in the dirt—six feet—
A spark struck out in the tinder
      Under his pyre,
A shot in his winding sheet.
No ceremonious tears,
      Nor the notes of a lyre.

Thus shall ye bury Love!

REWARD OF PATIENCE

They buried Job in heaven,
Where the angels watch his head;
Vega guards the coffin,
But poor old Job is dead.

Wisdom is in his grave;
Let him lie!
He was a dreary knave,
Cold and dry.

You were his droning slave?
So was I!
Wisdom is in his grave!
Let him lie.

This our cry:
We were too bold and brave,
Ready to starve and stave,
Live and die!

Wisdom is in his grave?
Pass him by.

FINIS

Formerly
I drew
No stoic breath.
I flew Epicurus' home
And too sequestered grove,
Passionately wooing Life that frights
The littlehearted; won her sumptuous breast
And crushed her lusty youth.
But Life has proved a sluttish bawd at best,
Promiscuous in her tawdry appetites,
Perverted in her love.
Divorced at last I come
To you, ambiguous Death,
And woo
With apathy.

He must have been all of twenty-three when he wrote this.

This brings us to a still briefer selection from

THE OUTLANDISH FIT

Its superscription is from Chaucer, "Sir Thopas," 117—1386.

Lo, lordes, heer is a fyt;
If ye wil eny more of it,
To telle it wol I fonde.

It is dedicated to the Lords

MY CHILDREN

Ercke, Ercke, Oethern Muthur

ANTEUS

Mother Earth, our hearts are breaking
With a thousand warring wills,
And the sun that would be waking
Smites us dizzy on the hills,

Where our passion led us groping
To explore the vaulted sky,
With the life you gave us, hoping
For a life that would not die.

Let us feel your arms beneath us
With the strength that shaped the clay,
And your love with courage sheath us,
And your wisdom end our day.

Then, with hearts that echo laughter,
We will welcome sombre night,
And the sleep it brings us after
Glories fade that crowned the fight.

Is Helen dead? Go tell the dead
And not the living; for we know
She is not dead while lips are red
And breasts are warmer than the snow.

The living ask of death no dream
Of vanished Helen's loveliness.
Only the dead have lost the gleam
In vanquished hope of her caress.

Tell me of Helen once again
Whose body is a Grecian joy.
Her beauty shall to us remain
Launching of ships and sack of Troy.

Go tell the dead that she is dead;
'Tis Helen still that lights the fire.
And, while we bleed as Grecians bled,
Her beauty is our heart's desire.

OBAN, SCOTLAND

1922

I know the ways of little men
Who, like the brook that brawls the glen
Till echo cataracts again
    Without a pause,
Down tumble, though I guess nor when
    Nor what the cause.

I know the ways of lazy louts,
Like marshes where the mallow pouts,
Lizards sprawl and the iris floats
    Her Tyrian show.
A gutter swaggers water spouts
    But they? Lord no.

I know the ways of shallow fools,
Who spread themselves as sandy pools,
Whose ferny bank the willow cools.
    How smooth they lie!
But when day's heat takes up her tools,
    How soon gone dry!

I know the secrets of the deep,
Where surges bosom and tides creep.
I know the silences they keep
    In midmost motion;
And, when the weary heart would sleep,
    I'll home to ocean.

The Natural Fit

TO TAFFY ON MY SHOULDER

(about 1928)

If I could sing
With the breath of spring
When the moon is full and fair,
I would carol my love
To the stars above
Till the night let down her hair,
For over the brink of the brimming soul
I would pour the wine of song
Till the night was drunk with the sparkling sound,
And the moon had sunk to the silvery ground
To live in the sea of song.

If I had eyes
As the bird that flies
Through the evening leaves and dew,
I would paint my dream
'Till the stars should seem
But a part of a larger view.
The curtain that covers a greater sky
Would fall from the glowing west,
And the dwindling day, as it glided down,
Would linger and lay its lustrous crown
At the feet of a better best.

'Tis great to live
With a life to give
And the duty of heart and hand
Where color and song and the amorous throng
Of beauty have plundered the land,
Till one with the lip of the whirlwind
And one from the radiant star
Have met in the midnight, and under the moon
The dream of the twilight is granted its boon,
And the song has ravished the star.

The world was made for fools.
Their reckless laughter leaps the facts
And acts
Ere passion cools.

Were but the wise as brave!
Their ponderous judgments wait for speech
Till each
Is in his grave.

Then call the fools the wise.
They're better fitted to the earth
With mirth
Than wisdom's sighs.

There is no sin
For me but this,
That I should win
A minor bliss,

That I begin
And end amiss:
There is no sin
For me but this.

To take a kiss
To please the skin,
And be within
My heart remiss;
There is no sin
For me but this.

But yesterday,
　If you had come!
I cannot stay
　So frolicsome;

My heart's away,
　And I am dumb.
But yesterday,
　If you had come!

All Christendom
Can never stay
The hearts that stray
　To martyrdom;
But yesterday,
　If you had come!

Dear Dreams of mine, whose thwarted eyes
Behold Despair and mock her cries,
　You have forgot your mother's care,
　Her leaden eyelids and her stare
That puzzled the imprisoning skies.

You were the children of her sighs;
In you she lives, in all else dies;
　And yours her wisdom, if you dare,
　Dear Dreams of mine.

Silvery silence and golden tongue,
Which of the wares of love will buy?
Fire in the eye, breath in the lung,
Fairest of dreams; then forth they fly.

Tears in the eye and songs unsung,
Death in the heart that may not die;
Silvery silence and golden tongue,
These are the wares of love they buy.

Twilight is creeping over the sky,
Silver replacing the gold of the young;
Silence is hearing the dull sighs wrung
Still from our hearts by tongues that lie;
Silvery silence and golden tongue,
These are the wares of love they buy.

I need no sign to summon you
From ferny hillocks starred with dew,
Forever in the daily round
Some droning labor loses ground
To fancies neither faint nor few.

Again returns the touch I knew,
Again the eyes look through and through,
And then, as on that starry ground,
    I need no sign.

We build our castles in the air,
And from the air they tumble down,
Unless we carry them up there
Until they crack the pate they crown.

And we must lug them everywhere,
From garden walk to crowded town;
We build our castles in the air,
And from the air they tumble down.

And lucky, if when sere and brown,
Before our eyes too lofty stare,
We scape with life and pate, though bare,
On which to plant an honest frown.
We build our castles in the air,
And from the air they tumble down.

I cannot paint the days I've seen
When, through the prism of the dawn,
The haze, vermilion, ochre, green,
Leaves gossamers upon the lawn
To catch the cobalt symphonies.
They hold my senses in their spell.
Speak, twilight's lapis lazuli,
Is Heaven secret?   So is Hell.

I cannot speak the love I feel
When pulsing blood in aching brain,
In trembling hands and knees that reel,
Is mad with an exulting pain
That holds the panting breath uppent
In patience that she cannot tell.
Speak passion, waiting, still unspent,
Is Heaven secret?   So is Hell.

I cannot name the God I serve,
While down the furrow of my days
I goad a life that shall not swerve
For senses' sweet nor love's warm ways.
I serve in truth the King of kings,
The Name of names that none may spell.
Speak Reason, emptiest of things,
Is Heaven secret?   So is Hell.

Prince, for the Idiot, cold and blind,
I would not ask thy clemency,
But by my eyes, my heart, my mind,
I do implore thee set me free.
Then would I welcome friendly death,
And praise the Prince that willed me well,
Should this not haunt my dying breath,
Is Heaven secret?   So is Hell.

So we come to

THE NATURAL FIT

Its superscription is from Samuel Johnson's The Prince of
Abyssinia, *xi*

"To be a poet," said Imlac, "is indeed very difficult."
"So difficult," returned the Prince, "that I will at present hear
no more of it."

*The form of the sonnet is difficult, but the required compression
of his enthusiasm was natural to his way of thinking hot.
The samples are a few from many; their arrangement, roughly
chronological.*

As when before the sculptor's eye there gleams
The vision of a form within the stone,
He grasps the chisel and he swings the mall
Till muscles ripple on the rough-hewn bone.

So I, with newborn thoughts of larger themes,
Have chiseled the first portion of my days
To a crude semblance of the broad and tall
And stalwart wanderer through all earth's ways.

Yet, even when this rough-hewn figure seems
Balanced to walk the earth and not to fall,
I may not polish part lest it betray
The form's entirety, and in my stone
One small perfection be the death of all,
And I, no sculptor, but the dupe of dreams.

There was a lovely lady and she died.
The barons for her flesh relinquished life.
The statesmen for her favor fostered strife.
For her very fame historians lied.

When I was in my teens, I even tried
To find me such a lady for a wife;
Victory, I dreamed, the envious knife
That followed Mary, faring by my side.

Tony, beware the error of my way,
Looking for beauty whither none has gone,
Nor hope a miracle of stone today.

No loveliness like hers was ever born
To catch the brutish eye of furtive clay,
But Fancy, paranoid, and Poem, forlorn.

What shall I call you? Be content with Eve.
I know no other name would suit so well.
I was a child until you came to me
And all my little heaven took its leave.
I never wondered that it went away,
And, though I loved its sweet simplicity,
The coming of your love meant so much more
To me, I never asked that it should stay.

There was a song you sang within the garden
Ere the gates were closed, and then before
The gates you sang it. God it may offend,
But we never sued for peace or pardon.
Love with us from Eden's pleasure fell.
Sing then, for love shall conquer in the end.

Knowest thou a young man diligent with old women? Lo—
LITTLE NIETZSCHE IN THE ARMS OF AUTUMN

Through hazy hours of autumn somnolence
And russet leaves that sifted slowly down
We lay along the sward and, with a hand
That promised soft repose, you stroked my brow.
I longed to sleep, admit feigned impotence,
And buy my peace. There's no release from frown
And furrowed forehead. They are me and stand
Unchanged, though all else change, to seal my vow.
"More life," I cried, "more hours before the dark
For love and fighting. I will wear the mark
Of any God who gives both grit and guile;
Too long I've dawdled here!" You sighed and pressed
My panting lassitude against your breast
And pitied me with autumn's wistful smile.

For such a year as this was Antony,
Who else had ruled all earth, contemned by earth:
For such a summer Tristan bent the knee
And never rose again to war and mirth:
For less than this Leander's struggling arms
Were broken by the stormy Hellespont:
And, for an instant's grip on all her charms,
Porphyria's lover dared his God confront.
All may not be too great a price to pay
For such a transient heaven as these have known.
Each one, transfigured ere he went his way,
Each one, knew glory that was his alone:
But Cleopatra, who can tell of her?
Of Iseult? Hero? Lost Porphyria?

The Natural Fit

I want a woman with a windy cheek
And eyes as steely as a leveled gun;
A woman, wooer of the bronzing sun,
Who listens to the open heavens speak.
I care not if her hair of oakum reek,
Or of the earth as woods where rivers run.
I need her mind that flashes to its fun
As salmon leaping in the rapid creek.

Fair ladies, dressed, perfumed with studied grace,
That preen yourselves upon your subtle ways,
How many seasons will you clog my sight
Till she, with frank intent, lifts face to face,
Demanding furrows in a field of days
And beds of love beneath the leafy night.

SANG REAL

There is a Secret Glory in whose train,
Marshaled, the Captains of a thousand creeds,
Templar on crested steed, the turbaned Moor,
Flame, Cross and Crescent, o'er the rim of day;

And virile prophets in whose purple vein
Ran wine for gods as yet unknown to deeds,
The pride to suffer and be sick and poor,
To replant Eden in the wastrel clay.

Yet I who raise the scarlet throat's refrain
And marvel how the heart still beats and bleeds,
Yes, I who to the end might still endure,
And humbly tramp the palmers' holy way,
I may no longer in their ranks remain,
Who glory not in that divine amour.

To the Great War that hallows every cause
I yield my panting breath and turbulent blood.
Not for the silence of oblivious night
Was I engendered in a flesh so free—
Not for the short sleeping or the final pause
Am I so conscious of the primal flood
Of Passion. Youth is Spring. Life at its height
Wars with the lethal nothingness to be.

Cry "Reason" to the fool, for I am wise
With the first wisdom of humanity.
Cry "Peace" to cowardice till strife be o'er.
What boots the Cause of Battle so it rise
To hate's red harvest or love's ecstasy.
The world's too small a field—too short the War.

Like that stupendous and amazing light
That breaks on captives and on captive kings
When dungeon wall and palace draperies go down,
And the sun shines suddenly into their night,

Abruptly leaps the End upon our own
Habit-hoodwinked following of strings,
Our dickering with a familiar plight,
Our tribute to dead selves, our slavery.

But we, the manumitted of old things,
Stand and are silent, bewildered, blind but stark
Until we see—and in that second sight
Our portraits' passionless fidelity
Lifts the new-found eternal 'till it sing
Palace and Dungeon down—and the Sun's Height.

The sonnet sequence that follows is too easily dated after the war, while there was still hope (in the hopeful generation) for a league of nations. He had entitled it sometimes "Communication" and sometimes "Communion."

It is consoling to recall that we once felt so well about our one world, and it is interesting to note how ingeniously this builder dovetailed these sonnets, sense and sound.

Sweet Language, child of human Loneliness
Engendered in the ravished soul of Sound,
Long keeper of the keys of paradise,
Open it quickly to the dumb heart of man.
Beneath your gaze melt years whose moments seemed
Unending through the gloom of solitude.
These could not tell what depth of consciousness,
What wealth of life, in man was yet unfound,
What agonies of parting, what surprise,
What rage, what glorying in battle of the strong.
Warder of paradise, Music began
In the first sigh of the first soul that dreamed;
Music continually yourself has wooed;
Welcome him to your breast and give our world our song.

Oh, ancestry of silence, though I scan
For ever your obliterated page,
I cannot learn when first the seed was sown,
And the heart's agony began.
But this I know, that some succeeding age,
The soul, no longer mingling in the sea,
A self, an entity to prescience grown,
Had more to give. But still the heart fore ran
The laggard tongue, and silence mocked the sage,
No confluence of the soul, no ecstasy,
Just sorrow's old dream, was there, without a plan.
That was the passion that we plead—our own,
Artist or artisan, whose pilgrimage
Is ever onward toward United Man.

We know no motive in symphonic time
As poignant as religion or as bold,
Where deep disconsolation and dear hope,
Contending in the lonely prison cell,
Murdered the mind, till men held nature crime
And thundered dreams as fact a thousandfold.
No answer yet awarded to that prayer
With confirmation crowns their martyrdom.
They loved too well and would with love sublime
The lonely heart out of earth's mould,
Recrystallized from death on Heaven's slope,
In reuniting flame go up God's stair.
Nor can we answer them that loved so well
Till earth is ours, and love's communion come.

Not with our loneliness, not with our dream,
Can earth be taken and our heaven won,
But with our toil and ponderous reasoning,
And with our little changing of the cosmic stream.
Slow science patiently from law and fact
Designs the implements for laboring,
And love's proud home, our earth, which man
   shall build,
A temple to the happiness he so long lacked.
Land and sea and sky, with careful thought
And toiling hand controlled, shall soon be filled
With the calm pulse of our united peace;
And Time and Space, no longer feared and fought,
Drop back neglected in the course we run
To be forgotten ere our daylight cease.

Sing then to the men that make the road
And tunnels through the hills and bridges slung
Over the wide valley and the deep ravine,
Till streets are crowded with the whirling cars,
And the long-leveled track rumbles to the train.
Sing to the men that left some safe abode
And gazing fixedly on distant stars
Conquered the sea's tumultuous domain.
With oar and sail and steam, gallant they clung
To their wide quest, over unfathomed green
Bearing the timorous body and the heart's load,
Till now through space the wireless word is flung,
And the skilled pilot guides the soaring plane.
With these we win the world. To these my ode.

And we who feel the deeper solitude
Of our lone souls and know our speech too crude
To tell the nature and the strength of love
Seek for some medium to share our mood,
And in the studied gestures of the stage
Commune with you. Rhythmic as dancers move
Our music and our words, for love beats time.
This is the magic of the printed page,
Of canvases that glow with subtle feeling,
The poignancy of statues and towers that climb
Halfway to heaven: Some man in silence' cloud
On Lethe's shore, with all his art appealing,
Into your lonely heart would cry aloud
The rich notes of his love, rending Death's shroud.

In sad humility we learn of death,
Of lonely tears and half the world at war,
With our dimmed eyes we come again to read
The lesson that we should have learned of home,
Among familiar needs whose every breath,
Inspired with love's beatitude, far more
Than all the prophecies of all the years,
Was panting for the union of the race.
But we to little State and transient God
Gave all our souls and let our loved ones bleed.
Thus have we bought again the vanished grace
Of nature's moral law. Again we come
Out of our lesser loyalties, in tears,
To build love's well-earned city in the rich sod.

Lift up your hearts and sing! Gather the clan,
The human brotherhood. Bend to the clay.
Build with exultant song and eager cry
Our desolation's dream, our nature's plan,
Our earth, a temple to the yearning heart,
A city for the Soul. Let love hold sway,
And stupid selfishness and lonely lie
In silence end; while beauty that fore ran
Our wisdom shares in the language of a finished art
Its tranquil mood 'till work is one with play;
And we, the transients of life's finite span,
Make room for greater man and gladly die,
Leaving to them the wages of our day,
The deep communion of the whole of man.

Years later of this sequence

he wrote

a sonnet in a single sentence

to

POSTERITY—RADAMANTHOS OF POESIE

348

Though this remain until that time of which
As yet there is no prophecy worth so
Much trust as one might put in seed to grow
On stone, in fire or in the winds that switch
Loam, clay and sand from the unwatered ditch,
That time may only reap of what we sow,
In days now dying and in ways we know
Are little like to make men more than itch
Impatiently for times that faster go,
Of that which grows, or stock or stalk or switch,
The same we planted, though to them it show
Of our intent, worn threadbare, not one stitch
To tell them of the glamour or the glow
With which we wrought to make them poor or rich.

COMMAND PERFORMANCE ON THE LINCOLN PENNY

One from the many made, of many one,
And one among that many of whom made:
This is the mystery love's mint has laid
On every penny. It's a pigmy pun
To make the lined face lift to mighty fun
As, to his last of nights, life's masquerade
Enticed him to delight, for which he paid
But silence to the sound of one small gun.

One of the many made, from many one,
And one among that many whom he made;
He smiled while hell was freezing in the sun
And laughed when heaven melted in the shade.
For death had ceased to count where he'd begun
A love whose mystery our lives evade.

If after I have ceased to percolate
Clean wit through grounds of drugging rhyme,
There still is left some pure, quiet time
I'll spend it drinking to my puny fate.

For I am one of those insatiate
Whom pepper makes no thirstier for slime,
Being by nature born for such hot climb
That even critics make me not irate.

How far from festive is my silly song,
Having no theme beyond its void distress,
And that's not only devious but wrong!

It wants the venison that good men bless,
With graces godly—ay—but never long,
Which I, naïve, forgot and now confess.

Leafless November now into her leaden dome
From damp and pungent fires exhales grey smoke
To soot the winter's toga and to soak
Into its coming candor death's black loam.

Now, like barbarians at sack of Rome,
Nor'easters swirl them in the purple cloak,
While the white beards of fathers of the folk
Fall on denuded shoulders like dried foam.

Comes so the festival of harvest home
When labor falls beneath the last load yoke
And gobblers' wattles wilt as the cock's comb;

While, unconsoled, they fast whom sorrows choke,
Their eyes too blurred for comfort of time's tome
And likest leaves that cling still to the oak.

The Natural Fit

Why now you turbulent and tardy ghost
Do you, like some ill-omened bird of prey,
Dart up betwixt me and the molten sun
To fall a cinder from your flaming post?

Too late, black augury for my bold wings,
You clutter the frail pathways of the day;
For ere my wings in earth's dull labyrinth were done,
My heart, close harbored in yon glistening coast,
Swept me abandoned up the breathless way,
Where to the unachieved the godhead clings.

Though more in cunning and in craft my boast,
Who, more than Daedalus could dream, have done,
My dream that lent the strength to my frail clay
Fails utterly and quits its frustrate host.

If I addressed you at a time and place
More certain than this earth and century,
Belittling so the brilliant wizardry
That beckons couriers to your bright face,

I should be guilty of my own disgrace,
For such explicit linking, you to me,
Would prove a gesture of humility
Too large for truth, too low for your embrace.

Clumsy the brain that speaks as brawn and bone
To wit that needs no signpost by the way
And hastens eagerly unto its own.

So take in silence what I would not say
Though I could crush the earth to us alone
And crowd whole centuries into our day.

Since you have seen how each, my yesterday,
Back to its yesterday no tribute sent,
But, as today, in living all were spent,
Leaving tomorrow richer for their stay,

You will not frown and from me turn away,
Nor curse as faithless one who never meant
More honor than love's irony has lent
To lust's impatience of the least delay;

So I am coming, as I only may
Who count the wit that is with beauty blent
The priceless gist of its complete display,

And know that none with this ingredient,
Whose loveliness is worth love's disarray,
While joys remain to taste, would rest content.

Like every man who writes English, faced with the many meanings of his words and the many constructions of his sentences, he had to train himself to speak so that, whatever sense we give to his successive sounds, his sonnets say one and the same thing to us all. He came to hate constraints of sense that written words with jots and tittles put so relentlessly upon the ambiguities of sound. In spoken English, sequences of words are so familiar that, having heard some, we rightly hear the rest and understand with half a mind and half an ear. Words that he knows we have anticipated we find only when their sense is unexpected. More often we encounter something that at most recalls the words we had imagined. He means us to hear both. By this compression he can tie ever more complexions of emotions into fourteen knottier lines. His sonnets grow well-nigh intolerable. His early poems fairly picture their origins in all the gratuitous particularity of sensory experience. We feel at home in them, for we know what he was doing. But this is irrelevant to the impassioned ideas which are in fact ambiguous as to their occasions. Was he experimenting? was he in love? was he thinking? was he building? when he wrote

We know not when for us to know will break
That surest of all days of sure desire
When certainty will flame of certain fire
And dreams, defeated, find the dream awake.

Does it matter? It does—but not what he was doing. So I read you only a few of these, the last of his sonnets.

Since, after I have lost faith's fairest form,
And certain am of my uncertainty
Of aught of evidence to comfort me,
My forte must evidently be this storm
That rises now to raze old verity
Back to the dust of such a backward lee
As was where silt, from the Sahara blown,
Sanding the blood that Saracens had strown
Instead of roses in red Tripoli,
Started the brig upon the startled sea;
Brigand and I emboldened by this storm
To boldest blows entrust security
And, on the instant, launch as instantly
A faith as fair as it is free of form.

Now from my rifted wreck seek I the reef
And nearer strive to what strove once too near,
Fearless for finding the well-founded fear,
Thankful to time that is my dear time's thief.

Out of a loneliness, alone in grief,
From tears that spring because they sprung no tear,
Comes joy that none are joyless now to hear
Of this my loneliness, its lone relief.

Up from a depth too deep to height too high,
Of breadth too broad and of a strength too strong,
I heaved and sprang into the vacant sky.

But from that vault I fell as falls the song
Sung by delighted singers that will die
Only as life has length to live too long.

He was a physician

These short words speak those wounds that wrung from men
The grunts and groans of pain, which not the grace
Of God had strength to stop nor held hope space
To mend. But death's self stills that sound, till then
Life's clutch and grasp on breath else forced out when
Quits flesh near flesh, rifts heart from hearts close place.
Now worst—time takes you! Sweet my brain bulge case!
Burst bone! Bleed stress! Woe's word lasts out care's ken.

Vain sigh and sweet life's waste with these words bid
Time hold back, cease to rend from us the moon
We most loved. More than vain to sob so, rid
The breast of short breath but to gasp too soon
For lack air lung to cramp the heart that hid
Lost love's night ache too long from death's dark noon.

He was a psychiatrist, and this was his prayer

"Ordine quest 'amore, O tu che m'ame"

Why pressed hard heart hide ostrich head in habit?
Estopped so, grief outshrieks stark silence. Thought,
Cliché-cozened, siezes—throat—singeth naught.
Lip, mine, my lips press, wanting kiss to (strange) stab it.

Never mine, God, pour now in place Babbit?
Why? Idles worldaxle well oiled. What's caught
'S else. Other's the woe we would . . . have . . . sought;
But it, flame teuyere-blast—I, handfast—how grab it?

Frenzied of Love, how to council He calls come?
Mum as inchoate or, wracked redeless, scry wise?
Never! Not either! Nor absent, but sing:
Praise life (contagious) that to Love's every-home
Hails all worths, eeriest guests in earth's guise,
Among whom to abide us *shall* time bring.

I had thought this character was dead, but the other day I found this on my desk, unpunctuated and the ink wet.

farewell sweet morrows hopes deferred and all
crisp years fat earnest in defect of youth
indian summers quicken to keen fall
as brisk october blazons times no ruth

i cry no quarter of my age and call
on coming wits to prove the truth
of my stark venture into fates cold hall
where thoughts at hazard cast the die for sooth

from me great days are gone and after none
array the ardour that i scarce compress
in temperance terrible   charged i abide
the desperate victor of my last race run
wanting bold challenge to lifes dread excess
to fire that frenzy i must else wise hide

A Historical Introduction to the Postulational Foundations of Experimental Epistemology* WARREN S. McCULLOCH

I shall sketch a theory of knowledge compatible with our modern physiology of the knower. For all its appeal to epistemic correlates,[1] physiology has, from its beginning, been largely a hypothetical and deductive system in terms of postulated recognizables constructed to explain the causal relations of perceived events.

The Haemic Theory of Knowledge

In that beginning one finds several postulated entities called "mixtures." One, sometimes called by Aristotle the "conate pneuma," an airy blood, is postulated by the Hippocratic school to explain quickening five months before the first breath. The Atomists supposed pure air pumped from the lung directly to the foetus, at variance with anatomy; the Empiricists, that quickening only occurred at birth, at variance with both hearing and feeling!

The second, or perfect, mixture was postulated to account for generation. This mixture specifies to the female the form of her progeny, thus conserving kind. Thus the perfect mixture is the natural cause of the conception, formation, and growth of the

* This work was supported in part by the National Institutes of Health (Grant NB–01865–05); in part by the U.S. Army, the Air Force Office of Scientific Research, and the Office of Naval Research; in part by the U.S. Air Force (ASD Contract AF33(616)–7783); in part by The Teagle Foundation, Inc.; and in part by Bell Telephone Laboratories, Inc.

progeny; its bound cause. Clearly it is the precursor of the shuffling of genes postulated by Mendel to explain frequency of occurrence of traits in phenotypes.

The postulation of the determinants of pure form to be embodied by a process of development, leading to the adult, and ultimately to its death by natural causes, gives us the law of the conservation of species, much as potential energy gives us a law of the conservation of energy. Because the bound cause is sharply distinguished from accidental, or casual, causes, it carries with it a value judgment, those things being good which are to the ends of the living thing and all else either indifferent or evil to it. The former promote health; the latter produce disease. To physiology the idea of the bound cause has contributed the notion of a function as the end in, and of, an operation. We return to it later.

The third mixture is postulated to explain knowledge. With much help from my most scholarly friends, I think I have begun to understand the origin of that postulate. In the continuum of sensation and perception, the world is this up to where it is that. Of this continuum Aristotle says "each this and that contains its end points." When a hand grasps an object, it conforms to the object, "the fulls of the one filling the hollows of the other," as the seal impresses the signet on the wax. In the form and proportions determined by the impression, the elements (earth, air, fire, and water) of the known mix with those of the knower. This mixture forms in the blood of the knower. The veins, anastomosing, mix the blood from various parts of the knower, and the final mixture takes place in the heart. Such was the cardiocentric theory of knowledge. The nerves were only reins to govern the muscles, and the brain a phlegm to cool the blood. The last time I heard this haemic theory taken seriously, except for hormones and immune reactions, was in the nineteen-twenties, when the neurosurgeon, Dandy, declared that he knew to his sorrow that consciousness was in the left anterior cerebral artery. Any psychiatrist, working with poor immigrants from backward rural areas, could tell you that to "think with one's blood" is still an ordinary notion. At its best, in the old days this notion yielded theories of contagion and infection, and so gave us quarantine and sanitation about two thousand years before Paracelsus postulated that a disease was a living thing, a virus that could be poisoned without killing the patient, thus laying the theoretical foundation for antibiotics. Pasteur was the first to see a pathogenic bacterium. Only in the last year has electron microscopy depicted what is thought to be the smallest virus.

Please note that the germ, the postulated bound cause of a disease, is a mixture of the second kind, prescribing a process leading to its own multiplication; whereas the reaction of the host, in forming specific agglutinin, and antibodies generally, makes the blood a mixture of the third kind, one that knows the antigen. Since the beginning of this theory, it has been postulated that the protein of the host, the antibody, is specifically shaped to grasp the antigen. No one has yet seen the shape, but we may expect it to be deduced rather soon, as we have the shape of the molecule of hemoglobin, which, with oxygen, forms the mixture of the first kind: the *conate pneuma*, the vital air.

The genetic structure of a cell is carried by deoxyribonucleic acid. It specifies ribonucleic acid, which, in turn, specifies the protein to be made. When a cell that makes antibodies to a given antigen first encounters it, within half an hour there is a great rise in ribonucleic acid, and the requisite protein synthesis is under way. That cell may live a matter of days before it divides and its daughter cells inherit the specification for making that antibody. In the case of the virus for smallpox, the immunity may last some seven years. Such is the memory in the savant mixture of the blood. Even more, the immunity can be conferred by inoculation with a strain of virus attenuated for that host. We use cowpox to protect ourselves from smallpox, and we made vaccination a legal requirement for entry into the U.S.A. while the virus and the antibody were still postulates, leading by deduction to hypotheses which checked with experience.

In various places in the Hippocratic corpus, and in a fragment of the words of Empedocles, there are two kinds of attraction to be noted. One is the attraction of likes for each other, as in our notion of gravity, which he calls "strife." It is to be seen when the rich come together on one side and the poor against them on the other. The second attraction is called "love," for it resembles that of opposite electrical charges. It is therefore love that begets knowledge, by mixing things which are in some way unlike. In the mixture that which is shared is a pure form or shape. In Pylus, the dry sand is soft and the water is soft, but close to the tideless sea the beach is hard where, by capillary attraction, the water fills the voids of the sand exactly. Thus the mixture, wet sand, has properties which are not proportioned between those of the components, as in the mixture of wine and water. This applies to all three kinds of mixture, and it led Aristotle to reject these entities because, he argued, there would then be small enough parts to be entirely the one or entirely the other of the components. Had he been an Atomist, he would have said the same for wine and water; nor would it have saved him had he imagined chemical combinations. The rejection of these mixtures left *idos* and *telos* without postulated things to embody them, so that they seem little more than rules of right speaking about living things. Hence his biology remains marvelous in description and classification, but useless in inquiring into the underlying mechanism and hence a poor basis for a physiological theory of knowing. Unfortunately, as Aristotle was the schoolmaster of the Western world, epistemology has been slow to become an experimental science.

The theory of the savant mixture, which served well for smell, taste, and feeling, began to fail for sight, in which a ray from the eye was supposed to touch the known, much as a blind man might with his cane. Democritus is believed to have said that all our senses were a kind of feeling. Without a theory of geometrical optics, which had to wait for Kepler, the alternative theory, that lighted things shed shells, some of which entered the eye, did not really work. It is here that a new approach was tried, some say first by Democritus' dissection of animals to learn the seat of madness. This ultimately transposed knowing from the blood to the brain. This may sound extreme; but, although on a careful rereading of the Hippocratic texts on epilepsy and on head injuries we see symptoms correctly attributed to loci in the brain, we still find the brain regarded only as an organ to cool the blood.

The Nervous Theory of Knowledge

There is a disease called sympathetic ophthalmia, in which infection in one eye leads to blindness of both. In 450 B.C., Alcmeon of Croton excised the human eye successfully. He held that the optic stalks carried vision from the eye to the brain. He thought that fire was intrinsic in the eye and water in it passed to the brain carrying the light with it, and thence the water came back to the eye. Moreover, he studied the optic chiasma and concluded correctly that it explained the fusion of the images of the two eyes and had something to do with their yoked motions. He said: "Things human are two," as black and white, and so on, and perhaps based his whole theory of opposites on similar operations, although Aristotle says that he threw them out at random. Finally I should add that, according to Theophrastus, Alcmeon thought that the seat of all sensations was in the brain "which somehow fitted them together." Here also, he thought, was the "governing faculty" and "intelligence," which is more than animals have in "perceiving by the senses." Either he or his followers seem to have traced hearing from the ear to the brain, and perhaps did the same for touch in the face.

But, be that as it may, dissection grew up slowly, culminating in a school in Alexandria which finally gave a good gross anatomy of the nervous system. When it died, the picture deteriorated so that even the ventricles were grossly distorted. This was corrected by Leonardo da Vinci.

Based on eight years of dissection of eyes and brains in Leiden, René Descartes postulated that (1) nerves were composed of parallel tubes too fine for him to see them individually even under his magnifying glass; (2) each tube was filled with liquid in which pulses of hydraulic pressure went from the brain and spinal marrow to muscles causing them to contract; and (3) each tube had a fine thread in it which, as the muscle contracted, signaled back to the central nervous system to close down the valve.

In the *Dioptrices*, Descartes, following Kepler, shows that the optical properties of the cornea, lens, and vitreous humor produce a picture of the world on the retina, and then he argued correctly that there were enough tubes from eye to brain to transmit the picture. Next he argued that thence to the master valve of his hydraulic system, the pineal gland, he did not believe there could be enough parallel tubes to convey the picture; he therefore postulated that it had to be conveyed by temporal sequences of pulses which need look no more like the picture than our word must resemble the thing we describe. This is the first great coding hypothesis of nervous activity based on the postulated nervous impulse. By it he gave his automata ideas, departing signally from the signet.

Recently, there has in fact been some evidence that a mechanical pulse is present in the nervous impulse. Galvani, however, turned attention in another direction by postulating animal electricity to explain nervous impulses and muscular contraction. In the last century, with the invention of the capillary electrometer, it became possible to detect activity in a peripheral nerve, and in 1875 Caton was able to demonstrate to the Royal Society of Medicine electrical waves of the brain. Only with the help of the vacuum tube amplifier could Forbes in 1924 and Adrian in 1926 see the postulated electrical nervous impulse in a single tubule. By "see" I mean deduce it and its temporal form from the temporal fluctuations of a record from a capillary electrometer driven by the electronic amplifier.

Long before that time the microscope had revealed tubules, and it had been found that when one excited a whole nerve electrically, after the exciting current reached a certain value, no greater pulse appeared in the nerve. This led to the postulation that the impulse in the single fiber was of a size independent of the current that evoked it. This is the so-called all-or-none law: that once the stimulus exceeded the threshold, the propagated impulse was determined in size and shape by local conditions—the tubule doing all that it could then do there.

Today much is known of the rate of propagation and form of the pulse, of its refractory periods, and of its sources of energy, but not enough yet of its physical and chemical basis. There are, in these tubules, fine threads of hyaluronic acid, whose function is not known, but it is certainly not that which Descartes proposed and which ultimately let his automata become purposeful.

Early in the nineteenth century Magendie defined the function postulated by Descartes for his threads as a reflex, supposing that when a process, such as the contraction of a muscle, occurred in some part of the body, impulses passed to the central nervous system, from which they were reflected to that part of the body where they arose, and there stopped or reversed the process that gave rise to them. By 1819, he had proved that these impulses always entered the spinal cord by the dorsal roots, or sensory roots, and emerged over the ventral roots. Hence evolved reflexology, beautifully clear in the writings of Sechenov, which, as a side line, produced the homeostasis of Cannon and Rosenblueth. A similar class of systems had grown up in the form of governors of prime movers, and in the controllers of telephonic relays. Once Julian

Bigelow noted that it did not matter how the information was carried, but only that the machine be informed of the outcome of its previous act, cybernetics was born, and teleology had its proper mechanistic base in engineering and in biology. The operation of such systems generally is such that the output decreases the input. When they act over a path that closes within the body, they regulate it; and when they act over paths closed by way of targets in the external world, they account for appetition. With the appearance of Wiener's cybernetics, the basic notions became rapidly popular. Russia woke up late, but now has five institutes of cybernetics, and may soon have three more. It will be taken for granted by their high school graduates in a few years. Its great importance for our present purposes is first that, by accounting for purposeful behavior in a general manner, it makes a sharp distinction between those things which are useful and useless to the built-in ends of the machine or animal; and, second, that it poses the question of how utility is mediated specifically in the physiology of particular anatomical structures.

Near the end of the last century Ramon y Cajal postulated (1) that all the nervous tubes were outgrowths of nerve cells, and (2) that it was only these cells and their processes that carried nervous impulses. The remaining cells, or glia, he thought served only metabolic or mechanical functions. His first postulation was proved by his own beautiful histology; and his second, confirmed by ' microelectrode techniques for neurons, is generally accepted, even if a few neurophysiologists suspect glia may have something to do with memory or may serve as passive conductors.

Following our direct line of descent in experimental epistemology, from Helmholtz, Rudolf Magnus, and Dusser de Barenne, my group decided to sharpen our hypotheses as much as possible, to adhere strictly to an electrical hypothesis of excitation and inhibition, and to see how far it would suffice to guide an experiment. Such a hypothesis requires that, from known anatomy and precise location of pick-up electrodes, one should be able to predict the outcome of an experiment. This postulate has worked well for us and led us to an understanding of the interaction of impulses afferent along separate fibers on their way to a terminal cell or cells. This possibility frees a real nervous system from the restriction to "threshold logic," from which imitations have suffered, and allows any cell to compute any logical function of the signals that approach it from any number of sources. This may seem trivial, for, with a neuron having only two inputs, all but two of the 16 logical functions (namely ⌐ . . . if and only if . . . ⌐ and the exclusive ⌐ . . . or . . . ⌐) are computable without interaction. But when one comes to functions of three arguments, only 104 out of the 256 functions can be had with threshold logic; and, for any reasonably large number of arguments, the fraction computable becomes negligible.

The importance of this interaction became obvious to us in our two-year experimental study of what the frog's eye tells the frog's brain. The known anatomy was sufficient for us to try to assign to each of the five kinds of ganglion cells in the retina the function it computes and of which it informs the brain. The connections between these five kinds of ganglion cells of the retina and the frog's brain are such that they map the four form functions in four discrete levels—one visual part of the frog's brain—and the four maps are in register. The fifth form is concerned with color and goes to another part. If the optic stalk is cut, the fibers re-generate, reconstituting the four maps in register.

I should mention two things. First, the frog's eye is built to detect things in motion and reports their presence for at most a short time once they stop. This is important for a beast who lives by catching insects. Second, the things that his ganglion cells do report, such as the radius of a spot, are obviously useful in this pursuit. My group of collaborators is inclined to agree with White-head's theory of percipient events, in this case the life of the frog, that perception requires cognizance of spots, be they large or small, by adjective; and cognizance, among spots, by relation, here preserved by the maps in register. In this instance, the frog's rods and cones, his transducers from light to nervous impulses, single out different wave lengths to respond to them; next, the bipolars single out certain patterns of signals from rods and cones; and finally, the ganglion cells single out still more elaborate patterns of their input from the bipolar cells. The frog's brain cannot see around, but only through, these channels. They yield his adjectives of the spots—in his case, moving spots. Small dark objects in motion in given directions are thus elementary constructs for him, and his four maps, preserving spatial relations, enable him to capture a fly. Let me say it this way: A fly in motion is one of the simplest things sensible to him. Literally he has no, and he needs no, cerebral cortex to generate the idea of a fly regardless of time, position, direction, and velocity of flight. Similarly, he has an "AAH" resonator built into his ears by which to find his mate.

When one studies the carnivore, all this changes. He can be shown to recognize a tune regardless of pitch and a square regardless of size. For these he requires his cerebral cortex, without which he can still distinguish sounds and somehow see enough to get about. Using the word "universal" in the sense of Aristotle, of the *Isagoge* of Porphyry, of the commentary on it by Boethius, and so in the sense of Peter Abélard, of Duns Scotus, and of William of Occam, which became formalized in the universal quantifier, $(x)\phi x$, Pitts and McCulloch showed how brains could embody these universals. Our article may have been wrong in any particular attribution of function to local anatomy or local physiology; but it cannot be wrong in its all-important proof that for a man to know such universals as shape regardless of size or chord regardless of key it would be sufficient for his brain to compute enough averages. Each average is an Nth of the sum, for all N transforms belonging to the group (say, dilations or translations), of the value attributed by some functional to each transform as a figure of excitation in the time and space of an appropriate matrix of relays. Thus the mechanism derives an invariant under that transformation, and so shape can be seen regardless of size and chord heard regardless of key.

So much new experimental evidence has been accumulating that in the next few years I expect a formulation to appear, new in almost every particular, but in no way that affects the sufficiency of our argument. So much for the perceived universals.

The Knowing Automaton

William of Occam, for all he would not have entities multiplied beyond necessity, stated bluntly that man thinks in two kinds of terms. The first, or natural, terms man shares with other animals. It is of these we have been speaking, even when the term was a natural universal, like a chord regardless of pitch. The second, or conventional, terms are enjoyed by man alone; and Occam somewhere adds that the greatest of these is number.

I think it was about 1929 that Gödel arithmetized logic, proving that the deduction of a proposition from a finite set of premises was precisely equivalent to computing a number. Within ten years Turing had shown that a finite machine with a finite number of states, working on a tape as long as need be, could compute any number that a man could compute.

In 1942, Pitts and McCulloch wrote "A Logical Calculus of the Ideas Immanent in Nervous Activity."[2] In it they considered a net of formal neurons with two inputs each, each neuron having a threshold that determined whether one input was sufficient or both were necessary to fire it and each neuron being liable to absolute inhibition. They showed that, with a proper circuit, a net of such neurons could compute any computable number, and hence could reach any conclusion given by a finite set of premises, or abstract any figure given in the excitation of the net. From the Turing machine have evolved our vast digital computers, and from the proposed logical calculus has sprung the deluge of automata studies.

To ask whether these computers can think is ambiguous. In the naive realistic sense of the term, it is people who think, and not either brains or machines. If, however, we permit ourselves the ellipsis of referring to the operations of the human brain as "thinking," then, of course, our computers "think," their primary language being that of number. Turing designed his machine for computation, which is deductive; but, because he made the value of the operand effective in determining the next operation, his machines are also capable of induction and are now so used.

What these machines lack by contrast with the human brain is the ability to operate in our natural terms. For this they require very special programing even to resemble simple perceptive automata. It is really an abuse of a Turing machine to compel it to "think" in our natural terms, but the very complexity of the programing required for such an abuse supplies a clue to the nature of the ordinary perceived universal.

The original Turing machine had no memory beyond the state it was in and its marks on the tape. The latter, or passive, storage had this great advantage, that what was stored, say, the Nth digit, was stored in the $(N + K)$th place; and its location was so related to it that one did not have to have a stored system of addresses to find it. Storage of this kind is often called associative, and has many advantages in long-term retention. W. Ross Ashby postulates it in his *Design for a Brain*,[3] which makes what is to be sought, and where it is to be sought, functions of the sequence of learning. It, and its invasions always deeper into the central nervous system, all too well known in the case of causalgia, brings us to the question of dynamic storage.

Before 1930, no spontaneous activity of neurons and no activity that was regenerative over a closed path were known. In 1930, Kubie[4] proposed both to account for thinking, which he did not believe required activity over a path through effectors and receptors. Within six weeks Ranson had proposed it for an entirely different reason. Next I proposed it, as occurring over a regenerative loop, to account for fits and certain kinds of facilitations. Lorente de Nó suggested it to account for a prolonged nystagmus following a single volley over the vestibular nerve. In both forms, within cells and among them, these representative neural activities are well known today. In the cat's somatic afferent system, a single volley sent into certain cells in the spinal cord produces a burst of eight or more impulses about one thousandth of a second apart. A similar performance is noted in the sensory cortex. Here the impulses are not necessarily equally spaced; and in the associative cortex it seems as if their patterns in time depend upon their place of origin in the cortex. This is in line with what MacKay and I proposed years ago, pointing out that by pulse interval modulation one could get far more information through a nervous junction than just one bit per pulse, as in my scheme with Pitts.

I have mentioned these things, and could mention many others which can only enrich the properties Walter Pitts and I attributed to our abstracted neurons. The ability of a single neuron with interaction of afferents to compute any logical function of its input is another example. But all of these are beside my point in the creation of a logical theory of nervous activity. Thanks to Gödel it is well known that, for a formalist logical theory, the only hardware one needs is the natural numbers. The only operations necessary are addition, subtraction, or division. It was for this reason that we abstracted from real neurons everything irrelevant. In a nervous system composed of such neurons, a closed regenerative path can sustain a sequence of impulses patterned after its input, provided only that the sequence in the input is of shorter duration than the time around the loops. A network composed of such elements can sort out and respond to any one figure in the sequence of impulses. The signal chasing itself around the loop represents an idea, presented once, but repeated at all subsequent times until the action is quenched. The process is a dynamic memory, making an invariant under translation in time, which issues in what Whitehead calls "Primary Recognition." What is more important is this: It is completely indifferent as to whether the signal embodies a perceived universal or a proposition concerning a postulated scientific object. Many men, working in automata studies, have put a sharp limit on what can, and cannot, be computed by such a closed reverberant path. They say that such circuits and subassemblies can compute the form of all definite, and no indefinite, events. Ten thousand ones is a definite sequence, a definite event; but one followed by any number of zeros followed by one is an indefinite event, although the sentence that describes it can be shown to be a definite event. Hence, we may put it this way: whatever may be defined by a finite sequence of symbols can be defined indefinitely by such a loop. Thus in finite loops, as long as they continue to reverberate, our brains "trap" any universal that can be defined in a finite and unambiguous manner. But when we get a bump on the head or go to sleep or simply switch our attention to something else entirely, the circuit ceases to reverberate, and the universal would be lost to us if the reverberation had not made some enduring alteration in the brain. Modern evidence indicates that all our acquired ideas, or learned generalizations and specifications, are carried on for nearly half an hour by regenerative activity, of which there is beginning to be some electrical evidence. If this activity is interrupted during that time, no memory remains. From the evidence to date it seems that if the process has not been interrupted, and if one looks at the appropriate neurons half an hour later, one finds that there is a great rise in ribonucleic acid, and protein synthesis is under way. So, while we do not yet know how or where this building material will be distributed, we may see nature using the same trick as in the immune reactions. Whatever the details of this process, it is clear that it must determine local changes in the electrical properties of neurons, which will fit together in some new fashion at some places. There is much of clinical interest which might be said here but it is beside the point. What matters is that universals, represented first by reverberating circuits whose activity persists for half an hour, may become embodied in anatomical structures and so fix future performance in accord with the learned idea.

The Prospect

Let us summarize the present state of experimental epistemology. It seems that, by postulation, we have created for ourselves the right kind of scientific objects to handle ideas and purposes in terms of circuit actions of oversimplified components in known relations. This has been done in terms of a most general notion of excitation and inhibition relating effects to locations or connections. It has served us well in the brain and spinal cord and in the frog's eye. If we are right, we have an algorithm to determine from anatomy those functions of its inputs that a given neuron can compute. These are sufficiently well substantiated for us to attribute one of the four shape functions, that we know are computed by ganglion cells in the frog's eye, to each of four kinds of ganglion cells. The projections to the brain preserve spatial relations. Whitehead's cognizance by adjective and cognizance by relation are thus anatomized. We have theories, perhaps wrong in details, to account for the perception of universals like squares and triangles as mediated by mammalian brains; and we have a general theory of reverberating activity that can account for the trapping of universals of any kind. There is evidence that if these activities persist for half an hour, the universals may become anatomically embodied.

In short, the central problem of experimental epistemology seems in principle to be soluble along lines sufficiently well verified to reduce every particular question of the physiology of knowledge, however intricate experimentally, to a strictly parochial problem.

FOOTNOTE REFERENCES

1. Northrop, F. S. C., "Toward a Deductively Formulated and Operationally Verifiable Comparative Cultural Anthropology," in F. S. C. Northrop, and Helen H. Livingston (eds.), *Cross-Cultural Understanding*, Harper & Row, New York, 1964, chap. 12.

2. McCulloch, Warren S., and Walter H. Pitts, "A Logical Calculus of the Ideas Immanent in Nervous Activity," *Bulletin of Mathematical Biophysics*, vol. 5, 1943, pp. 115–133.
3. Ashby, W. Ross, *Design for a Brain* (2nd ed.), Wiley, New York, 1960.
4. Thanks to Jerome Y. Lettvin we are able to trace the idea of circular paths a few years further back. For Kuhlenbeck wrote in 1957 as follows:
I am well aware of the objection, voiced by Rashevsky and others, that a single neuron cannot form a self-reexciting circuit because the excitation will fall within its own refractory phase. When, in 1927, I formulated the concept of a true self-reexciting circuit, such circuits were assumed to consist at least of two neurons. Nevertheless, since a great number of unknown variables may be involved, I do not consider Rashevsky's objection cogent, and I see no reason why, for theoretical purposes, single neuron self-reexciting circuits should not be assumed. Such arrangements might actually be realized in the central nervous system. The objection is furthermore immaterial, because it can easily be avoided by only slightly more complicated constructions, involving internuncials.
Kuhlenbeck, Hartwig, *Brain and Consciousness, Some Prolegomena to an Approach of the Problem*, Supplement to vol. 17, *Confinia Neurologica*, S. Karger, Basel and New York, 1957, pp. 242, note 40.

PHYSIOLOGICAL PROCESSES UNDERLYING PSYCHONEUROSES

By WARREN S. McCULLOCH

I am inclined to sympathize with the good Saint Thomas Aquinas, that patient ox of Sicily, who lost his temper and died of the ensuing damage to his brain, when he met in Siger of Brabant the arch-advocate of two incompatible truths. In his time the schism was between revelation and reason, as in ours it is between psychology and physiology in the understanding of disease called 'mental'.

As we follow down the long trail of neurophysiology from Alcmaeon to Sir Charles Sherrington, we find it leading blindly to the conclusion that 'in this world Mind goes more ghostly than a ghost'. It were tedious to trace the alternative tradition, which begins in Plato's political psychology, conceived in the image of the state to end in Freud's trichotomy of the soul. His epigoni, the latter day illuminati, those new perfectibilians, have dethroned reason but to install social agencies, analytic interviews and transference in the places of espionage, confession and conversion, and fail to add a cubit to our stature. Just as Galileo and the Inquisition were both wrong in the one thing they both believed, that motion is absolute, so these two warring sects both accept as real the separation of body and mind, although there is none in nature. If it were real, it could not be bridged by coining compound adjectives out of 'psyche' and 'soma'.

The real bridge we have is the science of signals, newly developed out of the art of communication. For a signal has a double nature; it is a physical event, which happens only once in a singular world, yet it is essentially capable of being true or else false. Whether the signals are closures of telegraph-relays or impulses in neurons, it is possible for the nets they traverse to have general ideas, in the sense of recognizing universals presented in experience shorn of accidental peculiarity. In recent papers we have shown how nets perform this function in the superior colliculus and in certain parts of the cerebral cortex.

Signal-bearing nets also exhibit purposes in the sense of ends in operation. A purpose is given in any condition of the inputs to a net, such that a deviation from it produces a change in the output that, directly or indirectly, returns into the input so as to reduce the deviation from the chosen condition. In physics, we should call this a state of stable equilibrium. Some circular paths lie wholly inside the nervous system; thus, as cortical excitement increases, the indirect paths returning from it to the thalamus inhibit the further transmission of signals to the cortex. Other circuits go outside the nervous system, but stay inside the organism. This is true of the reflex, defined by Magendie and Bell as a process begun by a change in some part of the body, initiating impulses that proceed over dorsal roots to the spinal cord, whence

373

they are reflected over ventral roots to the part where they arise, and there stop or reverse the change from which they spring.

In our appetitive circuits, only part of the path lies within us, the rest outside us in the world. These, cast in the molds of our ideas, mark out what we call purposive behavior. They are error-operated, driven toward their goals by some measure of the difference between the end and its attainment. It is the same device which the engineer uses routinely under the name of a *servomechanism*, whenever he wants to embody purpose in a machine. It would be strange indeed if he, himself, worked on a very different principle.

As psychiatrists, it is natural for us to try to carry the analogy further. If animal and machine operate in the same way, they ought to suffer from some of the same diseases, or *gremlins*, as the engineer calls them, namely, the ones common to all circular mechanisms. The diseases of such systems, the gremlins, defy dimensional analysis. Energy, time, and length are not their measures. Pure numbers and the logarithms of numbers are but the ground on which they figure. At the moment, I am not concerned with finding out their precise anatomical location. The properties of nervous circuits are greatly affected by changes in quite different ones which may have a part in common with them. The central nervous system performs nearly all its operations many times over in parallel, and proceeds to the next step according to a general agreement of its signals. If one part is disordered or preoccupied, it performs the same function elsewhere. Of the input it receives, it filters out and discards all but one part in 10^7. It is not surprising that it should defy the best neurologist, for all but the grossest defects. That is their misfortune and not yours.

On more than one occasion I have said, not quite in jest, that in their essence gremlins and neuroses are demons, sentient and purposive beings, exercising in their own right properties more mental and more physical than any psychoanalyst has yet had the courage and clarity to claim for them, as much when they haunt machines as men. I speak tonight of the nature of demons.

Half-way between the inner feedbacks of the brain, whose diseases are convulsions, tremors, and rigidities, and those outer, appetitive disorders that frequent the public world, be they 'isms' or neuroses, there is one particular demon I shall describe at length, partly because he produces wellnigh intolerable suffering, and partly because his ways and doings are better known than those of any other. He is called *causalgia* – burning pain. I do not say this demon is all soul, though you will find him embodied now one place and now another. To torture us at all he must exist somewhere, somehow, as a perversion of some function in some nervous structure.

Causalgia begins as a perversion of a reflexive circuit. If you thrust a hand into hot water, or into water so cold that it seems to burn, the sensory receptors for pain and extreme temperature are excited. Their impulses, coming by fine fibres of the sensory roots to their own segments of the cord, excite the small internuncials that play upon preganglionic neurons of the sympathetic system. These, in turn, excite the sympathetic ganglia whose axones, running in mixed nerves and plexus about blood vessels, descend to the burning hand. Their barrage shunts the blood from the skin through the muscle and the bone, thereby conserving temperature within by decreasing the thermal conductivity of the skin. To maintain the proper temperature of the affected part is the function of this reflex. Its perversion is causalgia.

Let us see how the perversion happens. We used to demonstrate by placing a clamp upon the left internal mammary artery how changes in the circulation of a portion of a nerve may alter its excitability: for then the left phrenic nerve responds with a hiccup to the heart's electrical systolic pulse. We are all familiar with the paraesthesia and the cramp that comes from sitting on the blood supply of the proximal portion of the sciatic nerve. The standard history of causalgia is injury to nerve sufficient to damage, but not to sever it. Thereafter it responds to almost anything.

In 1944, Granit stimulated the sympathetic fibres to a limb of a cat, and recorded the afferent impulses from it to the cord, before and after crushing the mixed nerve. The experiment is easily repeated, and the outcome what you would expect: only after the injury, a volley of impulses over the post-ganglionic sympathetic fibres provokes a volley returning by the dorsal root. From what we know of cross-talk of signals generally, we should expect coupling to occur principally between conductors of comparable resistance and capacity, and, consequently that sympathetic efferents, being fine fibres, would excite fine-fibre afferents reporting pain and temperature from the peripheral distribution of the affected nerve. We do not need to jump from fibres to sensations, or from cats' brains to men's. Earl Walker, in curing causalgia of the arm, cut all preganglionic fibres of the cervical sympathetic chain, leaving the peripheral connexions intact, and delivered the chain itself into a glass tube through the wound. The patient, on coming out of anaesthesia, was without his pain; but for several days, as long as the ganglia were still somewhat alive, stimulation of the chain evoked again the burning pain in the old place.

This, then, is how the reflex was perverted. Injury to the nerves permitted cross-talk from the post-ganglionic sympathetic nerves to the nerves reporting burning pain. This is a vicious circle. Efferent impulses which should have decreased the number of afferent impulses have increased their number. The reflexive circuit has become regenerative. This is a self-perpetuating active memory projecting the pain upon the peripheral distribution of the afferent nerve that it invaded. When the injury is recent, and the nerve healing well, causalgia may be terminated by temporarily blocking the reverberation in any part of the closed path. But if the wound remains an artificial synapse, the trouble starts again. What is far more interesting is that sometimes simply blocking the nerve distal to the lesion relieves or terminates causalgia, for this bespeaks the role of other afferents in maintaining a background of activity in the internuncial pool.

Now the patient keeps his white and glossy hand moist and cool, for every jolt, touch, rub, or tickle turns to burning pain. How came this perversion of sense? Strike the back of your hand against your chair and attend to the sensation. There is first a quick pain carried by fast fibres, then the late burning pain which comes by the fine fibres slowly to the cord. Whenever we do anything vigorously, these impulses are present, but the faster tactile or proprioceptive fibres get their impulses first to the cord, where they determine the pattern of internuncial activity before the impulses for burning pain arrive. In causalgia, the story is reversed. The painful impulses are always there, and all other impulses augment the process already under way. Here is

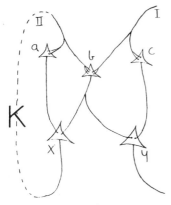

Gasser's diagram

Gasser's diagram of how such things can happen. Suppose the threshold of each neuron is just two synchronous impulses upon it. Then afferents of system *I* will fire *b* and *c* in phase and these will converge on *y* to fire it. But now let *II* get under way, and *b* will be swept into phase with *a*, convergence will occur on *x*, and it will fire. If this happens, the threshold of *b* must rise until *I*, which has but two synapses upon *b*, will become unable to fire *b* at any time. *II* has stolen the necessary internuncial *b* from *I*. But in causalgia, *x* feeds back to *II* and shuts *I* out forever. Obviously the scheme is oversimplified. *I* has many synergic fellows, and if enough of them can be got going at a time, they may be able to steal *b* from *II* and so break up causalgia. Among the best results that I, myself, have seen in the treatment of causalgia are Livingston's cases, in which good surgery of the wound was combined with early consistent and powerful persuasion to make use of these other afferent paths. He provided his patients with a whirlpool, into which they could put the painful part while they, themselves, controlled its rate of stirring. Those who were able to get other sensations through their burning pain usually recovered without further surgery. Here, at the reflex level, a kind of psychotherapy, by which I mean a use of afferent channels adequately stimulated, has exorcised the devil.

Unfortunately, if we wait too long, this method, as well as temporary and permanent nerve-blocking and section of the dorsal roots and section of the sympathetics fail, for the devil has moved into the cord. That he has not yet gone higher is clear; for spinothalamic section at that time will shut him out of our heads. I remember such a case after bilateral tractotomy and blocking of nerve proximal to the lesion. His affected foot was still obviously the recipient of a sympathetic barrage, which could come from no other thing than persistent activity reverberant in the cord. At this stage, instead of cutting the spinothalamic paths, the limb may be cut off – I have seen it done only too often – and it but substitutes a painful phantom for the real limb whereon the pain was formerly projected. This state has been imitated in experimental animals by Dr Margaret Kennard, who injected alumina cream into the sack around the cord. This produces no lesion apparent grossly or microscopically with ordinary stains. Yet the beast behaves as if he had causalgia of the corresponding regions.

Finally, there comes a time when section of the spinothalamic tracts is of no avail: the devil has moved upstairs and is reverberating there. Here we are confronted with new difficulties, for lesions dissociate aspects of pain, which, to the normal man, seems an elementary sensation. As the spinothalamic tract passes through the midbrain, fibres leave its main stream, and passing medially, terminate among the cells lying between the periaqueductal grey matter and the deepest layer of the superior colliculus. Mid-brain tractotomy at the level of the inferior colliculus prevents all pain and suffering; whereas, at the level of the superior colliculus, although the sensation of pain disappears, the suffering is as great as ever. In such a man, I am told that noxious stimuli produce suffering, fainting, sweating, and pupillary dilatation as if nothing had been done to interrupt their paths. The ascending spinothalamic tracts play into appropriate portions of the thalamic nuclei, whence relays extend into the cortex devoted to corresponding portions of the body. What is most important here is that in some cases of causalgia and of painful phantom limb, stimulation of the proper part of the postcentral convolution is sometimes perceived as pain. Among these cases are the few who seem to profit by excision of that part of the cortex. It seems unlikely that this cortex is part of a closed path through which the demon rings his changes. More probably, the improvement in these patients resembles the one achieved by peripheral block, and the cortical area in question only contributes to the sustaining excitation.

Finally, lobotomy, which has removed neither the sensation nor the primary affective component in any case that I have seen, does prevent the agony of worrying that makes distress a part and parcel of the typical character of such a patient. Only in this sense does the causalgia matter less to him, that he minds it only when he feels it. It may well be the demon haunts these cerebral paths, but they are certainly the last place where we ought to try to break his circle. I strongly suspect we shall find his last retreat in a certain small region of old and ill-defined structures near the core of the neuraxis, that stretch through the mid-brain and the thalamus. For lesions here affect the very springs of caring and of mattering. With this region left intact after all in front is gone, animals still learn, to the extent to which, without a cortex they can have ideas and control their movements. Whereas, with large lesions here, all else intact, they bother little if at all to respond, and do not learn.

Let us consider the demon from a slightly different point of view. Gasser's diagram represents the normal condition also, as long as we take the circuit K to be degenerative. In that case a certain fraction, smaller than unity of the afferents in II is fed back to them by K and subtracted ; this process keeps up until the circuit has come to rest at a definite level of activity directly proportional to the original input from II, if less variable than it. This level of activity is transmitted upward from x to communicate the sensory information from II; similarly from I by way of y. In causalgia, where K is regenerative, any input from II is amplified and added to itself, not subtracted. The level of activity in K then grows geometrically, until it is bearing all the activity it can bear; in this state it remains, to decline very slowly by attrition of fatigue. No matter how small the primary input, as long as there is any, the output is always the same: the maximum possible at x. The same thing happens if it was a collateral input, say from I, that triggered K. Furthermore, the proper response y from I will usually be prevented, either by Gasser's effect, already described, or else by direct inhibition from x when the latter is greatly excited. In the affected part the causalgic cannot distinguish among heat, touch, and pain, nor can he tell a greater degree of one of them from a lesser: in every case he experiences only the maximum of burning pain.

In this way the demon, causalgia, suppresses practically all the information formerly transmitted over II and every other circuit even partly connected with it. He does it by a kind of imperialism, substituting his own characteristic, repetitive, stereotyped, impertinent response for a whole range of infinitely varied and subtly adaptive responses to the actual facts of the situation. As we have seen, he takes time to get himself ingrained, like a skilled act. Thereafter he moves in on us, no longer requiring for his maintenance the particular structures from which he sprang.

These properties together describe more exactly what Lawrence Kubie has called the 'repetitive core' of every psychoneurosis. The difference is that the latter begins elsewhere, in the appetitive circuits.

In common with other psycho-analysts, Kubie makes a sharp distinction between processes which are conscious, and others which were or might have been conscious, but are now shut out of consciousness. In the latter he puts the core of the neurosis. Now the psycho-analytical use of the term unconscious, if somewhat indefinite, is quite a special one. In essence, I believe, it is nothing but the supression of information as we have just described it. The memories and learned reactions subserved by circuits connected with the regenerative circuit can no longer be evoked, not because anything has happened to them, but simply because all the stimuli which once evoked them, feeding secondarily into the regenerative circuit, now produce only the invariable neurotic response, which displaces all the others. In effect, such memories and such learning become inaccessible, although they return as soon as the circuit ceases to regenerate. The process looks like an active repression, particularly when combined with the secondary effect the psycho-analyst calls resistance. A man usually finds the output of the regenerative circuit disagreeable, so he learns to avoid stimuli which feed into the circuit in any way, as well as situations where such stimuli are probable. Thus the causalgic guards his hand even from his doctor. This development may go extraordinarily far.

But in some respects the psycho-analyst's metaphor is misleading. We cannot say the neurosis, or its root, is 'walled off' from the rest of the organism – quite the reverse. The regenerative circuit pours its output into other structures very strongly and usually distressingly. Again, it is only too easy for impulses from elsewhere to trigger the circuit and produce its characteristic maximal output. But that is all they can do: they cannot make it do anything different, they cannot stop it once it has started. We may say the neurosis is autonomous, almost completely so; it is not isolated.

377

So far I have spoken of the invasion of demons. But they can go outward and over-work a reflex path until its effectors or receptors are distorted or destroyed, as in *pruritus ani* and in gastric ulcer. I shall give you a different example because my knowledge of it is first hand. Franz Alexander became interested in a group of erstwhile energetic people whose living is crystallized about some goal made un-attainable by Fate. Thereafter they do their daily chores without zest. They are always tired. A few hours after eating they feel faint, warm, and sweaty. They eat too much and sleep too much and turn their food to fat. When Alexander came to me, he and his friends, following Szondi and Laz, had studied the glucose-tolerance curves of these people and found them abnormally low. What he asked me was whether these patients suffered from an under-activity of the sympathetic system or an over-activity of the parasympathetic system or both, for he knew that atropinizing the patient prevents the weariness and the postprandial faintness, although it does not restore the zest. For this reason he names the condition 'vegetative retreat'. So far our studies of their sympathetic system are far from complete; but of an excessive vagal excitement of the pancreas there can be little doubt.

Reliable statistics have shown us that neurotic patients are significantly more sensitive to insulin than is normal for their age and diet. Not so Alexander's patients. In their cases, to account for the increased speed of removal of sugar from the blood and the abnormal smallness of the final values after they receive sugar by vein, one must suppose an excessive secretion of insulin caused by excessive vagal excitation of the islands of Langerhans. Thanks to DeWitt Stetten, there is an easy way to check this; for he showed that with an excess of insulin, water made with heavy hydrogen, given concurrently with glucose, left heavy hydrogen in the fatty acids that are then produced because the patients turn their foods to fat. The odds are many to one that, on receipt of sugar, though their body temperature remains constant, their uptake of oxygen declines by an amount proportional to the amount taken from the sugar as it goes to fatty acid. If all of the sugar we injected went that way, we might expect a fall of 50% in oxygen uptake while the sugar was disappearing from the blood. In these patients we encountered falls as great as 30%, meaning 3/5 of the sugar went that way; in a normal man there is no change.

Let me rehearse, then, the doings of this devil. Springing from the tedium of life, he has produced an exaggeration of anabolic processes to a degree which has actually enfeebled his host and only fatigued him the more, thereby preventing him from developing a luxury of energy sufficient to extricate himself from his intolerable plight.

At this point I ought to hold my peace where I would in all conscience admit my failure and cry for help. For years I have tried and failed to find out how the brain knows how much sugar is in the blood; all I can be sure of is that it tastes it in some place other than the brain, for I can fool it. For years I have been trying to find all the ways by which the brain affects that quantity, but one eludes me. For the brain can still control blood sugar when the pituitary is removed, the vagi cut, the spinal cord transected above the topmost outflow of the sympathetic system. So much for my incompetence.

Causalgia exemplifies two modes of transition from an inverse feedback to a regenerative action. It begins by an injury which is equivalent to throwing a switch that reverses the sign of the feedback from negative to positive. Its ingression into the spinal cord is equivalent to a change in the ratio of output to input, or gain, of an amplifier, which overloads it. This change in gain is obviously the result of oft-repeated over-activity in the circuit. Now, in general, gain depends upon frequency. For a circuit whose action is inverse at the frequencies it is intended to handle, there will exist certain other frequencies, higher and lower, for which it is resonant. To be alerted to anything is to increase the gain in some circuit. If this circuit is excited at a frequency for which it is resonant, great overactivity can be produced, and like causalgia in the cord, may permanently augment its gain, so that it goes into self-sustained activity.

Telephone switchboard operators used to be subjected to a signal alerting them to plug in a line, ask and hear a number, make a connexion, and listen until they hear both parties speak, cut themselves out of the circuit, and stand by to receive the next alerting signal. Lively girls of high intelligence, doing this at busy switchboards, became tense or nervous, had rapid hearts, sweaty hands, and nightmares. This form of nervous breakdown became a serious industrial hazard, requiring months of care in a sanitorium. The expense to the company was great enough to prompt the development of the dial system.

This genesis of neuroses has been studied thoroughly in sheep and goats by Liddell. These beasts respond by lifting the fore-paw to a barely perceptible electrical shock. If the stimulus is repeated at equal intervals of one or several minutes, the sheep soon gives the response at the proper time, even if a single stimulus is omitted. That is all that happens. If he is taught that the beat of a metronome at one per second is followed by the shock, he tilts and raises his head and pricks up his ears whenever he hears the click, and may even raise his leg before the shock arrives. He can be taught to respond similarly to touch or sight instead of sound as the alerting signal. This is neither a painful nor a distressing experiment, nor one in which there is any task to require a difficult discrimination. Nevertheless, if the signal and shock are repeated at intervals of one minute or of four minutes, the beast becomes neurotic. With the shorter interval, he stiffens the fore-limb, breathes slowly, has a slow pulse and somewhat narrower pupils. With the longer interval, he begins to shake or paw with his fore-limb, pants, has a fast pulse and dilated pupils. Once firmly established, by a few runs each day for a few weeks, the reaction becomes so fixed that it lasts at least five years without reinforcement. Moreover, the beast ceases to be normally gregarious, and his fast irregular heart and respirations and much moving about continue permanently, even during sleep. Obviously the frequency of stimulation determines not only the existence of the neurosis, but also whether the sympathetic or parasympathetic system is the one involved.

Beside the neuroses that are generated by repetitive experience, there are some which clearly spring from a single, intense psychological insult. I have in mind what the American Army calls 'Blast'. A man near an explosion, but not so near as to suffer organic damage to his brain, starts to run in frenzy. After being stopped, say long enough to smoke a cigarette, he has lost all memory of the events from just before the blast until he smoked the cigarette. Thereafter he is startled easily, is terrified by the sound of airplanes or the back-fire of a passing car, and dreams of battle frighten him. He comes to resemble a hound gone gun-shy. From Walker's work we know that acceleration of head as great as in these patients produces throughout the central nervous system, an electrical disturbance which resembles that recorded in an epileptic fit. The blast itself can never be recalled. Again, the neurosis is an active reverberation, as shown in the autonomic outflow and the dreams. Why a single blast is able to set up such a process is not obvious. One would naturally suspect that the applied force, rather than the host of simultaneous signals over many nerves, was the cause, except that similar pictures appear in men too far removed from the explosion; merely as a consequence of seeing and hearing their companions killed in battle. Things of these kinds have easy access to a kind of memory other than either of those apparent in causalgics, neither mere reverberation nor the one that mediates our oft-repeated acts, but the one that stores our glimpses of the world, making it seem like a pack of photographs of things that happened once. Here each attempt to look again at these horrors, or anything that might incite him to revive them brings back the frenzied fear. The content of these snapshots is not itself the fear, and if the fear could be forestalled, they could be seen for what they are. I do not know when first man had it in his power by drugs to quiet these churning fears. In our Civil War, the patients were made drunk, and, as they sobered, were allowed to relive and discuss the things that racked them most. But we forgot the art of treating them, and re-discovered it in our war with Spain, when it was christened Hypnotic Therapeutics. In World War I we learned it once again, this time with ether, and in World War II barbiturates came into vogue, under the name of Narcoanalysis or Narcosynthesis. Next time, if there must be a next, I hope we have the grace to acknowledge the good works of our forebears, and have the skill to stand upon their shoulders.

To my mind, Fabing's trick[1] of following amytal by coramine seems an improvement, at least statistically in its results, and scientifically, for, inasmuch as the bulk of his patients lost their terrors and their amnesia without analysis, synthesis or intentional suggestion by any fellow man, his success ought to be attributed to the sequential action of these chemical agents on the central nervous system. The amytal brought many processes to rest; a violent reliving of the accident ensued, and this was suddenly converted to the waking state by the generalized excitation of the brain by coramine. Fear was swamped out by normal activities, among which were the memories themselves of the accident, now quite innocuous.

For all our hypotheses, of the majority of neuroses that begin in civil life, the origin seems to me undiscovered – probably undiscoverable. But the history of any case suggests that early in the process they may be broken up as easily as if they depended for their existence upon little more than mere reverberation, and only later became so fixed as to start up again once they are stopped.

Another origin of neuroses is instanced by conditions in which the gain is increased by the sudden withdrawal of various things, usually narcotic or soporific to the nervous system. I do not mean the convulsion that not infrequently follows the withdrawal of barbiturates. I am thinking, first, of the jitters of the alcoholic who tries to stop, and becomes unable in his tremor and terror to lift a glass to his mouth; second, of the violent autonomic discharge that ensues when morphine is withheld from those physiologically addicted, including the decorticated dog; and last, that all-pervading anxiety which comes when we lose the most wholesome of soporifics, a convivial bed-fellow. Fortunately, thanks to your British drug, myanesin, these problems have become simply and safely manageable. Henneman in our laboratory has most elegantly demonstrated that myanesin will prevent the activity of internuncials necessary for multisynaptic arcs, including the nociceptive flexion reflexes and the facilitation and inhibition produced by direct stimulation of the reticular formation of the mid-brain and hind-brain or by torsion of the head on the trunk. It was these experiments which led Dr Cooke to suggest trying it against the overactivity of masses of small cells produced in the aforesaid withdrawals, and so to experiments at Manteno State Hospital on large numbers of patients with sympathetic symptoms.

I have purposely dodged the term 'anxiety'; for it is now applied to any state of the central nervous system giving excessive sympathetic activity. I have already described three such states, which are clinically and experimentally distinct: the first induced by repetition in telephone operators and in sheep, the second by single fright in a blasted man and gun-shy dog, the third by withdrawal of certain drugs in man and dog. All three conditions show exaggerated startle, and respond, at least temporarily, to myanesin. A good instance is my old dog Puck, who was early frightened by fireworks. Every thunderstorm puts Puck into a state of terror: he shivers continuously, hides under the bed, and refuses food for many days. The slightest stimulus startles him. Myanesin will not prevent thunderclaps from frightening him, nor does it completely suppress the startle; but after the storm passes he eats, and instead of hiding, comes to be petted without shivering. Myanesin has evidently damped the

[1]Fabing, H. D. (1947) *Arch. Neurol. Psychiat.*, **57**, 14.

regenerative process. In the remaining case of the sheep, experiments with myanesin are now under way, although we do not yet know the results.

Besides all these, there is a fourth condition like the apprehension felt by a man about to visit the dentist, except that it often wants any well-defined object. The sympathetic system is evidently overactive, but mere noise will not augment its output further. The man shows no great exaggeration of startle, and his feelings are not much affected by myanesin, although his sympathetic output may decline a little. Masserman's cats appear to furnish the corresponding condition in animals. They are put into the ordinary experimental set-up for conditioning, where they learn to perform some response rewarded by food. Thereafter, when they perform the response, they receive instead of the food, or accompanying it, a blast of air in the face, like a cat spitting. Such cats will not eat, fight against being put into the conditioning box, and become unsociable. But they have no exaggerated response to startle, do not increase their sympathetic activity in response to noise, and, as I have just heard, are not measurably affected by myanesin. They seem anxious – but I suspect their apprehension is more like that of the ordinary neurotic patient.

Every treatment of causalgia has its counterpart in handling neuroses in general, at the proper stage. But, at the moment I am chiefly interested in one resembling the newest treatment of blast. We have had nearly five years' experience with it to date. Of the first 117 whose treatment ended some four years ago, 79 are still well today, and 2 who relapsed have recovered on repetition of the treatment.

For its rationale let me recall to you Gasser's diagram when the circuit K is regenerative. If we raise the threshold of *b*, we shall be able to halt the reverberation temporarily. When the threshold falls again, the normal input *I* may be able to pre-empt the necessary common internuncial, so *II* will not get going as before. Whether this happens depends upon the exact times at which signals from *I* and *II* arrive. A second way of doing this would be to make *b* temporarily indefatigable; for then *I* could fire it at any time and be on an equal footing with *II* in the race for possession of *b* at every round. A third possibility lies in the background of excitation and inhibition, not indicated in the diagram, but always there in the living nervous system. For, any shift that might fail to excite *II* or inhibit it or do the reverse to *I* might upset the balance. In fact, merely to excite both maximally or inhibit both maximally would tend to equalize their chances for possession of *b*.

Lorente de Nó has shown that CO_2 raises the voltage and threshold of all axones, and also, what may be most important here, it renders them almost indefatigable. The effect of this on the activity of various structures is diverse. The cortex, normally so far from fatigue as to be capable of an epileptic discharge whenever it is electrically excited, has its normal level of activity controlled by inverse feedbacks which keep its afferent impulses down to a small established average. Consequently, the effect of CO_2 on fatigability is here without effect, but the rise in threshold it induces puts a stop to cortical activity. In the respiratory mechanism the opposite is true, for its fatigued neurons are always the recipient of more impulses than they can relay. They are too tired to have a convulsion, no matter how frequently we excite them electrically. CO_2, by raising the threshold, can make little difference, but because it also prevents fatigue, it will cause a vast increase in respiration. Other structures of the thalamus, mid-brain, and hind-brain exhibit intermediate conditions.

Whether this is the complete story, or whether there is also a chemical specificity, remains to be proved. At the moment, we can only add that respiration of $15\% \ CO_2$ in O_2 prevents the seizures normally induced cortically by electrical stimulation or by metrazol or similar substances, whereas it augments the effect of bis-beta-chlor-nitrogen mustards, which start fits in the hind-brain, notable in the cerebellum. It follows that the respiration of $30\% \ CO_2$ in O_2 will alter, briefly but extremely, the background of excitation for neurotic reverberant feedback loops, and for normal

Physiological Processes Underlying Psychoneuroses

inverse ones. This alteration may halt reverberation. Over and above this shift, by rendering b indefatigable, CO_2 gives I and II equal chances for the necessary internuncial; in some of them I will succeed.

In giving, say forty treatments of say forty respirations each, of 30% CO_2 in O_2, one cannot avoid the suggestive effect of a doctor, a nurse, a mask, and submission to transient loss of consciousness. Still, in view of our contagious incredulity, particularly in the first series, the score is too high to attribute to psychological factors. Others now have longer series and better scores than we. In fact, their enthusiasm is somewhat alarming – particularly their reported success in treating gastric ulcer. I have been most surprised by the results in disorders of speech, commencing in childhood and treated.in the twenties or late teens. If we exclude stutterers – the people who say I did – – I did – – I did – – etc., who often have additional signs of damage to the brain, such as an arm that fails to swing normally in walking, or too fixed a stare – and accept only stammerers – those who say I – – – – – – – – I did it – then, of 50 cases the successes numbered more than 25. Having seen my sister, a teacher, and my cousin, a surgeon, bring on stammering by learning the one to write, the other to shave with the left hand, I am not altogether satisfied with supposititious psychic skeletons in the unconscious. It is enough to know that the devil is a reverberation who succumbs to CO_2.

Unfortunately causalgia and great anxiety are prepotent demons. Under CO_2 they are intensified, as if fatigue alone had limited their sway. The patient never leaves the doctor long in doubt on this score. He simply refuses a second or third treatment.

Beside prepotent demons, there is another condition that resists – or is unaffected by – CO_2. I hesitate to speak of anankastics – obsessive or compulsive – again at this meeting. The only experiments that have produced a condition which may be compulsive are Kurt Richter's on rats, poisoned once severely and thereafter required to select their diet from samples of various foodstuffs, of which, now one now another contained a little of the odorous poison. They hang on to the wires of their cages, wrap their tails around a wire and, even in sleep, hang on as if this would insure their not eating the poison in a moment of relaxation. This behavior persists for at least sixty days when the poison is withheld. If a similar picture can be produced in primates, we may be able to work out the complete circuit. In man mayhem must be less radical, but obviously there has been enough of it already to show that some portions of the fore-brain contribute to or constitute the closed path, or reiterative core, of obsessional stereotopy. I only hope that while neurosurgeons still have the operations on their consciences, psychologists will have an opportunity to study the way leucotomy, topectomy, and thalamotomy destroy the force, and finally the ideas, of those troublesome sentiments, for until we know more than we do today of the nature and boundaries of the consequent psychopathy we are in danger of robbing the patient of some of the ends of life which make it in the long run socially worth while.

DISCUSSION

The CHAIRMAN, Professor F. L. Golla, said that there was one point which struck him and that was whether a mechanistic approach to the neuroses was a possibility. Somewhere about 11 o'clock at night, standing in one of the highways, one would see a lot of people passing along in a great variety of moods; it was the hour at which the public houses closed. He could not think that very much would be learned from the sight of the effects of the poison but from the fact that each had a different system, a different stratum at which the alcohol worked. Professor McCulloch might be asking too much, it might be that they would ultimately have to correlate the mechanistic account with introspection to make it intelligible. As living beings they could do something which no mechanical thing could ever do – they could objectify themselves.

Physiological Processes Underlying Psychoneuroses

Dr DEREK RICHTER wished to pay a tribute to the most erudite and stimulating account which Professor McCulloch had given. Professor McCulloch had described, particularly in his writings and to some extent in his Address, the electrical mechanisms in the brain, and he would like to ask if there was any recent evidence of an interrelation of the electrical rhythms of the brain and behaviour at the higher levels. The previous work by Adrian and the work done in the Burden Institute were a little disappointing in that they showed a negative rather than a positive relationship between the electrical rhythms which one could pick up and actual behaviour. It was known that the *alpha* rhythm disappeared if conscious behaviour was started. They had been particularly interested in that problem at Cardiff and had recently been working on the relations between the actual phase of the electrical rhythms and behaviour. Some of the evidence might appear to give confirmation of the views of Professor McCulloch. The actual effect which he wished to mention was the relation of the phase of the *alpha* rhythm and the moment of initiation of a voluntary movement. The *alpha* rhythm could be shown very easily in an individual who was sitting relaxed with closed eyes, and the moment when he initiated any voluntary movement appeared to bear a relation to the phase of his *alpha* rhythm. Every tenth of a second the probability of his starting a movement increased, showing, in effect, a working relation between one of the rhythms and psychomotor behaviour (Kibbler, Boreham and Richter, 1949).

Was there any other evidence which would point to an active relationship between the rhythms rather than the negative type of relationship which had generally been described?

REFERENCE

KIBBLER, G. O., BOREHAM, J. L., and RICHTER, D. (1949) *Nature*, **164**, 371; Reports of 2nd Internat. Congress of EEG (1949), Paris.

Dr DENIS HILL thanked Professor McCulloch for a most interesting Address covering so many fields in which they were all concerned. He was surprised to hear him use the word 'demon' in describing the development of neuroses. He referred to reverberating processes of activity which might move towards the cortex and he referred to the state for such reverberating activity as the demon: 'the demon moves'. Keeping to his mechanical terminology it seemed to the speaker that Professor McCulloch was suggesting that the attention of the rest of the brain was directed towards the movement and activity of this electrical 'demon'. If that was so, there was a lot left after the reverberating circuit was accounted for.

Dr D. A. POND (London) said with reference to the idea of feedback, it was clear from Professor McCulloch's talk how nerve injury could produce 'cross-talk' and positive feedback in cases of causalgia. However, it was not clear what was the analogous explanation for the development of positive feedback mechanisms in the C.N.S., where there was no evidence of structural damage. The concepts of circular reflexes, the laying down of new pathways, etc., had a long history in psychology and physiology, and he was not clear how far Professor McCulloch's description of positive feedback as a functional disturbance in an electronic machine, threw light on what were the possibly comparable disturbances in the nervous system in cases of mental disorder.

Dr F. A. PICKWORTH (Birmingham) had studied the nature of nervous processes in mental disorders, and in this had profited much by reading Professor McCulloch's publications.

He (Dr Pickworth) wished to distinguish between mental and neurological processes. As far as the mind was concerned there was plenty of evidence that the central nervous system was not the 'master tissue' of the body. For example, the brains of schizophrenics were in his experience often better structurally than those from non-mental cases. Schizophrenics could be taken as typical since they occupied half the mental hospital beds throughout the world. Freeman [1] applied the terms 'particularly normal' to such brains. Dr Pickworth had known intimately several persons whose minds and personalities were not grossly altered by large cerebral destructive lesions. He had seen in Institutions, quadriplegic idiots who had minds and even characters of their own, although handicapped in the development and expression of them. Cerebral stimulation can restore function in long-standing mental abeyance, which fact establishes the integrity of the subservient central nervous system. The conditioned reflex, contrary to general acceptance, was not typical of a mental emotional state, since so much automatic (robot-like) behaviour was devoid of mental-emotional component. Attempts to identify unity of mind with the paired structures of the central nervous system were therefore doomed to failure. By contrast, all intense mental-emotional processes were regularly accompanied by vascular changes in the body. Corresponding mental changes were to be noted with physiological changes of blood pressure, which altered the local cerebral blood flow. Similar changes of both could be induced with drugs, toxins, or hormones acting over a period of time. He had been able to show, by a specially devised staining technique, structural alterations of the cerebral blood flow in cases of mental disorders. These changes were very evident in early general paralysis. The lantern slide shown indicated clearly congestion and gross structural lesions of the cerebral blood vessels of the motor cortex. He believed that, if cerebrovascular lesions were accepted as the pathogenesis of general paralysis, one could apply Osler's dictum of 'know syphilis in all its manifestations and all things clinical shall be added unto you', to other mental diseases, including the psychoneuroses. The aetiological agent may differ, but the pathogenesis is the same, namely pathological deviations of the local cerebral vascular flow, details of which are given in a pending publication [2]. The dependence of reflex nerve function upon the local blood flow was first shown by Sir F. W. Mott [3]. The blood flow abnormalities in schizophrenia have been likened to ergot poisoning. Those in early and late encephalitis are readily demonstrable, and in his opinion easily correlated with the sleep disturbances and mental symptoms. The literature contained most of the facts necessary, when read from the above aspect, to enable us to make drastic changes in our conception and treatment of mental disorders, and to acquire a better understanding of the mind itself.

REFERENCES

[1] FREEMAN, W. (1933) Neuropathology, p. 256. Philadelphia and London.
[2] PICKWORTH, F. A. (1950) New Outlook on Mental Diseases. Bristol.
[3] MOTT, F. W. (1900) The Degeneration of the Neurone, p. 50. Croonian Lecture, London.

Professor MCCULLOCH, in reply, said that he left his research, in problems raised by Organic Neurology while he was at Bellevue Hospital, for less than two years which he had spent in Psychiatry at Rockland State Hospital and from it returned to the laboratory with enough problems to keep him busy for the rest of his life. What he had done in his lecture was to rehearse the classical problems of neuroses, outlining for each neurosis the corresponding experimentation in animals in so far as he knew how to do it. It was his hope that some of his audience would begin to be interested in what one could do with a patient who could not confuse the doctor by his vocabulary.

He took up the questions in the order they were asked. The first concerned the mechanistic approach to the problem of neurosis or of any other psychological activity. One often heard that this or that property of the nervous system could be imitated by machines. Since he had shown that machines can and do have ideas and purposes it did not seem to him to be any great matter to design a machine that objectified itself, which is to have reflective knowledge of its own thinking.

Next, in answer to Dr Richter, who had asked concerning new evidence of resonant circuits, notably the relation of the *Alpha* activity of the brain to the output by mouth, or by hand and to perceptions. The man, Craik, who held most promise for the world in this direction unfortunately was dead and his work was so buried in Governmental reports that except for his little book it was not accessible. Among his most brilliant work were certain observations of the times during which man took in that amount of information on which he based a predicting response. Craik showed that in some cases it took 2/10ths second, and in others 3/10ths second with a rather sharp break between them, and thereafter the man took in no information during the next 1/10th second. John Stroud, now working with the U.S. Navy, had followed this same line. He showed that man perceived in moments of about 1/10th second each, lacking internal temporal structure and movement, and Stroud was correlating these moments with the electro-encephalographic records. He had shown that these 1/10th second visual moments could be locked in by auditory activity. Anyone who worked with the cathode ray oscilloscope trying to hold a pip in the center of the screen and put the click of the fly-back to his ears by earphones, and turned the frequency to a convenient setting found that he set to his own alpha frequency. The evidence on this was just beginning to come in. There was but one thing he would like to persuade his audience to do namely to collect Craik's work and get it published soon.

With regard to the demons: a demon is not a structure, or a gremlin is but a circuit-action. It is in almost all cases regenerative circuit-action which should be a kind of servomechanism – inverse or negative feedback. It was the peculiar property of complicated circuits like the nervous system that one usually could not precisely locate gremlins in them. Certainly the gremlin is never in a single item without a circuit but always in a closed path. What he had tried to point out was that this gremlin, this resonance, could begin in a disturbed reflex and, if it lived long enough, it modified some other loop and so could give birth to a second demon; whereafter the first demon could die, but, as far as his character or his soul is concerned, receives the same gremlin. He was not sure whether the difficulty the questioner had had was that the lecture attributed mental properties to gremlins who certainly have ideas and intentions.

To Dr Pond's question as to cross-talk and what turns up the gain, the answer was that the cross-talk in a causalgic nerve made it act repetitively and repetitive activity if persistent in some way, turned up the gain of the circuits in the cord. So when we learn to skip or to play a piano, erstwhile inadequate stimuli become adequate though we do not know how repetition turns up the gain. It is difficult to imagine how this happens in the spinal cord where one would expect all connexions to be firmly established by the time one can walk. Yet it seemed now clear that new pathways might be formed or old ones lost under unusual circumstances. This was first reported by Coller and Shurrager, but an excellent neurosurgeon, A. A. Ward, and a psychologist, Donald Marquis, were unable to teach the spinal cord. This suggested to Dr Lettvin that the difference might lie in rough handling, destroying some paths afferent to the motoneuron, thereby leaving it accessible to other impulses. Lettvin, therefore, cut the dorsal roots of a two neuron reflex arc, stimulated afferents normally inhibitory to this arc and simultaneously stimulated antidromically the motoneurons of this two neuron arc. Thereafter the erstwhile inhibitory afferents excited the motoneurons. The reason this work has not been published yet is that we do not know the histologic details nor are we certain the new path is monosynaptic. In any case it shows that the behaviour of the cord can be modified so that formerly inadequate stimuli become adequate. This is one kind of memory. The changes that occur higher in the nervous system may all be due to the kind of memory which preserves snapshots of the world to be re-evoked whenever this is required.

The last question was a crucial one. He did not join in the discussion that morning when Gellhorn lectured although he had wanted to cry 'hear, hear' because Gellhorn was on the right track. He thought neuropsychiatrists had habitually looked to the cortex for things actually in the brain-stem. Gellhorn was persuading them to look in the right direction. However, the brain-stem was not necessarily the master tissue of the body because there is no one master tissue. Meduna's work had shown that about two-thirds of so-called schizophrenics were biochemically abnormal, being unable to handle glucose properly when given it by vein, and unable to convert levulose into glucose, having something in the blood rendering them resistant to insulin, and putting out in their urine a substance that raised blood sugar in animals. About 1 mg. of this material when purified doubles the blood sugar of a 250-gramme rat. In these disorders of the brain we are dealing with a biochemical disorder which is almost as obscure as diabetes mellitus was when Professor McCulloch was in medical school.

"What's in the Brain
That Ink May Character?"*

Warren S. McCulloch

SINCE WE have come together as scientists who would become
a bit wiser as to the process of our art, it is proper for us to ask
what are the enduring qualities of our activities and what are our
present problems. Whether he would create poetry, fiction, or
science, the American is apt to think first of Mark Twain's law:
"You have to have the facts before you can pervert them." Which
are *the* facts? They are those that puzzle us—and not even all of
them, but those that arouse in us one and the same sort of uneasiness in various contexts of experience. From a vague sense of
there being something similar in these facts, we become curious as
to exactly what it is that is similar in them, and we define them with
increasing clarity, doing all of this before we are able to phrase a
single question to put to nature. At that stage we are uncertain
whether we really have one question or several questions.

You will find this difficulty explicit in the writings of Galileo,
who, in founding physics, speaks of two new sciences where we
now find only one. Kepler, in the act of putting physics into the
sky to produce elliptical orbits, was actually up against two questions, one in geometrical optics, and the other in mechanics, where
he originally thought them one question. At the end of the last

* Presented at the International Congress for Logic, Methodology and
Philosophy of Science, Jerusalem, Israel, August 28, 1964.

This work was supported in part by the Joint Services Electronics Program under Contract DA36-039-AMC-03200(E); the National Science
Foundation (Grant GP-2495), the National Institutes of Health (Grants
NB-04985-01 and MH-04737-04), the National Aeronautics and Space Administration (Grant NsG-496); and in part by the U.S. Air Force (Aero-
nautical Systems Division) under Contract AF33(615)-1747.

century, it looked as though physics was only a matter of pushing one decimal point to have a tidy theory of the universe. Only three awkward items had to be explained. These were the precession of the perihelion of Mercury, the drag of a moving medium on refracted light, and the absence of an aether drift. They raised three apparently separate questions, and no one expected that he had a single answer in the theory of relativity before that answer was forthcoming. Today there is a similar uneasiness in physics, perhaps foreshadowed by the want of a general field theory. It arises from the multiplication of the strange particles of subatomic physics, from the behavior of ballistic missiles, from transitions from streamline to turbulent flow, and from reports of an enormous object, a-fifth-of-the-age-of-the-universe away, which pulsates so fast that it requires a physical transmission immensely faster than light to keep it going.

The role of the projectile, and of its impact, in the development of physics may be of more than historical importance. In Galileo's hands, it proved fatal to the Greek doctrine of natural places. It disproved Descartes' attempted solution in terms of a plenum with a conservation of motion, and Leibnitz' plenum with a conservation of force. It now threatens Newton's conservation of momentum. For macroscopic projectiles and their impacts, there seems to be an intrinsic time, or τ, during which they absorb or deliver energy but during which they are incapable of a conservation of momentum in the macroscopic sense, and thus require a third temporal derivative. Its introduction has also served to explain both varieties of turbulence, the quasiperiodic and the hyperbolic, or explosive, in our rockets. Davis has pointed out that, without this assumption, these can only be explained away by distinct hypotheses *ad hoc*. Several of my friends have been asking whether or not atoms and particles may have a τ that accounts for some of their strange properties; and, at the other extreme of size, whether or not the gravitational field, like the electromagnetic field, may propogate, thereby giving a τ to gigantic structures. In short, it looks as though physics is again about to enjoy a new resolution, or at least a new revolution, and whether there be one question or many remains to be seen.

Since this is so in the most advanced of sciences, there is no need to apologize for the state of our own, for we are Johnnies-come-lately into the hypothetical and postulational stage of knowledge. Just as chemistry got off to a bad start in the rigid doctrine of alchemy and was saved only by the "puffers," so psychology was hindered by doctrinaire epistemology and saved only by biologists. To make psychology into experimental epistemology is to attempt to understand the embodiment of mind. Here we are confronted by what seem to be three questions, although they may ultimately be only one. It is these which we should like you to consider.

The three exist as categorically disparate *desiderata.* The first is at the logical level: We lack an adequate, appropriate calculus for triadic relations. The second is at the psychological level: We do not know how we generate hypotheses that are natural and simple. The third is at the physiological level: We have no circuit theory for the reticular formation that marshals our abductions.

Logically, the problem is far from simple. To be exact, no proposed theory of relations yields a calculus to handle our problem. When I was growing up, only the Aristotelian logic of classes was ever taught, and that badly. The *Organon* itself contains only a clumsy description of the apagoge—perhaps from the notes of some student who had not understood his master. Peirce says that when he was making the *Century Encyclopedia,* he understood the passage so badly that he wrote nonsense. "The apagoge," ordinarily translated "the abduction," is explained by Peirce as one of three modes of reasoning. The first is *deduction,* which starts from a rule and proceeds through a case under the rule to arrive at a fact. Thus: All people with tuberculosis have bumps; Mr. Jones has tuberculosis; *sequitur*—Mr. Jones has bumps. The second, or *induction,* starts from cases of tuberculosis and patients with bumps and guesses that the rule is that all people with tuberculosis have bumps. Peirce calls this "taking habits"; and properly it leads only to probabilities, coefficients of correlation, and perhaps to factor analysis. The guess at the rule requires something more—a creative leap—even in the most trivial cases. The third, or *abduction,* starts from the rule and guesses that the fact is a case under that rule: All people with tuberculosis have bumps; Mr. Jones has bumps; perhaps Mr. Jones has tuberculosis. This, sometimes mistakenly called an "inverse probability," is never certain but is, in medicine, called a diagnosis or, when many rules are considered, a differential diagnosis, but it is usually fixed, not by a statistic, but by finding some other observable sign to clinch the answer.

Clear examples of abduction abound in the Hippocratic corpus but are curiously absent in Aristotle's own writings, where one finds only genus, species, and differentia.

What seems even stranger in the Greek writings is a total absence of our notions of *a priori* or *a posteriori* probability. The ancients had only a possibility and a guess. Probability as we know it was still nearly two thousand years in the future. Possibility appears in Aristotle's problematic mode but was even more sharply handled by the Stoics and by the physicians. Both groups questioned whether a possible proposition can be said to be true if it never happens to be fulfilled. One thing is clear, then—the mind makes a leap from the cases and facts to the rule, and Mill's attempt to bridge this gap, and the attempts of all of his followers, slur over it too easily. We do not know how we even make the jump and come up with a simple and natural hypothesis—certainly not from probabilities.

When I was young, it was fashionable to sneer at Stoic logic as mere pettifoggery; at that very time it was being slowly and laboriously re-created under the alias of the logic of propositions. Thanks largely to Northrop and to Sambursky, I have recently become familiar with its tenets. Had I known it forty years ago, it would have saved me much wasted labor. In the first place it is, as Peirce points out, both pansomatic and triadic in its propositions. There are always three real related bodies: One is the utterance, the *flatus vocis* of Abelard; one is that which it proposes; one is something in the head like a fist in the hand called the *Lekton*. Shakespeare, at about the age of twenty-five, had it clear and wrote for a lawyers' club:

> What's in the brain that ink may character,
> Which hath not figur'd to thee my true spirit?
> What's new to speak, what new to register,
> That may express my love or thy dear merit?

The lawyers for whom he wrote it were concerned with writing lawyers' law, which grows out of Stoic logic, giving us our contracts, corporations, and constitutions, created as postulated entities and hypothetical relations, much as we inherited this structure from the Greeks to start the renaissance of science. What's in the brain is the Stoic *Lekton*. Stoic law contemplates possible alternatives but never probabilities, and time enters, allowing no contract without date of termination, no bond without date of redemption, and no elected office but for a limited term.

Time appears in Stoic logic in the relation of the necessary to the possible, and I have heard lawyers discuss this as a probable source of this aspect of contractual law. There are three statements attributed to Diodorus, called the Master, of which any two may be true and the third false: Every possible truth about the past is necessary; an impossible proposition may not follow from a possible one; there is a proposition possible that neither is true nor will be true.

Diodorus rejected the third and defined the "possible" as that which is or will be true. This is in keeping with his notion of implication, which is concerned with time. He held that *A* implied *B* only if, for *all* time, *A*, as a function of time, materially implied *B*, as a function of that time. For the last of the great Stoic logicians, Philo, implication was our material implication. There were at least two other forms of implication used by the Stoics, one resembling strict implication, and the other perhaps requiring analyticity. Unfortunately, none of these is the implication that we really want for our purposes, and, as you will see, we have had to turn to biology for the notion of a bound cause. A signal should be said to imply its natural cause, which is bound, and not its casual cause; for when it arises ectopically, it is false for the receiver. The communication engineer calls such a false signal "noise." Again, the trouble is that we are dealing with a triad of Sender, Signal, and Receiver, and with the Stoic triad: *A* means *B* to *C*. The signal means to the receiver what the sender intended.

In order to avoid paradoxes and ambiguities, the Stoics not only would not allow any self-reference, as in the famous Cretan's "This statement is a lie," but would not allow a proposition to imply itself and, as an added precaution, would not allow a negation within a proposition. This left them with *implication,* and an exclusive *or,* and with a *not both,* the last of which is one of Peirce's *amphecks,* or a version of Sheffer's stroke. Hence, they needed exactly five figures of argument to form a complete logic of atomic propositions.

In about 1920, I attempted to construct a logic to handle the problems of knowledge and action in terms of a logical analysis of propositions involving verbs other than the copulative, and found it worse than modal logic. One has to distinguish those verbs in which the physical activity described by the present tense begins in the object and ends in the subject, such as verbs of sensation, perception, etc.; those in which it begins in the subject and ends in the object, such as the verbs of action; the group of so-called intransitive and reflexive verbs in which the events begin in the subject and end in the subject, called the verbs of behavior; and finally, a group of verbs that in the present tense refer to no action but define some kind of action that will be taken if thus-and-so happens—verbs of sentiment, which are like propositional functions rather than propositions. In perception, time's arrow points to the past; in action, to the future; in behavior, it becomes circular; and in sentiment, it simply does not exist. Literally, one deals with a state. I gave up the attempt because I realized that I had been trapped by the subject-predicate structure of language into supposing I was dealing with diadic relations, whereas they were irreducibly triadic. My hypothesis was simple and natural, but I had mistaken the *flatus vocis* for the *Lekton*.

I next attempted to construct for myself a simplest psychic act that would preserve its essential character; you may call it a "psychon" if you will. It was to be to psychology what an atom was to chemistry, or a gene to genetics. This time I was more fortunate, probably thanks to studying under Morgan of fruit fly fame. But my psychon differed from an atom and from a gene in that it was to be not an enduring, unsplittable object, but a least event. My postulated psychons were to be related much as offspring are to their parents, and their occurrence was in some sense to imply a previous generation that begat them. There is perhaps no better understood triadic relation than family structure. Even the colligative terms are clearly specified. There is scarcely a primitive tribe but has a kinship structure. So I was fortunate in this hypothesis in the sense that it gave a theory of activity progressing from sensation to action through the brain, and even more so in this, that the structure of that passage was anastomotic, whereby afferents of any sort could find their way by intersecting paths to any set of efferents, so relating perception to action. The implication of psychons pointed to the past, and their intention foreshadowed the proposed response. In those days the neuronal hypothesis of Ramòn y Cajal and the all-or-none law of axonal impulses were relatively novel, but I was overjoyed to find in them some embodiments of psychons. There was a *Lekton* in the head like a fist in the hand, but it took me out of psychology through medicine and neurology to ensure my pansomatism. Thereafter, in teaching physiological psychology at Seth Low Junior College, I used symbols for particular neurons, subscripted for the time of their impulse, and joined by implicative characters to express the dependence of that impulse upon receipt of impulses received a moment, or synaptic delay, sooner.

But even then I could not handle circularities in the net of neurons, for which I lacked a genetic model. They were postulated by Kubie, in 1930, to explain memory and thinking without overt activity in the supposititious linked-reflexes of the behaviorists. Circles were well known as regulatory devices, as reflexes, in which the action instead of being regenerative was an inverse, or negative, feedback. My major difficulty was having insufficient knowledge of modular mathematics. This, Walter Pitts could handle, and we published our paper on a logical calculus for ideas immanent in nervous activity. Chicago in those days was under the spell of Rudolf Carnap, and we employed his terminology, although it was not most appropriate to our postulates and hypotheses. Quite apart from misprints, this has made it unduly difficult for all but a few like Bar-Hillel, who worked with Carnap, and we shall always be grateful to Kleene for putting it into a more intelligible form. I still feel, however, that he treated closed loops too cavalierly and so left open questions that we had raised, and neglected certain distinctions that, in Papert's hands, may prove a source of new theorems relating nets to the structure of the functions that they compute. The history of the ensuing developments in automata theory is certainly familiar to you.

As geometry ceased to be the measurement of the earth, so automata theory is ceasing to be a theory of automata. Recently, in Ravello, I was told that an automaton or a nerve net, like me, was a mapping of a free monoid onto a semigroup with the possible addition of identity. This is the same sort of nonsense one finds in the writings of those who never understood the *Lekton* as an embodiment. It is like mistaking a Chomsky language for a real language. You will find no such categorical confusion in the original Pitts and McCulloch of 1943. There the temporal propositional expressions are events occurring in time and space in a physically real net. The postulated neurons, for all their oversimplifications, are still physical neurons as truly as the chemist's atoms are physical atoms.

For our purpose of proving that a real nervous system could compute any number that a Turing machine could compute with a fixed length of tape, it was possible to treat the neuron as a simple threshold element. Unfortunately, this misled many into the trap of supposing that threshold logic was all one could obtain in hardware or software. This is false. A real neuron, or Crane's neuristor, can certainly compute any Boolian function of its inputs— to say the least! Also, in 1943, the nets that we proposed were completely orderly and specified for their tasks, which is certainly not true of real brains. So, in 1947, when we were postulating a *Lekton* for the knowing of a universal, we began with a paragraph of precautions, that the function of the net be little perturbed by perturbations of signals, thresholds, and even by details of synapsis. All of this underlies the beginnings of a probabilistic logic to understand the construction of reliable automata from less reliable components, as is apparent in the work of Manuel Blum and Leo Verbeek. Finally, in the work of Winograd and Cowan, it is clear that, for an information-theoretic capacity in computation in the presence of noise, the logic has to be multiple-truth-valued, and the constructions require, for coding without fatal multiplication of unreliable components, not threshold elements, but those capable of computing any Boolian function of large numbers of inputs — that is, they must be somewhat like real neurons. The facts that worried us over the years from 1947 to 1963 were simply that real brains do know universals, are composed of unreliable components, and can compute in the presence of noise. The theory of automata has proved more provocative than the automata theory divorced from the automata.

Please note that, to this point, we have considered only deductive processes. The automata were not "taking habits." Our group has not been concerned with induction, either experimentally or theoretically. Soon after World War II, Albert Uttley produced the first so-called probabilistic perceptive artifact. It enjoyed what is now called a "layered computation" and could be trained to classify its inputs. He has stayed with the problem, and I happen to know that he has written, but not yet published, an excellent theoretical paper based on a specific hypothesis as to the events determining the coupling of neurons in succession; and, moreover, that physiological experiments performed by one of his friends indicate that his assumption is probably correct. I take it you are familiar with the writings of Donald MacKay, Oliver Selfridge, Marvin Minsky, Gordon Pask, Frank Rosenblatt, and a host of others on perceptrons, learning and teaching machines, etc., and that you know of the numerous studies on the chemical nature of the engram, which certainly involves ribose nucleic acid and protein synthesis.

The next step would obviously be to postulate a process of concept formation. This is the very leap from weighing probabilities to propounding hypotheses. Marcus Goodall, Ray Solomonoff, Marvin Minsky, and Seymour Papert, among my immediate friends, are all after it, and I think they all feel that it requires a succession of subordinate insights organized at successive superordinate levels or types. This is what Hughlings Jackson called "propositionalizing." This certainly cannot be left to variation and selection as an evolutionary process starting from chaos or a random net. That would be too slow, for it can be followed in ontogenesis, as Piaget has shown. The child does form "simple" and "natural" hypotheses, as Galileo called them. "Simple" and "natural" are evaluative terms and are based upon the evolution of the organism and its development in the real world, the natural world in which it finds itself. There again we come up against our logical limitation, for there simply does not exist any proper way to handle the triadic, or *n*-adic, relations of such relata. We cannot state our problem in a finite and unambiguous manner.

That man, like the beasts, lives in the world of relations rather than in a world of classes or propositions seems certain. He does not know the relative size of two cubes from a measurement of the lengths of their edges, or even from the area of their faces. If he can just detect a difference of one part in twenty of a length, he can do the same for areas and also for volumes. I happen to have spent two years in measuring man's ability to set an adjustable oblong to a preferred shape, because I did not believe that he did prefer the golden section or that he could recognize it. He does and he can! On repeated settings for the most pleasing form he comes to prefer it and can set for it. The same man who can only detect a difference of a twentieth in length, area, or volume sets it at 1 to 1.618, not at 1 to 1.617 or 1 to 1.619. So the aesthetic judgment bespeaks a precise knowledge of certain — shall I say privileged? — relations directly, not compounded of the simpler perceptibles. A sculptor or painter has sometimes told me he had added enough to a square so that the part he had added had the same shape as the whole. This example is pertinent here, for in this case we do have an adequate theory of the relations, namely ratio and proportion. But these apply only to the perceived object, not to its relation to the statement or the *Lekton* in the brain of the aesthete. Clearly, the concept of a ratio must be embodied before the concept of a proportion can be conceived as the identity of the ratio. Once formed, the concept endures in us as the embodiment of an eternal verity, a sentiment, like love. To quote from the same Shakespearean sonnet CVIII:

> What's new . . .
>
> ....
>
> Nothing, sweet boy, but yet like prayers divine,
> I must each day say o'er the very same,
> Counting no old thing old, thou mine, I thine,
> Even as when first I hallowed thy fair name.
> So that eternal love in love's fresh case,
> Weights not the dust and injury of age,
> Nor gives to necessary wrinkles place,
> But makes antiquity for aye his page,
>> Finding the first conceit of love there bred
>> Where time and outward form would show it dead.

Such is the beauty we still find, the pure form, the golden section, in the ruins of a Greek temple.

The golden section is a ratio that cannot be computed by any Turing machine without an infinite tape or in less than an infinite time. It is strictly incomprehensible. Yet it can be apprehended by finite automata, including us. Nor does it arise from any set of probabilities, or from a factor analysis of any data or correlation of observations, but as an insight — a guess, like every other hypothesis that is natural and simple enough to serve in science. It is nearer to the proper notions of classical physics than to the descriptive laws, the curve-fittings, that bedevil psychology.

This brings us to the problem of abduction, the apagoge. Evolution has provided us with reflexive arcs organized for the most part by what are called "half-centers," whose activities may alternate, as in breathing or walking, or synchronize, as in jumping. These are then programmed for more complicated sequences, and all of these are marshaled into a few general modes of behavior of the whole man. Psychologists and ethologists count them on their fingers or at most on their fingers and toes. These modes of behavior are instinctive, and only the manner of their expression and their manner of evocation are modified by our experience. The structures that mediate them have evolved in all linear organisms, like us, from an original central net, or reticulum, and while they may be very dissimilar from phylum to phylum, the central core of that reticulum has remained curiously the same in all of us. It is distributed throughout the length of the neuraxis and in each segment determines the activity of that segment locally, and relates it to the activity of other segments by fibers, or axons, running the long way of the neuraxis. The details of its neurons and their specific connections need not concern us here. In general, you may think of it as a computer to any part of which come signals from many parts of the body and from other parts of the brain and spinal cord. It is only one cell deep on the path from input to output, but it can set the filters on all of its inputs and can control the behavior of the programmed activity, the half-centers, and the reflexes. It gets a substitute for depth by its intrinsic fore-and-aft connections. Its business, given its knowledge of the state of the whole organism and of the world impingent upon it, is to decide whether the given fact is a case under one or another rule. It must decide for the whole organism whether the rule is one requiring fighting, fleeing, eating, sleeping, etc. It must do it with millisecond component action and conduction velocities of usually less than 100 meters per second, and do it in real time, say, in a third of a second. That it has worked so well throughout evolution, without itself evolving, points to its structure as the natural solution of the organization of appropriate behavior. We know much experimentally of the behavior of the components, but still have no theory worthy of the name to explain its circuit action. William Kilmer, who works on this problem with me, is more sanguine than I am about our approach to the question. Again, the details of our attempts are irrelevant here. The problem remains the central one in all command and control systems. Of necessity, the system must enjoy a redundancy of potential command in which the possession of the necessary urgent information constitutes authority in that part possessing the information.

The problem is clearly one of triadic or *n*-adic relations, and is almost, or perhaps entirely, unspecifiable in finite and unambiguous terms without the proper calculus.

We see, then, the same theme running throughout. We lack a triadic logic. We do not know how to create natural and simple hypotheses. We have, at present, no theory to account for those abductions which have permitted our evolution, ensured our ontogenesis, and preserved our lives. The question remains:

What's in the brain that ink may character?

Index

Abduction, *see* Apagoge
Alexander, Franz, 378
"All-or-none" character of nervous activity, 19–21, 35, 37, 76, 145, 159, 206, 256, 258–259, 364, 392
Alpha rhythm, 52, 68, 80, 81, 117–119, 124–131, 383
  in hysterical blindness, 134–135
Anxiety, 379–380
Apagoge, or abduction, 5, 8, 13–14, 389–390, 396
Appetitive circuit, *see* Choice; Feedback; Servomechanism; Values
Apter, Julia, 59–61, 64
Associationalism, 74, 83
Atomic proposition, 148–153
Audition, *see* Universals, and sound
Automata, theory of, 19–39, 393–394

Bacon, Roger, 5
Behavior
  and cerebral mechanisms, 112–141
  neurotic, 374–380
  and reticular formation, 396
  and social intercourse, 194–195
Bernard, Claude, 290
Bound cause, 360, 391
Brain, 220–221, 394
  circuit theory of, 3, 19–39
  negative feedback in, 78–79
  see also Computing machines;
    Memory; Reverberating circuits
Brown, Graham, 115–116

Carbon dioxide, and nervous activity, 381–382
Causalgia, 374–382
Causality, 6, 142, 148, 149–150, 291, 297
  in nets of neurons, 35–39
Cell types, 105–107, 109
Cerebral cortex
  functional organization of, 67–70, 78–

79, 85–86, 151
  lesions in, 101, 132, 374–377
  molecular structure of, 121–124, 138
Chemicals
  and neurons, 108–109
  and neuroses, 379–380
Choice, 268–270, 310–311
  see also Values
Circles in nets, *see* Nets
Circularity of preference, 196
Command and control systems, 397
Communications systems, 194
  see also Computing machines
Computing machines, 139–141, 144–145, 148–149, 155–156, 162–164
  and brains, 72–76, 77, 78–80, 83–85, 132–134, 137, 368
  ethical, 194–200
  as game players, 159, 197, 198–199
  moral, 199
  self-organizing, 217, 220–228
  self-reproducing, 160, 200
  thinking, 307–316, 367
  Turing machines, 9–10, 13–14, 35, 159, 197–198, 200, 220, 368, 393
Consciousness, 72, 84, 129–130, 147, 159, 162, 377
  see also Unconscious
Continuity, 148, 154–155
Cybernetics, 158, 163, 194, 216–229, 365
  in industry, 219–220, 221–222
Cyclic nets, *see* Nets
Cytochemistry, 108–109, 119–120

Descartes, René, 155, 363
Devil, 225, 228
Dorsal root interaction, 177–193, 375
Dromes, 40–44
  see also Choice; Reflex
Duns Scotus, John, 5, 6, 7, 8

Ear, 49–52
  see also Universals

399

Index